Networking Applications on UNIX® System V Release 4

MICHAEL PADOVANO

Prentice Hall, Englewood Cliffs, New Jersey 07632

Library of Congress Cataloging-in-Publication Data

Padovano, Michael.
   Networking applications on UNIX System V release 4 / Michael Padovano.
      p. cm.
   "An Alan R. Apt book."
   Includes bibliographical references and index.
   ISBN 0-13-613555-2
   1. Operating Systems (Computers) 2. UNIX System V (Computer file)
3. Computer networks. I. Title.
QA76.76.O63P33   1993
005.7'11--dc 20   93-22196
                                                          CIP

Publisher: Alan Apt
Production Editor: Mona Pompili
Cover Designer: Wanda Lubelska Design
Copy Editor: Peter J. Zurita
Prepress Buyer: Linda Behrens
Manufacturing Buyer: Dave Dickey
Editorial Assistant: Shirley McGuire

 © 1993 by Prentice-Hall, Inc.
A Simon & Schuster Company
Englewood Cliffs, New Jersey 07632

Printed in the United States of America

10 9 8 7 6 5 4 3 2 1

ISBN 0-13-613555-2

Prentice-Hall International (UK) Limited, *London*
Prentice-Hall of Australia Pty. Limited, *Sydney*
Prentice-Hall Canada, Inc., *Toronto*
Prentice-Hall Hispanoamericana, S.A., *Mexico*
Prentice-Hall of India Private Limited, *New Delhi*
Prentice-Hall of Japan, Inc., *Tokyo*
Simon & Schuster Asia Pte. Ltd, *Singapore*
Editora Prentice-Hall do Brasil, Ltda., *Rio de Janeiro*

To my parents.

Preface

The UNIX operating system is rich with powerful networking capabilities. UNIX System V Release 4 (SVR4) merges the networking facilities of the major variants of the UNIX system to form a single, comprehensive networking platform. It contains a variety of network applications and provides tools to create new network services.

This book explains the networking facilities available on SVR4 (and SVR4-based systems such as Solaris 2.0, Solaris 2.1, and SVR4.2), and shows how to use them to create new network services. It reveals how existing network applications work, describes how to incorporate them into new applications, and explains how to create programs using the SVR4 networking routines. It contains many practical examples of networking applications that use the Remote Procedure Call (RPC) interface, the Transport Level Interface (TLI), and the Socket interface.

Intended Audience

This book is intended for those who want to understand how the SVR4 networking utilities work, and those who want to develop network applications using SVR4 tools. It assumes

- a working knowledge of the UNIX system;

- the ability to write and understand shell scripts; and

- familiarity with the C programming language.

It does *not* assume network programming experience or knowledge of networking concepts. Networking ideas and concepts are presented throughout the book.

This book is intended for computer professionals who are interested in developing networking applications using SVR4, as well as computer professionals who are interested in understanding how networking applications work. It can also be used as a text for undergraduate and graduate students in computer science and computer engineering.

Organization

This book covers the networking facilities on SVR4 from an application developer's perspective. It describes how existing applications work and shows how to create new applications using shell scripts and C language programs.

It presents a top-down approach to creating network applications. SVR4 has many available network applications; the book starts by explaining how to create new network services by incorporating existing applications into shell scripts. It then works its way to creating more sophisticated applications by incorporating the SVR4 Remote Procedure Call (RPC) Facility and the SVR4 Transport Level Interface (TLI) routines into C language programs.

Chapter 1 begins by introducing network concepts and explaining the SVR4 networking architecture. It gives an overview of the networking model and presents the networking features of SVR4.

Chapter 2 describes the STREAMS framework and shows how to push STREAMS modules, open multiplexing devices, and use STREAMS-based devices. It also describes which STREAMS modules are available on SVR4.

Chapter 3 details the Transmission Control Protocol/Internet Protocol (TCP/IP) protocol suite and explains how TCP/IP applications work. This chapter also creates new applications by incorporating existing TCP/IP applications into shell scripts.

Chapter 4 explains the UNIX-to-UNIX Copy (UUCP) family of commands and shows the architecture of the UUCP services. It also shows how to incorporate UUCP commands into shell scripts to create new applications.

Chapter 5 explains Remote File Sharing (RFS) and the Network File System (NFS), the two distributed file systems available on SVR4. Many applications make extensive use of the file system, and this chapter explains how you can access files on a remote machine by using normal UNIX system calls. It also describes the differences between the two file-sharing systems, showing the pros and cons of each.

Chapter 6 describes how to create more sophisticated applications by using the SVR4 Remote Procedure Call (RPC) Facility. It gives examples of how to create C programs using RPC routines, and explains what types of applications are suitable for the RPC Facility.

Chapter 7 presents a lower layer of network programming by introducing the SVR4 Transport Level Interface (TLI). It provides an overview of TLI and presents the details of TLI routines. It also explains when you should use TLI instead of RPC.

Chapter 8 builds upon Chapter 7 by explaining how to create C programs that use TLI. It shows how to write programs that establish communication with remote services, transfer data, and shutdown network communication.

Chapter 9 explains the Network Selection and Name-to-Address Mapping facilities, two new features of SVR4 that help make applications work over any network. It shows how to incorporate these facilities into C programs.

Chapter 10 describes the socket interface, an interprocess communication interface prominent on BSD UNIX systems. It compares the socket routines to the TLI routines, and shows how to write applications using the socket interface.

Acknowledgments

Many people helped make this book possible. Many thanks to Art Sabsevitz at UNIX Systems Laboratories for his detailed comments on many of the chapters. His help contributed greatly to the final product. Thanks also to the other reviewers from UNIX Systems Laboratories: Bill Sherman, Mark Thomas, Bob Bowden, Bill Baker, and Dave Olander. Thanks especially to Dave Olander, who provided detailed comments on the TLI chapters.

I would like to thank the reviewers used by Prentice Hall: Steve Buroff, Mike Comer, Thomas Wood, Mike Garwood, and Ole Jacobsen. Steve Buroff and Mike Garwood gave many helpful suggestions on the initial draft of the book; Mike Comer and Thomas Wood provided detailed comments throughout the project.

I would also like to thank Jerry Keselman and Mary Ann Hondo for their insights and comments on the TLI, RPC, and socket chapters. Mike Milicia, Anne Milicia, Paul Krzyzanowski, Chip Christian, Don Milos, Ariadna Stroll, and Hai-Thi Khong also provided many helpful suggestions. Finally, thanks to Alan Apt, my editor at Prentice Hall, for his support and help while writing this book.

This book was produced by the author using `ditroff`, `tbl`, `pic`, and `xfig`, on an Intel 80486-based system running UNIX System V Release 4. The source code was written by the author from scratch, and was included in the text directly from the source files. The source code was formatted using a program written by the author.

The author would like to hear from readers with comments, bug reports, and suggestions. Please direct all comments to `padovano@remus.rutgers.edu`.

Michael Padovano

Contents

Chapter 1 Networking on UNIX System V Release 4   1

1.1 Introduction   1
1.2 Benefits of Networking   1
     Drawbacks of Networking   2
1.3 The Networking Model   3
     The Client/Server Model   7
1.4 Transport Providers on the UNIX System   8
1.5 Transport Independence   9
1.6 Transport Modes of Service   10
1.7 History of Networking on the UNIX System   12
1.8 Networking on SVR4   12
1.9 SVR4 Network Architecture   13
     The STREAMS Mechanism   14
     Network Selection and Name-to-Address Mapping   16
     Ports and Port Monitors   17
     The Service Access Facility   19
For Further Reading   20
Exercises   20

Chapter 2 Introduction to STREAMS   21

2.1 Introduction   21
2.2 Overview of STREAMS   21
2.3 Manipulating a Stream   23
     Other STREAMS Operations   31
2.4 Multiplexing Device Drivers   31
2.5 Clone Devices   36
2.6 STREAMS-Based Pipes   37
     Named STREAMS   38
2.7 STREAMS-Based Terminals   43
     The Autopush Facility   44

2.8	Pseudo-Terminal Devices	44
2.9	Which Modules are Available?	50
	connld	50
	ldterm	50
	pckt	50
	pipemod	50
	ptem	51
	sockmod	51
	timod	51
	tirdwr	51
2.10	Summary	52
	For Further Reading	52
	Exercises	52

Chapter 3 Applications Using the TCP/IP Protocol Suite   53

3.1	Introduction	53
	Why is TCP/IP so Popular?	54
3.2	Overview of TCP/IP	54
	IP Addresses	55
	Special Addresses	57
	The Internet Protocol	58
	Device Drivers	60
	The Address Resolution Protocol	60
	The Transmission Control Protocol	61
	The User Datagram Protocol	62
	The Internet Control Message Protocol	63
	Routing Protocols	63
	Applications	64
	TCP/IP Implementation in SVR4	64
3.3	Application Communication	65
	Application Ports	65
	Machine Naming	66
	Service Naming	68
	Communication Establishment	68
	Communication Establishment over UDP	70
	Determining a Transport Address	71
3.4	Remote Login via the Telnet Protocol	72
3.5	File Transfer: FTP	76
	Anonymous FTP	83
3.6	UNIX-Specific Remote Login: rlogin	84
3.7	UNIX-Specific Remote Execution: rsh	87
3.8	UNIX-Specific File Transfer: rcp 90	

3.9 Application: Remote Archive and Restore   91
    Remote Archive Using TCP/IP Tools   91
    Implementing the Archive Command Using ftp   96
    Implementing Restore Using rcp   100
    Implementing Restore Using ftp   104
3.10 Other Services   107
For Further Reading   107
Exercises   108

Chapter 4 Applications Using UUCP   109

4.1 Introduction   109
4.2 Overview of UUCP   110
4.3 Which Machines Can I Talk To: uuname   111
4.4 File Transfer: uucp   112
4.5 Simple File Transfer: uuto and uupick   115
4.6 Remote Execution: uux   118
4.7 The uucico Command   121
4.8 Application: Remote Archive and Restore   122
    Archive Using the UUCP Commands   123
    Restore Using the UUCP Commands   126
4.9 Summary   129
For Further Reading   129
Exercises   129

Chapter 5 Applications Using RFS and NFS   131

5.1 Introduction   131
5.2 Overview of RFS and NFS   132
5.3 Goals of RFS   133
5.4 Architecture of RFS   134
    RFS Name Service   136
    Client/Server Interactions   137
    State Information   138
    UNIX System Semantics   139
5.5 RFS Security Considerations   140
5.6 New Features of RFS in SVR4   143
5.7 Restrictions of RFS   144
5.8 Drawbacks of RFS   145
5.9 Goals of NFS   147

5.10 Architecture of NFS   148
     Client/Server Interactions   151
     The NFS File Handle   152
     Stateless Operations   153
     NFS Recovery   154
     NFS Path Name Parsing   155
     UNIX System Semantics   157
5.11 NFS Security Considerations   159
5.12 New Features of NFS in SVR4   160
5.13 Drawbacks of NFS   160
5.14 When to Use NFS and When to Use RFS   161
5.15 Remote Backup and Restore Using NFS or RFS   162
5.16 A Simple Remote Execution Application Using RFS   169
5.17 Summary   178
For Further Reading   178
Exercises   179

Chapter 6 Applications Using the Remote Procedure Call Facility   181

6.1 Introduction   181
6.2 Overview of RPC   181
     When Should You Use RPC?   183
     RPC Architecture   183
6.3 Overview of XDR   186
6.4 RPC Security Issues   188
6.5 Creating an RPC Program   190
6.6 Using the RPC Compiler   192
6.7 A Simple RPC Example   193
6.8 The RPC Definition Language   200
     Constants   202
     Structures   203
     Enumerations   203
     Unions   204
     Type Definitions   206
     Declarations of Arrays   206
     Declarations of Pointers   207
     Strings   208
     Boolean Values   209
     Void   209
     Opaque Data   209
     Summary   210

6.9	The Server Code	210
	XDR Routines	211
6.10	The Client Code	212
6.11	A Remote Users Service	216
6.12	Changing Authentication	222
	Incorporating Unix Authentication	225
	Incorporating Secure Authentication	229
	Overview of Secure Authentication	230
	Using Secure Authentication	235
6.13	Using SVR4 Port Monitors	240
6.14	Summary	242
	For Further Reading	242
	Exercises	242

Chapter 7 Introduction to TLI

245

7.1	Introduction	245
7.2	Overview of TLI	245
	When Should You Use TLI?	247
	Summary of TLI Routines	247
	Transport Addresses	249
	Transport Service Data Units	250
7.3	TLI Connection-Mode Service	252
	Synchronous and Asynchronous Modes	256
7.4	Transport Endpoint Events	258
7.5	Connection-Mode Transport Endpoint States	259
7.6	TLI Connectionless-Mode Service	264
	Synchronous and Asynchronous Modes	267
7.7	Connectionless-Mode Transport Endpoint Events	267
7.8	Connectionless-Mode Transport Endpoint States	268
7.9	Details of TLI Routines	269
	t_open()	269
	t_bind()	272
	t_unbind()	276
	t_close()	276
	t_getinfo()	277
	t_getstate()	277
	t_sync()	278
	t_look()	280
	t_connect()	281
	t_rcvconnect()	283
	t_listen()	285

t_accept()   287
t_snd()   288
t_rcv()   290
t_sndrel()   291
t_rcvrel()   292
t_snddis()   292
t_rcvdis()   294
t_sndudata()   295
t_rcvudata()   297
t_rcvuderr()   298
t_error()   300
t_alloc()   300
t_free()   302
t_optmgmt()   303
Example of the t_optmgmt() Routine   305
7.10 Summary   313
For Further Reading   314
Exercises   314

Chapter 8 Applications Using TLI   315

8.1   Introduction   315
8.2   The Presentation Layer   316
8.3   The Session Layer   320
8.4   A Simple Connection-Oriented Application   321
      The Server Code   322
      The Client Code   333
8.5   A Simple Connectionless-Mode Application   338
      The Server Code   339
      The Client Code   344
8.6   Applications With qlen Greater Than 1   352
8.7   Making Applications Transport Independent   361
8.8   Polling Multiple Transport Endpoints   363
8.9   A Read/Write Interface   368
8.10 A Transport-Independent Application: rpopen()   370
      The Server Code   379
      The Client Code   395
8.11 Using the SVR4 Listen Port Monitor   408
8.12 Summary   411
For Further Reading   411
Exercises   412

Chapter 9 Network Selection and Name-to-Address Mapping   413

9.1	Introduction	413
9.3	The Network Configuration File	415
	Example of the /etc/netconfig File	416
9.4	Network Selection	418
	Modifying the Loop	422
9.5	More Network Selection Routines	422
9.6	Name-to-Address Mapping Routines	424
	How It Works	426
	Example: Determining Addresses	427
	Special Values for Host Name	430
9.7	Miscellaneous Name-to-Address Mapping Routines	432
	netdir_getbyaddr()	432
	taddr2uaddr()	433
	uaddr2taddr()	436
	netdir_free()	437
	netdir_options()	437
	netdir_options(): ND_SET_BROADCAST	438
	netdir_options(): ND_SET_RESERVEDPORT	441
	netdir_options(): ND_CHECK_RESERVEDPORT	441
	netdir_options(): ND_MERGEADDR	441
9.8	Putting it All Together	443
9.9	Completing the rpopen() Function	444
9.10	Summary	448
	For Further Reading	448
	Exercises	448

Chapter 10 Applications Using Sockets   449

10.1	Introduction	449
10.2	Overview of Sockets	449
	When Should You Use Sockets?	453
	Summary of Socket Routines	453
	Transport Addresses	455
	Socket Implementation in SVR4	458
10.3	Sockets Using Virtual-Circuit Service	459
	Synchronous and Asynchronous Modes	463
10.4	Sockets Using Datagram Service	465
	Synchronous and Asynchronous Modes	467

10.5 Details of Socket Routines   468
       socket()   468
       socketpair()   472
       bind()   473
       connect()   474
       listen()   475
       accept()   475
       send()   476
       sendto()   478
       sendmsg()   479
       recv()   480
       recvfrom()   481
       recvmsg()   483
       shutdown()   484
       getsockname()   485
       getpeername()   485
       setsockopt()   486
       getsockopt()   490
       Example of sendmsg() and recvmsg()   491
10.6 A Simple Virtual-Circuit Application   502
       The Server Code   503
       The Client Code   509
10.7 A Simple Datagram Application   514
       The Server Code   514
       The Client Code   518
10.8 Processing Asynchronous Events   523
10.9 Selecting Multiple File Descriptors   525
10.10 Using inetd   532
10.11 Summary   536
For Further Reading   536
Exercises   536

Index   **537**

Chapter 1

Networking on
UNIX System V Release 4

1.1   Introduction

UNIX System V Release 4 (SVR4) offers a wide variety of interfaces and frameworks for writing network applications. It merges the networking facilities of the most popular versions of the UNIX system, including UNIX System V Release 3, SunOS, XENIX, and the Berkeley Software Distribution (BSD) versions 4.2 and 4.3. It also includes industry standard networking facilities, introduces new networking routines, and provides a flexible architecture. The result is a powerful networking platform that allows creation of sophisticated networking applications.

This book explains the networking features of SVR4 and uses them to develop network applications. It begins by explaining the benefits of networking, introducing networking concepts, and describing the SVR4 networking architecture.

1.2   Benefits of Networking

Networking is essential in today's computer environments. It turns isolated computers into integrated systems, providing an environment where resources are shared and capacity problems reduced.

The primary benefit of networking is **resource sharing**. Resource sharing allows users on different machines to share modems, printers, tape drives, and disk space. For example, users can send network messages requesting to use a central printer, allowing everyone to share that resource.

Another benefit is **communication**. Networking allows diverse systems to communicate. Users can send electronic mail and messages to colleagues across the room or across the world. They can also consult networked electronic bulletin boards to share ideas about a variety of subjects.

Networking allows **growth**. If a company needs more computing resources, a new computer can be installed, added to the network, and immediately accessed by other machines and users.

Networking provides **high reliability**. If applications share data, the data can be replicated across several machines. If one machine goes down, another can take its place and provide the data to the applications.

A further benefit is **distribution of applications**. By using networking routines, applications are not limited to a single machine. They can be distributed to machines that serve their needs in the most efficient way. For example, consider a computer-aided design application that requires a high-resolution graphics capability, a fast CPU for numeric calculations, and a large amount of disk space to store data. Networking allows you to partition the application and distribute it among machines that have the necessary capabilities.

Networked computers allow **load balancing**. Processes can float from one CPU to another within a cluster of machines, allowing an even distribution of the processing load across all machines in the cluster.

Users on the network realize the benefits of **sharing information**. Data files can be shared between machines on the network, allowing users to see invoices, results of surveys, company newsletters, and other information.

Networking also solves **capacity problems**. CPU processing can be reduced by distributing an application, disk space can be accessed from remote machines, and remote I/O ports can be utilized. Even main memory capacity problems can be solved; partitioning a task to work over a network results in several smaller programs instead of a single large program.

Most of all, networking results in **lower cost**. A single device can be shared by several machines, reducing the need to buy many peripheral devices. Networking also saves money because an installation can have several low-cost workstations accessing a single file server. That puts a lot of processing power on the user's desk without the expense of large mainframe systems.

Drawbacks of Networking

Networking has its pitfalls as well. One of the biggest disadvantages of networking is **security concerns**. When a network message arrives at a machine, it is important to authenticate the identity of the user sending the message. With a weak authentication scheme, a remote user can impersonate a local user and gain unauthorized access to private data.

A second disadvantage is **increased administration**. System administrators must tune the network, monitor the network, administer network database files, and ensure network integrity. When networking is introduced into an organization, the administrator must ensure that the network runs smoothly.

A further disadvantage is **network failure**. As applications increase their use of a network, network failure becomes catastrophic. Most applications are not coded to recover gracefully when a network goes down.

Another disadvantage is **virus attack**. When a system is connected to a network, it is vulnerable to destructive network messages. For example, a message that sparks a damaging activity (like erasing files) may enter the system via the network.

By far the greatest drawback of networking is the security concerns. A network can be a valuable tool, but it becomes worthless if it allows impersonators to steal or inappropriately access data. As we examine and develop network applications, we'll make network security a top priority.

1.3   The Networking Model

Most networks are divided into layers that perform well-defined functions. A layer is a logical unit that performs an operation on data and passes the data to the next layer, where each layer is independent of the layers below and above it.

A layered architecture is desirable because you can replace a layer without affecting the surrounding layers. To illustrate this, let's look at a hypothetical example. Suppose we have a German scientist that wants to use the telephone to talk to a Chinese scientist about computer theory. For this to occur, we need a translator. Let's suppose further that we can't find someone who can translate German into Chinese. So, we do the next best thing: we get a translator that translates German into another language, say, English, and another that translates English into Chinese. Let's further suppose that the translator refuses to operate the telephone. So, we bring in technicians that operate the phone and repeat whatever the translator says into it. We now have three layers of operations: the scientists, the translators, and the technicians. Figure 1.1 shows the configuration we contrived.

In this configuration, we can replace any of the layers without affecting the layers surrounding it. For example, we can replace the existing translators with others that translate from German to Spanish and from Spanish to Chinese. The scientists are not affected by this; they continue to speak in their respective languages. The technicians are not affected; they simply take what is said and repeat it into the telephone. Similarly, we can replace the phone technicians with Morse code operators without affecting the scientists or the translators.

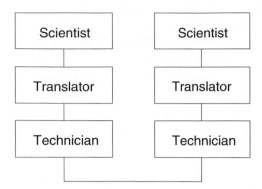

Figure 1.1 A Layered Architecture

The ability to replace functionality easily is why most networks are divided into layers. The International Organization for Standardization (ISO), an organization that develops international standards, has defined a layered architecture for networks. This architecture is called the Open Systems Interconnection (OSI) Reference Model, and it organizes the functionality of networks into seven distinct layers. The layers are shown in Figure 1.2, and consist of the following:

- The **physical layer** is responsible for transmitting raw data to the communication medium. It is concerned with the hardware and the details of transmission. It neither knows nor cares about what the data represent.

- The **data-link layer** detects and corrects any errors that may occur in the physical layer transmission. Typically, this layer organizes data into packets, passes the packets to the physical layer, and accepts acknowledgments from the receiver stating that the packet arrived.

- The **network layer** is responsible for relaying and routing information to its destination. For example, a message originating from a machine in New Jersey destined for a machine in California may have to go through several intermediate machines before reaching its final destination. The network layer manages this journey; if a message arrives at a machine that is not the final destination, the network layer sends the message to the next machine in the route.

- The **transport layer** provides a consistent interface for ''end-to-end'' communication. It frees the upper layers from the concerns of achieving data transfer. The transport layer is similar to a post office mailbox; if you write and address a letter, you can place it in a mailbox and not worry about how it reaches its destination. Similarly, you can create and address a network message, give it to the transport layer, and not worry about how it reaches its destination.

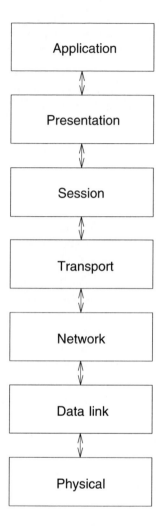

Figure 1.2   The OSI Reference Model

- The **session layer** provides the services needed to coordinate dialogue and manage data exchange. It is similar to radio communication where the conversing parties specify the keywords "over" or "over and out" to synchronize messages. The session layer manages a conversation by providing the means for each side to synchronize data exchange.

- The **presentation layer** is responsible for the selection of an agreed syntax to be used for the transfer of information. For example, some machines represent integers as 2-byte quantities and others as 4-byte quantities. The presentation layer translates the data into a common representation before passing it to the session layer. It is similar to the translator in the layered architecture we created in Figure 1.1.

• The **application layer** provides elements for managing resources. This is the layer associated with network applications. Examples include file transfer, distributed processing, and virtual terminal support.

Each layer defines a *protocol* between the two communicating sides. A protocol is simply a set of rules that the local and remote machines must follow. For example, we can define an application protocol that implements a "login query" mechanism (illustrated in Figure 1.3). This protocol specifies that a local machine calls a remote machine and sends it a single-word user name. The remote machine reads the name and sends back a "yes" or "no" depending upon whether that user is currently logged on. If the local machine does not send a name, or the remote system sends something other than a "yes" or "no," the protocol is violated.

ISO is defining international standard protocols for each layer of the OSI Reference Model, collectively referred to as the "OSI protocols." For example, ISO has defined an application-layer protocol for file transfer called File Transfer, Access, and Management (FTAM). This is a well-defined protocol that allows users to transfer files from one machine to another. Similarly, ISO has published the Transport Protocol Specification (ISO 8073) that defines protocols for the transport layer. These protocols are well-defined rules that the transport layer on the local and remote machines must follow.

The base SVR4 operating system does not provide the OSI protocols, although they are available from third party software vendors. However, as we will see later, the SVR4 STREAMS mechanism supports the OSI Reference Model, and the OSI Reference Model provides a good basis for describing network protocols that SVR4 does provide. Throughout this book, we refer to the OSI Reference Model when developing network applications.

Now that we have a model for layering a network, we can discuss the relationship between peers in a network application. Most network applications define *requesters* and *suppliers*, where the requester requests some action from the supplier. This relationship is called the *client/server model*.

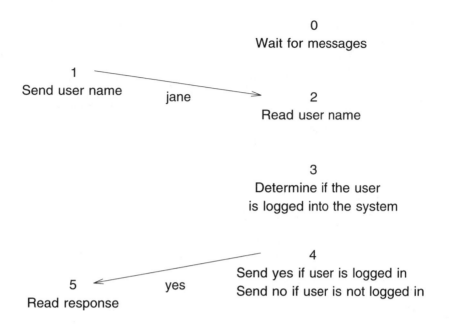

Figure 1.3   An Application-Layer Protocol

The Client/Server Model

The most common networking relationship for applications is the client/server model. The model defines a client, a server, and a service.

A service is a task that another machine performs for you. The service must be well-defined, that is, it must specify exactly what it does, the parameters it needs, and the results it returns.

A server is a machine that performs a service for you. The client is the machine that asks the server to execute the service on its behalf.

Typical services include file transfer, electronic mail, and remote command execution. Some services are machine-specific. For example, if a machine has a printer attached to it, it can offer a "remote print" service that accepts the contents of a file and sends the contents to the printer.

Clients and servers are not mutually exclusive. A machine can take on the role of a server by offering a file-transfer service, while taking on the role of a client by allowing users to access a file-transfer service on another machine.

There are several steps that must be done before communication can take place. They include the following:

1. The server must get a *transport address* for the service. A transport address is a well-defined location. It is similar to a telephone number, because you must get a unique phone number before people can call you. Applications work the same way. The server must associate the service with an address before clients can communicate with it.

2. The client must figure out the transport address of the service. There are several ways to do that. For example, the address can be hard-coded into the client side of the application or the application can query a database (similar to looking up a phone number in a telephone book). No matter how it's obtained, the client must specify the destination address when sending a message to a service.

In most cases, clients obtain addresses from a database. To accomplish this, servers and services are named, and entries exist in databases that map the names into associated addresses. As we will see in Chapter 9, SVR4 provides the Name-to-Address Mapping facility to make name-to-address translation easy for applications. It contains subroutines that take a name of a service and a server, and return the address of that service on the specified server. This makes obtaining an address as easy as looking up a phone number in a phone book; you simply specify the name of the service you want, and the routines present you with the address you need to communicate with it.

Network applications depend on *transport providers* to transmit data between machines. A transport provider is software that accepts a network message and sends it to a remote machine, freeing the application of the details of achieving data transfer (in other words, it performs the services of the transport layer of the OSI Reference Model). Over the years, several transport providers have been written for the UNIX system. Because this dependency exists, we present an overview of transport providers available on the UNIX system.

1.4   Transport Providers on the UNIX System

A transport provider is an implementation of a transport-layer protocol. There are many transport providers available on the UNIX system, the three most popular being TCP/IP, XNS, and the OSI transport protocols. SVR4 includes the TCP/IP protocol suite; XNS and the OSI protocols are available from third-party software vendors.

By far the most widely used transport provider on the UNIX system is TCP/IP. The term "TCP/IP" is short for an entire protocol suite based on the Transmission Control Protocol (TCP) and the Internet Protocol (IP). The Defense Advanced Research Projects Agency (DARPA) supported the development of TCP/IP to link its network with other research networks. The result was the Internet, a very large worldwide network based on the TCP/IP protocols. The popularity of TCP/IP grew because systems wanted to connect to the Internet and because a readily available implementation of the suite was distributed with the BSD UNIX operating system. Today, there exists hundreds of products based on TCP/IP.

Following TCP/IP in popularity is XNS. XNS refers to the Xerox Network Systems network architecture, a protocol suite developed by the Xerox Corporation. It contains several transport protocols, the most prominent being the Sequenced Packet Protocol (SPP). The popularity of XNS grew because Xerox made the protocols publicly available, and many software vendors implemented them.

Although not as prominent as TCP/IP and XNS, the OSI protocols are growing in popularity. ISO has been working on the OSI protocols since the 1970s, and, since their publication in 1988, governments and private organizations have increasingly required that all new networks use them. ISO defines five protocols for the transport layer, OSI Class 0 through OSI Class 4, more commonly referred to as TP0 through TP4. These protocols specify different levels of reliability; TP0 is the least reliable and TP4 is the most reliable. The one to use depends upon the reliability of the network-layer protocol; if you have a very reliable network-layer protocol, you can use TP0, and if you have an unreliable network-layer protocol, you should use TP4.

UNIX System V had OSI in mind in 1986 when it introduced STREAMS and the Transport Level Interface (TLI). STREAMS is a modular communications framework; it reflects the OSI Reference Model by allowing network developers to separate functionality into distinct layers. TLI is based on the ISO Transport Service Specification (ISO 8072), and consists of routines that allow easy migration from existing transport providers into OSI transport providers. Details of STREAMS are given in Chapter 2, and details of TLI are given in Chapters 7 and 8.

1.5 Transport Independence

Applications are ''transport-independent'' if they can work over any transport provider without modification. This is important when there exists several transport providers on a single system or if a site is migrating from one transport provider to another.

To illustrate the need for transport-independent applications, consider the move toward OSI protocols. The large installed base of TCP/IP applications means that the period of migration to the OSI protocols will be lengthy, and most sites will run TCP/IP and the OSI protocols simultaneously. Transport-independent applications will continue to work during this transition.

There are several reasons why users will migrate to the OSI protocols. The main reason is **government standards**. ISO is composed of standards organizations from many countries. Standards established by these organizations often carry the force of law in government purchases.

Another reason is **industry standardization**. Companies installing computer networks are concerned with protecting their investment. The use of the OSI protocols guarantees that equipment and software will work together. Migrating to the OSI protocols also reduces the proliferation of incompatible networks.

A third reason is **OSI existence**. Many European wide-area networks are already based on the OSI protocols, and recent graduates are trained in the ISO protocols.

Lastly, users will migrate to OSI because of its **functional richness**. Applications such as the Message Handling System (X.400), which allows messages containing ASCII text and digital voice to be sent via electronic mail, and FTAM, which allows users to access remote files, are essential in the computer market. Granted, most of this functionality exists in other network protocols (for example, TCP/IP), but the OSI versions carry the stamp of international standardization. For more details on the OSI protocols, see *The Open Book—A Practical Perspective on OSI*, listed in the **For Further Reading** section at the end of this chapter.

As mentioned earlier, the large installed base of TCP/IP applications means that the period of migration to the OSI protocols will be lengthy. Applications that are transport-independent can handle this migration to OSI. The routines presented in Chapters 7, 8, and 9 focus on making applications transport-independent.

1.6   Transport Modes of Service

Transport providers offer two modes of service: connectionless service and connection-oriented service.

Connectionless transport is similar to sending a message via the post office. The application must address each network message separately before passing it to the transport provider. The client can be reasonably sure that the message reached its destination, but can't be positive. Also, if the client sends two messages, there is no guarantee that the first message will arrive before the second. This type of transport is often called **datagram service** because of its similarity to telegram service.

Connection-oriented transport is like a telephone call. The client establishes a connection (similar to dialing a phone number), and sends all data to the server over the connection. It is like creating a direct link between the client and the server; the client does not have to address every message, but simply sends the data over the link. All messages are guaranteed to arrive at their destination, and the sender can be sure that they arrive in the order in which they were sent. This type of transport is also called **virtual-circuit service** because it resembles a connected circuit between two parties.

Connection-oriented transport can have the characteristic of "orderly release." This provides the user a way of sending an orderly release indication, stating that the user is finished sending data. Not all transports have this capability. Most notably, the OSI Class 4 transport protocol (TP4) does not support orderly release.

Transport providers can be further qualified by reliability. For example, consider a connectionless transport provider that sends an acknowledgment indication upon receipt of each message, somewhat like registered mail at the post office. This is sometimes referred to as reliable datagram service, because the sender is sure of the receipt of the message.

There are advantages and disadvantages to each mode of service. Some users dislike virtual-circuit transport providers because of the overhead required to set up the connection. Others dislike datagram transport providers because each message must be separately addressed. Users in favor of virtual-circuit transport providers claim that application development is easier because the transport provider does the work of guaranteeing delivery. Users in favor of datagram transport providers argue that virtual-circuit setup is too time-consuming, particularly when an application doesn't care if packets arrive in sequence.

There is no clear winner in this debate. Applications use connectionless or connection-oriented transports depending upon their particular needs. If an application can afford to resend a lost message, then connectionless transport will do. If an application demands that messages arrive intact and in order, then it must use connection-oriented service.

For example, connectionless service is adequate for an application that implements the ''login query'' protocol described in Section 1.3. If the client does not receive a response after a certain period of time (because the client's query request was lost or the server's response was lost), the client simply resends the query request.

On the other hand, applications that manage complicated sessions with a remote machine (for example, a remote login application) should use connection-oriented service. Applications like these send many messages, and coding the application to keep track of each message makes it unnecessarily complicated.

Note that connectionless transport providers may lose the server's response as well as the original request. Therefore, you should only use connectionless service for idempotent operations. An idempotent operation is one that can be repeated several times without affecting the final result. For example, the ''set counter to 1'' operation is idempotent. If the server's acknowledgment of this operation is lost, you can resend the request without affecting the result. On the other hand, the ''add 1 to counter'' operation is not idempotent. If the server's response to this operation is lost, resending the request causes the counter to be incorrectly updated.

Chapters 7 and 8 describe the SVR4 routines that manipulate connectionless and connection-oriented transport providers. As we will see, these routines are designed to work over any transport provider, a goal that SVR4 had from the start.

SVR4 builds on the networking facilities of many variants of the UNIX system. Before explaining the SVR4 networking architecture, we present a brief history of these networking facilities.

1.7   History of Networking on the UNIX System

Networking on the UNIX system began in 1975 with the UNIX-to-UNIX copy (UUCP) facility. The UUCP facility enables batched file transfer and remote command execution between UNIX systems. The UUCP facility can transfer electronic mail and files over low-speed, low-cost communications links.

In 1977, the Defense Advanced Research Projects Agency (DARPA) of the U.S. Department of Defense funded the development of the TCP/IP protocols. The TCP/IP protocols are powerful internetworking protocols that allow communication over a variety of physical media.

In 1981, the Berkeley Software Distribution (BSD) UNIX system included the TCP/IP suite and introduced the socket interface. The socket interface consists of routines that allow interprocess communication, both locally and over a network.

Sun Microsystems introduced the Network File System (NFS) and the Open Network Computing Remote Procedure Call (RPC) facility in 1985. NFS allows machines to transparently share file systems, and has become a de facto standard file-sharing mechanism for UNIX systems. RPC is a powerful programming paradigm that allows users to distribute applications across a network.

In 1986, UNIX System V Release 3 introduced the Transport Level Interface (TLI), Remote File Sharing (RFS), and the STREAMS mechanism. TLI is a transport-independent interface to transport providers based on the ISO Transport Service Specification. RFS allows transparent access to remote file systems and supports full UNIX system semantics. The STREAMS framework allows modular development of communication protocols, and provides the means to share software modules.

In 1990, UNIX System V Release 4 introduced the Network Selection and Name-to-Address Mapping facilities. These facilities provide generic routines for obtaining addresses and determining which transport providers exist on the system.

1.8   Networking on SVR4

SVR4 merges the networking facilities of UNIX System V Release 3, Berkeley Software Distributions 4.2 and 4.3, and SunOS. It also introduces new networking routines that help create transport-independent applications.

It provides the following from UNIX System V Release 3:

- the Transport Level Interface (TLI), a transport-independent interface that application programs use to access transport providers;

- the Remote File Sharing (RFS) mechanism, which provides transparent access to remote files and devices;

- the network listener, a facility for connection management;

- STREAMS, a framework for developing network protocols; and

- the UUCP family of commands.

It includes the following features of BSD Versions 4.2 and 4.3:

- sockets, a transport-layer interface for application programs;

- the TCP/IP protocols and associated TCP/IP applications;

- UNIX system-specific TCP/IP applications such as **rlogin**, **rcp**, and **rsh**; and

- the **inetd** facility, which manages TCP/IP server applications.

It has the following features of SunOS:

- the Network File System (NFS), a de facto standard for sharing files between machines in a network;

- the Remote Procedure Call (RPC) facility, a programming paradigm for creating networked applications; and

- the External Data Representation (XDR), a machine-independent way of representing data passed between systems.

The new facilities introduced in SVR4 are as follows:

- the Network Selection mechanism, a set of routines that allow applications to figure out which transport providers exist on the system; and

- Name-to-Address Mapping, a facility that provides transport-independent routines to determine addresses of services.

The OSI protocols are not included in the base SVR4 system. However, the STREAMS mechanism provides the framework to implement those protocols. The OSI protocols are available from third-party software vendors.

1.9   SVR4 Network Architecture

The SVR4 Network Architecture consists of the STREAMS framework, port monitors, TLI, the Service Access Facility, the Network Selection mechanism, and the Name-to-Address Mapping facility. Figure 1.4 shows the relationship of these features. The client side of the application uses the STREAMS framework, TLI, the Network Selection mechanism, and the Name-to-Address Mapping facility. The server side of the application uses the STREAMS framework, TLI, a port monitor, and the Service Access Controller (SAC), an administrative piece of the Service Access Facility. These features work together to make application development easier. The following

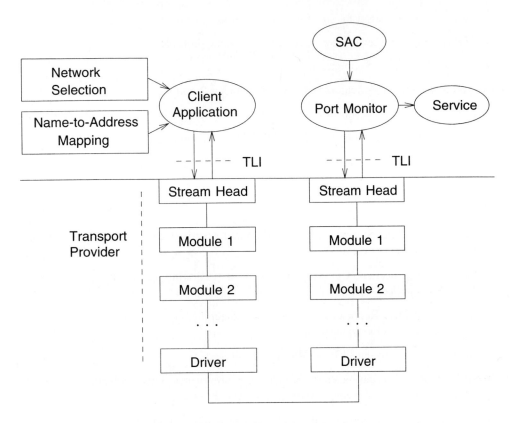

Figure 1.4 The SVR4 Network Architecture

sections briefly describe each of these elements, beginning with the STREAMS mechanism.

The STREAMS Mechanism

The STREAMS mechanism is a framework that lets you customize a data path. The framework consists of UNIX system calls, kernel resources, and kernel subroutines. Figure 1.5 shows the STREAMS model.

You can consider a ''stream'' to be a layered set of software modules that manipulate data as they travel from your application to a device driver and from the device driver to your application. Each module accepts data, performs an action on them, and sends them to the next module in the stream. It is similar to an information bucket brigade,

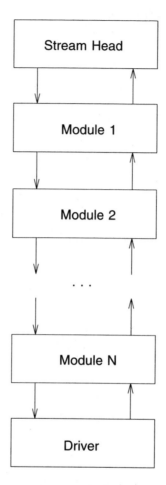

Figure 1.5   The STREAMS Model

but while the human units in a bucket brigade pass the pailfuls of water intact, the software modules in streams manipulate the ongoing messages before sending them on their way.

The stream has three parts: the stream head, the device driver, and streams modules.

The **stream head** is the beginning of the stream. It is responsible for translating the system calls generated by your application into messages that are sent down the stream.

The **device driver** is software that controls the hardware device. It must be written to the streams interface, meaning it must be able to accept messages from the stream and send messages up the stream.

The **streams modules** are units of software that manipulate the messages as they flow up and down the stream. Each stream can have zero or more modules, which are stacked between the stream head and the device driver. Each module accepts streams messages, performs an operation on them, and sends the modified messages on their way along the stream.

The best way to see the workings of a stream is through an example. Suppose you wanted a general mechanism that encrypts data before they leave your machine. Instead of modifying every application to do the encryption, you can create an "encryption module" to use on a stream. When this module gets a message flowing down the stream from the stream head, it encrypts the data contained in the message and passes the message down the stream (causing the data to be encrypted when they go out the wire). When the module gets a message flowing up the stream from the network device driver, it decrypts the data and passes the message up the stream. The module neither knows nor cares which modules are above and below it; thus it can be placed on any stream where encryption is needed. Allowing a module to perform terse, specific actions on data is the power of the STREAMS framework. Given a set of modules, you can choose which ones to use to customize a data path.

STREAMS-based networking allows protocol substitution and easy protocol migration. For example, if you had the TCP/IP protocol suite written to the STREAMS framework, you could easily replace the TCP modules with OSI modules. Chapter 2 presents details on how to manipulate a stream.

Applications access a STREAMS-based transport provider via the Transport Level Interface (TLI). TLI is a set of routines that allow you to initialize a transport provider, send and receive data, and perform other actions necessary to achieve data transfer. Details of TLI are given in Chapters 7 and 8.

Network Selection and Name-to-Address Mapping

The Network Selection and Name-to-Address Mapping routines provide the means to create completely transport-independent applications. The Network Selection feature lets applications select which transport provider to use for communication. The Name-to-Address Mapping facility provides routines for finding the transport address of a service over the selected transport provider.

Previous to SVR4, you had to "hard-code" into the application specific information such as the device to access the transport provider and the routines needed to find transport addresses. Embedding this information into an application makes it inherently transport-dependent. The Network Selection and Name-to-Address Mapping routines provide a way to get this information at execution time, freeing the application from having to specify it explicitly. Chapter 9 details these routines.

Ports and Port Monitors

As mentioned in Section 1.3, a network service must associate itself with a unique transport address before it can receive network messages. All messages sent to that transport address are delivered to the service. In this sense, you can consider a transport address to be an entry point into the machine.

SVR4 uses the term ''port'' to refer to any external access point into the system. This term normally refers to serial and parallel communication lines; but, because a transport address is also an external access point into the system, SVR4 uses this term to refer to a transport address as well.

Associating a service with a port is tedious. The service must perform the TLI operations required to attach itself to the port, wait for a client to communicate with it, and, if the port is over a connection-oriented transport provider, perform the TLI operations needed to accept the connection. Communication can take place only after these operations are performed.

SVR4 provides *port monitors* to make things easier for a service. A port monitor is a process that works on a service's behalf. It performs all the operations needed to establish communication for the service. It monitors one or more ports, waiting for messages to arrive. The ports must be of the same type, that is, a single port monitor can control serial lines or transport addresses, but not a combination of both.

When a port monitor controls a transport address on a connection-oriented transport provider, it greatly simplifies the service. The port monitor performs the TLI operations to associate *itself* with the transport address, and, when a connection indication appears, it performs the necessary operations to accept the connection. Once accepted, the port monitor passes the connection to the service. In this sense, the port monitor is like a secretary that monitors several phones, waits for one of the phones to ring, answers it, accepts the call, and passes the phone to the associated service. The service can then simply start communicating with the client.

Each port monitor reads a configuration file that specifies which ports to control, the service associated with each port, and other information. For example, the configuration file in Figure 1.6 instructs the port monitor to poll ports 1, 2, 3, 4, and 5. If a connection request comes in on port 3, the port monitor accepts the connection and passes it to the **/usr/sbin/serv_c** command, which implements the server side of an application protocol.

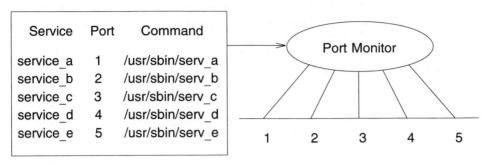

Port Monitor Configuration File

Figure 1.6   A Port Monitor

SVR4 supports three port monitors: **ttymon**, **inetd**, and **listen**. The **ttymon** port monitor controls terminal access to the system. Previous to SVR4, a separate **getty** process monitored each serial line and spawned a **login** process when it detected activity. SVR4 replaced the multiple **getty** processes with a single **ttymon** port monitor. The **ttymon** process listens on multiple ports, waits for line activity, and, when activity is detected, invokes a configured service. Usually, the service is the **login** program.

The **inetd** port monitor is used by the TCP/IP suite. As with all port monitors, it reads a configuration file to figure out which ports to control. The **inetd** program monitors ports for services that operate in connection-oriented and connectionless modes. For connection-oriented services, **inetd** attaches itself to the port, waits for a connection request, accepts the connection, and starts the service. For connectionless services, it attaches itself to the port, waits for a message to appear, and starts the appropriate service when a message arrives.

The **listen** port monitor is a general-purpose network listener. It can work over any connection-oriented transport provider, but cannot monitor ports on connectionless transport providers. It reads a configuration file to figure out which ports to control, attaches itself to each port, waits for a connection request, accepts the connection, and spawns the service. However, unlike other port monitors, the configuration file can specify which STREAMS modules to push onto the stream before spawning the service. Additionally, the **listen** process can pass the connection to an already running service, allowing a service to maintain state information between connections.

The Service Access Facility

SVR4 introduced a new feature called the Service Access Facility (SAF), which collectively refers to port monitors and processes to administer them. The SAF is a common administrative mechanism that allows the administrator of a machine to install and configure port monitors.

Figure 1.7 illustrates the high-level architecture of the SAF. The Service Access Controller (SAC) is a program that controls port monitors. It allows administrators to show port monitor status, add and remove a port monitor, start and stop a port monitor, and enable and disable a port monitor.

In writing networked applications, we are not concerned with the SAF, because it is an administrative mechanism. We are, however, concerned with STREAMS, port monitors, TLI, Network Selection, and Name-to-Address Mapping, since we use these features directly when developing applications.

Because the STREAMS framework is a key to network programming in SVR4, we begin by presenting the basic routines that manipulate a stream. We then show how to use the UNIX shell to paste existing tools into usable applications, and work our way to creating more sophisticated applications with the System V Release 4 network routines and interfaces.

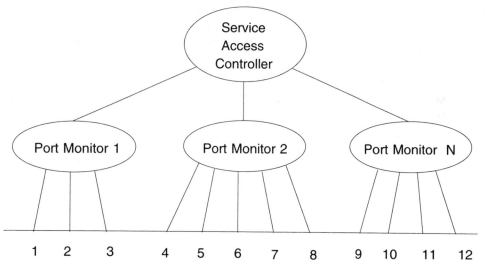

Figure 1.7   The SAF Architecture

For Further Reading

1. AT&T, *UNIX System V Release 4 Network User's and Administrator's Guide*, Prentice Hall, Englewood Cliffs, NJ, 1990.

2. Bartoli, A., ''The Application Layer of the Reference Model of Open Systems Interconnection,'' *Proceedings of the IEEE*, December 1983.

3. Rose, M., *The Open Book—A Practical Perspective on OSI*, Prentice Hall, Englewood Cliffs, NJ, 1990.

4. Stallings, W., *Handbook of Computer Communications Standards—Volume 1, The Open Systems Interconnection (OSI) Model and OSI-Related Standards*, Macmillan, New York, 1987.

5. Tanenbaum, A., *Computer Networks*, Prentice Hall, Englewood Cliffs, NJ, 1989.

Exercises

1.1   Describe the datagram service and virtual-circuit service. What are the pros and cons of each?

1.2   Consider an application protocol in which the client machine sends a file name to a server machine. If the file exists, the server machine removes the file and returns a **0** to the client machine. If the file does not exist, the server machine returns a **1** to the client machine. Is this an idempotent operation? Why or why not?

1.3   Describe some more benefits and drawbacks of networking other than those presented in this chapter.

Chapter 2

Introduction to STREAMS

2.1 Introduction

The STREAMS framework is a replacement of the traditional UNIX communications system. It reflects the ISO model by taking a layered approach to I/O, providing modules that manipulate data as they travel into and out of the computer.

SVR4 implements all character I/O devices via the STREAMS mechanism. Every form of communication is now STREAMS-based, including terminals, network protocols, and UNIX pipes. A basic understanding of STREAMS is helpful when developing networking applications. This chapter presents an overview of STREAMS and examines the framework from an application's point of view.

2.2 Overview of STREAMS

STREAMS is the framework for application communication in SVR4. It provides a full-duplex data path between your application and an I/O device. The data path is actually a set of software modules that manipulate data as they travel between your application and the device driver, and your application can customize the data path by choosing which modules it wants on the stream.

The STREAMS mechanism is like two fine-tuned assembly lines, one that goes from your application to the I/O device and one that goes from the I/O device to your application. Just as human elements in an assembly line modify widgets as they travel along a belt, STREAMS provides software modules that modify data as they travel up and down a stream. Each STREAMS module performs a terse, specific action on the data and passes the modified data to the next module on the stream. It is the modules that make STREAMS a powerful mechanism—modules can implement the layers of the seven-layer ISO model, encrypt and decrypt data, and perform many other useful functions.

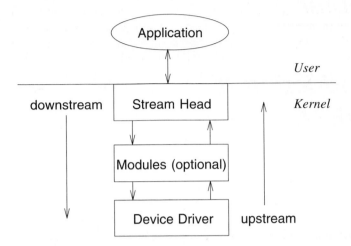

Figure 2.1   The STREAMS Framework

A stream has three parts: the **stream head**, the **device driver**, and optional **modules**. Figure 2.1 shows the structure of a stream. We use the term *downstream* to refer to the path from the application to the device driver and the term *upstream* to refer to the path from the device driver to the application.

The stream head is at the top of the stream. It resides in the SVR4 kernel, and applications interface with it via SVR4 system calls such as `open()`, `close()`, `read()`, `write()`, and `ioctl()`. The stream head interprets these system calls and performs the appropriate STREAMS actions. For example, if your application issues the `write()` system call to send data to the device driver, the stream head creates a STREAMS message containing the data and sends the message downstream. Similarly, if your application issues the `read()` system call, the stream head delivers data that the device driver sends upstream to your application.

The STREAMS modules sit between the stream head and the device driver. They perform actions on data as they travel up and down the stream. Each module accepts a data message, performs an operation on it, and passes it to the next module on the stream. For example, consider the ''line-discipline'' module that performs terminal line-discipline actions. This module takes a data message as it travels along a stream, performs line-discipline functions (such as the processing of ''erase'' and ''kill'' characters), and sends the modified data on their way. This frees the terminal device driver from performing these actions and allows an application to choose alternate line disciplines by removing this module and pushing a different one onto the stream. Each application can customize the data path by pushing whatever modules it requires onto the stream.

The device driver is at the bottom of the stream. It can be a real device driver, which handles physical hardware, or a pseudo-device driver, which emulates a real device without having physical hardware associated with it. The device driver accepts messages sent downstream and interfaces with the device. It also processes interrupts from the device and sends messages upstream.

2.3 Manipulating a Stream

Applications manipulate a stream with SVR4 system calls. An application gains initial access to the stream the same way it gains initial access to any device—by using the `open()` system call. Each STREAMS device is represented by a file name in the UNIX file system. Applications specify this file name when opening the stream. For example, the Ethernet Media Driver may be represented by the device file named **/dev/emd**, and applications open it to establish a stream to that device.

The `open()` system call initializes the stream head and sets up the device driver. Your application uses the file descriptor returned from the `open()` system call on subsequent accesses to the stream. Figure 2.2 shows the stream after an application opens a device file.

```
fd = open("/dev/device", flags);
```

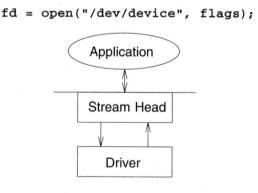

Figure 2.2 The Result of an Open

Once opened, your application can push modules onto the stream via the `ioctl()` system call with the **I_PUSH** parameter. The third parameter to the `ioctl()` system call is the name of the module you want on the stream. Once pushed, the module resides between the stream head and the device driver.

Figures 2.3 through 2.5 show how your application can modify the stream by adding and removing modules. Figure 2.3 shows the stream after your application uses the

```
ioctl(fd, I_PUSH, "module1");
```

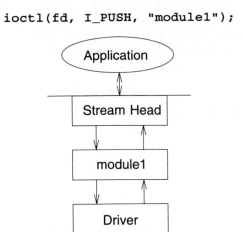

Figure 2.3   The Result of Pushing a Module

```
ioctl(fd, I_PUSH, "module2");
```

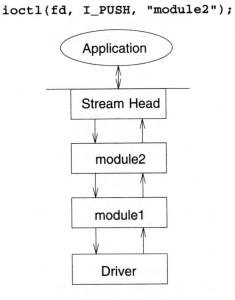

Figure 2.4   The Result of a Second Push

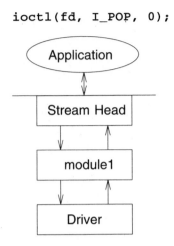

Figure 2.5   The Result of Popping a Module

I_PUSH operation to push **module1** onto the stream, and Figure 2.4 shows the result of subsequently pushing **module2** onto the stream.

Once a module is on the stream, it cannot be bypassed. For example, if you push **module1** onto the stream, there is no way to say "send this data down the stream, but pass it directly from the stream head to the device driver."

Your application can push as many modules as it wants, and as illustrated in Figure 2.4, modules are pushed in a stacklike fashion. After your application pushes the second module, data sent downstream are processed by **module2**, which passes them to **module1**, which in turn passes the data to the device driver. For efficiency reasons, the STREAMS framework does not copy the data from one module to the next. Instead, it passes a pointer to the data between modules.

Modules can be removed from the stream by using the **ioctl()** system call with the **I_POP** parameter. Figure 2.5 shows the configuration after your application removes **module2** from the stream. Only the top module can be popped, so your application may have to issue several **I_POP** requests to delete all modules on the stream.

Your application sends and receives data by using the normal **read()** and **write()** system calls. Figures 2.6 and 2.7 illustrate how these system calls interact with the stream.

When your application issues the **write()** system call, the stream head interprets the system call, copies the data from your application into the SVR4 kernel, translates the data into a STREAMS message, and sends the message downstream.

`write(fd, data, nbytes);`

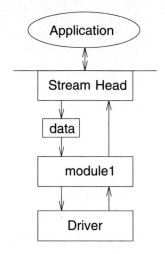

Figure 2.6   Sending Data with `write()`

`read(fd, buffer, nbytes);`

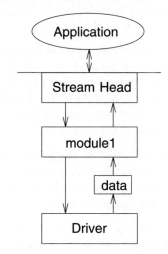

Figure 2.7   The `read()` System Call

Your application reads data with the **read()** system call. Reading data from a stream works the same as with any other device, for example, the **read()** call blocks until data are available (unless your application specified the **O_NDELAY** flag on the **open()** system call). If data are at the stream head and your application does not issue the **read()** system call, the data remain queued at the stream head awaiting consumption. When your application exits, all unread data associated with the stream are freed.

SVR4 has four more system calls for STREAMS I/O: **putmsg()**, **putpmsg()**, **getmsg()**, and **getpmsg()**. Each works similarly to **read()** and **write()**, but they provide more powerful functionality.

Figures 2.8 and 2.9 illustrate **putmsg()** and **getmsg()**. The **putmsg()** system call lets you pass control information with data to the stream head. Control information is interpreted by the modules on the stream. For example, when a network application sends data over a connectionless transport provider, it must specify the destination address along with the data. The destination address is control information, and is separate from the data. So, if the transport provider is implemented using the STREAMS framework, an application can use the **putmsg()** system call to send the destination address and data to the transport provider.

The **putmsg()** system call also lets you mark a message as "high priority." The STREAMS framework places high-priority messages ahead of normal messages. It does that on a first-in, first-out basis. So, if there are several messages waiting to be processed by a module, the STREAMS framework puts a high priority message in front of all normal messages but behind any existing high-priority messages.

The **getmsg()** system call reads messages containing control information and data from the stream. For example, when a network application receives a datagram from a connectionless transport provider, the sender's address is returned with the data. The sender's address is control information. If the transport provider is implemented using the STREAMS framework, an application can use the **getmsg()** system call to receive the data and the address associated with a datagram.

If there are several messages queued at the stream head, the **getmsg()** system call returns the message at the front of the queue. It also tells you if the message was marked as "high priority." If desired, you can tell the **getmsg()** system call to read the next message only if it is a high-priority message. In that case, the system call reads the message if it is of high priority and leaves the message queued at the stream head if it is not.

The semantics of the control information are defined by the STREAMS modules that generate or receive the message. Most networking applications do not use **putmsg()** and **getmsg()** directly; they usually use the Transport Level Interface (TLI) routines that generate these system calls on the application's behalf.

`putmsg(fd, cntrlp, datap, flags);`

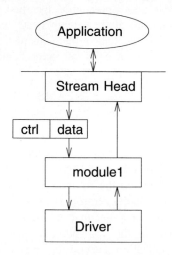

Figure 2.8   Sending Messages with `putmsg()`

`getmsg(fd, cntrlp, datap, flagsp);`

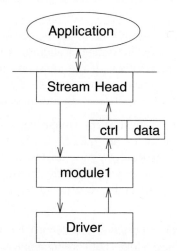

Figure 2.9   The `getmsg()` System Call

The `putpmsg()` system call is very similar to the `putmsg()` system call, that is, it lets you pass control information with data to the stream head. However, it also lets you specify a "priority band" for the message.

A priority band is an indication of the urgency of the message. The SVR4 STREAMS mechanism uses the priority band of a message to figure out where to put the message on a queue. STREAMS defines three types of messages and puts them on a queue with the following precedence:

1. **High-priority messages**. A high-priority message is an urgent message. As mentioned before, the STREAMS framework puts a high-priority message in front of all normal messages but behind any existing high-priority messages.

2. **Priority messages**. A priority message is not as urgent as a high-priority message, but it is more urgent than a normal message. A priority message is associated with a priority band. The STREAMS framework defines 256 priority bands, numbered from `0` to `255`. Messages in priority band `0` are the least urgent, and messages in priority band `255` are the most urgent. If you use the `putpmsg()` system call to send a message in priority band `n`, the STREAMS framework puts it ahead of all messages in band `(n-1)` or lower and after all high-priority messages and messages in band `n` or higher.

3. **Normal messages**. A normal message is not an urgent message. If there are several messages waiting to be processed by a module, the STREAMS framework puts a normal message at the end of the queue. Normal messages are placed in priority band `0`.

The `getpmsg()` system call works the same as the `getmsg()` system call, that is, it reads messages containing control information and data from the stream. But, unlike the `getmsg()` system call, the `getpmsg()` system call lets you specify that you want messages only in a given priority band.

If there are several messages queued at the stream head, the `getpmsg()` system call returns the message at the head of the queue. It also tells you if the message was marked as "high priority" or, if the message is not of high priority, it tells you the priority band associated with the message.

If desired, you can tell the `getpmsg()` system call to read the next message only if it is a high-priority message or if it is in a specified priority band. In those cases, the system call reads the message if it is high priority or if the priority band is greater than or equal to the requested priority band. It leaves the message queued at the stream head otherwise.

As with `putmsg()` and `getmsg()`, most networking applications do not use `putpmsg()` and `getpmsg()` directly; they usually use the Transport Level Interface (TLI) routines that generate these system calls on the application's behalf.

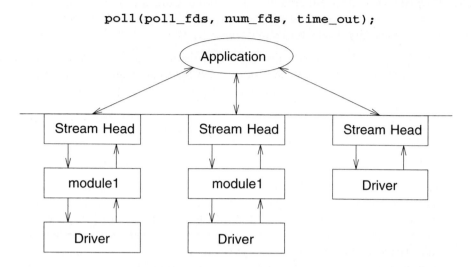

Figure 2.10   Polling Streams

SVR4 also provides the `poll()` system call that allows your application to monitor
multiple streams, waiting for messages to arrive. For example, suppose your application were monitoring a terminal, waiting for the user to enter data, and monitoring two
network connections, waiting for network messages to arrive. Issuing a `read()` system call on one of the three streams would not work correctly because the `read()`
system call would wait for data to arrive, potentially delaying the processing of data
that appeared on one of the other two streams. The `poll()` system call solves this
problem by allowing you to monitor several streams simultaneously. The `poll()`
system call monitors the specified streams and returns when data appear on any of
them. Your application can then query on which stream the data appeared.

Figure 2.10 illustrates an application polling three streams. In this configuration, the
application opened a stream, pushed a module, opened another stream, pushed the
same module, opened a third stream, and then polled all three streams for incoming
data. The `poll()` system call returns when data appear on any of the streams. If
desired, you can set a time-out parameter to limit the amount of time the `poll()`
system call waits for data to arrive.

Other STREAMS Operations

Besides pushing and popping modules, SVR4 provides other STREAMS `ioctl()` operations that your application can use. They include the following:

- **I_LOOK**, which returns the name of the module just below the stream head;

- **I_FLUSH**, which lets you flush data out of the stream;

- **I_FIND**, which, given the name of a module, returns 1 if that module exists anywhere on the stream and 0 otherwise; and

- **I_LIST**, which lists all the modules on the stream.

Other functions are also available that perform control functions on a stream. These are presented as the overview continues.

2.4 Multiplexing Device Drivers

STREAMS provides a multiplexing capability. This gives a device driver the ability to accept messages from several streams simultaneously and funnel data to several streams below it. This is very important for networking applications, because there can be many applications on the machine that want to create a stream into a network device driver.

The simplest form of multiplexing is N-to-1 multiplexing, as shown in Figure 2.11. An N-to-1 multiplexing driver accepts data from several streams and passes the data to the device. Multiplexors of this type include network device drivers that can accommodate streams from several applications simultaneously.

As stated earlier, applications gain initial access to a stream by opening a device file name. Every device file has a major number and a minor number associated with it. The major number identifies the device, and the minor number identifies a subunit of that device. With a STREAMS multiplexing device, each minor number identifies a unique stream into the multiplexor. When your application opens the device file, the multiplexing driver uses the minor number to identify the stream.

For example, Figure 2.11 shows three applications accessing a multiplexing device. For this to occur, each application must open a device file with a unique minor number. So, if the major number of the device were **56**, there could be three device files, each with a different minor number:

```
crw-rw-rw- 1 root bin  56, 1  Dec 19 09:27 /dev/mux01
crw-rw-rw- 1 root bin  56, 2  Dec 19 09:27 /dev/mux02
crw-rw-rw- 1 root bin  56, 3  Dec 19 09:27 /dev/mux03
```

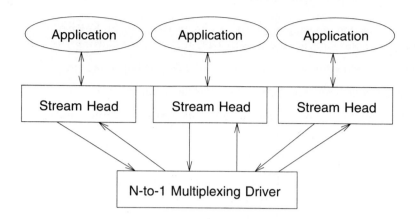

Figure 2.11   N-to-1 Multiplexor

Each of those device files represents a unique stream into the multiplexing device driver. Note that in most networking environments, a device driver requires that each application create a separate stream to establish communication (because havoc may arise if two applications try to establish connections over the same stream, similar to two parties trying to make a phone call using the same telephone). In this case, the multiplexing device driver will only allow one open to occur per minor number (that is, it returns an error condition when an application attempts to open a device file that is already opened by another application). So, to gain a unique stream into this type of device, an application would first try to open `/dev/mux01`, and if the `open()` system call fails, it would try `/dev/mux02`. The application must continue in such a fashion until the `open()` system call succeeds. As we will see shortly, SVR4 provides ''clone devices'' to make the search for a unique stream easier.

Each stream into the multiplexor can push whatever modules it chooses. As illustrated in Figure 2.12, one application can push a module without affecting the other streams into the multiplexor.

Multiplexing drivers can also be 1-to-M, as shown in Figure 2.13. Here, a driver accepts messages from one stream and passes the data to one of several streams beneath it. This form of multiplexing is essential for internetworking drivers that must channel data from an application to one of several other networking device drivers.

Applications see the 1-to-M multiplexing driver as the end of the stream. Internally, the multiplexing device driver creates a new stream to each of the device drivers below it.

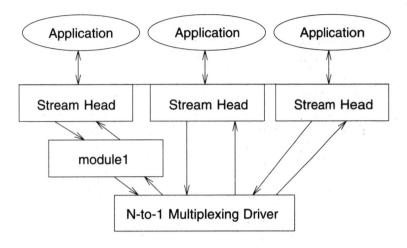

Figure 2.12   Pushing a Module

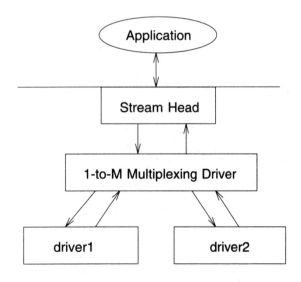

Figure 2.13   1-to-M Multiplexor

The STREAMS mechanism also supports N-to-M multiplexors. As shown in Figure 2.14, this type of multiplexing driver accepts input from several streams and channels the data to several streams below it. As with 1-to-M multiplexors, applications see the N-to-M multiplexor as the end of the stream.

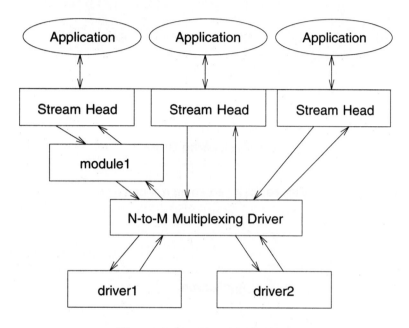

Figure 2.14   N-to-M Multiplexor

An administrative application must explicitly set up 1-to-M and N-to-M multiplexors. For example, to set up the configuration in Figure 2.13, an administrative application must first open the 1-to-M multiplexing device driver and then open **driver1**. Once opened, the administrative application issues the **ioctl()** system call with the **I_LINK** parameter, passing the file descriptors from the two **open()** system calls. This links **driver1** under the multiplexor. The application then opens **driver2** and links it under the multiplexor as well. The **I_LINK** call passes a ''mux identifier'' to the multiplexing device driver, and the driver uses that value to identify each stream under it.

A good example of multiplexing device drivers is the STREAMS-based Transmission Control Protocol/Internet Protocol (TCP/IP) suite. Details of TCP/IP are given in Chapter 3, but from a high level, we can view the TCP/IP suite as four parts:

1. TCP, the Transmission Control Protocol;

2. UDP, the User Datagram Protocol;

3. IP, the Internet Protocol; and

4. one or more device drivers.

Figure 2.15 shows the drivers involved with the STREAMS-based implementation of TCP/IP. The setup must be done by an administrative application, and it is usually done when the system initializes. The administrative application first links all the network device drivers under the IP driver; it then links the IP driver under the TCP and the UDP drivers.

The TCP and UDP drivers are N-to-1 multiplexors, because they accept data from several streams simultaneously and pass the data to the IP driver. Applications see the TCP or the UDP driver as the end of the stream, and, as with all STREAMS-based devices, they gain access to the stream by opening a device file associated with the driver (in this case, by opening a device file associated with TCP or UDP). The IP driver is an N-to-M multiplexor, taking data from the higher-level drivers and passing them to one of the network device drivers beneath it. Chapter 3 presents the details of TCP/IP.

Normally, the SVR4 kernel tears down the multiplexor configuration when the last stream into the multiplexor closes. So, if the configuration is to persist, the administrative application that sets it up must be a daemon process that keeps at least one stream open.

That may cause an unwanted amount of daemon processes on a system. SVR4 provides a ''persistent link'' feature that allows a multiplexing configuration to remain even if there are no applications that hold streams into it. To create a persistent link, the administrative process uses the **ioctl()** system call with the **I_PLINK** parameter instead of the **I_LINK** parameter when linking a device driver under a multiplexor. In that way, the administrative application can exit without dismantling the configuration. Persistent links can be dismantled later when another administrative process issues the **ioctl()** system call with the **I_PUNLINK** parameter.

As described earlier, multiplexing device drivers use the minor number of the device file to differentiate streams. If you want to create a unique stream into the device, your applications must open a device file that is not held open by another application. Since finding such a device file is a time-consuming task, SVR4 offers the clone device to help applications gain a unique stream into a multiplexor. Our overview of streams continues with a high-level view of the clone device.

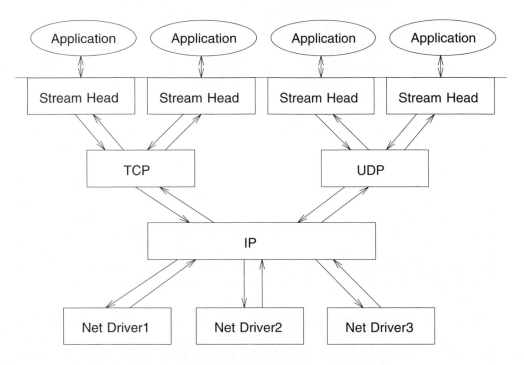

Figure 2.15   STREAMS-Based TCP/IP

2.5   Clone Devices

The clone device is a STREAMS-based pseudo-driver. Just like any other device, it is accessed by opening a device file that has a major and minor number. But, when you open the device file for the clone device, the clone device creates a unique stream into the device whose major number corresponds to the *minor* number of the clone device file you opened.

Here's how it works. Suppose the major number of the clone device is **63**, and your application opens the device file with major number **63** and minor number **40**. Opening this file causes the clone device to do the following:

1.   It looks at the minor number, and, because the minor number is **40** in this case, it finds the device that corresponds to *major* number **40**.

2.   It calls the open routine of the device at major number **40**, passing it the special **CLONE_OPEN** flag.

3. The device at major number **40** recognizes the **CLONE_OPEN** flag and finds an unused minor number (for this example, assume the driver finds that minor number **23** is not used by any other application). The driver then goes through its normal processing as if your application had opened the device file with major number **40** and minor number **23**. When this processing is complete, the driver returns the minor number (that is, a value of **23** in this example) to the clone driver.

4. The clone driver returns a stream to the application as if the application had opened the device file with major number **40** and minor number **23**. This is a unique stream into the device driver at major number **40**.

Clone devices simplify the search for a unique stream into a multiplexing device driver because they find a unique stream for you. To illustrate, suppose the multiplexor for the **tcp** networking driver had the following device files:

```
crw-rw-rw- 1 root bin  40,  1 Dec 19 09:27 /dev/tcp01
crw-rw-rw- 1 root bin  40,  2 Dec 19 09:27 /dev/tcp02
crw-rw-rw- 1 root bin  40,  3 Dec 19 09:27 /dev/tcp03
crw-rw-rw- 1 root bin  40,  4 Dec 19 09:27 /dev/tcp04
```

To gain a unique stream into the **tcp** driver, your application would first try to open **/dev/tcp01**, and if that failed, would try to open each of the other device files. Now, suppose there were a device file for the clone device:

```
crw-rw-rw- 1 root bin  63, 40 Dec 19 09:27 /dev/tcp
```

Here, your application would only have to open **/dev/tcp**. Because this device file accesses the clone device, the clone device driver would call the **tcp** driver (at major number **40**). The **tcp** device finds an unused minor number and continues as if your application had opened the device file with that minor number. When the **open()** system call completes, your application has a unique stream into the **tcp** driver.

As mentioned earlier, even UNIX pipes and terminals are STREAMS-based in SVR4. The following sections present an overview of STREAMS-based pipes and terminals.

2.6 STREAMS-Based Pipes

A pipe is a facility that allows processes to communicate, and SVR4 implements them using the STREAMS framework. Applications create a pipe the same way they did in previous releases of the UNIX system—by using the **pipe()** system call. Once created, applications can use the pipe for interprocess communication.

The STREAMS implementation of pipes does introduce one difference in semantics. Previously, pipes were unidirectional—one end of the pipe was opened for reading and the other end was opened for writing. In the STREAMS implementation, pipes are bidirectional, that is, your application can read and write from both ends. Data written to one end are read by the other. So, if your application wants to use the pipe in a unidirectional manner, it still can.

The STREAMS implementation also allows your applications to push modules onto a stream. That lets you customize the data path between the two processes communicating over the pipe. However, if you choose not to exploit the features of STREAMS, your application can manipulate the STREAMS-based pipe in exactly the same way as in previous releases of the UNIX system.

Figures 2.16(a) and 2.16(b) show how to create two processes that can communicate over a STREAMS-based pipe. Your application first issues the **pipe()** system call, which creates a pipe and returns two file descriptors. The pipe is full-duplex, so data written to the first file descriptor are available for reading on the second, and data written to the second file descriptor are available for reading on the first. All data appear in a first-in, first-out basis.

Figure 2.16(b) shows the results of your application creating a child process via the **fork()** system call. The parent process closes the first file descriptor returned by the **pipe()** system call and the child process closes the second. The parent and child can communicate with each other through the pipe.

Your application must be aware of one subtle point when using STREAMS-based pipes. If you want to use the **ioctl()** system call with the **I_FLUSH** parameter to flush all data in the pipe, you must first push the **pipemod** module onto the stream. This is because the STREAMS framework has no way to figure out the ''midpoint'' of the STREAMS-based pipe, that is, the place where the direction of the flush messages should be switched from downstream to upstream. The **pipemod** module specifically marks the midpoint of the stream and changes the direction of the flush messages. It must be the first thing pushed on the stream, and it can be pushed onto either end. If your application does not use the **I_FLUSH** call, the **pipemod** module is not needed on the stream.

Named STREAMS

The Named STREAMS feature is the ability for an application to attach a stream to a file. Once attached, another application can access the stream by opening the file.

This is particularly useful with STREAMS-based pipes. An application can create a pipe, attach one end to a file, and have unrelated processes communicate with it by opening the file.

Figures 2.17(a) through 2.17(c) show how this works. As illustrated in Figure 2.17(a), your application creates a pipe with the **pipe()** system call. Then, as shown in Figure 2.17(b), it attaches one end of the pipe to a file with the **fattach()** routine.

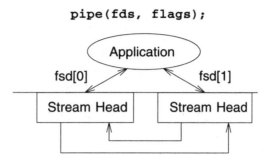

Figure 2.16(a)   The Result of a `pipe()` System Call

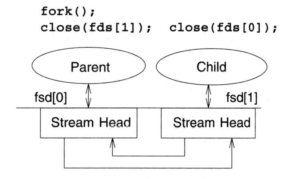

Figure 2.16(b)   After a `fork()` System Call

The file must exist in the file system, and it cannot already have a stream attached to it. Next, as shown in Figure 2.17(c), any process that opens the file can communicate with your application through the pipe.

Named STREAMS provide an easy way for two unrelated processes to communicate. But there is a drawback in the scenario presented in Figures 2.17(a) through 2.17(c)— if two processes opened the attached file, they would both send messages down the stream, and your application could not distinguish which messages came from which process. It would be much better if each process that opened the file obtained a unique pipe into your application.

Fortunately, SVR4 provides "file-descriptor passing" to do this. An unrelated process can create a new STREAMS-based pipe, pass one of the pipe's file descriptors to your application, and begin communicating over the new pipe. The sending and receiving of file descriptors are done with the **I_SENDFD** and **I_RECVFD** parameters, respectively, to the **ioctl()** system call.

Here's how it works:

1.   Your application creates a pipe and attaches one end of the pipe to a file.

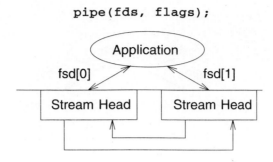

Figure 2.17(a)   Creating a Pipe

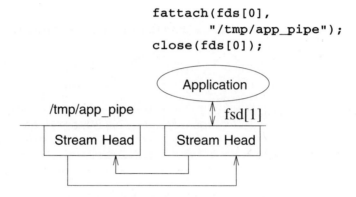

Figure 2.17(b)   Attaching the Pipe to a File

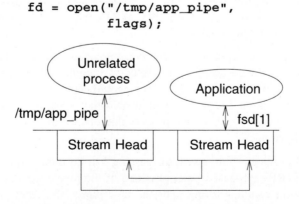

Figure 2.17(c)   An Unrelated Process Opens /tmp/app_pipe

2. It issues the `ioctl()` system call with the `I_RECVFD` parameter. This sleeps waiting for a message containing a file descriptor to arrive over the pipe.

3. An unrelated process opens the file that is attached to your pipe (this gives it access to the pipe that your application created). The unrelated process then creates a new pipe via the `pipe()` system call. Next, it sends a message to your application (through the pipe your application created) that contains one of the file descriptors of this new pipe. The process does that by issuing the `ioctl()` system call with the `I_SENDFD` parameter, specifying one of the file descriptors of the new pipe.

4. Your application wakes up from the `I_RECVFD` call, reads the message containing the file descriptor for the new pipe, and uses that file descriptor to communicate with the unrelated process.

Using `I_SENDFD` and `I_RECVFD` lets an unrelated process communicate with your application over a unique pipe, but requires a lot of extra processing. So, to simplify things, SVR4 offers the `connld` module that gives an unrelated process a new pipe when it opens the attached file.

The `connld` module can be used only on a STREAMS-based pipe that has one end attached to a file, and is used to create automatically a new pipe whenever an unrelated process opens that file. To use it, your application creates a pipe, pushes `connld` onto one end of the pipe, attaches that end to a file, and issues the `I_RECVFD` call. Then, when an unrelated process opens this file, the `connld` module creates a new pipe, generates the `I_SENDFD` call to send one end of the new pipe to your application, and returns the other end to the process that opened the file.

Figures 2.18(a) through 2.18(c) illustrate how this works. As shown in Figure 2.18(a), your application creates a pipe and pushes the `connld` module onto one end of the pipe. Next, as shown in Figure 2.18(b), your application attaches that end of the pipe to a file. It then issues the `ioctl()` system call with the `I_RECVFD` parameter, waiting for file descriptors to arrive over the pipe.

Now, as shown in Figure 2.18(c), an unrelated process can open the file. When that happens, the `connld` module recognizes the `open()` system call, generates a new pipe, and generates the `I_SENDFD` call to send one end of the new pipe to your application. When your application has one end of the new pipe, the `connld` module completes the `open()` system call by returning the other end of the pipe to the unrelated process. The unrelated process simply opens the file and obtains a unique pipe to your application.

Named STREAMS and the `connld` module let your application easily establish communication with unrelated processes on your machine. As we will see in Chapter 5, the Remote File Sharing feature of SVR4 allows your application to use Named STREAMS and the `connld` module to communicate with remote processes as well.

```
            pipe(fds, flags);
    ioctl(fds[0], I_PUSH, "connld");
```

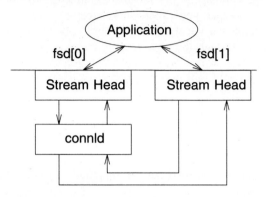

Figure 2.18(a)   After Pushing the `connld` Module

```
    fattach(fds[0],
            "/tmp/rendezvous");
    close(fds[0]);
    ioctl(fds[1], I_RECVFD,
            &new_strfd);
```

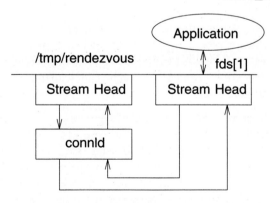

Figure 2.18(b)   After Attaching the Stream

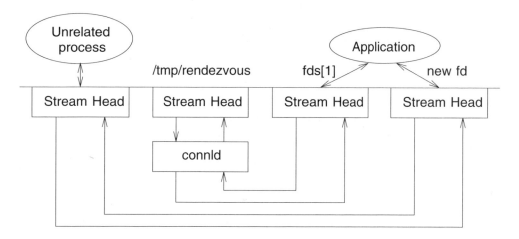

Figure 2.18(c)   Unrelated Process Opens `/tmp/rendezvous`

2.7   STREAMS-Based Terminals

Terminal devices are also STREAMS-based in SVR4. And, as with STREAMS-based pipes, STREAMS-based terminals work the same as their non-STREAMS counterparts if your application does not take advantage of the new STREAMS features. But, if desired, you can now customize the data path from your shell to the terminal by pushing modules onto the stream.

Figure 2.19 shows a STREAMS-based terminal device. The line-discipline functions, such as the processing of ''erase'' and ''kill'' characters, are now handled by the `ldterm` module. That frees the terminal device driver from implementing line-discipline functions, and lets you replace **`ldterm`** with another line-discipline module if desired.

Unfortunately, implementing the line-disciple functions within a module poses a problem: You must push the line-discipline module before you can get full terminal semantics. To access a terminal, you must first open the terminal device (for example, **`/dev/tty01`**) and then push the **`ldterm`** module. This breaks applications that expect to open a device such as **`/dev/tty01`** and immediately get full terminal functionality. So, to ensure that terminals work the same way as their non-STREAMS predecessors, SVR4 provides an ''autopush'' facility that automatically pushes modules onto a stream when an application opens the STREAMS device.

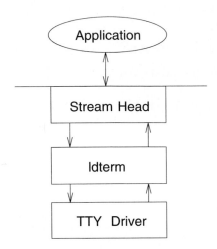

Figure 2.19   STREAMS-Based Terminals

The Autopush Facility

The autopush facility is an administrator-controlled mechanism that automatically pushes modules on a stream when an application opens a device file. This is essential for STREAMS-based terminals, because line-discipline functions are implemented via a STREAMS module and must be present on the stream to gain full terminal semantics.

To use this feature, the administrator specifies the modules that are to be pushed onto a stream when a specified device is opened. The stream head consults this list when the driver is opened for the first time and pushes the specified modules onto the stream. This lets the administrator specify that the `ldterm` module is automatically pushed on the stream when a terminal device is initially opened.

The SVR4 terminal subsystem also includes the pseudo-terminal feature. A pseudo-terminal is a device that emulates terminal functions. They are STREAMS-based in SVR4, and so an overview of pseudo-terminals is presented.

2.8   Pseudo-Terminal Devices

Pseudo-terminals are a powerful feature that network applications can use. They let you set up an environment where an application thinks it is interfacing with a STREAMS-based terminal, but instead of reading and writing to a terminal device, it interfaces with another application. This is ideal for remote login applications, because they allow the server side of the application to create an environment where a remote shell appears to be interfacing with a user at a terminal.

Figure 2.20 shows the high-level pseudo-terminal architecture, which consists of a master side and a slave side. The slave side appears as a normal STREAMS-based terminal to the application. However, instead of having a real device associated with it, the slave side has another application manipulating it through the master side. All data written to the slave side are sent to the application on the master side, and all data written to the master side appear as input to the application on the slave side.

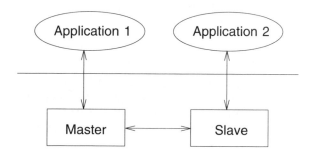

Figure 2.20   Pseudo-Terminals

This is particularly useful for remote-login applications. A remote-login application is one where a user creates a remote shell on a server machine. Since several UNIX commands must interface directly with a terminal to work correctly, the server process can use pseudo-terminals to give remote commands a terminal interface.

To illustrate, consider the remote-login setup in Figure 2.21. Here, the client side of the application sends all data entered by the user to the server side of the application. The server process reads the data from the network and writes them to the master side of the pseudo-terminal. The remote shell sees the data as input from a terminal—it does not realize that the data were originally obtained from the network. All data that the remote shell writes to the slave side of the pseudo-terminal are read by the server process, which in turn sends them over the network to the client process. The client process then displays that data to the user. Using this setup, the user interfaces with the remote shell by sending and receiving data over the network, and the remote shell sees a fully functional terminal interface.

There is a direct one-to-one correspondence between the master side and the slave side of a pseudo-terminal. Each master side has only one slave side and vice versa. SVR4 implements both sides as STREAMS devices.

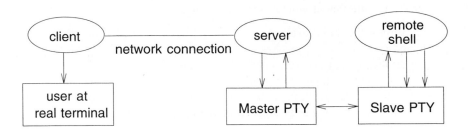

Figure 2.21   Remote Login Application

Figures 2.22(a) through 2.22(d) show the steps involved in setting up a pseudo-terminal. First, as shown in Figure 2.22(a), your application must open the **/dev/ptmx** device file. This file is a clone device with a minor number corresponding to the major number of the pseudo-terminal master device. And, because it is a clone device, opening this file returns an unused stream into the master side of a pseudo-terminal.

Now, your application has an unused stream into the master side of a pseudo-terminal. Thus, you must open the slave side. As shown in Figure 2.22(b), several steps are necessary to do this:

1. Your application calls the **grantpt()** routine, passing it the file descriptor obtained by opening the master side of the pseudo-terminal. This changes the mode of the slave device to **620** and changes the ownership of the slave device to that of the user running your application.

2. Next, your application issues the **unlockpt()** routine. This clears a lock associated with the slave side. This lock is set by the master side when the master side is opened and is used to stop other applications from creating a stream into the slave device. Only the application that opened the master side can remove this lock.

3. Now, because your application has an unused stream into the master side, it must determine exactly which device file it must open to gain access to the slave side. It does this via the **ptsname()** routine, passing it the file descriptor of the stream into the master side. The **ptsname()** routine returns the name of the device file to use when creating a stream into the slave device.

4. Finally, your application opens the device file returned by **ptsname()**. This creates a stream into the slave device.

Next, as shown in Figure 2.22(c), your application must push the modules that emulate terminal semantics onto the slave side. There are two modules needed: **ldterm** and **ptem**. The **ptem** module keeps track of the terminal parameters, for example, whether your terminal is in raw mode or canonical mode, and the **ldterm** module performs terminal line-discipline actions. The **ldterm** module is the same module used by normal STREAMS-based terminals.

```
fdm = open("/dev/ptmx", O_RDWR);
```

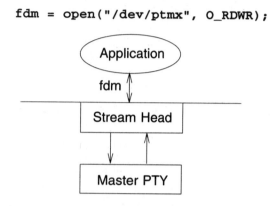

Figure 2.22(a)   Opening the Master Side

```
grantpt(fdm);
unlockpt(fdm);
slavenm = ptsname(fdm);
fds = open(slavenm, O_RDWR);
```

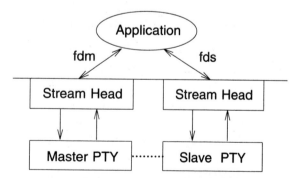

Figure 2.22(b)   Accessing the Slave Side

```
ioctl(fds, I_PUSH, "ptem");
ioctl(fds, I_PUSH, "ldterm");
```

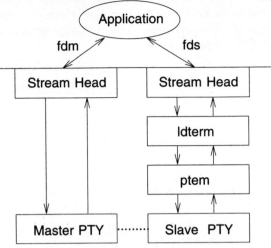

Figure 2.22(c)   Pushing Necessary Modules

```
fork();
```

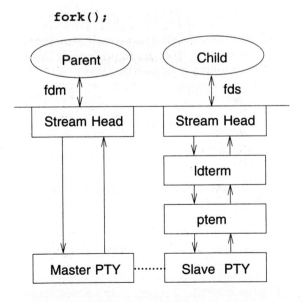

Figure 2.22(d)   Creating a Child Process

Next, your application issues the **fork()** system call to create a child process. The child process can change standard input, standard output, and standard error to reference the slave side. At this point, anything the parent process writes into the master side will appear as terminal input to the child process, and anything the child process writes can be read by the parent process. The child can exec another process, and that process will see full terminal semantics on standard input, standard output, and standard error.

There is one other thing to consider when using pseudo-terminals. SVR4 has the notion of a *controlling terminal*, which is the terminal associated with a login session. When a user on the controlling terminal enters certain input sequences (for example, the **break** key), it causes signals to be sent to foreground processes associated with the login session. Also, if a process writes to the **/dev/tty** device, the data are sent to the controlling terminal.

When using pseudo-terminals, you may want the process accessing the slave side to start a new session and establish the slave side as its controlling terminal. This would divorce the process from its existing controlling terminal and stop it from receiving signals from that terminal. It would also cause data written to **/dev/tty** to go to the slave side of the pseudo-terminal.

To set up a new session with a new controlling terminal, the order of operations presented in Figures 2.22(a) through 2.22(d) must be slightly changed:

1. Your application would still open the master pseudo-terminal device and set up the slave via the **grantpt()** and **unlockpt()** routines.

2. Next, before opening the slave device, it would issue the **fork()** system call to create a child process.

3. The child process would then issue the **setsid()** system call. This system call creates a new session for the child process and divorces it from its current controlling terminal.

4. Next, the child process opens the slave side of the pseudo-terminal and pushes the **ptem** and **ldterm** modules. In SVR4, if a process lacks a controlling terminal and it opens a terminal device (such as the slave side of a pseudo-terminal), that terminal device automatically becomes its controlling terminal. So, because the **setsid()** system call divorced the child process from its controlling terminal, opening the slave side of the pseudo-terminal device causes it to become the controlling terminal for the child process.

We revisit pseudo-terminals throughout the book as we examine networking applications. This chapter concludes with a brief description of the STREAMS modules that are available on SVR4.

2.9   Which Modules Are Available?

SVR4 provides several STREAMS modules. The following sections briefly describe
the modules available on the base SVR4 system. Other modules are available from
third-party software vendors.

connld

The `connld` module is used on SVR4 pipes and provides a unique communication
path between two processes. Your application creates a pipe, pushes `connld` onto
one end of the pipe, and attaches that end to a file (this process is described in Section
2.6). When another process opens this file, the `connld` module creates a new pipe,
returns one end of the new pipe to your application, and returns the other end to the
process that opened the file. This gives your application a unique pipe to every process that opens the attached file.

ldterm

The `ldterm` module provides terminal line-discipline functions. These include processing "erase" and "kill" characters. This module is used on streams to real terminals and on streams to pseudo-terminals.

pckt

The `pckt` module is used on the master side of a pseudo-terminal and implements a
feature called *packet mode*. The packet mode is used to inform the process using the
master side of the pseudo-terminal whenever a state change occurs on the slave side.

For example, if the application on the slave side changes the state of the pseudo-
terminal from the raw mode to the canonical mode, the `pckt` module creates a message indicating the new state and sends it to the application on the master side. That
allows the application on the master side to keep complete track of the state of the
slave side of the pseudo-terminal.

pipemod

The `pipemod` module is used on STREAMS-based pipes when applications want to
flush data on the pipe via the `I_FLUSH` parameter of the `ioctl()` system call.
This module marks the midpoint of the pipe, that is, the point where data stop flowing

downstream and starts flowing upstream. When it receives a flush message, it changes the direction of the message from downstream to upstream and vice versa.

ptem

The **ptem** module processes terminal **ioctl()** calls and keeps track of the terminal parameters. When used with the **ldterm** module (which performs terminal line-discipline actions), applications see full terminal semantics when using the pseudo-terminal subsystem.

sockmod

As we will see in Chapter 10, SVR4 provides the socket interface, a set of programming subroutines that let your applications access a transport provider. The **sockmod** module helps supply the semantics of the socket routines in SVR4. When you use the socket routines, they push this module onto the stream.

timod

The **timod** module provides operations necessary for networking applications to interface with STREAMS-based network protocols through TLI, the Transport Level Interface (details of TLI are given in Chapter 7). The **timod** module translates certain **ioctl()** operation into network protocol messages. When you use the TLI routines, they push this module onto the stream.

For example, as we will see in Chapter 7, TLI provides routines that obtain the default settings of a transport provider. The TLI routines issue an **ioctl()** system call to get this information. The **timod** module intercepts this **ioctl()** call, creates a protocol interface message to request the information from the transport provider, and sends the message downstream. When the transport provider returns the requested information, the **timod** module completes the **ioctl()** call and delivers the information to the TLI routines.

tirdwr

The **tirdwr** module provides a ''read/write'' interface for network applications that use TLI. As we will see in Chapters 7 and 8, network applications use the TLI **t_snd()** and **t_rcv()** routines to send and receive data, respectively, over a network. If your application pushes this module onto the stream, it can use the **read()** and **write()** system calls instead.

2.10 Summary

The STREAMS framework allows an application to customize a data path by pushing modules onto a stream. SVR4 implements all character-based I/O as streams, including UNIX pipes, terminals, pseudo-terminals, and networking protocols.

One of the networking protocols implemented using the STREAMS framework is the Transmission Control Protocol/Internet Protocol (TCP/IP) suite. TCP/IP is one of the most popular networking protocols used by UNIX systems, and it contains many useful applications. Details of TCP/IP are presented in the next chapter.

For Further Reading

1. AT&T, *UNIX System V Release 3.2—STREAMS Primer*, Prentice Hall, Englewood Cliffs, NJ, 1989.

2. AT&T, *UNIX System V Release 4 Programmer's Guide: STREAMS*, Prentice Hall, Englewood Cliffs, NJ, 1990.

3. Olander, D., McGrath, G., and Isreal, R., ''A Framework for Networking on System V,'' *USENIX Conference Proceedings*, Summer 1986.

4. Ritchie, D., ''A STREAM Input-Output System,'' *AT&T Bell Laboratories Technical Journal*, vol. 63. no.8, 1984.

5. Stevens, R., ''Interprocess Communication,'' Chapter 3, *UNIX Network Programming*, Prentice Hall, Englewood Cliffs, NJ, 1990.

Exercises

2.1   Suppose a STREAMS module encrypts data as they traveled down the stream and decrypts data as they traveled up the stream. Because encrypting data requires a key, what system call could you use to send a key to this module?

2.2   Describe the differences between the various type of multiplexing device drivers. What are the benefits of persistent links in multiplexors?

2.3   After an application opens a clone device, how can it find out the major and minor numbers of the actual device it holds open? Why would an application want this information?

2.4   Suppose application A opens a file and passes that file descriptor through a pipe to application B. Does this pose a security problem? If this capability were disallowed, could application A still grant file access to application B?

Chapter 3

Applications Using the
TCP/IP Protocol Suite

3.1 Introduction

The TCP/IP protocol suite is one of the most popular networking protocols available today. It can be found on a variety of machine architectures and is the prominent networking protocol for UNIX systems.

The term ''TCP/IP'' refers to an entire communication protocol family based on the Transmission Control Protocol and the Internet Protocol. It is not an OSI protocol, but a complete protocol implementation in itself. Developed in the early 1970s for the U.S. Department of Defense, it allows diverse systems to communicate over a variety of physical media.

This chapter does four things:

1. Provides an overview of the protocol suite, showing how the various components fit together to create an internetworking environment.

2. Describes what applications must do to establish communication using the TCP/IP protocol suite.

3. Explains how to use some of the TCP/IP applications and shows how they work.

4. Shows you how to integrate TCP/IP applications into new services.

We begin by explaining why TCP/IP is a popular networking protocol.

Why Is TCP/IP So Popular?

There are three reasons why TCP/IP is popular. The first is simply because TCP/IP is a **powerful internetworking protocol**. It allows a machine to attach to several communications media simultaneously, providing the ability to connect networks together. TCP/IP can be configured to run over almost any type of communications media, including Ethernet local area networks, Token Ring local area networks, X.25 public data networks, and point-to-point links.

A second reason for its popularity is **connectivity**. The original funding of the TCP/IP protocols came from the U.S. Defense Advanced Research Projects Agency (DARPA). It was developed to link DARPA's network (the ARPANET) with other research networks, resulting in the Internet, a worldwide network based on the TCP/IP protocols. Many installations adopted TCP/IP because they wanted to join the Internet.

The third reason is that TCP/IP is a **mature, readily available protocol**. It has been in use for over a decade, and many people are familiar with it. It was an integral part of the Berkeley Software Distribution version 4.2, and it exists on almost every variant of the UNIX system. Today, there are many products based on TCP/IP, and its popularity continually drives the development of new application services.

3.2   Overview of TCP/IP

The functionality of TCP/IP is divided into well-defined distinct layers. Unfortunately, TCP/IP does not fit into the OSI Reference Model cleanly, because its functionality is divided differently. Figure 3.1 shows the structure of the TCP/IP protocol suite and its relationship to the OSI reference model.

The TCP/IP model has six basic elements: Applications, the Transmission Control Protocol (TCP), the User Datagram Protocol (UDP), the Internet Protocol (IP), auxiliary protocols like the Internet Control Message Protocol (ICMP) and the Address Resolution Protocol (ARP), and one or more network device drivers. Applications interface with TCP or UDP, which in turn interface with IP, which interfaces with the network device drivers.

The most distinctive feature of the protocol suite is that *IP can be configured to interact with several network device drivers simultaneously*. It is this feature that allows internetworking; a machine attached to several networks can forward packets from one network to another.

This feature makes IP the most important part of the protocol suite. When an application sends a data packet to another machine, IP determines to which network the packet should go, and if necessary, routes the packet from one network to another. IP figures out where to send a packet based on the *IP address* of the recipient. IP addresses are essential to the workings of TCP/IP, and they are described first.

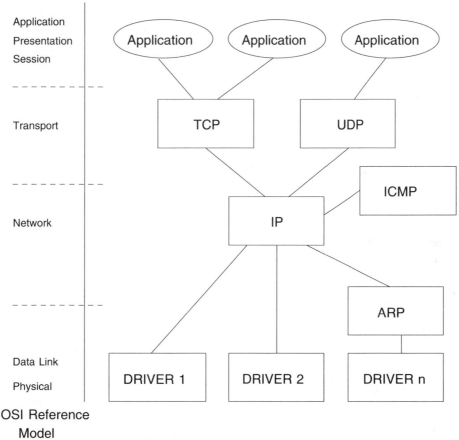

Figure 3.1   Structure of TCP/IP

IP Addresses

Every machine running TCP/IP has a 32-bit IP address. When an application sends data to a remote machine, it must specify the IP address of the recipient. An IP address has two parts, a network number and a host number. The network number identifies the network a machine is on, and the host number identifies a machine on that network. The number of bits representing the network number depends upon the *class* of the address, which is determined by the high-order bits.

Here's how it works. There are three primary classes of addresses: Class A, Class B, and Class C. Table 3.1 shows the relationship of the class to the network number. If the first bit of an IP address is `0`, then the IP address is a Class A address. A Class A address has the network number in the next 7 bits and the host number in the remaining 24 bits. If the first 2 bits of the address are `10`, then the IP address is a Class B address, and reserves the next 14 bits for the network number and the remaining 16 bits for the host number. If the first 3 bits are `110`, then the IP address is a Class C address, using the next 21 bits for the network number and the remaining 8 bits for the host number.

Class	Leading Bits	Number of Bits in Network Number	Number of Bits in Host Number
A	0	7	24
B	10	14	16
C	110	21	8

Table 3.1 TCP/IP Address Classes

As mentioned before, the network number identifies the network a machine is on, and the host number identifies a machine on that network. When an application issues a request to send data to another machine, it must specify that machine's IP address. The IP module uses the network number of the address to figure out which network the destination machine is on and passes the packet to the device driver for that network. If the destination is not on a directly-accessible network, IP consults internal tables to select a machine that can complete the delivery and forwards the packet to that machine. The details of how IP forwards packets is given in the description of IP presented later in this section.

An application must specify the IP address of the recipient when it sends a network message. Therefore, it is essential that no two machines have the same IP address. This is somewhat easy to enforce if the network is small and contained within one organization. However, if a machine wants to join the Internet, a worldwide network based on the TCP/IP protocols, special actions must be taken to ensure uniqueness of IP addresses. Your network administrator must request a network number from the Network Information Center (NIC) at Network Solutions, Incorporated, located in Chantilly, Virginia. The NIC is the central authority that assigns network numbers. Once the network number is obtained, the network administrator creates IP addresses by assigning host numbers to individual machines on the network. Your network administrator should request a network number from the NIC, even if your organization has no immediate plans to join the Internet. That will greatly ease the pain, should your organization join at a later date.

The class of the address directly relates to the size of the network. Class A networks have 24 bits to use for host numbers, Class B networks have 16 bits, and Class C networks have 8 bits. So, if an installation has less than 255 machines, the administrator can request a network number that corresponds to a Class C address (because up to 255 host numbers can fit in the 8 bits). Similarly, if an installation has between 256 and 65,535 machines, the administrator must request a network number that corresponds to a Class B address.

IP addresses are usually represented in "decimal-dot" notation. Decimal-dot notation is a period-separated sequence of bytes, where each byte is specified in decimal form. For example, the address

$$\texttt{1100 0000 0000 1010 0001 0101 0001 1011}_2$$

has the hexadecimal representation of

$$\texttt{C0 0A 15 1B}_{16}$$

and therefore would be written as

$$\texttt{192.10.21.27}_{10}$$

This address is a Class C address, because the 3 three bits are $\texttt{110}_2$. The network number is $\texttt{A15}_{16}$ (specified in the next 21 bits), and the host number is $\texttt{1B}_{16}$ (specified in the last 8 bits).

As mentioned before, the network number identifies the network a machine is on, and the host number identifies a machine on that network. So, *a single machine attached to several networks will have several IP addresses*. Normally, a machine has an IP address for each network interface.

This poses a problem for applications: If a server machine has several IP addresses, which address should you use? The answer: You can use any IP address of the server, since IP forwards packets that are not on a directly accessible network. However, for performance considerations, you should try to figure out if the server machine is on a network attached to your machine, and use the address corresponding to that network. Unfortunately, SVR4 does not provide routines to help you figure this out. So, given a list of addresses for a server, most applications simply use the first IP address in the list.

Special Addresses

TCP/IP places special meaning on some addresses. These addresses have reserved semantics and cannot be assigned to a machine on the network:

1. **An address with all bits 0**. Neither the network number nor the host number can be zero. A value of zero is interpreted to be "this host." As mentioned

earlier, a single machine can have several network interfaces and hence can have several IP addresses. Therefore, the address `0.0.0.0` means "all addresses for this machine."

2. **An address with the host number of all bits 1**. A host number with all bits `1` is reserved as a "broadcast address." So, sending a message to address `192.10.21.255` means "send the message to all machines on Class C network `192.10.21`." Similarly, sending a message to address `35.255.255.255` means "send the message to all machines on the Class A network `35`."

3. **The address with *all* bits 1.** The special address `255.255.255.255` refers to "all machines on every directly attached network." A message sent to this address will go to all hosts on all networks connected to your machine. The message will not be forwarded to machines on networks not attached to your machine.

TCP/IP supports another address called a *muticast address*. A packet sent to a multicast address is delivered to a set of machines in a specified group. A multicast address has its own class (Class D) and is of the following form:

Class	Leading Bits	Remaining Bits
D	1110	Group Identification (28 bits)

The first 4 bits (`1110`) identify an address as a multicast address, and the remaining 28 bits identify a multicast group. If a machine is a member of a multicast group, it gets all packets sent to that group. A machine may join or leave a multicast group at any time.

Now let's examine the elements of the TCP/IP suite. Each element of the TCP/IP protocol suite performs a terse, specific action. IP is essential to the workings of the suite, and it is described next.

The Internet Protocol

IP is the heart of the protocol suite. The higher-level protocols and the lower-level device drivers interact only with IP. Given a packet from a higher-level protocol, IP examines the destination address, looks at the network number of the address, figures out the network to which the packet should be delivered, passes it to the corresponding device driver, and routes packets from one network to another. Because IP relays and routes packets, it corresponds to the network layer of the OSI model.

If the recipient is not on a directly accessible network, IP sends the packet to an appropriate host that can deliver the packet to its final destination. Similarly, if the IP module on your machine receives a packet that is destined for another host, it forwards the packet to that host or sends it to another machine that can complete the delivery.

To see how all this works, consider the configuration in Figure 3.2. In this configuration, host X is connected to two networks. Host Y can send a message to a machine on network B by first sending the packet to host X. When host X receives the message, the IP module realizes the packet is destined for a host on network B and passes it to the device driver for that network. In this sense, host X acts as a router between the two networks.

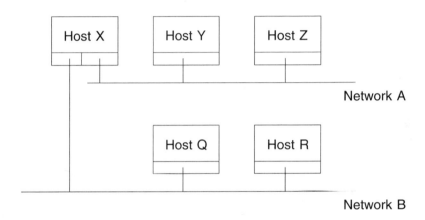

Figure 3.2   Multiple Networks

The destination address plays a major role in forwarding messages, because IP chooses which network to forward a packet to based on the network number in the destination address. IP also keeps information about routers to which to send packets if the destination host is on a network that is not directly attached to your machine.

IP provides datagram service. It does not retransmit lost packets, does no error checking of data consistency, and does not ensure that packets arrive in sequence (the TCP layer, described later, provides those services). IP is responsible for figuring out which network to route the packet to and sending the packet on its way.

IP does, however, provide some error detection. It performs a checksum validation of the IP packet header and verifies that the length of the packet matches the value stored in the header. It also ensures that a packet does not loop continuously through the network trying to reach its destination. It does this by decrementing a ''Time to Live'' counter in the header every time the packet passes through a router machine and discarding the packet when the counter reaches zero. IP sends a special error packet to the originator when it detects one of these errors. It does this via the Internet Control Message Protocol (ICMP), described below.

IP performs other operations as well. For example, different networks have different requirements on packet size; thus, IP must occasionally fragment packets when routing them between networks. It does this based on the Maximum Transmission Unit (MTU) of the network. The IP module at the final destination is responsible for reassembling the packets.

Device Drivers

The device drivers manage the network hardware and therefore correspond to the data link and physical layers of the OSI model. A device driver carries IP packets out of the machine to the network. Examples include Ethernet drivers, Token Ring drivers, X.25 drivers, and point-to-point link drivers.

Virtually any type of communications media can be used, as long as the network hardware or the device driver software meets the following requirements:

1. The device must be able to transmit datagrams.

2. Some method of packet framing must be supplied; IP packets are discrete units and not continuous streams.

3. The device need not do any type of error detection.

The first requirement is easy for datagram-based networks like Ethernet and Token Ring. It is more difficult for circuit-based networks like X.25, because circuit-based drivers require connection establishment before any data can be sent.

This requires special processing for X.25 networks. When IP sends a packet to an X.25 driver, X.25 makes a connection to the destination, holds the circuit open, and uses the circuit for subsequent packets. The circuit is held open for some length of time after a packet is sent or received, where the length of time depends upon the cost of the circuit.

The Address Resolution Protocol

As described above, each host running the TCP/IP suite has a 32-bit IP address. When an application sends a packet, it specifies the 32-bit IP address of the recipient. This presents a problem for device drivers that have their own addressing schemes. For example, each machine on an Ethernet network has a 48-bit Ethernet address, which bears no resemblance to its 32-bit IP address. When IP sends a packet over an Ethernet local area network, the 32-bit IP address is meaningless; the 48-bit Ethernet address must be used when sending the packet.

One way to solve this problem is to configure tables that map a host's IP address into its Ethernet address. As you might suspect, this becomes unmanageable as the network grows. The Address Resolution Protocol (ARP) provides a more elegant solution. ARP implements a "dynamic discovery" procedure of mapping IP addresses into hardware addresses, and it is usually used on Ethernet and Token Ring local area networks.

Here's how it's done. Suppose a network connected to your machine is an Ethernet local area network. Before IP sends a packet to that network, ARP consults a local table to see if a mapping exists between the destination IP address and the destination Ethernet address. If it doesn't, ARP sends a broadcast packet requesting the Ethernet address of the machine with the given IP address. Because it is a broadcast packet, every machine in the network receives it. The host with the requested IP address sends a reply, stating its Ethernet address. The originating machine receives the reply, adds an entry into its mapping table that associates the IP address with the Ethernet address, and sends the packet to its destination.

ARP doesn't fit cleanly into any on the OSI layers. It is not a network-layer protocol as it does no routing or other operations of network protocols. Nor does it belong to the data-link layer as it doesn't detect and correct errors that occur in the physical-layer transmission. Because it is used after network-layer actions are performed, it falls between the network and data-link layers.

Other networks have similar problems. For example, X.25 uses addresses that are different from IP addresses. ARP cannot be used on X.25 systems because X.25 systems are circuit-based (that is, a client must call a server to set up a circuit before any data can be sent). Fortunately, IP addresses can usually be mapped directly into X.25 addresses. If not, static tables must be used.

The Transmission Control Protocol

The Transmission Control Protocol (TCP) corresponds to the transport layer of the OSI model. Applications interface directly with TCP when sending and receiving data.

TCP provides virtual-circuit service. It handles flow control by ensuring packets are received intact and in order, checks for errors in received packets, and retransmits packets that are lost or damaged.

The destination TCP module sends an acknowledgment for every packet received. If the TCP module on the originating machine does not receive the acknowledgment, it retransmits the packet. If the acknowledgment is not received after several retransmissions, TCP assumes the data cannot be delivered and passes an error indication to the application.

Every TCP packet contains a checksum that covers the TCP header and the data in the packet. If the checksum is valid, the TCP module on the destination machine sends the acknowledgment to the TCP module on the originating machine. If the checksum is not valid, no acknowledgment is sent, causing the TCP module on the originating machine to eventually resend the packet. There are no ''negative acknowledgments'' in TCP/IP, that is, the TCP module on the destination machine does not send a message if it detects an error in the packet. If the TCP module on the originating machine does not get an acknowledgment, it assumes the original packet was never received, the packet was corrupt, or the acknowledgment was lost. In all cases, the TCP module on the originating machine resends the packet.

There are several aspects of TCP that applications must be aware:

- TCP provides virtual-circuit service. The client must establish a connection with the server before any communication can take place.

- TCP connections are full-duplex. Data may be transmitted simultaneously in both directions.

- TCP maintains no record markers and transmits no information about how many bytes were written. So, an application may have to do several read requests to obtain all the data sent with a single write request.

The User Datagram Protocol

The User Datagram Protocol (UDP), a peer to TCP, also corresponds to the transport layer of the OSI model. Applications can interface with UDP to send data; however, UDP only provides datagram service. It does not do any error correction or retransmissions. The UDP module on the destination machine can check for errors in packets, but it only delivers error-free packets to the application. Erroneous packets are dropped.

There are several aspects to UDP that applications must be aware:

- *Data sent may be lost.* If your application sends a message to a service and expects a response, it must be coded to time out and resend the request if it does not receive the response.

- Data may arrive out of sequence. If your application sends two messages to a service, the service may not receive them in the order sent.

- The application must specify the recipient address on every message. Connection establishment is not necessary. UDP is datagram-based, so every message is a discrete unit.

The Internet Control Message Protocol

The Internet Control Message Protocol (ICMP) is responsible for generating control messages. ICMP is a datagram-based protocol and is directly tied to IP. It sends a message to the originator whenever IP drops a packet, unless the packet is an ICMP message (errors occurring in ICMP packets are never reported). A packet can be dropped because it is corrupt, but most of the time a packet is dropped because a router has a disabled network or because problems occur while a router is trying to access a network.

ICMP also generates advisory messages. For example, a router can send an ICMP message to tell a host to slow down its transmission rate. A router can also use ICMP messages to inform a host of a better router to a particular network.

If desired, applications can interface with ICMP directly. For example, the `ping` command is a TCP/IP application available on SVR4. It sends an ''echo'' packet to a specified server machine via the ICMP protocol. That causes the destination to respond to the packet, allowing the `ping` command to note when the reply arrives and to display how long it takes to send a packet.

Although applications can interface with ICMP directly, it is not a transport-layer protocol. It does not provide a consistent interface for end-to-end communication. ICMP is not a network-layer protocol either, because it does not relay and route information to its destination. It falls somewhere between the two, reporting errors and advisory messages to IP.

Routing Protocols

Although not shown in Figure 3.1, the TCP/IP protocol suite has several routing protocols. Among them are the Gateway-to-Gateway Protocol (GGP), the Exterior Gateway Protocol (EGP), and the Routing Information Protocol (RIP). They are used between router machines to pass and establish routing information, and they are generally of little concern to applications.

Each router protocol has a scope of functionality. For example, when the ARPANET existed, a central authority maintained a small set of core router machines to connect the ARPANET to other Internet networks. Those core routers used GGP to propagate routing information. Within each Internet network, groups of smaller networks are formed characterized by administrative authority. Each of these smaller networks are called autonomous systems. EGP is used between routers of different autonomous systems, and RIP is used between routers within autonomous systems.

Applications

Applications using the TCP/IP protocol suite must take on the operations of the application, session, and presentation layers of the OSI Reference Model. TCP/IP does not provide session and presentation services. Applications are responsible for coordinating dialogue and translating data into a common representation.

Applications are also responsible for security features. TCP/IP does not provide any information about the identity of a user sending a packet. This may seem odd for a protocol that was developed by the U.S. Department of Defense, but the rationale was to let each application determine its own security requirements. Each application must implement the identification and authentication features and the security constraints it deems appropriate.

SVR4 provides several standard TCP/IP applications. These include the File Transfer Protocol for transferring files and the Telnet protocol for remote login. SVR4 also provides nonstandard, UNIX system-specific applications ported directly from the 4.3 BSD operating system, such as **rsh**, **rcp**, and **rlogin**.

TCP/IP Implementation in SVR4

SVR4 implements the TCP/IP protocol suite using the STREAMS mechanism. This is different from the implementations of other UNIX systems. However, the functionality conforms completely to the TCP/IP protocol specification, and the STREAMS implementation gives the added benefit of customizing the data path with STREAMS modules.

SVR4 applications access the protocol suite via the System V Transport Level Interface (TLI). They use the TLI **t_open()** routine, specifying the **/dev/tcp** or the **/dev/udp** device file as a parameter, to open the transport provider. The **t_open()** routine returns a file descriptor to use with subsequent TLI calls. Chapters 7 and 8 present the details of TLI.

BSD implementations of the TCP/IP suite provide the socket interface to access the transport providers. Applications do not specifically open a device file such as **/dev/tcp** when using the socket interface. Instead, they use the **socket()** routine, specifying a protocol family, a mode of service, and a protocol number. The **socket()** routine returns a file descriptor that applications use with subsequent socket calls.

To provide compatibility for applications written to the socket interface, SVR4 provides a socket library that maps all socket routines into TLI routines. Chapter 10 presents the details of the socket routines.

3.3   Application Communication

As mentioned in Chapter 1, each network service has a transport address. Earlier, we described how an IP address uniquely identifies a machine on a network. Unfortunately, we can't use the IP address to form a complete transport address, because you must also specify the service on the server machine with which you want to communicate.

TCP/IP solves this problem by assigning a 16-bit *port number* to each service. A complete transport address for a TCP/IP service consists of a 32-bit IP host address and a 16-bit port number. The 32-bit IP address identifies a machine, and the 16-bit port number identifies a service on that machine.

The following sections describe application port numbers and explain how a client can find the transport address of a service.

Application Ports

Both TCP and UDP provide 16-bit port numbers that services use when listening for messages. A service associates itself with a port number, and all messages sent to that port number are delivered to the associated service. In this sense, you can consider the IP address as the address of a home and the port number as the name of a person in that home. To form a complete address, you must specify both the name of the person and the home address.

The TCP/IP protocol reserves ports **1** through **255** for ''standard'' services. A standard service is one that has been approved by the Internet Engineering Task Force, a group of users and implementors that meet several times a year. Once approved, the Internet Assigned Numbers Authority at the Information Sciences Institute of the University of Southern California assigns a port number to the service.

For example, the **ftp** service allows file transfer using the TCP/IP protocol. It is approved by the Internet Engineering Task Force and is assigned the port number **21**. Every system offering the **ftp** service has it available on port number **21**.

The TCP/IP specification states that port numbers over **255** are not reserved. However, SVR4 restricts these port numbers by using the following BSD conventions:

- Port numbers **1** through **1024** are considered ''privileged ports.'' Your application can use these ports only if your effective user-id is **0**. These are used for UNIX-specific services like **rlogin** (a UNIX-specific remote login service) and **rsh** (a UNIX-specific remote shell service). As we will see in Section 3.6, privileged ports may be used to ensure that a connection attempt is made by a trusted user.

- Ports `1025` through `5000` are used by applications that want to get an arbitrary, unused port. Although these are sometimes used by server processes (for example, server processes utilizing the Remote Procedure Call facility, described in Chapter 6), they are usually used by clients. When the client side of an application connects to a service, the client must have a "return address" to which the service sends responses. Therefore, the client must obtain a port number. Because it doesn't care what port number it obtains, any unused port number will suffice. When an application requests an arbitrary, unused port number, SVR4 returns one between `1025` and `5000`.

- Ports over `5000` are reserved for site-specific services. If you create a service, you can be assured that ports over `5000` are not used by applications wanting arbitrary ports. So, if you attempt to use a port number over `5000` for your service, there is a good chance that the port will be available. Of course, the port will not be available if another service is using it.

The TCP and UDP protocols do not share port numbers. One application can associate itself to a port number over TCP, and another can associate itself to the same port number over UDP. This doesn't pose a problem, because applications must choose to use either TCP or UDP for communication.

Figure 3.3 illustrates the relationship of services and port numbers. In this configuration, a client application uses the combination of IP address `192.11.108.95` and port number `23` as the transport address of the `telnet` service on machine `farside`.

This brings up the issue of naming hosts and services. It is much easier to say, "I want to connect to the `telnet` service on machine `farside`" than "I want to connect to the service on port number `23` on the machine with IP address `192.11.108.95`." Specifying a machine and service name is much easier than specifying an IP address and port number because names are easier to remember. This led most TCP/IP applications to accept machine names instead of IP addresses and map the names into IP addresses internally. Consequently, machine and service names became an integral part of applications using the TCP/IP suite.

Machine Naming

Most TCP/IP applications allow you to specify a machine name instead of an IP address. These applications consult databases to translate machine names into IP address. Because of this, machine names must be unique.

Ensuring unique names is straightforward for small networks, but becomes unmanageable as the network grows. To solve the problem of name collisions in large networks like the Internet, the ARPANET Domain Name System (DNS) associates *domain*

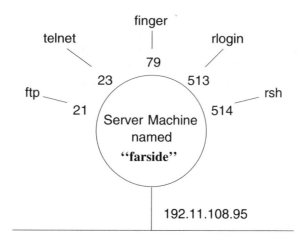

Figure 3.3   TCP/IP Ports

names with machines. A domain name is a period-separated list of names that represent administrative authorities, and it is read right to left.

For example, the machine name

```
farside.att.com
```

shows that an initial administrative authority has created the name **com** and given the responsibility for the name space of **com** to another administrative authority. The administrative authority for **com** has created the name **att** and delegated responsibility for that name space to yet another administrative authority. Finally, the administrative authority for **att** has created the name **farside**. Each administrative authority must ensure that the names it creates are unique.

The highest level of administrative authority creates names based on types of organizations. Examples include

- **com** for commercial institutions,
- **edu** for educational institutions,
- **net** for network providers,
- **mil** for military organizations, and
- **org** for other organizations.

The next level of administrative authority creates names based on specific organizations. For example, the **com** administrative authority created the name **att.com** for AT&T, **sun.com** for Sun Microsystems, Inc., and **ibm.com** for IBM. Similarly, the **edu** administrative authority created the name **berkeley.edu** for the University of California at Berkeley and **rutgers.edu** for Rutgers University. Tripping on in such a fashion, the administrative authority for **rutgers.edu** could create the name **remus.rutgers.edu** for a machine at Rutgers University.

Service Naming

Naming a service is easier than naming a machine, because the name space is much smaller. Service names generally correspond to the service provided, such as **ftp** for the file-transfer protocol and **rlogin** for the remote-login protocol.

New services must come up with unique names. If a new service is approved by the Internet Engineering Task Force, the name and port number are assigned by the Internet Assigned Numbers Authority at the Information Sciences Institute of the University of Southern California. If a new service is a local service used only at your installation, the name can be any string that does not conflict with other services.

Communication Establishment

Once we have translated the names into an IP address and port number, we can establish communication. Communication establishment differs depending upon whether you are using TCP or UDP.

Communication establishment over TCP is similar to setting up a phone call. Figure 3.4 shows the steps involved. The server side of the application does the following:

1. **Open a transport endpoint**. The service does this by opening the STREAMS device file associated with the TCP transport provider. Opening the device does not automatically associate the service with an address, so this step is like getting a telephone without a phone number.

2. **Attach to its transport address**. This establishes an address for the service, similar to obtaining a phone number. As mentioned earlier, the transport address consists of the service's port number and the IP address of the machine on which it is running.

3. **Wait for connections**. The service must wait for a client application to make a connection, similar to waiting for the phone to ring.

When the service is waiting for connections, the client side of the application can make the call. The client side of the application must do the following:

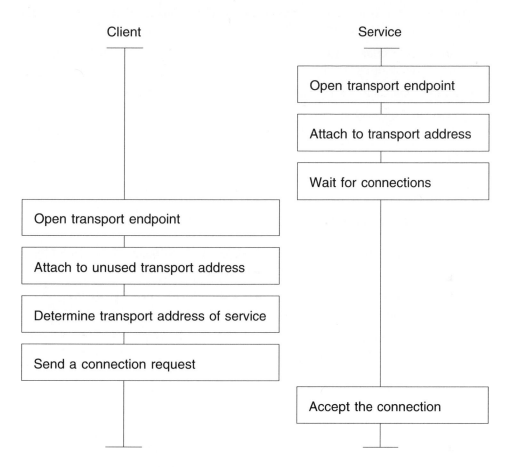

Figure 3.4 Communication Establishment Using TCP

1. **Open a transport endpoint**. The client side of the application does this by opening the STREAMS device file associated with the TCP transport provider. Again, this is like getting a telephone without a phone number.

2. **Attach to an unused transport address**. This establishes an address for the client side of the application, similar to getting a phone number. This is necessary because the server sends acknowledgments and data back to the client, so it must have an address to which to send the information. The transport address is formed by combining the client's IP address with an unused port number. When the application requests an unused port number, SVR4 assigns one between `1025` and `5000`.

3. **Determine the transport address of the service**. This is similar to looking up the server's telephone number. The way to do this is described shortly.

4. **Send a connection request to the service**. This is similar to dialing the telephone number of the service.

Upon receipt of the connection request, the service must do the following:

1. **Accept the connection**. This is similar to answering the telephone.

2. Once accepted, the service and the client side of the application can send and receive data. The TCP protocol guarantees that all data will arrive intact and in order.

Communication Establishment over UDP

If the service is available over UDP, communication establishment is easier. Figure 3.5 shows the steps involved. The service must do the following:

1. **Open a transport endpoint**. The service does this by opening the STREAMS device file associated with the UDP transport provider.

2. **Attach to a transport address**. As mentioned earlier, this gives the service an address to which the client side of the application can send messages. The address is formed by combining the service's port number with the IP address of the machine on which it is running.

3. **Wait for datagrams to arrive**. When a datagram arrives, it has the transport address of the client, allowing the service to send responses if necessary.

The client side of the application must do the following:

1. **Open a transport endpoint**. The application does this by opening the STREAMS device file associated with the UDP transport provider.

2. **Attach to an unused transport address**. This is necessary because every datagram has a return address associated with it. The client side of the application forms the transport address by combining the IP address of the machine on which it is running with an unused port number.

3. **Determine the transport address of the service**. The way to do this is described shortly.

4. **Send a datagram to the service**. If you expect a reply, you must wait for the reply to arrive on the transport address to which you have attached. However, because UDP does not guarantee delivery, applications must be coded to time out and resend the datagram if a response is not received.

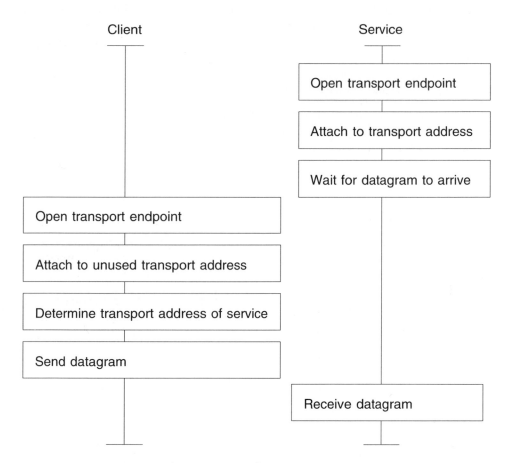

Figure 3.5   Communication Establishment Using UDP

Determining a Transport Address

It is the sole responsibility of the client side of the application to obtain the transport address of the service. The server machine does not communicate this information to the client in any way. Fortunately, SVR4 applications can use the Name-to-Address Mapping facility (described in Chapter 9) to obtain the transport address of a service. You specify the name of the service and the name of the machine providing the service, and the Name-to-Address Mapping facility reports the transport address of the service on the specified machine.

For the TCP/IP suite, the Name-to-Address Mapping facility obtains a transport address by consulting the `/etc/hosts` and `/etc/services` files. The `/etc/hosts` file has entries that map machine names into IP addresses. Each entry has an IP address followed by the name of the machine with that address, followed by zero or more aliases for that machine. Given a machine name, the Name-to-Address Mapping facility searches this file to obtain the associated IP address.

The `/etc/services` file maps the service name to its port number. Each entry in this file contains a service name, the port number of the service, and an indication of whether the service is offered over TCP or UDP.

If these files do not contain the requested machine and service name, the Name-to-Address Mapping facility queries the *Domain Name System*, a distributed database developed for the ARPANET. If the information cannot be obtained from the distributed database, the routines return an error condition to the application.

For compatibility with other versions of the UNIX system, SVR4 also provides routines to search the `/etc/hosts` and `/etc/services` files directly. We show how to use those routines in Chapter 10.

With this overview of the TCP/IP suite, TCP/IP applications can be examined. The remaining sections describe some of the TCP/IP applications available on SVR4 and show how to incorporate these applications into new services.

3.4   Remote Login via the Telnet Protocol

The Telnet protocol implements the TCP/IP standard for logging into a remote machine. Telnet implements remote login via a *Network Virtual Terminal* (NVT). The NVT gives you a terminal interface into a remote system.

Here's how it works. When you start up a Telnet session, each side of the connection attaches itself to a NVT. The NVT is not a real device. It is a simulation of a very simple terminal interface with a mechanism to negotiate for more powerful terminal functionality.

To clarify, consider a real terminal device, which is a device that has an input component (usually a keyboard) and an output component (usually a monitor). The NVT is a simulation of a real terminal device that has a keyboard as its input component and a printer as its output component. The printer prints any incoming messages, and the keyboard generates outgoing messages. Each side of the Telnet connection maps its real terminal characteristics into the NVT.

Because users are accustomed to more elegant features than those provided by the NVT, the Telnet protocol allows negotiation of options. The options provide more (or different) functionality of the NVT. For example, you can use options to

- change the character set of the NVT;

- have the server echo back the characters it receives;

- negotiate whether the client sends data a line at a time or a character at a time; or

- have the client send specific information about its real terminal to the server.

Either side may request an option from the other. The request can be positively or negatively acknowledged, indicating whether the machine receiving the request agrees to perform the option. The negotiation of options consists of a WILL, WON'T, DO, and DON'T sequence:

- The "**WILL option_name**" message is sent by either side of the connection when that side offers to do the specified option. It is acknowledged positively with "**DO option_name**" and negatively with "**DON'T option_name**."

- The "**DO option_name**" message is sent by either side when it requests that the *other* side do the specified option. The receiver responds with either "**WILL option_name**" or "**WON'T option_name**," indicating whether it agrees to perform the option.

SVR4 implements the Telnet protocol via the `telnet` command on the client machine and the `telnetd` process on the server machine. SVR4 ported these commands directly from the BSD operating system, and they work exactly the same as their BSD counterparts. Figure 3.6 shows the interaction of `telnet` and `telnetd`.

To initiate the Telnet protocol, you issue the `telnet` command, specifying the name of the server with which you want to communicate. The `telnet` command uses the TCP protocol to make a connection to the `telnetd` process on the server machine.

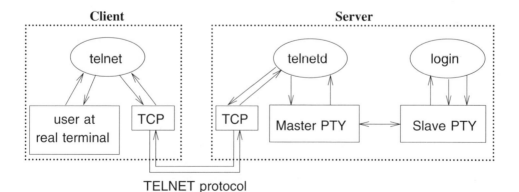

Figure 3.6 The Telnet Model

After a connection is established, the `telnet` command on the client machine and the `telnetd` process on the server machine negotiate the options they will perform. Next, the `telnetd` process on the server machine allocates a pseudo-terminal device. As explained in Chapter 2, a pseudo-terminal is a master/slave pair. The slave appears to be a real terminal to the process using it. However, unlike a real terminal, any data written to the slave are sent to the master. A process monitoring the master can read these data. Similarly, any data written to the master side appear on the slave as if they had been typed on a real terminal.

Once `telnetd` allocates a pseudo-terminal device, it forks a child process. The child process sets up the file descriptors for standard input, standard output, and standard error to access the slave side of the pseudo-terminal, and execs the `login` command. The parent process monitors the master side of the pseudo-terminal, reads all data the `login` command writes, and sends them to the client machine over the network connection. The parent process also monitors the network connection, reads all data the client sends, and writes them to the master side of the pseudo-terminal for consumption by the `login` command. The `login` command performs its normal authentication sequence and starts a shell.

Back on the client, the `telnet` command monitors your terminal and the network connection, sending data from your terminal to the server and displaying data from the server to your terminal. With this configuration, anything you enter will be read by the shell on the server machine, and anything written by the shell will be displayed on your system.

The `telnet` command provides interactive commands to modify the NVT. Once you issue the `telnet` command, you get a `telnet>` prompt. You can establish a connection by specifying the **open** *machinename* command (or, if preferred, you can establish a connection immediately by specifying a server machine name on the `telnet` command line).

Once a connection is established, the `telnet` command enters the input mode and sends all data you enter to the remote machine. The input mode will be either character-at-a-time, sending every character immediately to the server, or line-at-a-time, sending data only after you enter a newline character. The mode `telnet` uses depends upon the server machine. Not every server machine supports both modes.

In the line-at-a-time mode, the `telnet` command catches the *interrupt*, *erase*, and *kill* characters locally and sends them as Telnet protocol sequences to the remote host. In the character-at-a-time mode, `telnet` sends these characters directly to the server. The distinction is important when input sequences have special meaning. For example, the `vi` editor interprets the backspace key as ''go back one character,'' not as the shell interpretation of ''erase the previous character.'' If you are running `vi` within a Telnet session, you must be in character-at-a-time mode so you don't send a Telnet erase character to the server when you enter a backspace key.

Telnet modes and options can be modified when you are in the interactive mode. You can enter interactive mode at any time by entering **Control-]**. Once entered, **tel-net** presents the **telnet>** prompt.

There are several commands you can use in the interactive mode. They include

- **open** *servername*, which initiates a new connection to the given server machine;

- **close**, which closes the connection; and

- **mode**, which toggles between the line-at-a-time mode and the character-at-a-time mode.

A sample session follows:

```
$ telnet
telnet> open farside.att.com
Trying...
Connected to farside.att.com.
Escape character is '^]'.

login: padovano
Password: enter your password

Welcome to farside.

$
```

At this point, you are logged into the remote system **farside.att.com**. You could have entered the command **telnet farside.att.com**, which would connect immediately to **farside** and eliminate the need for the **open** command.

You can enter the Telnet interactive mode again by typing **Control-]**. At the **telnet>** prompt, you can issue the **help** subcommand to see information about other available commands:

```
$ ^]
telnet> help
Commands may be abbreviated.  Commands are:

close     close current connection
display   display operating parameters
mode      enter line-by-line or character-at-a-time mode
open      connect to a site
```

```
quit       exit telnet
send       transmit special characters ('send ?' for more)
set        set operating parameters ('set ?' for more)
status     print status information
toggle     toggle operating parameters ('toggle ?' for more)
z          suspend telnet
?          print help information
telnet>
$
```

If you enter the **Control-]** character while logged into the server, you can enter a carriage return at the **telnet>** prompt to return to the remote session.

3.5   File Transfer: FTP

The File Transfer Protocol (FTP) is the TCP/IP standard for transferring files. It is a powerful protocol that allows the transfer of files between diverse systems. The protocol provides commands to retrieve files, store files, change the current working directory, and specify the data type of files transferred.

As shown in Figure 3.7, FTP has two connections, a data connection and a control connection. FTP uses the data connection to transfer files and the control connection to send FTP protocol messages. The client side of the protocol is implemented with the **ftp** command and the server side is implemented with the **ftpd** process.

The protocol consists of requests and replies. The client process generates all requests, and the server process generates all replies. Requests include

STOR, to copy a file from the client machine to the server machine;

RETR, to copy a file from the server machine to the client machine; and

APPE, to append data to a file that exists on the server machine.

Certain operations are done via a sequence of requests. For example, FTP authenticates your identity at the beginning of a FTP session. To do this, the client issues the **USER** request to send your user name to the server, followed by the **PASS** request that carries your password, and if required, an **ACCT** request that specifies any account information needed by the server.

The server machine reads each request, performs an action, and generates a reply. A reply is a three-digit number, followed by text. The text is for human consumption, and is used for informational purposes only. If the server wants to send more than one line of text, the first response contains a three-digit number immediately followed by a hyphen (-), and the last line has the same three-digit number followed by a space.

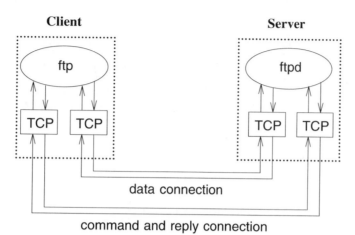

Figure 3.7 The ftp Model

Each digit of the response has a special meaning. The first digit can have one of the following five values:

1 A positive preliminary reply; the requested action is in progress, and you should expect another reply.

2 A positive completion reply; the requested action has completed successfully.

3 A positive intermediate reply; the requested action has completed successfully, but the server expects more information. FTP uses this for sequences of commands, such as user authentication.

4 A transient negative reply; the requested action did not complete successfully, but you may send the request again. If you were in the middle of a command sequence, the sequence should be restarted.

5 A permanent negative reply; the requested action did not complete successfully and you should not resend the request.

The second digit has six values that qualify the first digit:

0 A syntactic response, implying that a failure happened because your request was syntactically incorrect or because the server did not recognize your request.

1 An informational response, meaning the reply is associated with a request for status or other information.

2   A connection response, indicating the reply is associated with a request for connection setup or teardown.

3   An authentication or accounting response, specifying the reply is to an authentication procedure.

4   Currently not used.

5   A file response, meaning the reply is associated with a request to manipulate files.

The third digit further qualifies the second digit. For example, suppose the first two digits of the response are **50**, meaning the request failed because of a syntax error. In this case, the last digit will be **0** if the request is simply not recognized, **1** if there is an error in the parameters, or **2** if the command is not implemented on the server. If a request is associated with authentication of a user, the last digit is **0** if no more information is needed, **1** if a password is needed, or **2** if account information is needed.

To illustrate the protocol, let's walk through an FTP session. First, attempt to connect to the server. The server can respond with one of three values: **220**, indicating the service is ready; **120**, indicating the service is almost ready and the client should expect **220** shortly; or **421**, indicating the service is not available yet and the client should try later. The second digit is always **2**, because the response is to a connection request. The first digit is either **1**, meaning the server accepted the request but is not ready to process it yet; **2**, meaning the connection is ready; or **4**, meaning the service is not ready. The first digit cannot be **3**, because a connection establishment is not a series of commands. Nor can the first digit be **5**, because a permanent negative reply to a connection request means the server is not running, and there would be no process on the server machine to generate the reply.

Now let's go through the authentication steps. Suppose the client sends a **USER mary** request. The server processes the request and sends one of the following replies:

230 The user is logged in; proceed.

530 The user is not allowed in.

500 The command is not recognized.

501 The server sees a syntax error in the command.

421 The service is not available now.

331 The user name is valid; supply a password.

332 The user name is valid; supply account information.

If the response is **331**, the client must supply a password. It does this by sending the **PASS** *password* request to the server (where *password* is mary's password on the server machine). The server can respond to this request with one of the following:

230 The user is logged in; proceed.

530 The user is not allowed in.

500 The command is not recognized.

501 There is a syntax error in the command.

503 This is not the proper command in the sequence.

421 The service is not available now.

202 The command is not needed.

332 The user name is valid; supply account information.

If the server sends **332**, the client must supply account information via the **ACCT** request. This will not happen on SVR4 servers, but may occur on non-UNIX system servers. The **ACCT** request causes the server to respond with one of the following:

230 The user is logged in; proceed.

202 The command was not needed.

530 The user is not allowed in.

500 The command is not recognized.

501 There is a syntax error in the command.

503 This is not the proper command in the sequence.

421 The service is not available now.

If the client receives a **230**, then user **mary** is authenticated on the server machine and can proceed with the file transfer.

Earlier, we mentioned that FTP uses a separate connection for data and commands. This has the advantage of simultaneously sending commands and data. Unfortunately, there are two problems with this approach. First, each subsequent transfer must wait for the previous connection to close, causing an unnecessary delay. SVR4 uses the BSD solution to this problem: Before a transfer occurs, the client issues the FTP **PORT** request. The **PORT** request generates a unique data connection, allowing you to create a new data connection for each transfer request.

The second problem arises when the data connection closes because of a server crash. Normally, the server closes the connection after it transfers the file. When the client sees the closed connection, it assumes it has received the entire file. However, if a server crashes in midtransfer, the client sees a closed connection and cannot distinguish this from a normal end-of-file indication. The FTP protocol provides a solution to this problem by defining a "block mode" that allows an end-of-file marker to be sent. Unfortunately, SVR4 does not support this mode of transfer. It only supports the stream mode, where the end of file is implied by a closed connection. Therefore, SVR4 lacks a solution to this problem.

As stated earlier, SVR4 implements the client side of the FTP protocol via the `ftp` command. The `ftp` command is interactive, allowing you to specify commands that directly correspond to the FTP protocol. When entering `ftp`, you connect to a server with the following subcommands:

- **open** *machinename*—establishes a connection with the specified server machine. If auto-login is on (the default setting on SVR4 machines), you will be prompted to log into the server machine. If not, you must issue the `user` command to log into the server machine.

- **user** *username*—sends the `USER` request to the server and proceeds with the login sequence. It is required only if auto-login is off,

Once connected, you must prepare for file transfer by using the following commands:

- **ascii**—specifies that the files to be transferred are ASCII files (this is the default mode of transfer).

- **binary**—specifies that the files are non-ASCII files.

- **cd** *remotedir*—changes the working directory on the server to *remotedir*.

- **lcd** *directory*—changes the current working directory on the local machine to *directory*.

- **ls** or **dir**—lists the contents of the remote directory.

- **pwd**—prints the current working directory on the server machine.

- **prompt**—toggles interactive prompting. You use this to modify the behavior of the `mget` and `mput` subcommands, described below.

When transferring files, you can use the following `ftp` subcommands:

- **get** *remotefile* [*localfile*]—retrieves the specified remote file from the server machine and stores it on the client machine. If you do not specify a local file name, it will be the same as the remote file name.

- **put** *localfile* [*remotefile*]—stores the specified local file on the server machine. If you do not specify a remote file name, it will be the same as the local file name.

- **append** *localfile* [*remotefile*]—appends the local file to the end of a file on the server machine. If the remote file name is not specified, the local file name will be used.

- **mget** *remotefiles*—expands wild-card characters (such as the "*****" character) in the specified remote files and does a **get** for each name produced. Files are expanded the same way as with the UNIX shell. Each file is expanded separately on the server machine, and all files are transferred into the local working directory. If interactive prompting is on (set with the **prompt** command), **ftp** prompts you before any transfer occurs.

- **mput** *localfiles*—expands the wild-card characters in the specified files and does a **put** for each name produced. If interactive prompting is on, **ftp** prompts you before any transfer occurs. In this case, the client machine does the expansion.

- **mkdir** *directory_name*—creates a directory on the server machine.

Commands exist to close the connection. They are

- **close**—terminates the FTP session with the server machine and returns to the **ftp** command interpreter.

- **bye**—terminates the FTP session with the server machine and causes the **ftp** command to exit.

To illustrate the use of these commands, consider the following sample execution:

```
$ ftp
ftp> open farside.att.com
Connected to farside.att.com
220 farside FTP server ready.
Name (farside:padovano): padovano
331 Password required for padovano.
Password: enter password
230 User padovano logged in.
ftp> get file1
200 PORT command successful.
150 Opening data connection for file1 \
          (192.11.109.8,4047) (9007 bytes).
226 Transfer complete.
local: file1 remote: file1
9103 bytes received in 0.04 seconds (203.91 Kbytes/s)
ftp> get file2
200 PORT command successful.
150 Opening data connection for file2 \
          (192.11.109.8,4100) (51719 bytes).
```

```
226 Transfer complete.
local: file2 remote: file2
53051 bytes received in 0.19 seconds (278.87 Kbytes/s)
ftp>
```

There are several things to note in the above session:

1. Auto-login is on, so **ftp** prompts you for a user name without having you explicitly issue the **user** command. If an error occurs while logging in, you can use the **user** command to start the login sequence again.

2. Each server response is displayed. For example, the connection request resulted in a **220**, indicating the server is ready.

3. We are in the default mode, which is **ascii**.

4. After the **get** subcommand, the **ftp** command automatically issues a **PORT** request to get a new data connection to the server machine (notice the "**200 PORT command successful**" message). The data connection for the first **get** request used port number **4047**, and the data connection for the second **get** request used port number **4100**. The full transport address of the data connection is displayed as **IP_Address,Port**, and appears immediately after the message indicating the server is opening the data connection.

5. The **get** request did not specify a local file name; **ftp** assumed it to be the same as the remote file name.

6. The preliminary response to the first **get** subcommand command shows the file is **9007** bytes. However, the client reports that it received **9103** bytes. The discrepancy arises because we are in **ascii** mode. In this mode, the server sends a carriage-return character and a new-line character whenever it reaches the end of a line (this behavior is specified by the FTP protocol). Because files on the UNIX system only use the new-line character, the server sends an extra character on every line. The client strips the extra carriage-return character when storing the file, so the file stored on the client machine will be exactly the same as it is on the server machine.

The example continues:

```
ftp> ls
misc
net
notes
rfs
sccs
```

```
src
systems
226 Transfer complete.
ftp> cd net
250 CWD command successful.
ftp> ls
file1
file2
file3
file4
226 Transfer complete.
ftp> binary
200 Type set to I.
ftp> get file2 /tmp/rem.file2
200 PORT command successful.
150 Opening data connection for file2 \
               (192.11.109.8,1056) (516 bytes).
226 Transfer complete.
local: /tmp/rem.file2 remote: file2
516 bytes received in 0.02 seconds (25.20 Kbytes/s)
226 Transfer complete.
ftp> close
221 Goodbye.
ftp> bye
$
```

The continuation of the **ftp** session uses the **cd** command to change the directory on the server machine and the **ls** command to display the contents of that directory. We set the transfer mode to **binary**, causing the server to send data verbatim. In this case, the server does not send the extra carriage-return character after each line, so the number of bytes received by the client is exactly the number of bytes in the file.

Anonymous FTP

Many servers have publicly accessible files. These servers support *anonymous FTP*, which allows you to log into the machine without having an account. To do this, you specify **anonymous** when asked for a user name. You will be prompted for a password, and you should enter a string that identifies who you are. Usually, you enter your login name.

An example of a machine that has publicly accessible files is **ftp.uu.net**. To access that machine, you enter the following:

```
$ ftp
ftp> open ftp.uu.net
Connected to ftp.uu.net
220 ftp FTP server ready.
Name (ftp:padovano): anonymous
331 Guest login OK, send ident as password.
Password: any string to identify yourself
230 User anonymous logged in.
ftp>
```

Once logged in, you are free to transfer files to your local machine. Many of the machines with publicly accessible files have an index file that describes what is available. Usually, you have to transfer the index file onto your local machine, view it locally, and then reissue the **ftp** command to transfer the files you want. However, because you can specify any local file with the **get** subcommand, you can view a file immediately by transferring the file to **/dev/tty**. Therefore, the command

get file /dev/tty

transfers the file to **/dev/tty**, which writes the contents to your terminal screen.

3.6   UNIX-Specific Remote Login: rlogin

Although the Telnet protocol is the TCP/IP standard for remote login, most UNIX system users prefer the **rlogin** command for logging into remote systems. The main reason for this is because the **rlogin** command allows preauthorized connections, that is, you are not prompted for a password if the server specifically sets up preauthorized access.

Invoking the rlogin command is straightforward. The syntax is simply

rlogin host [-l user]

where the **-l user** option specifies your user name on the server machine. If you omit the **-l** option, your user name on the client machine will be used.

Figure 3.8 shows the structure of the **rlogin** command. The following actions set up this structure:

1. You issue the **rlogin** command, optionally specifying a remote user name. If you don't specify a remote user name, **rlogin** will use your local user name.

2. The **rlogin** command makes a connection to the **rlogind** process on the server machine.

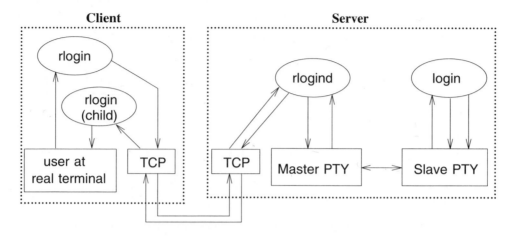

Figure 3.8   The rlogin Model

3. The **rlogin** command sends the local user name, the remote user name, the terminal type, and, if you have a windowing terminal, the size of the current window to the **rlogind** process on the server.

4. The **rlogind** process creates a pseudo-terminal and forks a new process. The parent monitors the master side of the pseudo-terminal. The child attaches standard input, standard output, and standard error to the slave side of the pseudo-terminal, and execs the **login** command. The **login** command is started with the **-r** option, causing the following to happen:

    a. The **login** command checks the **/etc/hosts.equiv** file. This file contains the list of machines that are "equivalent" to the server. A machine is equivalent to the server if it has exactly the same users on it. The server machine makes a bold assumption about these machines: If a user has logged into an equivalent client machine, that user need not specify a password when attempting to remotely log into the server machine. The server assumes that the client machine has already authenticated the user's identity, so there is no need for the server machine to authenticate it again. So, if the client machine appears in the **/etc/hosts.equiv** file, and the local user name is identical to the remote user name, the **login** command does not prompt for a password and immediately starts a shell.

    b. If the client machine name is not in the **/etc/hosts.equiv** file, the **login** command checks the **.rhosts** file in the home directory of the specified remote user. This file lists client machine names and users on those client machines in the following format:

```
client1      username1
client2      username2
```

If the local user name on the client machine is listed in this file, **login** does not prompt for a password. So, a remote user's **.rhosts** file states specifically which users on the client machine are allowed into the remote user's account without a password.

5. Back on the client machine, the **rlogin** command forks. The child process reads from the connection and writes to the terminal. The parent process reads from the terminal and writes to the connection. The parent process does not buffer the data. Each character typed is immediately sent to the server.

Using the **/etc/hosts.equiv** and the **.rhosts** file, although convenient for the user, is inherently dangerous. If a user breaks into one system, that user has access to all equivalent systems. These files should be used with caution, and should only contain entries for trusted clients.

There are two problems with this preauthorization scheme: The server must believe the **rlogin** command when it sends the local and remote user names, and the server must trust that the client machine is who it says it is.

SVR4 uses the BSD solution to the first problem. It restricts the use of ports **1** through **1024** to processes running with the effective user ID of **0**. The **rlogin** command is set-uid to **0**, giving it the ability to attach to one of these reserved ports. When the **rlogind** process on the server machine receives a connection, it checks that the client side of the application is using a port number that is less than **1024**. If it is, the **rlogind** process assumes that the connection was generated by the real version of the **rlogin** command and therefore assumes that the local and remote user names are not fabricated. Otherwise, the **rlogind** process assumes the request was generated by a bogus version of the **rlogin** command and immediately closes the connection.

The restriction of having a privileged user (such as user ID **0**) attach to a port under **1024** is not in the TCP/IP protocol specification. Therefore, a host should not be in the **/etc/hosts.equiv** file unless the administrator of the server machine is sure that host follows this convention.

The second problem, the ability to believe that a client is who it claims to be, is more difficult to solve. The **rlogind** process on the server machine attempts to solve this by obtaining the client name directly from the TCP/IP protocol suite. The client does not send its name to the server. Instead, the server asks the TCP/IP protocol to inform it of the IP address of the client. Once obtained, it maps the IP address into the client machine name.

Unfortunately, it is possible (although difficult) for one machine to impersonate another by changing its IP address. The general solution is to be very selective of which users you preauthorize into your account.

3.7   UNIX-Specific Remote Execution: rsh

TCP/IP lacks a standard application for remote execution. However, SVR4 offers the nonstandard UNIX-specific **rsh** command to do remote execution. When using **rsh**, you specify a command to be executed on the server. The **rsh** command has the following syntax:

```
rsh [-n] [-l user] remote_host [command] [argument ...]
```

The **rsh** command creates a shell on the server machine to execute the specified command. The **-l** argument allows you to specify the user name to use while running the command. You can use the **-n** option to disable standard input, as we will see later.

The **rsh** command only works on equivalent machines. Therefore, the client machine name must appear in the **/etc/hosts.equiv** file on the server machine, or your user name must appear in the **.rhosts** file in the home directory of the remote user. The server immediately disconnects if the client machine is not equivalent.

The remote shell is not associated with a pseudo-terminal. This means commands that require a terminal (for example, the **vi** editor) will not work correctly when executed via the **rsh** command.

Figure 3.9 shows the structure of the **rsh** command. There are several steps involved when setting up this communication:

1. You issue the **rsh** command on the client machine, specifying a server machine name. The **rsh** command checks if you specified a remote command. If not, it executes the **rlogin** command, creating a remote session on the server machine.

2. If you specify a remote command, **rsh** connects to the **rshd** process on the server machine and sends it your local user name, the remote user name, and the specified command and arguments.

3. The **rsh** command attaches to a new, unused port. It then sends a message to the **rshd** process, stating the new port number to which it is attached.

4. The **rshd** process reads the message containing the client's new port number, forms a transport addresses by combining the client's IP address and the new port number, and makes a connection to that address. There are now two connections: the original connection that the **rsh** command made to the **rshd**

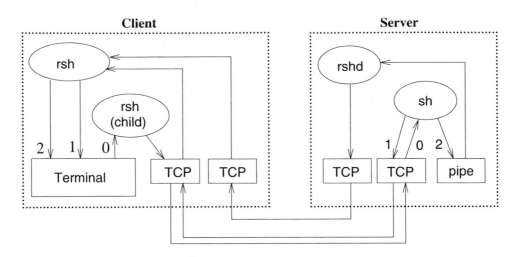

Figure 3.9 The rsh Model

process and the new connection that the **rshd** process made to the **rsh** command. The **rsh** command uses these two connections to separate standard output and standard error.

5. The **rshd** process on the server machine creates a pipe and forks a child process. The child assigns file descriptors **0** and **1** to the initial connection and file descriptor **2** to the pipe.

6. The child process figures out whether you are preauthorized by checking the **/etc/hosts.equiv** file and the remote user's **.rhosts** file. If you are preauthorized, the child changes its identity to the specified remote user and execs the UNIX shell, passing it the command and arguments. (If you are not preauthorized, the child process exits, causing the **rshd** process to close the connection.)

7. The shell reads standard input from the first connection, writes standard output to the first connection, and writes standard error to the pipe. The **rshd** parent process reads all data from the pipe and sends the data to the client over the second connection.

8. The **rsh** command on the client forks a child process. The child process reads from the terminal and writes to the first connection.

9. The **rsh** parent process reads all data from the two connections. Data it receives on the first connection are written to file descriptor **1**, and data received

on the second connection are written to file descriptor **2**. That provides a separation of standard output and standard error. The **rsh** command uses the first connection for the remote shell's standard input and standard output, and uses the second connection for the remote shell's standard error.

This setup allows you to use remote commands the same way you use local commands. For example, to display the contents of a remote file, you can execute the following command:

```
rsh farside cat /tmp/file1
```

Or, if desired, you can use it in a pipeline:

```
rsh farside cat /tmp/file1 | grep pattern
```

Standard output and standard error can be redirected separately, as in the following:

```
rsh farside cat /tmp/file1 >/tmp/out 2>/tmp/err
```

The **rsh** process passes the specified command and arguments to a shell on the server, so shell metacharacters are processed normally. However, it is important to realize where this processing takes place. For example, the command

```
rsh farside ps -ef >outfile
```

creates **outfile** on the local system, where

```
rsh farside "ps -ef >outfile"
```

creates **outfile** on the server system.

Because the **rsh** command transfers all input to the server machine, it does not handle typeahead characters. The **rsh** command sends everything you enter to the server machine, even if the command running on the server machine does not want input. For example, consider the following sequence:

```
$ rsh ed file
a
hello world
.
w
q
date
```

Here, **rsh** sends all data to the server, even though the **date** command was meant for the local shell.

The **rsh** command reads input from the terminal; it has problems if another process wants to read from the terminal as well. This is where the **-n** flag comes in. If you specify the **-n** flag, it is the same as redirecting the standard input of the **rsh** command to /dev/null. That stops the rsh command from reading input from the terminal.

3.8   UNIX-Specific File Transfer: rcp

Though FTP is a powerful file-transfer protocol, it is somewhat cumbersome to use. Therefore, SVR4 offers the BSD rcp command to copy files between UNIX systems. The rcp command is a UNIX-specific command that is easy to use and similar to the UNIX system cp command.

You can use rcp to copy a file from your machine to a remote machine:

rcp file1 server:file2

or from a remote machine to your machine:

rcp server:file1 file2

or from one remote machine to another:

rcp machine1:file1 machine2:file2

The rcp command uses the rsh facility, so it only works between equivalent machines. As stated earlier, your machine is equivalent to a server machine if appropriate entries appear in the server's /etc/hosts.equiv file or the remote user's .rhosts file.

If your user name is different on the server machine and there is preauthorized access via the .rhosts file, you may specify the server name as user@machine. This changes your identity to the specified user on the named server machine.

Because rcp uses rsh, its setup is the same as in Figure 3.9. The rcp command connects to the rshd process on the server machine to perform the file transfer. For efficiency reasons, rcp performs the rsh protocol itself and does not invoke the rsh command directly.

The normal cp command supports the -r flag to recursively copy files; the rcp command supports this option also. To copy a directory tree recursively from a server machine to the local machine, you simply have to execute the following:

rcp -r server:directory .

Just as with the local cp command, the rcp command can copy a list of named files into a directory.

Now let's create a new application by using the file-transfer applications described above. This application serves as an example of how to use some of the TCP/IP commands available on SVR4.

3.9   Application: Remote Archive and Restore

Armed with tools for file transfer, we can create two applications: one that archives files to a server machine and another that restores them to the client machine. We begin by developing the code to archive files onto the server.

Remote Archive Using TCP/IP Tools

There are several things to consider when creating an application to archive files to a server machine:

1. We will be storing files on server machine. Therefore, we must have an account on the server machine.

2. We want the ability to archive a single file or an entire directory. To make this easier, we will package all objects we want to archive into a single file and store that file on the server machine.

3. A user may want to create archives several times per day. So, we must store the archives on the server machine in a way that can be easily restored to the client machine.

4. We must keep a local record o the archives. This record must contain the name of the file or directory archived, the name of the server machine on which we stored the files, and the directory on the server where we stored the archive. This record is used to restore the files back to the client machine.

Because several TCP/IP commands are available for file transfer, we can implement the archive application as a shell script. We'll implement it two ways: the first using the UNIX-specific **rcp** command and the second using the TCP/IP standard **ftp** command. The code shows the TCP/IP-specific routines in bold font and other commands in normal font.

The UNIX system provides the **cpio** tool that packages files into an archive. This tool fits our needs. We can use it to create an archive and then transfer the archive to the server machine.

Where to place the archive on the server machine is a more difficult problem. We must put it in a directory that will not clash with other archives. We must also label the archive on the server machine in case our local record becomes corrupted.

Any user can archive his or her files. Therefore, we will store all information in the home directory of the user. Under a user's home directory, we will create a directory called **backup**. This directory will contain everything necessary to archive and restore files.

On the client machine, the **backup** directory will contain the **client.log** file, which records all of the user's archives. On the server machine, it will have subdirectories corresponding to the names of client machines. Under each of these directories, we will have directories that correspond to the date of a particular archive. Under the date, we will have another directory that contains the exact time the user created the archive. Under that directory, we place the archive file and an auxiliary file that contains the name of the archived directory. Figure 3.10 shows this directory structure.

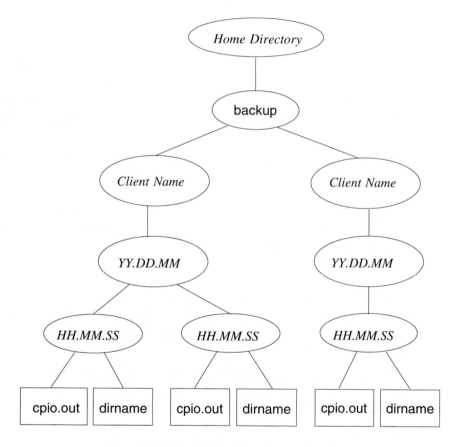

Figure 3.10   Archive Layout on the Server

Using the UNIX-specific **rcp** command poses a problem: The server must be equivalent to the client. As mentioned earlier, this raises security issues. On an equivalent machine, the server does not prompt for a password, potentially opening your account to intruders. However, implementing the archive application with the **rcp** command is straightforward and provides a basis for implementing it with the standard TCP/IP tools later.

To begin, let's trap signals to clean up any temporary files that we create. Next, we create the **backup** directory if it doesn't already exist, because it will contain the log of what we archived to the server machine.

```
trap 'rm -f /tmp/$$.*; exit 0' 0 1 2 3 4 5 6 7 8 10

if [ ! -d $HOME/backup ]
then
    mkdir $HOME/backup 2>/dev/null
    if [ $? -ne 0 ]
    then
        echo "$0: ERROR: could not create the $HOME/backup"
        echo "$0:         directory. This directory is"
        echo "$0:         necessary to log your backups"
        exit 1
    fi

fi
```

Next, we prompt for the file or directory the user wants archived. If it doesn't exist, keep prompting until the user specifies one that does exist.

```
echo "Please enter the file or directory you want to"
echo "back up: \c"
read DIR
while [ ! -f "$DIR" -a ! -d "$DIR" ]
do
    echo "$DIR does not exist!"
    echo "Please enter the file directory you want to"
    echo "back up: \c"
    read DIR
done
```

We can now prompt for the name of the server machine on which the user wants to store the archive. Unfortunately, SVR4 does not provide commands to check the validity of a server machine name. But, if the server name is invalid, the **rcp** command we execute later will fail.

```
echo "Please enter the server machine name: \c"
read SERVER
```

Because the user can specify a relative path name, let's check whether the first character of the specified directory is /. If it isn't, generate the full path name.

```
FIRST_CHAR=`echo $DIR | cut -c1`
if [ "$FIRST_CHAR" != "/" ]
then
     DIR=`pwd`/$DIR
fi
```

Next, we create a **cpio** file containing the files we want archived. We have to do the
following:

1. Start a child shell. This allows us to change directories within the new shell
    without affecting our current working directory in the parent shell.

2. If the user wants to archive a single file, we echo the file name into
    /tmp/$$.bkup. Otherwise, we use the **find** command to list all files under
    the specified directory and we put that list into **/tmp/$$.bkup**.

3. Inform the user as to which files we are backing up.

4. Use the **cpio** command to create the archive file. But, before we create the
    file, we strip the leading / from the path name. That lets us restore the files to
    a directory other than / if the user desires.

5. Write the name of the directory we're archiving into the **/tmp/$$.dname** file.

```
(
cd /
if [ -f $DIR ]
then
     echo $DIR >/tmp/$$.bkup
else
     find $DIR -print >/tmp/$$.bkup
fi
```

```
echo "Backing up the following files:"
cat /tmp/$$.bkup
cat /tmp/$$.bkup | sed 's/^.//' | cpio -odc >/tmp/$$.cpio
echo $DIR >/tmp/$$.dname
)
```

Now that we've created the **cpio** file, let's create the directory structure on the server machine. We'll get the time and date, and use **rsh** to execute the **mkdir** command on the server machine. Because some of these directories may already exist on the server machine, we cannot use the return value of **mkdir** to indicate success or failure. So, we use the **rsh** command to execute the **ls** command on the server to figure out if we created the directories properly.

```
DATE=`date +"%y.%m.%d"`
TIME=`date +"%H.%M.%S"`
CLIENT=`uname -n`

rsh $SERVER "mkdir backup \
                backup/$CLIENT \
                backup/$CLIENT/$DATE \
                backup/$CLIENT/$DATE/$TIME; \
            ls -d backup/$CLIENT/$DATE/$TIME" \
            2>/dev/null >/tmp/$$.rsh

if [ "`cat /tmp/$$.rsh`" != "backup/$CLIENT/$DATE/$TIME" ]
then
    echo "error in creating the directory"
    echo "backup/$CLIENT/$DATE/$TIME on $SERVER"
    exit 1
fi
```

We can now transfer the archive to the server machine. We use the **rcp** command to transfer both the archive file and the file containing the name of the directory.

```
rcp /tmp/$$.cpio \
    $SERVER:backup/$CLIENT/$DATE/$TIME/cpio.out &&
rcp /tmp/$$.dname   \
    $SERVER:backup/$CLIENT/$DATE/$TIME/dirname

if [ $? -ne 0 ]
then
    echo "error occurred during transfer"
    exit 1
fi
```

Finally, let's record what we've done so we can restore the archive later. The record contains the name of the server, the directory backed up, and the location of the archive on the server machine.

```
echo $SERVER $DIR $CLIENT/$DATE/$TIME/cpio.out \
                    >>$HOME/backup/client.log

echo "Transfer complete."
echo "Files saved in cpio format in"
echo "$SERVER:backup/$CLIENT/$DATE/$TIME/cpio.out"
exit 0
```

Implementing the Archive Command Using ftp

As mentioned earlier, using the **rcp** command requires that the server and client be equivalent. This poses security problems, because you have unauthenticated access to equivalent machines.

A more secure solution is to use the **ftp** command to implement the archive application. Unfortunately, the **ftp** command is interactive, making it hard to incorporate into a shell script. But there are some details of the SVR4 implementation of the **ftp** command that we can exploit:

1. The **ftp** command writes all messages to standard output except authentication prompts, which it writes to standard error. So, we can redirect standard output to a file and still see the password prompt.

2. The **ftp** command reads your password by opening your terminal device, not by reading from standard input. So, if we redirect standard input from a pipe, the **ftp** command will still read your password directly from the terminal.

3. The **ftp** command prints the string ''**unknown host**'' when it is given an invalid server name.

The first two points allow us to pipe subcommands into the **ftp** command and still be prompted for a password before any file transfer occurs. The third point allows us to figure out if an invalid server name was specified.

So, let's start the same as before, by obtaining the name of the directory and the name of the server:

```
trap 'rm -f /tmp/$$.*; exit 0' 0 1 2 3 4 5 6 7 8 10

if [ ! -d $HOME/backup ]
then
    mkdir $HOME/backup 2>/dev/null
    if [ $? -ne 0 ]
    then
        echo "$0: ERROR: could not create the $HOME/backup"
        echo "$0:         directory.  This directory is"
        echo "$0:         necessary to log your backups"
        exit 1
    fi

fi

echo "Please enter the file or directory you want to"
echo "back up: \c"
read DIR
while [ ! -f "$DIR" -a ! -d "$DIR" ]
do
    echo "$DIR does not exist!"
    echo "Please enter the file directory you want to"
    echo "back up: \c"
    read DIR
done

echo "Please enter the server machine name: \c"
read SERVER
FIRST_CHAR=`echo $DIR | cut -c1`
```

```
if [ "$FIRST_CHAR" != "/" ]
then
    DIR=`pwd`/$DIR
fi
```

Now, because the **ftp** command asks for your user name on the server machine, we prompt for it here. Once obtained, we create the **cpio** archive as we did with the **rcp** version.

```
echo "Please enter your user name on $SERVER: \c"
read NAME

(
cd /
if [ -f $DIR ]
then
    echo $DIR >/tmp/$$.bkup
else
    find $DIR -print >/tmp/$$.bkup
fi

echo "Backing up the following files:"
cat /tmp/$$.bkup
cat /tmp/$$.bkup | sed 's/^.//' | cpio -odc >/tmp/$$.cpio
echo $DIR >/tmp/$$.dname
)

DATE=`date +"%y.%m.%d"`
TIME=`date +"%H.%M.%S"`
CLIENT=`uname -n`
```

Now that we have created the archive, let's transfer it to the server machine. First, we tell the user that we are going to store the files on the server machine, and explain that they will be prompted for a password. Next, we create the FTP subcommands and pipe them into the **ftp** command. We will redirect the output of the **ftp** command to a file, so the user will not see the **ftp** specific messages (the **ftp** messages are cryptic to the inexperienced user, so displaying them would only cause confusion to users of this application). The following actions occur:

1.   We echo FTP subcommands into the **ftp** command. The first thing echoed is
     the user name obtained earlier. Auto-login is on (this is the default setting in
     SVR4); the **ftp** command thus reads the name and sends a FTP **USER** request
     to the server machine.

2.   Because the next step in the sequence is to send an FTP **PASS** request, the
     ftp command prompts for a password. The prompt goes to standard error
     (which is not redirected, so the user will see it), and the **ftp** command opens
     the controlling terminal to read the user's password. The **ftp** command does
     no further processing until the user enters a password.

3.   After a password is obtained, the **ftp** command continues to read standard
     input. We echo **ftp** subcommands to create the directory tree on the server,
     changing the directory to each directory we create.

4.   Once we get to the correct directory on the server, we use the **put** subcommand
     to transfer the archive file and the file containing the directory name.

5.   Finally, we issue the **ls** subcommand to list the contents of the remote direc-
     tory. This is used later to verify that the transfer happened correctly.

```
echo "About to store files on $SERVER"
echo "You will be asked the password for $NAME on $SERVER"

echo " $NAME
mkdir backup
cd backup
mkdir  $CLIENT
cd $CLIENT
mkdir  $DATE
cd $DATE
mkdir $TIME
cd $TIME
put /tmp/$$.cpio cpio.out
put /tmp/$$.dname dirname
ls
quit" | ftp $SERVER >/tmp/$$.ftp.out
```

Now let's check that the file transferred correctly to the server machine. If the file was
listed in the output of the **ls** command, the transfer happened correctly. Otherwise,
tell the user that an error occurred. If the string "**unknown host**" appears in the
output, it means the user specified an invalid server name.

```
if grep 'cpio.out' /tmp/$$.ftp.out >/dev/null 2>&1
then
    : OK!
else
    echo "ERROR in creating the directory"
    echo "backup/$CLIENT/$DATE/$TIME on $SERVER"
    if grep 'unknown host' /tmp/$$.ftp.out >/dev/null 2>&1
    then
        echo "ERROR: $SERVER is an unknown host"
    fi
    exit 1
fi
```

Now let's record what we've done so we can restore the archive later. The record contains the name of the server, the directory backed up, and the location of the archive on the server machine.

```
echo $SERVER $DIR $CLIENT/$DATE/$TIME/cpio.out \
                    >>$HOME/backup/client.log

echo "Transfer complete."
echo "Files saved in cpio format in"
echo "$SERVER:backup/$CLIENT/$DATE/$TIME/cpio.out"
exit 0
```

Implementing Restore Using rcp

Now let's implement the other side of the application: restoring files back to the client machine. As with the archive application, we can implement the restore application as a shell script. We'll implement it two ways: the first using the UNIX-specific **rcp** command, and the second using the TCP/IP standard **ftp** command.

The **restore** script assumes the user archived a file or directory with our archive application. It asks the user which archive they want restored, copies the archive to the local machine, and unpackages the archive.

Several archives of a single directory can exist. Therefore, the **restore** script must be able to ask which archive to restore. The **ksh** shell, a standard shell with SVR4, provides the **select** feature that makes this easier. So, we will use the **ksh** shell to take advantage of the **select** feature.

To begin, we start the script with the **#!/usr/bin/ksh** line, causing SVR4 to invoke the **ksh** shell when executing the script. We then trap signals to clean up any temporary files we create, and prompt the user for the archive they want restored.

```
#!/usr/bin/ksh
trap 'rm -f /tmp/$$.*; exit 0' 0 1 2 3 4 5 6 7 8 10

echo "Please enter the name of the"
echo "file or directory you want restored: \c"
read DIR
```

Next, we check the record of archives to figure out how many times the specified directory was archived. We set the **ALL_DATES** variable to the list of the dates to which the directory was archived.

```
CLIENT=`uname -n`
ALL_DATES=`grep " $DIR $CLIENT/" $HOME/backup/client.log |
           cut -d' ' -f3 | cut -d/ -f2 | sort -u 2>/dev/null`

if [ "$ALL_DATES" = "" ]
then
    echo "There is no record of archive $DIR"
    echo "Please check for the archive in the backup"
    echo "directory in your home directory on the server"
    echo "machine to which you archived to."
    exit 1
fi
```

Now, we count the dates associated with the archive. If the number is greater than 1, we use the **select** feature so that the user can select the date of the archive to restore. Because the date appears as **yy.mm.dd**, we translate the date into **yy/mm/dd** before displaying it to the user. After the date is selected, we change it back to its original form.

```
NUMBER_OF_BKUPS=`echo $ALL_DATES | wc -w`
if [ $NUMBER_OF_BKUPS -eq 1 ]
then
    DATE=$ALL_DATES
else
    echo
```

```
    echo "You have archived $DIR $NUMBER_OF_BKUPS times"
    echo "Please select the date of the archive you want"
    echo "restored"
    PS3="Please enter the number corresponding to the date "
    select DATE in `echo $ALL_DATES | sed 's/\./\//g'`
    do
        break
    done
    DATE=`echo $DATE | sed 's/\//./g'`
fi
```

Because the user could have created the archive several times on the specified date, we check the number of times the backup occurred. If it occurred more than once, we use the **select** feature to prompt for the specific archive that the user wants restored. Because the time appears as **hh.mm.ss**, we translate it into **hh:mm:ss** before displaying it to the user. After the time is selected, we change it back to its original form.

```
ALL_TIMES=`grep " ${DIR} ${CLIENT}/${DATE}"  \
                                $HOME/backup/client.log |
            cut -d' ' -f3 | cut -d/ -f3 | sort -u 2>/dev/null`

NUMBER_PER_DAY=`echo $ALL_TIMES | wc -w`
if [ $NUMBER_PER_DAY -eq 1 ]
then
    TIME=$ALL_TIMES
else
    echo
    echo "You have backed up $DIR $NUMBER_PER_DAY times"
    echo "on $DATE. Please select the time associated"
    echo "with the archive you want restored."
    PS3="Please select the time "
    select TIME in `echo $ALL_TIMES | sed 's/./:/g'`
    do
        break
    done
    TIME=`echo $TIME | sed 's/:/./g'`
fi
```

We now use the **rcp** command to copy the archive back to the local machine.

```
SERVER=`grep " ${DIR} ${CLIENT}/${DATE}/${TIME}"  \
             $HOME/backup/client.log | cut -d' ' -f1`
echo "About to restore files, please wait..."
```

**rcp $SERVER:backup/$CLIENT/$DATE/$TIME/cpio.out **
           /tmp/$$.cpio.out

```
if [ $? -ne 0 ]
then
    echo "error occurred during transfer"
    exit 1
fi
```

Now that we have a local copy of the archive, we ask the user where to restore it. The user may want to restore the files to a directory different from the original location.

```
echo
echo "Archive successfully restored."
echo "Please hit the return key if you want to copy the"
echo "files to their original location, or enter a new"
echo "directory to which to restore them: \c"
read NEWDIR

if [ "$NEWDIR" = "" ]
then
    NEWDIR=/
fi

(
cd $NEWDIR
echo "Restoring the following files to $NEWDIR"
cpio -idcvm </tmp/$$.cpio.out
)

exit 0
```

Implementing Restore Using ftp

As mentioned earlier, using the **rcp** command requires that the server and client be equivalent. This poses security problems, because you have unauthenticated access to equivalent machines.

A more secure solution is to use the **ftp** command to implement the restore application. We begin the same way we did with the **rcp** version:

```ksh
#!/usr/bin/ksh
trap 'rm -f /tmp/$$.*; exit 0' 0 1 2 3 4 5 6 7 8 10

echo "Please enter the name of the"
echo "file or directory you want restored: \c"
read DIR

CLIENT=`uname -n`
ALL_DATES=`grep " $DIR $CLIENT/" $HOME/backup/client.log |
           cut -d' ' -f3 | cut -d/ -f2 | sort -u 2>/dev/null`

if [ "$ALL_DATES" = "" ]
then
    echo "There is no record of archive $DIR"
    echo "Please check for the archive in the backup"
    echo "directory in your home directory on the server"
    echo "machine to which you archived."
    exit 1
fi

NUMBER_OF_BKUPS=`echo $ALL_DATES | wc -w`
if [ $NUMBER_OF_BKUPS -eq 1 ]
then
    DATE=$ALL_DATES
else
    echo
    echo "You have archived $DIR $NUMBER_OF_BKUPS times"
    echo "Please select the date of the archive you want"
    echo "restored"
    PS3="Please enter the number corresponding to the date "
    select DATE in `echo $ALL_DATES | sed 's/\./\//g'`
    do
        break
    done
```

```
    DATE=`echo $DATE | sed 's/\///./g'`
fi

ALL_TIMES=`grep " ${DIR} ${CLIENT}/${DATE}"  \
                                $HOME/backup/client.log |
        cut -d' ' -f3 | cut -d/ -f3 | sort -u 2>/dev/null`

NUMBER_PER_DAY=`echo $ALL_TIMES | wc -w`
if [ $NUMBER_PER_DAY -eq 1 ]
then
    TIME=$ALL_TIMES
else
    echo
    echo "You have backed up $DIR $NUMBER_PER_DAY times"
    echo "on $DATE. Please select the time associated"
    echo "with the archive you want restored."
    PS3="Please select the time "
    select TIME in `echo $ALL_TIMES | sed 's/./:/g'`
    do
        break
    done
    TIME=`echo $TIME | sed 's/:/./g'`
fi

SERVER=`grep " ${DIR} ${CLIENT}/${DATE}/${TIME}"  \
            $HOME/backup/client.log | cut -d' ' -f1`
```

Now that we know exactly what archive to restore, we attempt to transfer the archive from the server machine to the local machine. As we did with the FTP version of the archive command, we redirect the output of the **ftp** command to a file, so the user will not see the **ftp** specific messages. We do the following:

1. Prompt for the user's name on the server machine.

2. Echo data into the **ftp** command. The first thing echoed is the user name. Because auto-login is on, the **ftp** command reads the name and sends an FTP **USER** request to the server machine.

3. Because the next step in the sequence is to send a FTP **PASS** request, the **ftp** command prompts for a password. The prompt goes to standard error, and the **ftp** command opens the controlling terminal to read the user's password. The **ftp** command does no further processing until the user enters a password.

4. After a password is obtained, the **ftp** command continues to read standard
    input. We give it the **cd** subcommand to change the directory to the location of
    the archive on the server machine, and use the **get** subcommand to transfer the
    archive to the local machine.

```
echo
echo "Please enter your user name on $SERVER \c"
read NAME

echo "\nAbout to restore files"
echo "You will be prompted for the password for $NAME"
echo "on $SERVER"

echo " $NAME
cd backup/$CLIENT/$DATE/$TIME
get cpio.out /tmp/$$.cpio.out
quit" | ftp $SERVER >/tmp/$$.ftp.out
```

Now that the transfer is complete, we check whether the file arrived. If the file is not
on the client machine, we generate an error message and exit. If the archive did arrive,
we ask the user to which directory to restore the files, and unpack the files.

```
if [ ! -f /tmp/$$.cpio.out ]
then
        echo "error occurred during transfer"
        exit 1
fi

echo
echo "Archive successfully restored."
echo "Please hit the return key if you want to copy the"
echo "files to their original location, or enter a new"
echo "directory to which to restore them: \c"
read NEWDIR

if [ "$NEWDIR" = "" ]
then
    NEWDIR=/
fi
```

```
(
cd $NEWDIR
echo "Restoring the following files to $NEWDIR"
cpio -idcvm </tmp/$$.cpio.out
)

exit 0
```

3.10 Other Services

SVR4 offers many more of the TCP/IP services. For example, it contains the Simple Mail Transfer Protocol (SMTP) for sending electronic mail messages, the **finger** service to find out information about users on remote systems, and the Trivial File Transfer Protocol (TFTP), a file-transfer protocol that transfers files using the UDP protocol. Each of these applications provides unique services that together create a powerful internetworking environment.

For Further Reading

1. AT&T, *UNIX System V Release 4 Network User's and Administrator's Guide*, 1990, Prentice Hall.

2. Cerf, V., and Cain, E., "The DOD Internet Architecture Model," *Computer Networks*, October 1983.

3. Comer, D., *Internetworking with TCP/IP - Volume I*, Prentice Hall, Englewood Cliffs, NJ, 1991.

4. Narten, T., "Internet Routing," *Proceedings ACM SIGCOMM '89*, 1989.

5. Postel, J., "The Internet Protocol," *RFC 792*, 1981.

6. Postel, J., "The Transmission Control Protocol," *RFC 793*, 1981.

7. Postel, J., "The User Datagram Protocol," *RFC 768*, 1980.

8. Postel, J., and Reynolds, J., "File Transfer Protocol (FTP)," *RFC 959*, 1985.

9. Postel, J., and Reynolds, J., "Telnet Protocol Specification," *RFC 854*, 1983.

Exercises

3.1   What must an application do to establish communication over TCP? Over UDP?

3.2   Port numbers **1** through **1024** are considered "privileged ports" by SVR4. How are privileged ports used by **rlogin** and **rlogind**? What are the problems associated with the assumptions made by **rlogind** with respect to privileged ports?

3.3   If an application on a client machine sends 1000 bytes to an application on a server machine using TCP, will the application on the server machine receive all the bytes in one packet? Why or why not?

3.4   Can you use terminal-specific commands (for example, the **vi** editor) using the **rsh** command? Why or why not?   Can you use terminal-specific commands with **rlogin** or **telnet**? Why or why not?

3.5   Write a shell script that uses anonymous ftp. The shell script should take a file name and a server machine name as arguments, and use anonymous ftp to transfer the named file from the server machine to the local machine.

Chapter 4

Applications Using UUCP

4.1   Introduction

The UUCP facility is a set of user-level commands that provide file transfer and remote execution. But, unlike the TCP/IP file-transfer and remote execution commands, the UUCP facility provides queued operations.

In SVR4, you can use the UUCP commands over any transport provider, including the TCP/IP protocol suite and the OSI protocols. You can even use the UUCP commands to transfer files between machines connected by telephone lines or serial lines. Most systems use the UUCP facility to transfer files over low-cost communication links.

The UUCP commands provide queued file transfer. When you execute the UUCP file-transfer commands, they first copy the files to a local directory and then copy the files to their destination at a later time. If the destination machine is not running, the files remain queued on the local system and the UUCP commands try the transfer again later.

The UUCP remote execution commands are also queued. You specify a remote system name and a command that you want to execute, and the UUCP facility executes that command on the specified system later.

This chapter describes the UUCP facility, explains how to use the UUCP commands, and shows how to incorporate the commands into new applications. Unfortunately, discussing the UUCP facility is slightly confusing, because one of the UUCP commands (the UNIX-to-UNIX Copy command) is also named `uucp`. In this chapter, we use `uucp` in a constant-width font to mean the UNIX-to-UNIX Copy command, and UUCP in capital letters to mean the family of commands. We begin by giving and overview of the UUCP facility.

4.2   Overview of UUCP

The UUCP facility contains a set of file-transfer and remote execution commands. They are similar to some of the TCP/IP applications presented in Chapter 3. But, where the TCP/IP commands provide immediate access to remote machines, the UUCP commands give queued access to remote machines.

There are several reasons for using the UUCP commands:

1. If a remote machine is down, the UUCP commands keep file-transfer requests queued on the local system and automatically retry the file transfers later.

2. The administrator can tune the UUCP facility to do all transfers at night, reducing network traffic during the day.

3. Some machines support the UUCP facility, but do not support the TCP/IP protocol suite.

SVR4 supports the Honey-DanBer version of the UUCP facility. Named after its implementors (Peter **Honey**man, **D**avid **A**. **N**owitz, and **B**rian **E**. **R**edman), the Honey-DanBer version of UUCP is a complete reimplementation of earlier versions of the UUCP facility. It provides better performance and more functionality. In SVR4, the UUCP facility uses TLI, so it can work over any transport provider that SVR4 supports. We present the details of TLI in Chapters 7 and 8.

Figure 4.1 shows some of the UUCP commands. The commands fall into one of three categories:

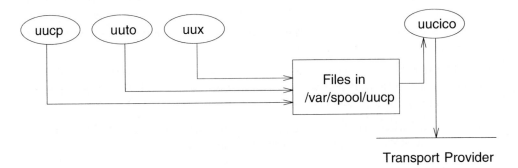

Figure 4.1   Some UUCP Commands

1. **Queued file-transfer commands**. These commands include the `uucp` command and the `uuto` command. When you execute these commands, they place the files in an intermediate directory. The files are transferred later.

2. **A queued remote execution command**. The `uux` command lets you execute commands on a remote UNIX system. When you issue the `uux` command, you specify a remote system name and a command that you want to execute on that system. Then, `uux` creates a file containing the requested command into an intermediate directory and executes it on the remote system later.

3. **Administrative commands**. These commands manage the data transfer. They include the `uucico` command and the `uuxqt` command.

The key to all UUCP operations is the `uucico` command (the name of the `uucico` command means ''UNIX-to-UNIX Copy-In, Copy-Out''). It manages all file transfers between machines. The machine administrator creates configuration files that describe an environment that the `uucico` command uses. For example, the configuration files tell when to contact a remote machine, the valid machines that can transfer files to the local machine, and other information.

The `uucico` command will be described along with various UUCP commands. The remaining sections describe some of the UUCP commands that are available on SVR4, and show how to incorporate them into new services.

4.3   Which Machines Can I Talk To: uuname

Before you can use any of the UUCP commands, you must figure out with which machines you can communicate. You can only communicate with remote machines that are running the UUCP facility.

The administrator keeps a list of the machines that your machine can contact in the `/etc/uucp/Systems` file. The UUCP facility provides the `uuname` command to print that list onto standard output. So, before you use any of the UUCP commands, you should issue the `uuname` command to figure out if you can contact the remote system. A sample execution follows:

```
$ uuname
farside
elvis
dopey
doc
sleepy
hera
$
```

In the above example, the `uuname` command displayed all of the machines that your machine can talk to via the UUCP facility.

4.4 File Transfer: uucp

The `uucp` command lets you transfer files from one machine to another. It has the following syntax:

---

uucp [*options*] source_file destination_file

The `uucp` command copies the specified source file to the destination file. If the source file and the destination file exist on the local machine, the `uucp` command acts like the SVR4 `cp` command. However, the source file and destination file can be of the following form:

system_name!path_name

Here, the `uucp` command uses the file on the specified system. If the source file contains a system name, the `uucp` command copies the file from the given machine. If the destination file contains a system name, the `uucp` command transfers the source file to the path name on the remote system.

If you specify a system name in the source and destination files, you must make sure you can contact that system. As mentioned earlier, you do that by using the `uuname` command. The `uuname` command lists all machines that you can talk to.

If you want to contact a machine that is not listed in the `uuname` output, you can specify a system route. For example, if your machine talks to machine `farside`, and machine `farside` talks to machine `zeus`, you can specify the following in your source file or your destination file:

farside!zeus!path_name

Here, the UUCP facility first contacts machine `farside` and then asks `farside` to contact machine `zeus`. In general, the source and destination files can be of the following form:

system_*1*!system_*2*!...!system_*n*!path_name

Unfortunately, SVR4 does not have a facility that lets you figure out machine routes. However, as we will see in what follows, the UUCP facility contains the `uux` command that provides remote command execution. So, if you can talk to machine `farside`, you can use the `uux` command to run the `uuname` command on that machine (provided machine `farside` allows it). That will tell you the machines to which `farside` can talk. We illustrate how to do that in Section 4.6.

The path name in the source file and destination file can have several forms. The forms include the following:

1. A full path name. If the file is on the local system, you can also specify a path name relative to your current working directory.

2. A path name preceded with *~user*, where **user** is a login name on the destination machine. Here, the UUCP facility replaces the *~user* string with the home directory of specified user on the destination machine.

3. A path name preceded with *~/destination*. Here, the UUCP facility appends the specified **destination** to the `/var/spool/uucppublic` directory on the remote machine.

4. Path names containing the shell pattern-matching characters (for example, `?`, `*`, and `[...]`). The system containing the files expands the patterns.

5. If the destination is a directory, the UUCP facility uses the base name of the source file, just like the SVR4 `cp` command. To make sure the UUCP facility interprets the destination as a directory, end the path name with the `/` character.

There are many options to the `uucp` command. The four most common are the `-C` option, the `-g` option, the `-n` option, and the `-m` option. They perform the following actions:

`-C`   Causes the `uucp` command to copy the source files into a spool directory. In that way, you can remove the original files if desired. Without the option, the `uucp` command uses the file specified in the path.

`-g`*n*   Lets you specify the "grade" of the file transfer. The UUCP facility has 62 grades. The first 10 grades are labeled grade `0` through grade `9`, the next 26 grades are labeled grade `A` through grade `Z`, and the final 26 grades are labeled grade `a` through grade `z`. Grade `0` is the highest grade, and transfers at that grade happen before any other. Grade `z` is the lowest grade, and transfers at that grade happen last.

`-n`*user*   Sends mail to the specified user on the destination machine when the file transfer completes. The mail message tells that user the names of the files transferred.

`-m`   Sends mail to the user that entered the `uucp` command when the file transfer completes.

The `uucp` command provides other options. The manual page for the `uucp` command details their actions.

Figure 4.2 shows how `uucp` transfers files. The file transfer is in two stages:

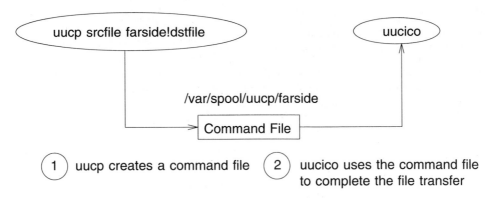

Figure 4.2 The uucp Command

1. The **uucp** command creates the following command file:

    /var/spool/uucp/*system*/C.*systemNxxx*

    This file contains information about the transfer, including the path names of the source and destination files and the login name of the user doing the transfer. In the file name, the *system* name is the machine to which to send the request, *N* is the grade, and *xxx* is a job ID that the UUCP facility uses. If you gave the -C option to the **uucp** command, it also creates the following data file:

    /var/spool/uucp/*system*/D.*xxx*

    This file contains a copy of the source file. The *xxx* in the file name is the job ID.

2. After the **uucp** command puts the files in the spool directory, the **uucico** command does the rest of the work. The **uucico** command checks the C. files, and for each file, attempts the file transfer. If the remote machine is down, the **uucico** command tries again later. We present the details of the **uucico** command in Section 4.7.

When the file arrives to its destination, the UUCP facility sets the owner of the file to the **uucp** login. And, because the file transfer occurs under the **uucp** login, the final destination directory must give full-access permission for any user to write into it.

To illustrate how to use the **uucp** command, let's look at some examples. To transfer the file named **file1** on the local system to **/u/mike/pub/newfile** on machine **farside**, enter the following command:

`uucp file1 farside!/u/mike/pub/newfile`

In this example, the `/u/mike/pub` directory on machine `farside` must allow all users to write into it (that is, it must have permissions of `777`). The `uucp` command takes `file1` from the current working directory on the local machine.

To copy a file named `/usr/mike/file2` from machine `zeus` into the `/tmp` directory on the local machine, enter the following command:

`uucp zeus!/usr/mike/file2 /tmp`

In this example, `/tmp` is a directory. So, the UUCP facility forms the destination file using the base name of the source file. In the example, the UUCP facility copies the source file to the `/tmp/file2` file.

As a final example, suppose a file named `file1` exists in the home directory of user `mike` on machine `frodo`. If you wanted to copy that file to `/var/spool/uucppublic/newfile` on machine `bilbo`, you would use the following command:

`uucp frodo!~mike/file1  bilbo!~/newfile`

Now let's examine the `uuto` command. The `uuto` command is an alternate, simpler form of file transfer.

4.5   Simple File Transfer: uuto and uupick

The UUCP facility contains two more file-transfer commands: `uuto` and `uupick`. The `uuto` command is a simplified interface to the `uucp` command. It lets you send files to a specified user on a given machine, and uses the `uucp` command to do the actual file transfer. It also lets the recipient use the `uupick` command to process the files they receive.

The `uuto` command has the following syntax:

`uuto [-m] [-p] source_files username`

If you specify the **-m** option, the **uuto** command sends you mail when the file transfer completes. If you specify the **-p** option, the **uuto** command copies the source files into the local spool directory (it is the same as the **-C** option of the **uucp** command).

You specify the source files the same as with the **uucp** command. You can specify a local file or a remote file. And, as you did with the **uucp** command, you specify a machine route as follows:

system_*1*!system_*2*!...!system_*n*!path_name

The system names specify a route that **uuto** uses to get to the destination machine. The path name can contain any of the forms used in the **uucp** command. If a path name is a directory, then **uuto** uses the entire directory subtree as the source files.

The **username** in the **uuto** command contains a machine name followed by a login name on that machine. It has the following form:

system_*1*!system_*2*!...!system_*n*!user

The **uuto** command delivers the source files to the specified user on the destination system (that is, **system_*n***). On the destination machine, the UUCP facility copies the source files to the following directory:

/var/spool/uucppublic/receive/*user*/*machinename*

The *user* in the above path is the user you specified in the **uuto** command, and the *machinename* is the machine you were on when you entered the **uuto** command.

As mentioned earlier, the **uuto** command executes the **uucp** command to do the file transfer. For example, suppose you executed the following command on machine **farside**:

---

uuto /usr/local/file2.c hera!mike

In that case, the **uuto** command executes the following **uucp** command:

---

uucp -nmike /usr/local/file2.c hera!~/receive/mike/farside/

That, in turn, tells the **uucp** command to copy the file named

`/usr/local/file2.c`

to the file named

`/var/spool/uucppublic/receive/mike/farside/file2.c`

on the machine named **hera**. The **-n** flag also tells the **uucp** command to send mail to user **mike** on machine **hera** when the transfer completes. If you specified the **-m** option on the **uuto** command, you would get mail as well.

The UUCP facility also provides the **uupick** command that let's you accept or reject files that someone sent via the **uuto** command. The **uupick** command has the following form:

`uupick [-s` *machine*`]`

If you specify the **-s** option, the **uupick** command only looks for files sent from the given machine. Otherwise, it looks for all files that were sent to you.

The **uupick** command searches for files and directories of the following form:

`/var/spool/uucppublic/receive/`*username*`/`*machine*`/`*entry*

That path name, of course, is to where the **uuto** command transferred the files. The *username* is the user issuing the **uupick** command, and the directory after the *username* is the machine that sent the files.

The **uupick** command is interactive. When you execute the **uupick** command, it searches for files of the above form, extracts the machine name, and prints the following message:

`from system` *machine*`: file` *entry*`:`

If the last element of the path is a directory instead of a file, the **uupick** command prints the following message:

`from system` *machine*`: dir` *entry*`:`

After printing the message, the **uupick** command waits for you to enter a command. The command can be one of the following:

*   Prints a summary of all available commands.

`<Return>` Tells the **uupick** command to proceed to the next file or directory.

a *[dir]*   Instructs the **uupick** command to move all files from the listed *machine* into the *dir* directory on the local system. If you do not specify a directory, the **uupick** command moves the files to the current working directory. The directory can be a full path name or a relative path name.

m *[dir]*   Instructs the **uupick** command to move the listed file into the *dir* directory on the local system. If you do not specify a directory, the **uupick** command moves the files to the current working directory. And, as with the **a** command, the directory can be a full path name or a relative path name.

d   Tells the **uupick** command to remove the file.

p   Prints the file onto standard output.

q   Exits the **uupick** command.

! *command*   Creates a shell and executes the specified *command*.

Now let's look at the **uux** command. The **uux** command provides queued remote execution.

4.6 Remote Execution: uux

The **uux** command lets you execute commands on remote systems. However, unlike other remote execution facilities, the **uux** command provides queued remote execution. You specify a command to execute, and the UUCP facility executes the command later.

For security reasons, the administrator of the server machine restricts the commands that remote users can execute. If you try to execute a command that is not allowed on the remote system, you will receive mail telling you it is not allowed.

If the command you want to execute takes files as arguments, you can tell the **uux** command to gather those files from remote systems. You can also tell it to direct its output to a file on a remote system.

The **uux** command has the following format:

---

uux *[options]* *command_string*

The ***command_string*** looks like a normal UNIX system command line, except you can prefix the command and arguments with a system name, as follows:

`system!path`

You can specify a null `system` that defaults to the local system. For example, consider the following command:

`uux "farside!uuname > !/tmp/out"`

That executes the `uuname` command on machine `farside` and places the output into the `/tmp/out` file on the local system. It lets you figure out all the machines that `farside` can access via the UUCP facility.

As with the `uucp` command, the file names in the command string have several forms:

1. A full path name. If the file is on the local system, you can specify a path name relative to your current working directory.

2. A path name preceded with *~user*, where ***user*** is a login name on the destination machine. Here, `uux` replaces the *~user* string with the home directory of the specified user on the destination machine.

3. A path name preceded with *~/destination*. Here, `uux` appends the specified ***destination*** to the `/var/spool/uucppublic` directory.

To illustrate, consider the following command line:

`uux "hera!troff -mm zeus!~mike/f1 > zorro!~/mike/out`

Here, the `uux` command gets file `f1` from the home directory of `mike` on machine `zeus`, executes the `troff` command on machine `hera`, and puts the output in the file `/var/spool/uucppublic/mike/out` on machine `zorro`.

The `uux` command transfers the files to the machine that does the remote execution. In the foregoing example, the `uux` command transfers the `f1` file on machine `zeus` to machine `hera` before executing the `troff` command. When the `troff` command completes, the UUCP facility transfers the output to the specified file on machine `zorro`.

The `uux` command takes several options. For example, you can specify a grade with a `-g` flag and you can force the copy of local files into a spool directory with the `-C` flag. The `uux` manual page gives the details of all options.

Figure 4.3 shows the how `uux` does remote execution. The remote execution happens in several stages:

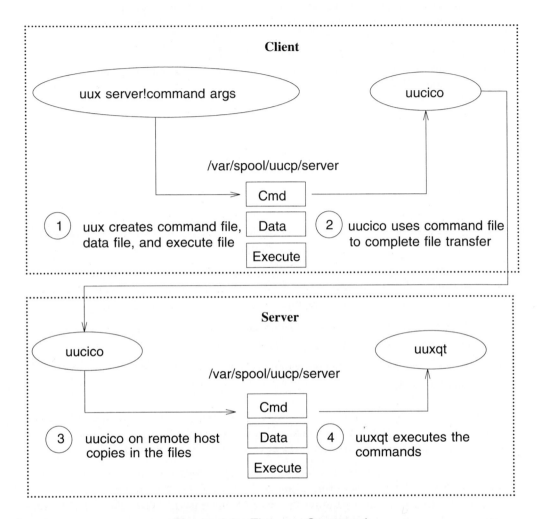

Figure 4.3 The uux Command

1. The **uux** command creates the following file:

/var/spool/uucp/*system*/X.*systemNxxx*

This file contains information about the command that will be executed on the remote system. In the file name, the *system* name is the machine to which to send the request, *N* is the grade, and *xxx* is a job ID that the UUCP facility uses.

As with the `uucp` command, the `uux` command also creates a command file (that is, a `C.` file) and data file (that is, a `D.` file) in the spool directory. The command file contains the same information that `uucp` uses. The data files contain the data needed for the remote execution.

2. After the `uux` command puts the files in the spool directory, the `uucico` command takes over. It contacts the remote system and transfers the files.

3. On the remote system, the `uucico` command copies the files into the spool directory.

4. Then, the `uuxqt` command on the remote system executes the specified command. It searches the spool directory, and for each execute file, it does the following actions:

   a. Reads the file to figure out which data files it needs to complete the command execution;

   b. Checks that the required data files are available; and

   c. Reads an administrative file to figure out if the specified command can be executed. Usually, the administrator of the machine restricts the commands that remote users can execute. As mentioned earlier, you will receive mail if you try to execute a command that is not allowed on the remote system.

5. If the administrator allows the execution of your command, the `uuxqt` command executes it. The `uuxqt` command then transfers the output to the file on the system you specified.

A key piece of the UUCP facility is the `uucico` command, which is examined in the next section.

4.7   The uucico Command

The `uucico` command transfers files between machines. When the `uucp` and the `uux` commands put files in the spool directory, they execute the `uucico` command to complete the transfer. Also, the system starts the `uucico` command periodically.

The `uucico` command does the following:

1. Scans the `/var/spool/uucp` directory on the local system looking for transfer requests;

2. Determines the network protocol to use for communication (administrative files have this information);

3. Establishes a connection with the remote system;

4. Invokes the login sequence with the remote system, logging in as a special UUCP user ID;

5. Transfers all files; and

6. Notifies an administratively designated user when the transfer completes.

Both the local system and the remote system run the `uucico` command. When the `uucico` commands starts on the local system, it makes a connection to the remote system and performs the login sequence (as mentioned before, the `uucico` command uses a special UUCP login ID that the administrator of the server machine establishes). Upon a successful login, the remote system starts the `uucico` command as the login shell.

On the local system, the `uucico` command performs the ''copy-out'' functions, that is, it copies the files to the remote system. On the remote system, the `uucico` command performs the ''copy-in'' functions, reading files and placing them into their destination directory. After the data transfer completes, the two `uucico` commands can switch roles to allow the remote system to copy files into the local system if needed.

Now that we've seen how the UUCP commands work, let's incorporate them into an application. We'll create a remote archive and restore application that uses the UUCP facility.

4.8 Application: Remote Archive and Restore

In Chapter 3, we implemented a remote archive and restore application using the TCP/IP file-transfer commands. To illustrate how to use the UUCP commands, we'll implement the same applications using the UUCP file-transfer commands.

The difference between the application created in Chapter 3 and the application presented in what follows is that the UUCP commands provide queued file transfer. So, where the TCP/IP commands transferred the files immediately, the UUCP commands transfer the files at a later time.

Queued file transfer has the advantage of robustness. If the server machine is down, the UUCP facility will keep the files in a local spool directory and attempt the transfer again later. The disadvantage, of course, is the delay in transferring the files.

We'll use the same directory layout used in Chapter 3. Figure 4.4 illustrates that layout. And, as in Chapter 3, we'll create a `cpio` file locally and transfer it to the appropriate directory on the server machine. We begin by presenting the script for the archive application.

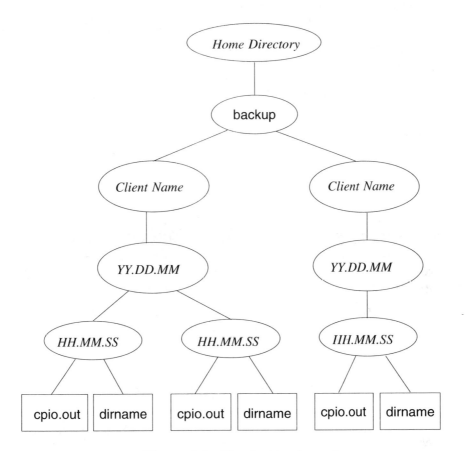

Figure 4.4   The Archive Layout

Archive Using the UUCP Commands

We'll begin the same way we did in Chapter 3:

1. Trap signals to clean up all the temporary files we create.

2. Create the **backup** directory that will contain the log of all archive operations we perform.

3. Prompt for the file or directory the user wants to archive.

4. Prompt for the server machine to which the user wants to archive. We use the **uuname** command to check that the specified server is accessible through the UUCP facility.

5. Prompt for the user name on the server machine. We do that because we will transfer the archive to the user's home directory on the server machine.

6. Create the archive using the **cpio** command.

The script follows:

```
trap 'rm -f /tmp/$$.*; exit 0' 0 1 2 3 4 5 6 7 8 10

if [ ! -d $HOME/backup ]
then
    mkdir $HOME/backup 2>/dev/null
    if [ $? -ne 0 ]
    then
        echo "$0: ERROR: could not create the $HOME/backup"
        echo "$0:         directory.  This directory is"
        echo "$0:         necessary to log your backups"
        exit 1
    fi
fi

echo "Please enter the file or directory you want to"
echo "back up: \c"
read DIR
while [ ! -f "$DIR" -a ! -d "$DIR" ]
do
    echo "$DIR does not exist!"
    echo "Please enter the file directory you want to"
    echo "back up: \c"
    read DIR
done

echo "Please enter the server machine name: \c"
read SERVER
CHECKNAME=`uuname | grep "^${SERVER}$"`
while [ "$CHECKNAME" != "$SERVER" ]
then
    echo "$SERVER is not known to the UUCP facility"
    echo "Please enter the server machine name: \c"
    read SERVER
    CHECKNAME=`uuname | grep "^${SERVER}$"`
fi
```

```
FIRST_CHAR=`echo $DIR | cut -c1`
if [ "$FIRST_CHAR" != "/" ]
then
    DIR=`pwd`/$DIR
fi

echo "Please enter your user name on $SERVER: \c"
read NAME

(
cd /
if [ -f $DIR ]
then
    echo $DIR >/tmp/$$.bkup
else
    find $DIR -print >/tmp/$$.bkup
fi

echo "Backing up the following files:"
cat /tmp/$$.bkup
cat /tmp/$$.bkup | sed 's/^.//' | cpio -odcm >/tmp/$$.cpio
echo $DIR >/tmp/$$.dname
)

DATE=`date +"%y.%m.%d"`
TIME=`date +"%H.%M.%S"`
CLIENT=`uname -n`
```

Now that we have created the archive, let's transfer it to the server machine. We can do this with the **uucp** command. We specify the following parameters:

1. The **-C** option. That causes the **uucp** command to copy the archive to the spool directory, letting us remove the original file.

2. The **-m** option. That causes the **uucp** command to send mail to the user when the transfer completes.

3. We prefix the destination file with **server!**. That causes the **uucp** command to transfer the file to the specified server machine. Also, we precede the path name with **~user**, which expands to the home directory of the specified user.

After we issue the **uucp** commands, we check the return code. A successful return code says the files are queued for transfer. The script follows:

```
uucp -C -m /tmp/$$.cpio \
    ${SERVER}!~$NAME/backup/$CLIENT/$DATE/$TIME/cpio.out &&
uucp -C -m /tmp/$$.dname \
    ${SERVER}!~$NAME/backup/$CLIENT/$DATE/$TIME/dirname

if [ $? -ne 0 ]
then
    echo "ERROR in transferring the directory"
    echo "backup/$CLIENT/$DATE/$TIME on $SERVER"
    exit 1
fi
```

As in Chapter 3, let's record what we've done so we can restore the archive later. The record contains the name of the server, the directory backed up and the location of the archive on the server machine.

```
echo $SERVER $DIR $CLIENT/$DATE/$TIME/cpio.out \
                    >>$HOME/backup/client.log

echo "Transfer successfully queued."
echo "Files will saved in cpio format in"
echo "$SERVER!~/backup/$CLIENT/$DATE/$TIME/cpio.out"
exit 0
```

The application that restores the archive to the local machine using the UUCP facility follows.

Restore Using the UUCP Commands

As with the archive application, we'll implement the same restore application created in Chapter 3. However, in this version, we use the UUCP facility for file transfer.

We begin that same as we did in Chapter 3:

1. Start the script with the `#!/usr/bin/ksh` line. That causes SVR4 to execute the script with the Korn Shell. The Korn Shell has the `select` feature used in the script.

2. Trap signals to remove all temporary files we create.

3.   Prompt the user for the archive to be restored. And, as in Chapter 3, we use the **select** feature of the Korn Shell to prompt the user for the specific archive they want restored.

The script follows:

```
#!/usr/bin/ksh
trap 'rm -f /tmp/$$.*; exit 0' 0 1 2 3 4 5 6 7 8 10

echo "Please enter the name of the"
echo "file or directory you want restored: \c"
read DIR

CLIENT=`uname -n`
ALL_DATES=`grep " $DIR $CLIENT/" $HOME/backup/client.log |
           cut -d' ' -f3 | cut -d/ -f2 | sort -u 2>/dev/null`

if [ "$ALL_DATES" = "" ]
then
    echo "There is no record of archive $DIR"
    echo "Please check for the archive in the backup"
    echo "directory in your home directory on the server"
    echo "machine on which you archived."
    exit 1
fi

NUMBER_OF_BKUPS=`echo $ALL_DATES | wc -w`
if [ $NUMBER_OF_BKUPS -eq 1 ]
then
    DATE=$ALL_DATES
else
    echo
    echo "You have archived $DIR $NUMBER_OF_BKUPS times"
    echo "Please select the date of the archive you want"
    echo "restored"
    PS3="Please the number corresponding to the date "
    select DATE in `echo $ALL_DATES | sed 's/\./\//g'`
    do
        break
    done

    DATE=`echo $DATE | sed 's/\//./g'`
fi
```

```
ALL_TIMES=`grep " ${DIR} ${CLIENT}/${DATE}"  \
                                $HOME/backup/client.log |
            cut -d' ' -f3 | cut -d/ -f3 | sort -u 2>/dev/null`

NUMBER_PER_DAY=`echo $ALL_TIMES | wc -w`
if [ $NUMBER_PER_DAY -eq 1 ]
then
    TIME=$ALL_TIMES
else
    echo
    echo "You have backed up $DIR $NUMBER_PER_DAY times"
    echo "on $DATE. Please select the time associated"
    echo "with the archive you want restored."
    PS3="Please select the time "
    select TIME in `echo $ALL_TIMES | sed 's/./:/g'`
    do
        break
    done
    TIME=`echo $TIME | sed 's/:/./g'`
fi

SERVER=`grep " ${DIR} ${CLIENT}/${DATE}/${TIME}"  \
            $HOME/backup/client.log | cut -d' ' -f1`
```

Now that we know exactly what archive to restore, we try to transfer the archive from the server machine to the local machine. Unfortunately, because the UUCP facility provides queued file transfer, we can only queue the transfer request. However, we set the **-m** option on the **uucp** command, instructing **uucp** to send mail to the user when the file transfer completes.

We issue the **uucp** command to transfer the archive to the **backup** directory in the user's home directory on the local machine. Then, we instruct the user that they must unpack the archive with the **cpio** command when the archive arrives.

The code follows:

```
echo
echo "Please enter your user name on $SERVER \c"
read NAME
```

**uucp ${SERVER}!~$NAME/backup/$CLIENT/$DATE/$TIME \
            $HOME/backup/$DATE.cpio**

```
echo
echo "File transfer queued."
echo "You will receive mail when the archive is transferred."
echo
echo "To restore the archive, enter the following command"
echo "in the directory in which you want to restore"
echo "the files:"
echo
echo "        cpio -idcvm <$HOME/backup/$DATE.cpio     "
exit 0
```

4.9 Summary

The UUCP facility is one of the original networking applications written for the UNIX system, and it provides powerful file-transfer and remote execution facilities. Unlike other file-transfer mechanisms, the UUCP facility provides queued operations. You issue a UUCP request, and the operation is carried out later.

In SVR4, the UUCP facility works over any communication medium. It can work over telephone lines, TCP/IP protocols, and any other transport protocol.

For Further Reading

1. AT&T, *UNIX System V Release 4 System Administrator's Guide*, Prentice Hall, Englewood Cliffs, NJ, 1990.

2. O'Reilly, T., and Todino, G., *Managing UUCP and USENET*, O'Reilly and Associates, Sebastopol, CA, 1992.

3. Redman, B., ''UUCP UNIX-to-UNIX Copy,'' *UNIX Networking*, Macmillan, New York, 1989.

4. Todino, G., and Dougherty, D., *Using UUCP and USENET*, O'Reilly and Associates, Sebastopol, CA, 1986.

Exercises

4.1 Explain the differences between the `uucp` command presented in this chapter and the `ftp` command presented in Chapter 3. What are the advantages and disadvantages of each?

4.2   Explain how the `uux` command works. Show an example of how to use the
`uux` command to figure out who is logged into a remote system.

4.3   Explain the roles of the `uucico` command and the `uuxqt` command. Why
are these commands needed in the UUCP facility?

4.4   What are the security implications of the UUCP facility?

Chapter 5

Applications Using
RFS and NFS

5.1 Introduction

Although powerful tools exist to copy data from one machine to another, many applications also need the ability to *share* data between machines. For example, consider a bank teller application that is running on several machines in a network. All instances of this application must share the bank database file—if one instance of the application updates the database file, the modifications must be seen by the others. SVR4 allows applications to share files in this way through RFS and NFS.

Remote File Sharing (RFS) and the Network File System (NFS) are two file-sharing systems available on SVR4. They let applications running on one machine transparently access files and directories that exist on another.

With RFS, machines running System V can selectively share directories containing all types of UNIX files, including regular files, directories, and device files. RFS supports full UNIX semantics, so anything applications can do on a local file can also be done on a remote file.

Using NFS, the de facto standard file-sharing system, you can share files and directories between UNIX and non-UNIX operating systems. This makes NFS essential for applications that want to share files in a heterogeneous operating system environment. In addition, NFS can provide initial disk space for diskless workstations.

In this chapter, we present the architecture of both file-sharing systems, show the strengths and weaknesses of each, and explain how applications can use RFS or NFS to transparently access files over a network. We begin by presenting an overview of RFS and NFS.

5.2   Overview of RFS and NFS

RFS and NFS are distributed file systems. From an application's point of view, a distributed file system looks like any other file system, that is, it is simply a collection of files. However, where as regular file systems access local files, distributed file systems access files that exist on another machine. This lets your applications transparently access files and directories across the network. Because many applications make extensive use of the UNIX file system, using a distributed file system lets you use the network without modifying your application.

RFS and NFS follow the *remote mount model*. Using this model, the administrator of a server machine makes a directory available to client machines, and the administrator of a client machine attaches that directory to the local file tree. Once attached, applications running on the client machine see the remote files as if they existed on the client machine, even though the files physically reside on the server machine. Figure 5.1 shows the remote mount model.

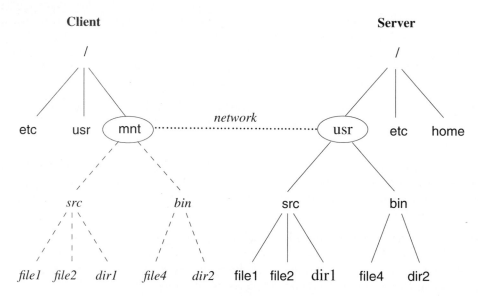

Figure 5.1   The Remote Mount Model

It is important to realize that the files are actually shared between the machines, not copied from one machine to the other. So, if an application running on either the client machine or the server machine modifies a file, the modifications are seen by the other.

Because both RFS and NFS follow the remote mount model, they are often viewed as competitors. The questions often arises: ''Of RFS and NFS, which is the better distributed file system?'' This is an unfair question, because RFS and NFS derive from differing goals and therefore provide solutions to differing problems. The question is similar to the query: ''Which tool is better, a hammer or a screwdriver?'' As we will see when we examine the goals of RFS and NFS, the answer to both questions is the same: ''It all depends on what you want to use it for.''

5.3 Goals of RFS

The RFS distributed file system had several goals. First and foremost, RFS was *to provide transparent access to remote files and devices* and **preserve full UNIX system semantics** on remote files. This meant RFS had to maintain the standard UNIX system interface and allow applications to access a remote file in the same way as a local file.

This goal implies full transparency of operation. It meant all operations that could be done on a local file could also be done on a remote file, including mandatory and advisory file and record locking, opening a file with append mode, and all other UNIX system semantics.

A second goal was *to allow applications to access a remote file independent of the file's physical location*. This goal meant that a directory could move from one server machine to another without affecting client-machine operations. For example, if a server machine containing the official source code for a project went down for repair, the network administrator could move the source code to another server machine (or maintain a backup copy of the source code on another server machine) without affecting the administrative process of a client machine.

As we will see in the description of the RFS architecture, RFS meets this goal by letting the administrator of the server machine give a symbolic name to a directory. RFS provides a name service to resolve the symbolic name into a server machine's identity. The administrator of the client machine simply specifies the symbolic name when it wants to attach to a remote directory and lets the name service figure out which server machine has the directory available.

Next, RFS wanted *to support all UNIX file types*, including device files and named pipes. This would allow applications *to share devices like printers and tape drives*. If a server machine had a printer and shared a directory containing a device file for that printer, then every application that opened the device file would access the printer on the server machine.

A fourth goal was *to preserve binary compatibility*. Existing applications would not have to be modified or recompiled to make use of remote files and directories. For example, if the administrator chose to put a database on a server machine, an application on the client machine would not have to be modified to access the remote database files.

Another goal was *to operate independent of network media*. RFS was to be completely transport-independent and operate over a variety of networks ranging from local area networks (LANs) to large concatenated networks.

RFS also wanted *to provide full data-cache consistency*. Caching data increases performance—when an application reads data from a remote file, the client machine can keep a copy of the data in a local data cache. By doing this, the next application on the client machine that wants to read the data can do so without accessing the network. As we describe later, RFS provides full cache consistency by guaranteeing that the data cache on the client machine is always in sync with the data on the server machine.

Finally, RFS was designed *to achieve easy portability*. This goal was to minimize and localize the changes to the UNIX kernel. RFS meets this goal by isolating most of its functionality to a configurable, separate module in SVR4.

RFS met every one of its goals. It provides applications with full UNIX semantics when accessing remote files and directories and provides full cache consistency. It works over any connection-oriented transport provider and supports every type of UNIX file. It lets applications on a client machine use devices on a server machine (such as printers and tape drives) simply by accessing the remote device file. From an application's point of view, remote files can be manipulated in exactly the same way as local files.

Now that we've seen the goals of RFS, let's take a closer look at the RFS architecture. We present the architecture of RFS from an application's point of view.

5.4   Architecture of RFS

The RFS architecture has client machines, server machines, and resources. A *resource* is a directory (that may contain files, directories, device files, or named pipes) that is shared between two or more machines. The server is a machine that physically owns a resource, and a client is a machine that accesses the resource over the network.

The administrator of a server machine *advertises* a directory to make it available for sharing. After the resource is advertised, client machines can access it. All files and directories under the resource are available to a client machine—the server machine does not "end" the resource at any point. For example, if the administrator of a server machine advertised the root directory, then applications on client machines could access the entire directory tree on the server machine.

As mentioned earlier, RFS subscribes to the remote mount model. Figure 5.2 shows this model as used by RFS. The following steps set up the RFS configuration:

1.   The administrator of the server machine advertises a directory by issuing the **share** command, giving the directory a symbolic resource name.

2.   The administrator of the client machine attaches the directory onto the local directory tree by issuing the **mount** command, specifying the symbolic resource name and the local mount point.

3.   Once mounted, applications on the client machine see the remote directory as part of the local directory tree. They can access files, directories, and named pipes from the server machine's advertised directory in the same way as if they were local files.

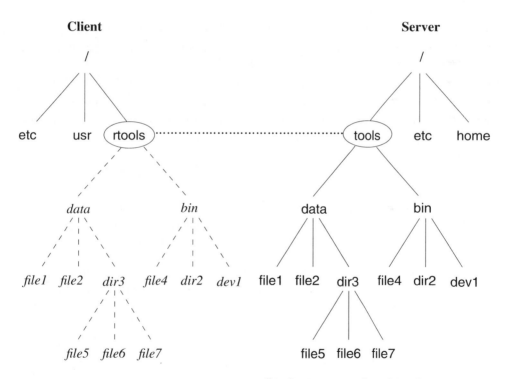

```
                                          # share -F rfs /tools TOOLSDIR
# mount -F rfs TOOLSDIR /rtools
```

Figure 5.2 The RFS Model

Note that the **mount** command in Figure 5.2 does not contain the server machine's name. It only contains the symbolic resource name. This lets administrators move resources from one machine to another. For example, if a server machine was to go down for repair, the contents of the directory could be moved to another server machine. This new server machine could then advertise the directory, and the administrators of the client machines would not have to modify their actions—they would still simply specify the symbolic resource name when they issued the **mount** command.

The process of resolving the symbolic name into the identity of the server machine is done via a series of cooperating processes, collectively called the RFS name service. Because the RFS name service is important to the architecture of RFS, an overview is presented.

RFS Name Service

The RFS name service gives RFS its feature of location independence. It lets the administrator of the server machine symbolically name a resource, freeing administrators of client machines from figuring out on which server machine a resource resides.

The RFS name service works by having each machine in the RFS environment run a name-server process. One of the machines is administratively classified as the "primary name server." The name-server process on the primary name server is responsible for maintaining a table that maps the symbolic names into transport addresses.

Here's how it works. When an administrator of a server machine advertises a resource via the **share** command, he or she assigns the resource a symbolic name. The **share** command sends a message to the local name-server process, telling it the resource being advertised. The local name-server process sends a message to the name-server process on the primary name server machine, informing it of the symbolic name, the server machine's identity, and the transport address the client machine should use to establish communication. The primary name server records this information in a table and sends an acknowledgment to the name-server process on the server machine.

When the administrator of a client machine mounts the resource, he or she specifies a symbolic resource name. The **mount** command sends a message to the local name-server process, identifying the resource to be mounted. The name-server process sends a query to the name-server process on the primary name server, requesting the identity of the server machine that advertised the resource and the corresponding transport address. The name-server process on the primary name server sends the requested information to the client machine, allowing the client machine to make a network connection to the server machine.

So, the name-server process on the primary name server is the central point when advertising and mounting resources. It is responsible for resolving symbolic resource names into transport addresses. However, once a client machine gets the required transport address, the primary name server is not involved in the communication between the client machine and the server machine.

The name-server process on the primary name server is essential to the operation of RFS. Havoc would result if the primary name-server machine crashed. To avoid this single point of failure, RFS lets other machines act as secondary name servers. An RFS administrator can define one or more secondary name servers, which will automatically assume primary name-server responsibility if the primary name server goes down.

Once the client machine obtains the address of the server machine, it must establish communication with the server machine to share files and directories. We now present this interaction between the client machine and the server machine.

Client/Server Interactions

The RFS architecture uses virtual-circuit connections between the client machine and the server machine. RFS uses the Transport Level Interface (TLI), so it can use any virtual-circuit transport provider (details of TLI are given in Chapter 7).

The client machine establishes the virtual-circuit connection with the server machine when the administrator issues the first **mount** command. This virtual circuit is used on all subsequent accesses. If the administrator of the client machine issues another **mount** command to get another resource from the same server machine, RFS uses the virtual circuit established on the first **mount** command.

Using virtual circuits has several advantages. First, the server machine knows when the client machine goes down (because the virtual circuit breaks). Next, the RFS code need not retransmit packets, because a virtual-circuit transport provider guarantees delivery. This simplifies the RFS implementation.

After the client machine establishes the virtual circuit, applications on the client machine can access files on the server machine. When an application attempts to open a remote file, the client machine performs the following:

1.   When parsing the path name of the file, the client machine detects that the file exists on the server machine.

2.   The client machine forms a network message that contains an indication of which system call is being performed (the **open()** system call in this case), the parameters, and the rest of the path name. It then sends the message to the server machine and waits for a response.

3. The server machine receives the message from the client machine and does the following:

    a. Completes the system call (in this example, the server machine completes the `open()` system call).

    b. Formulates a response (containing results or error information) and sends the response to the client machine.

4. When the client machine receives the response, it returns the results to your application.

So, the RFS protocol consists of UNIX system calls. When your application issues a system call, the client machine begins its execution. When it reaches a remote mount point, it sends the system call to the server machine for completion. That is why RFS provides full UNIX semantics—anything that can be done on a client machine can be done on the server machine because the server machine actually completes the system call on your application's behalf.

To work correctly, the server machine must keep information about which applications on client machines are using its resources. This is called *maintaining state information* and is described next.

State Information

The server machine maintains state information in an RFS environment. This means the server machine knows exactly which client machines are using its resources. The server machine keeps local file reference counts, file and record locks, and all other information associated with its files.

Figure 5.3 illustrates an example of the state information kept on the server machine. In this illustration, the server knows that one application from machine A, three applications from machine B, and one local application have the file open.

Maintaining state information lets the server machine maintain file lock information. For example, if an application on a client machine wanted to lock a file on the server machine, it is essential that the server machine record this information to prevent other applications from locking the same file.

State information also lets the server machine provide complete data-cache consistency. When a client machine reads a file, it caches the data locally. When the file is updated (either by an application on another client machine or by an application on the server machine), the server machine tells all client machines caching the data to invalidate their cache. The server machine can do this because its state information tells it exactly which client machines are using the file.

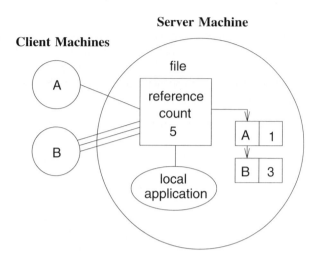

Figure 5.3   RFS Server State

Now let's look at some specific UNIX system semantics. Because some semantics do not work well when files exist on a remote machine, RFS must take certain actions to ensure consistent operation.

UNIX System Semantics

There are some UNIX system semantics that must be specifically addressed by RFS. One such semantic is **time skew**. The UNIX system lets the administrator of a machine set the time and date. Unfortunately, the time of day on the server machine may be different from the time of day on the client machine. Even though the difference may be only a minute or two, the difference breaks some UNIX commands that rely on the time stamps of UNIX files to perform tasks.

For example, the **make** command looks at the time a source file was last modified to figure out whether to rebuild an executable object. If the **make** command was accessing files via RFS, it would be essential that the time of day on the server machine and the time of day on the client machine be exactly in synch.

To address this problem, the server machine keeps the time delta between its idea of time and each client machine's idea of time. The delta is calculated when the virtual circuit is set up between the client machine and the server machine, and it is updated when the time is explicitly reset by either machine.

The server machine uses the time delta when returning results to the client machine. Here's how it works. When an application on the client machine makes a system call on a remote file, the server machine completes the system call. But, before returning the results to the client machine, the server machine adjusts time-based information (for example, the time a file was last modified) using the time delta. This compensates for any time inconsistency between itself and the client machine and lets applications see a consistent view of time across a network.

Another semantic is status information returned from the `stat()` system call. In the UNIX system, applications figure out whether two files are the same by comparing the `st_dev` and `st_ino` elements of the information returned by the `stat()` system call. Unfortunately, the `st_dev` and `st_ino` pair are guaranteed to be unique only within a single system. It is possible that the `st_dev` number and the `st_ino` number of a local file match that of a remote file. If an application used the `stat()` system call on a remote and local file, and the files coincidentally had the same `st_dev` and `st_ino` pair, that application would incorrectly conclude that the two files were the same.

RFS has the client machine fix this problem. When an application on the client machine issues the `stat()` system call on a remote file, normal operations happen— the client machine sends the request to the server machine and the server machine performs the operation and returns the results. But, when the results are received, the client machine modifies the high-order bits of the `st_dev` element to incorporate the identity of the server machine. This guarantees that the `st_dev` element from a file on a server is unique to applications on the client machine.

Other UNIX system file semantics come automatically because the server machine keeps state information. Applications on client machines can open a file with append mode, use mandatory and advisory file and record locking, access device files on the server machine, and access named pipes. This all occurs because the server machine completes the UNIX system calls on behalf of the application running on the client machine.

5.5 RFS Security Considerations

Security is always a concern when applications on a client machine access files on a server machine. The RFS philosophy on security is that the server machine has complete control over who can access its files. RFS provides the following security features:

1. The administrator of the server machine can choose which client machines can mount a resource. When administrators advertise a directory, they can specify an optional list of client machine names. The client machines in the list are the only ones that can mount the directory.

2. The administrator of the server machine can advertise a directory as "read-only," meaning applications on a client machine can read the files but cannot write into them.

3. The administrator of the server machine can enforce an optional password mechanism. Using this mechanism, a server machine can disallow access to a resource if a client machine does not carry a correct machine password.

4. The administrator of the server machine can enforce ID mapping. ID mapping lets the server machine map users from client machines into local users. This allows the server machine to map dangerous users from a client machine (for example, the **root** user) into less dangerous ones.

ID mapping is probably the most advantageous security feature of RFS. Here's how it works. The administrator of the server machine sets up a table that maps users from a client machine into local users. The administrator then issues the `idload` command to make the table active within the system.

Whenever an application on a client machine issues a system call that accesses a file on the server machine, RFS sends the user ID associated with the application. Before the server machine executes the system call, it checks the ID mapping table to figure out whether the user ID should be changed. If it should, the server machine maps the user ID before executing the system call.

Figure 5.4 illustrates ID mapping. Here, user **jane** has user ID **107** on machine **farside** and user ID **123** on the server machine. Also, user **mike** has user ID **107** on the server machine. RFS allows the administrator of the server machine map user ID **107** from machine **farside** into user ID **123**. This way, whenever user ID **107** from **farside** sends a system call to the server machine, the server changes the user ID to **123** before proceeding. This stops user **jane** on **farside** from gaining unauthorized access to files owned by user **mike** on the server machine.

RFS also provides *inverse ID mapping* to give a consistent file view to users on client machines. With inverse ID mapping, the server machine uses its ID mapping information to reverse a user ID before returning information about a file to a client machine.

To illustrate, consider the scenario in Figure 5.4. Suppose user **jane** on machine **farside** creates a file on the server machine. Because user **jane** on machine **farside** has user ID **107**, the server machine changes that user ID into **123** before completing the request (as directed by the ID mapping table entry). So, on the server machine, the owner of the file is user ID **123**. Now, if a user on client machine **farside** issues the `stat()` system call to obtain information about that file, the server machine does the following:

1. Obtains the information about the file.

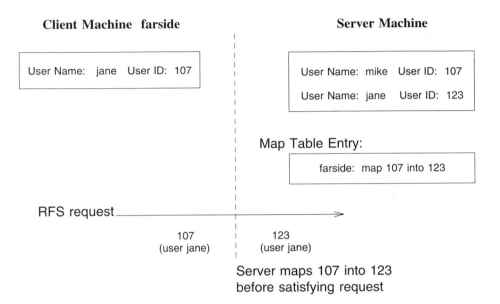

Figure 5.4   ID Mapping

2. Sees that user ID **123** owns the file and notes that a user on machine **farside** originated the `stat()` system call.

3. Looks at its mapping table and sees that user ID **107** from machine **farside** is mapped into user ID **123**.

4. Changes the user ID **123** to user ID **107** in the status information and sends the modified information to machine **farside**. That way, users on machine **farside** see that the file is accessible to user **107**.

ID mapping takes on one more twist when set-user-ID programs are involved. If a user on a client machine executes a set-user-ID program that resides on a server machine, the *client* machine maps the effective user ID (as directed by its mapping table for the server machine) before executing the program. RFS does that to close a security hole. Here is the potential danger:

1. Suppose user **mike** is the administrator on a server machine named **bilbo** and a normal user on the client machine named **farside**.

2. Also suppose the administrator of the client machine mounted the `/usr` directory from **bilbo** onto its `/mnt` directory.

3. Because user **mike** is the administrator of **bilbo**, user **mike** can log into **bilbo** as user **root**. User **mike** can then create a copy of the UNIX shell as set-user-ID to **root** and place the copy of the shell into the `/usr/xxx` file.

4. Now, user **mike** knows there is a copy of the shell with set-user-ID to **root** in the `/usr/xxx` file. Also, because machine **farside** has the `/usr` directory from **bilbo** mounted on its `/mnt` directory, user **mike** knows the file is available on **farside** as `/mnt/xxx`.

5. User **mike** can now log into **farside** and execute the `/mnt/xxx` file. With that, user **mike** has gained unauthorized superuser privileges on the client machine!

To close that security hole, RFS lets the client machine map users when it retrieves set-user-ID programs. So, if machine **farside** mapped user ID **0** from machine **bilbo** into user ID **60001**, the set-user-ID program would run on **farside** as set-user-ID to **60001**, not as set-user-ID to **0**. Because user ID **60001** has no special privileges, the security hole is closed.

The ID mapping feature and the other security features were introduced in UNIX System V Release 3 and are supported in SVR4. The new features of SVR4 are described next.

5.6   New Features of RFS in SVR4

RFS is enhanced in SVR4. Besides performance improvements and bug fixes, the RFS architecture in SVR4 uses an RFS name service that works over several transport providers simultaneously.

Although previous versions of the RFS name service could work over any virtual-circuit transport provider, it could only work over one transport provider at a time. So, if a machine had several transport providers available, the administrator would have to choose which one to use when running RFS.

That changed in SVR4. The SVR4 RFS name service can be configured to work over multiple transport providers, so you can run RFS in a true heterogeneous transport-provider environment. So, if you have more than one transport provider on your machine, the RFS name service can work over all of them simultaneously.

Another new feature is a simplified administrative interface. A new administrative architecture and menu-driven interface make setting up RFS much easier than in previous releases.

5.7   Restrictions of RFS

There are some restrictions enforced by RFS. First, RFS does not allow a multihop capability. A multihop capability allows a client machine to access files on a remote machine by going through an intermediate machine.

Figure 5.5 illustrates a multihop scenario. Here, machine C advertises the `/src` directory and machine B attaches it to its `/usr/src` directory. Next, machine B advertises the `/` directory and machine A attaches that to its `/mnt` directory.

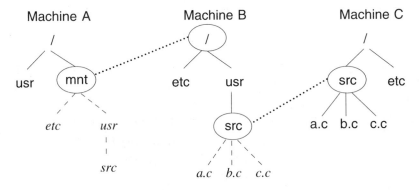

Figure 5.5   Multihop

Now, if an application running on machine A attempted to access `/mnt/usr/src/a.c`, the access would fail (the application would get an error indication stating ''Multihop attempted''). The reason for that restriction deals with security issues—machine C could have restricted access to machine B only. If machine B allowed applications from machine A to access files on machine C, it would violate the restrictions set up by machine C.

RFS also restricts where the administrator of a client machine can mount a resource. The administrator of a client machine can only mount a resource onto a local directory. This is because of the way RFS operates—when an application on the client machine attempts to access a remote file, the client machine sends the system call and the rest of the path name to the server machine for completion. The client machine does not have control of the path name after it sends it to the server machine, so the administrator of the client machine cannot mount another resource on the remote directory.

A third restriction deals with passing file descriptors through pipes. As described in Chapter 2, SVR4 lets your application attach a STREAMS-based pipe to a file. Once attached, an unrelated process can open the file and communicate with your application through the pipe. Now, if your application is running on a server machine and the attached file is accessible to processes on a client machine via RFS, then processes on the client machine can open the file. Once opened, the process on the client machine can communicate with your application on the server machine over the pipe. That provides a powerful interprocess communication facility between machines.

However, RFS does *not* allow a process on the client machine to pass an open file descriptor to the application on the server machine via the `ioctl()` system call with the `I_SENDFD` parameter. This function is reserved for applications running on the same machine. Instead, the application on the server machine must use the `connld` module to generate a unique file descriptor automatically when another process opens the file. An overview of sending file descriptors over pipes is given in Chapter 2. We show an example of how to use the `connld` module in Section 5.16.

5.8   Drawbacks of RFS

As you may expect, there are some drawbacks to RFS. First, because it provides full UNIX semantics, it can only be fully implemented on other UNIX systems. It is not designed to share files between UNIX and non-UNIX operating systems.

Second, it cannot be used to provide initial disk space to diskless workstations. This is because RFS lets you share devices, so a diskless workstation using RFS to obtain a root directory would not be able to access its own local devices.

Figure 5.6 illustrates why this is so. If a server machine wanted to provide the root directory for a diskless workstation, it must create a directory that contained all the files that the diskless workstation needed. One of those directories would be the `/dev` directory, containing the device files for the workstation's console, floppy drives, and other peripheral devices.

Now, suppose the diskless workstation used that directory as the root of its file tree. Because RFS shares devices, when an application on the diskless workstation wrote data to `/dev/console`, the data would go to the console on the server machine, not to the console on the workstation! So, even though letting a client machine access a device on the server machine is a powerful function, it stops RFS from providing initial disk space to diskless workstations. However, RFS can be used to share files and devices with diskless workstations after the workstation obtains initial file space by another means.

A third drawback is that RFS is administratively difficult to set up. It provides a name service to map symbolic resource names into server identities, and so the name service must be configured, administered, and maintained. Although SVR4 simplified the administrative interface to RFS, administrative action is still required.

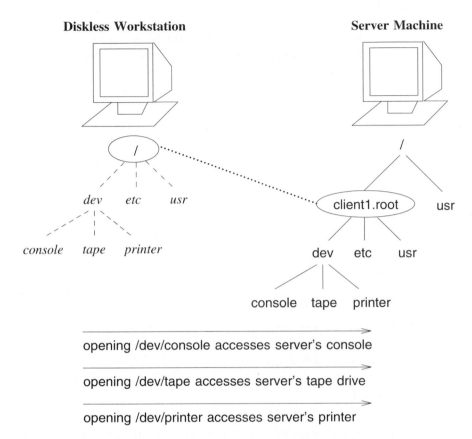

Figure 5.6   Problem with RFS and Diskless Workstations

Another disadvantage is that RFS does not handle server crashes well. If a server machine crashes, the client machine treats it like a disk failure. The client machine actions can be tuned by the administrator, but, by default, the client machine kills all applications using the remote directory when the server machine goes down.

Despite these drawbacks, RFS does do what it was set out to do. It allows applications to transparently access remote files and directories without modification.

Now let's look at NFS. Before we describe the NFS architecture, we examine its goals. The goals of NFS were different from the goals of RFS. Where as RFS was to provide full UNIX semantics, NFS was to provide semantics that would fit the UNIX model but could be implemented on non-UNIX systems. And, as we will see, differences in functionality reflect the differences in goals of these file-sharing systems.

5.9   Goals of NFS

As with RFS, a major goal of NFS was to provide transparent access to remote files. However, unlike RFS, the primary goal of NFS was *to provide transparent access to remote files and directories in a heterogeneous operating system environment.* This goal would allow applications to access remote files on UNIX operating systems and non-UNIX operating systems.

By reaching this goal, NFS is machine and operating system independent. This gives applications a powerful file-sharing ability. Unfortunately, there is a price to pay— sharing files with non-UNIX systems means that NFS cannot support UNIX system specific functionality. So, full UNIX system semantics are not supported. Section 5.10 describes the semantics your applications cannot assume when using NFS.

A second goal of NFS was to allow applications *to access a remote file in the same way as a local file.* This goal was to let applications access remote files by using the normal UNIX system calls.

Another goal was *to provide good recovery characteristics.* NFS wanted to recover easily from machine and network failures. A server machine offering files would not be sensitive to a crash of a client machine, and a client machine could recover easily from a server machine failure. Details of how NFS met this goal are presented in Section 5.10.

The next goal was *to achieve easy portability.* NFS certainly met this goal. The NFS protocol is very easy to port. It has been ported to many different operating systems and hardware architectures.

Finally, and perhaps most important, NFS was designed *to give diskless workstation file space.* NFS achieves this goal by handling device files locally. When an application running on the client machine accesses a device file on a server machine, it accesses the corresponding device on the *client* system. For example, if your application wrote a message to a device file corresponding to a remote console, the message actually goes to the *local* console. Figure 5.7 shows this functionality. This behavior gives a diskless workstation the ability to access remote files and directories while still being able to access local peripheral devices.

NFS met all its goals. It allows file sharing between UNIX and non-UNIX systems and provides file space to diskless workstations. From an application's point of view, NFS lets you access files from a variety of operating system platforms.

Now let's look at the NFS architecture. We present this from an application's point of view.

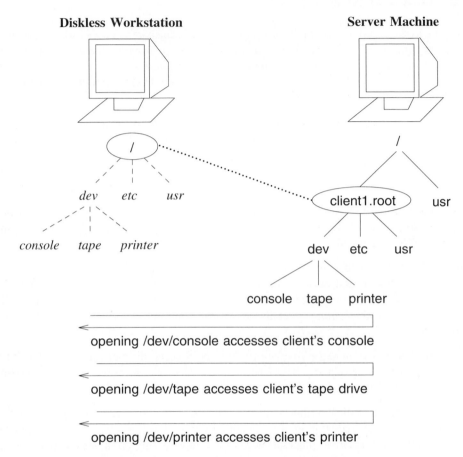

Figure 5.7   NFS and Diskless Workstations

5.10 Architecture of NFS

The NFS architecture has server machines, client machines, and file systems. A file system in the NFS sense is a logical grouping of files and directories. The server machine physically owns a file system that is shared across a network. A client machine uses a file system that belongs to a server machine.

Because NFS shares files on a file-system basis, it is important to realize exactly what a file system is on a UNIX system. A file system is a set of files on a single physical hardware device (for example, a disk device). The administrator of the UNIX machine attaches the file systems together (via the **mount** command) to form the directory tree that your applications see.

To illustrate, consider the configuration in Figure 5.8. Here, the UNIX machine has three separate file systems. The administrator mounts these file systems together, forming the complete UNIX directory tree. Applications are not aware that they cross the file systems when they travel along the tree.

Now let's look at an NFS environment. In an NFS environment, the administrator of the server machine *exports* a file system to make it available for sharing. Once exported, the administrators of client machines can mount it onto their local file tree. However, unlike RFS, only files and directories on the physical file system are available to the client machine—applications running on the client machine do not access files on any other file system on the server machine.

Figure 5.9 shows this model as used by NFS. The administrator of the server machine uses the **share** command to export a file system, and the administrator of the client machine uses the **mount** command to attach that file system to a local directory. Once attached, applications on the client machine can access files and directories on the remote file system.

Now let's look at what it takes to set up the configuration shown in Figure 5.9:

1. The administrator of the server machine exports a file system by issuing the **share** command.

2. The administrator of the client machine attaches the file system onto the local directory tree using the **mount** command. The administrator specifies the name of the server machine and the name of the file system. If desired, the administrator can specify a subdirectory under the exported file system.

3. Once attached, applications on the client machine can access files and directories on the remote file system as if they existed on a local file system.

It is important to remember that applications on the client machine can *only* access files and directories on the exported file system. Any other file systems on the server machine are inaccessible to the client machine.

It is also important to remember that applications running on the client machine can only access files and directories on the server machine. If an application tries to access a device or a named pipe on the server machine, it will access the corresponding device or named pipe on the client machine. So, if an application on the client machine writes to the **console** file on the server machine, the data will appear on the client machine's console. Although this prevents applications on the client machine from using devices on the server machine, it allows diskless clients to obtain disk space and still access local devices.

Now let's look at the interaction between the client machine and the server machine when an application accesses a remote file.

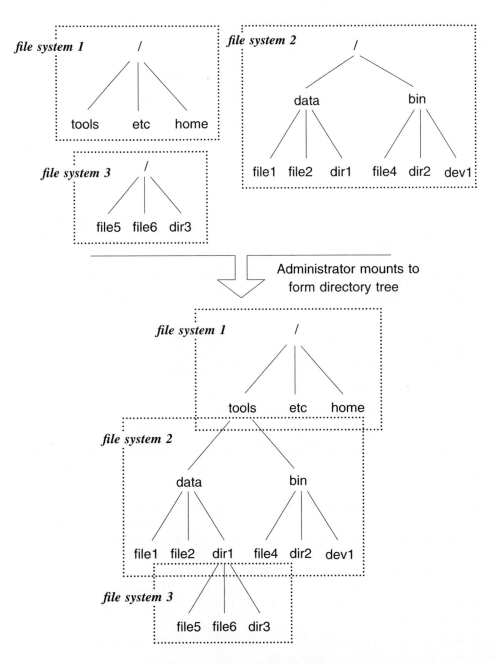

Figure 5.8 Mounting File Systems

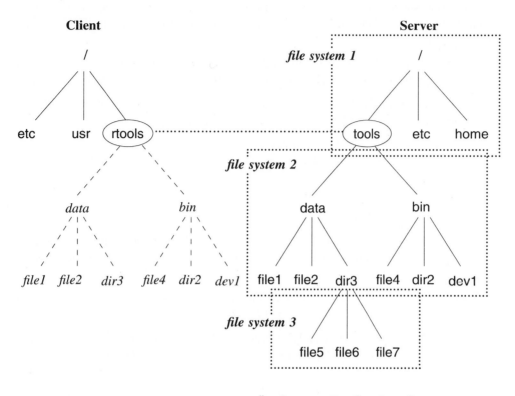

share -F nfs /tools

mount -F nfs server:/tools /rtools

Figure 5.9   The NFS Model

Client/Server Interactions

NFS uses a datagram transport provider. This means that the NFS implementation must retransmit lost packets. However, it saves the overhead of virtual-circuit establishment. In SVR4, NFS can work over any datagram transport provider.

When an application on the client machine attempts to access a remote file, the client machine obtains a *file handle* associated with the file. A file handle is a data structure that uniquely identifies a file on the server machine and is used for all NFS operations on that file.

To illustrate, suppose two machines established the configuration in Figure 5.9. If an application on the client machine opened `/rtools/data/file2`, the following would occur:

1. The client machine realizes that the `/rtools` directory is remote and sends a message to the server machine requesting a file handle for the directory `data`.

2. The server machine gets the request, creates a file handle for the directory `data`, and sends this to the client machine.

3. When the client machine gets the response, it sends a message to the server machine requesting a file handle for `file2`.

4. The server machine gets this request, creates a file handle for `file2`, and sends it to the client machine. The client machine uses that file handle for all future operations on `file2`.

The file handle is the most important element of the NFS implementation. It identifies a file on the server machine, and the client machine sends it to the server machine on all operations on the file.

For example, suppose the application on the client machine that opened the `/rtools/data/file2` issued a `read()` system call. The following would occur:

1. The client machine sends an NFS **read** request to the server machine, specifying the file handle, the number of bytes to read, and an indication of where to start reading.

2. The server machine gets the request, opens the file associated with the file handle, retrieves the requested data, closes the file, and sends the data to the client machine.

Similar actions take place for writing the file. The client machine sends an NFS **write** request to the server machine, specifying the file handle, the number of bytes to write, and an indication of where to start writing. The server machine gets the request, opens the file associated with the file handle, writes the data, and sends an acknowledgment back to the client machine.

Because the file handle is a key piece of NFS operations, let's take a closer look at it from the view of the client machine and the server machine.

The NFS File Handle

The file handle plays a key role in all NFS operations. Whenever an application on the client machine requests an operation on a remote file (such as reading or writing data), the client machine sends the file handle to the server machine to identify the file.

The client machine gets its first file handle from the server machine when the administrator issues the **mount** command. The client machine gets all other file handles in one of two ways: when an application opens a file that exists on the server machine or when an application creates a file or directory on the server machine.

The server machine creates the file handles. A file handle contains all information the server machine needs to identify the file. On SVR4 (as with most other UNIX systems), the file handle contains the device number of the file, the inode number of the file, and a "file instance number" of the file. The device number identifies a physical device (that is, a partition of the hard disk), and the inode number identifies a file on that device. Normally, a device number and inode number uniquely identify a file. But, because an inode number can be reused, the file instance number is needed.

Here's why: Assume file **/tools/data/file2** on the server machine had device number **115** and inode number **102**. If an application deletes that file, inode number **102** is available for reuse. So, another application can create a new file (for example, **file3**) with device number **115** and inode number **102**. Now, if the file handle contained only device number **115** and inode number **102**, it would now refer to **file3** instead of **file2**.

To solve this problem, SVR4 associates a file instance number with the inode. Whenever the inode is reused, SVR4 increments the inode's file instance number. In this way, the triple containing the device number, inode number, and file instance number uniquely identifies the file.

Server machines running non-UNIX operating systems can put whatever is necessary into the file handle. The only requirement is that the file handle contain enough information to uniquely identify a file.

The client machine, on the other hand, sees the file handle as a black box that it sends to the server machine when operations on that file occur. It neither knows nor cares what's in the file handle.

Because the file handle uniquely describes a file, the server machine need not remember to which client machines it gave file handles. When a client machine that has a file handle sends an NFS request to the server machine, the server machine uses the file handle to locate the file and performs the requested operation. Hence, NFS is said to have "stateless operations."

Stateless Operations

The server machine does not maintain state information. It has no notion of which client machines have its files open. The server machine simply creates and returns a file handle when an application on a client machine initially accesses a file.

This has several implications:

1. When a client machine issues an NFS request, the request must contain all information necessary to complete the operation. For example, when a client machine issues an NFS **read** request, the request must contain the file handle associated with the file, an indication of where to start reading, and an indication of how much data to read.

2. Operations that require state must be done via another network service. For example, locking a file requires state information. The server machine must keep track of which client machines hold locks on its files. Because this cannot be done in a stateless environment, file locking is not a part of NFS. File locking is supported through a separate locking service.

3. A datagram protocol can be used. Every NFS request contains all information needed to satisfy the operation; so, the client machine can simply resend the request if it does not get an acknowledgment from the server machine.

The stateless features of NFS make recovery from machine crashes very easy. We now present an overview of NFS recovery.

NFS Recovery

In a stateless environment, recovery is straightforward. If the client machine crashes, the server machine doesn't care (in fact, the server machine didn't even know the client machine was up in the first place). The server machine kept no record of what the client machine was doing, so it does not have to recover any information if the client machine crashes.

If the server machine crashes, the client machine simply keeps resending requests. This can be done because every NFS request is an autonomous unit. When the server machine comes back, it will satisfy the client machine's request. To illustrate, consider the following scenario:

1. An application on the client machine opens a file, causing the client machine to obtain a file handle for that file.

2. The application issues a **read()** system call. This causes the client machine to send an NFS **read** request to the server machine. The server machine gets the file handle, opens the file, retrieves the data, and returns the data to the client machine.

3. The server machine crashes.

4. The application on the client machine issues another **read()** system call.

5. The client machine sends an NFS **read** request to the server machine. Because the server machine is down, the client machine does not get the requested data. However, the packet could have been lost in the network (as may happen with datagram transport providers), so the client machine resends the request. Again, the client machine gets no response and continues to resend the request.

6. The server machine comes back online. It gets the request from the client machine (the client machine is continually resending the request), examines the file handle, opens the file, retrieves the data, and returns the data to the client machine.

7. The client machine gets the data and returns it to the application. The application did not realize that the server machine had gone down! It may realize that a lot of time has passed since it issued the **read()** system call, but it eventually got the data it requested.

If desired, the administrator of the client machine can specify the **soft** option when mounting the file system from the server machine. This option causes the client machine to time out and return an error condition to the application if several retry attempts fail.

There is an implication to this type of recovery: When a client machine issues an NFS **write** request, the server machine must write all data to disk before returning an acknowledgment to a client machine. If the server machine kept it in a buffer cache without writing it to disk, the data would be lost if the server machine crashed.

NFS Path Name Parsing

Using NFS, the client machine parses a path name one component at a time. This has an interesting side effect: A client machine can mount file systems anywhere, even on remote portions of the directory tree.

Figure 5.10 illustrates this. Here, the client machine mounts the **/tools** file system from **Server 1** onto the local **/rtools** directory. It also mounts the **/u1** file system from **Server 2** onto the **/rtools/data/dir2** directory. Here's what happens when an application opens **/rtools/data/dir2/file6**:

1. The client machine realizes that the **/rtools** directory is remote and sends a message to **Server 1** requesting a file handle for the directory **data**.

2. **Server 1** gets the request, creates a file handle for the directory **data**, and sends it to the client machine.

3. When the client machine gets the response, it sends a message to **Server 1** requesting a file handle for the directory **dir2**.

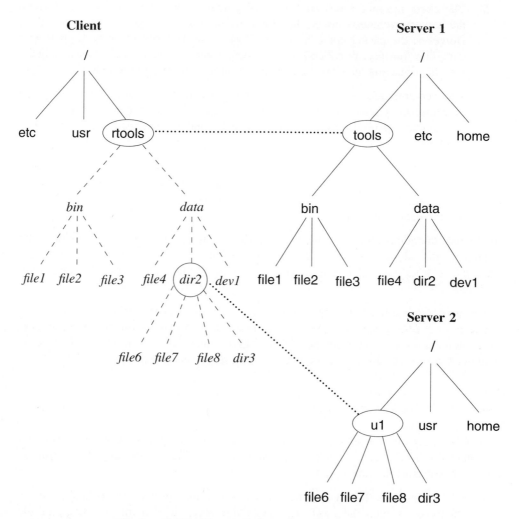

Figure 5.10   Mount Points Can Be Anywhere

4. **Server 1** gets this request, creates a file handle for **dir2**, and sends it to the client machine.

5. The client machine now realizes that there is another mount point on **dir2** and sends a message to **Server 2** requesting a file handle for **file6**.

6. **Server 2** gets the request, creates a file handle for **file6**, and sends it to the client machine.

7. The client machine now has the file handle for `file6` and sends all subsequent NFS requests on this file to `Server 2`.

Although this allows the administrator of a client machine to customize the directory tree any way he or she sees fit, it does have one disadvantage. If `Server 1` goes down, the applications on the client machine cannot access files on `Server 2`. This is because the client machine must go through `Server 1` to get to the files on `Server 2`.

UNIX System Semantics

Because of its stateless nature and because of its ability to run on non-UNIX operating systems, NFS does not support full UNIX system semantics.

For example, consider the UNIX semantic of accessing data after you open a file. After your application opens a file, it can access the contents of the file even if another application removes the file or if another application changes the permission bits associated with the file.

NFS does not fully support this semantic. Because NFS is stateless, the server machine must open the file every time an application on the client machine makes an NFS **read** or **write** request. If an application on another machine removes a file that your application holds open, the subsequent NFS **read** and **write** requests will fail (because the file no longer exists on the server machine).

The implementation of NFS on SVR4 (as well as other UNIX systems) tries to maintain as many UNIX semantics as possible. However, your applications must be aware of some restrictions.

First, NFS does nothing to handle time skew. NFS assumes all machines have the same time, and NFS does not modify time-based information in any way.

Next, the UNIX semantic of "open with append mode" is not fully supported. When an application opens a file with append mode, every subsequent `write()` system call writes data to the end of the file. However, because the NFS server machine is stateless, the client machine must specify where to write the data on each request. Therefore, a true append mode cannot be supported. Fortunately, the client machine does the next best thing: It implements an append mode as an "open and seek" operation.

Here's how it works. When your application opens a file with append mode, the NFS implementation figures out where the end of the file is. When an application writes data to the file, the client machine uses the current end of the file as the starting point. However, if an application on another machine writes to the end of the file, the client machine will not be aware that the end of the file has changed. If your application writes data, they will be written to where the client machine thinks the end of the file is. That means your application can overwrite data that an application on another machine has written to the end of the file.

File and record locking is also not supported through NFS. However, file and record locking is available through another service called the lock manager.

As mentioned earlier, NFS breaks semantics associated with open files. If your application opens a file, another application can unlink (that is, remove) the file and stop you from further access. This turned out to be a disaster for some applications. For example, the `tmpfile()` function creates a temporary file for your application to use, and works as follows:

1. It creates a unique file and opens it.

2. It unlinks the file, removing it from the directory tree. This stops other applications from opening the same file, but you can still read and write into it (because you have the file open).

This did not work over NFS. The `tmpfile()` function created a remote file, opened it, and unlinked it. But, because the file no longer existed on the server machine, all further accesses to the file failed!

To solve the problem, the UNIX implementation of NFS handles this case in a special way. When an application on a client machine attempts to unlink a file that it holds open, the client machine does not tell the server machine to unlink the file. Instead, it tells the server machine to *rename* the file and issues a remove request later when all local applications close the file. Because the file is not actually removed on the server machine, applications on the client machine can access the file even after the file was reportedly unlinked.

This solution is not foolproof, however. Applications running on the server machine or on other client machines can still remove a file that your application holds open. If that happens, your application gets an error indication stating the file handle is ''stale'' whenever it attempts to access the nonexistent file.

Finally, let's look at what happens if the permission bits of a file change after your application opens it. Again, every NFS **read** and **write** request causes the server machine to open the file, so the server machine must check file permission bits on every request. If your application opens a file and another application changes the permission bits of the file, you may be disallowed access.

To help solve this problem, the NFS server machine relies on the credentials contained in each request. The server machine allows the owner of the file to access a file without checking the permission bits. So, if a **read** request comes in from user `joe` to access a file owned by user `joe`, NFS allows the read to occur even if the permission bits on the file disallow read access. Again, this only solves part of the problem. If the permission bits of the file change *and* the owner of the file changes, subsequent **read** requests may be denied.

NFS does handle status information returned from the `stat()` system call correctly. As mentioned earlier, UNIX system applications figure out whether two files are the same by comparing the `st_dev` and `st_ino` elements of the information returned from the `stat()` system call. However, because the `st_dev` and `st_ino` pair are guaranteed to be unique only within a single system, it is possible that the `st_dev` number and the `st_ino` number of a local file match that of a remote file.

The client machine in the NFS environment solves this problem. It creates a unique device number each time the administrator issues the NFS `mount` command. This device number is local to the client machine and bears no resemblance to the real device number on the server machine. The client machine returns this unique device number whenever applications issue the `stat()` system call on a remote file.

5.11 NFS Security Considerations

NFS lets users from client machines access files on a server machine; therefore, security becomes a concern. NFS provides the following security features:

1. The administrator of the server machine can choose which client machines can mount a file system. When administrators export a file system, they can specify an optional list of client machine names. The client machines in the list are the only ones that can mount the file system.

2. The administrator of the server machine can export any directory on a file system, not just the root. And, as mentioned earlier, only the files and directories on the file system under the exported directory are available to client machines.

3. The administrator of the server machine can export a file system as ''read-only,'' meaning applications on a client machine can read the files but cannot write into them. Further, the administrator can export a file system as ''read-only'' to some client machines and ''read/write'' to others. In that way, the administrator of the server machine can allow full access to trusted client machines and restricted access to others.

4. The administrator of the server machine can unexport a file system at any time. When a file system is unexported, the server machine denies all access requests to that file system from client machines.

5. SVR4 supports the ''Secure NFS'' option. The Secure NFS option passes a user's network name and encrypted time stamp for verification on every NFS request. The Secure NFS option uses the secure flavor of RPC authentication, which is described in Chapter 6.

NFS on SVR4 does not support user ID mapping. By default, NFS assumes a global user-ID space, that is, it assumes that user IDs are the same across all machines.

However, the server machine does map user ID **0** from client machines into user ID **60001**. Also, when exporting a directory, the administrator of the server machine can have NFS map user ID **0** from client machines into an alternate user ID.

The security features presented are available on previous versions of NFS. Now let's look at the new features of NFS in SVR4.

5.12 New Features of NFS in SVR4

SVR4 did not modify the NFS protocol, but it made an improvement to the internal NFS implementation—SVR4 made NFS transport independent. In previous releases, NFS could only work over the the TCP/IP suite, specifically, the UDP transport provider. In SVR4, NFS can work over any datagram transport provider.

NFS also has a new administrative interface. It lets the administrator use common tools to administer multiple distributed file systems.

5.13 Drawbacks of NFS

NFS is not without its drawbacks. By far its greatest drawback is that NFS does not support full UNIX system semantics. Your applications may not see the same behavior on remote files as they do on local files.

A second drawback is the lack of data-cache consistency. Most client machine implementations of NFS (including SVR4) cache remote data locally. This reduces network traffic on subsequent read requests of the same data. Unfortunately, the server machine keeps no state information about which clients machines are caching data. That means the server machine cannot notify the client machine when the data change. So the client machine's data cache can become out of synch with the data in the remote file.

A third drawback is that NFS does not share devices like printers and tape drives. If an application on the client machine wanted to access a device on a server machine, it would have to use another network application to do it.

Another drawback is that NFS can raise security concerns. As mentioned earlier, NFS assumes a global user ID space, that is, it assumes that user IDs are the same across all machines in an NFS environment. By default, the client machine sends the effective user ID of the application making the NFS request. The SVR4 implementation of NFS does not give the server machine a way of mapping remote users into local ones.

However, SVR4 does provide the ''Secure NFS'' option, which uses encryption keys to authenticate a user's identity. Unfortunately, this slows down NFS operations and is administratively difficult to set up. However, it proves the identity of the user making the NFS request, giving the client machine and the server machine a more secure environment.

5.14 When to Use NFS and When to Use RFS

When it comes to choosing between NFS and RFS, you must ask yourself a series of questions:

- **Is diskless client support essential?**
  If it is, then NFS is the tool to use to obtain initial disk space. NFS allows a diskless client to obtain a root file system and still access local devices.

- **Does your application demand full UNIX system semantics?**
  If it does, then you should use RFS. RFS provides full UNIX system semantics across the network. However, NFS does provide a large, useful subset of UNIX system semantics.

- **Is it important that devices like printers and tape drives be shared?**
  If it does, then RFS wins. RFS allows applications on a client machine to access devices that exist on a server machine.

- **Is administrative complexity a big concern?**
  NFS is easier to administer than RFS, because RFS requires name-server setup and maintenance.

- **Is security a major consideration?**
  If it is, then RFS may be the right tool. RFS provides ID mapping to map dangerous users into less dangerous ones. If you must use NFS, use the Secure NFS option.

- **What type of recovery characteristics are suitable for your application?**
  If your application is a long-running one that should not abort if a server machine crashes, then NFS would be better to use. Due to its stateless operations, the NFS client machine will keep trying to reach a server machine, even if the server machine is down. When the server machine comes back, your application is not aware of the crash. Using RFS, applications see a server machine crash like a local disk failure—all file operations fail.

- **Need files be shared between different operating systems?**
  If so, then NFS is the tool to use. Because RFS provides full UNIX system semantics, it cannot be fully supported on non-UNIX operating systems. NFS was designed to provide services that can be implemented on any operating system.

- **Need files be shared over multiple transport protocols?**
  If so, you can use either RFS or NFS in SVR4. But, whereas previous versions of RFS were transport-independent, previous versions of NFS could only use the UDP transport provider.

However, it should be borne in mind that NFS and RFS can coexist on a single machine; together, they make one powerful tool.

5.15 Remote Backup and Restore Using NFS or RFS

Remote backup and restore is easy using a distributed file system. Because distributed file systems provide transparent access to remote files and directories, you can use the standard UNIX **mv** or **cp** command to transfer files between machines!

To illustrate, let's look at the backup and restore shell scripts developed in Chapter 3. In those shell scripts, we used the **rsh** command to create the directory structure on the server machine and the **rcp** command to copy files.

If the remote directory was mounted on the client machine over RFS or NFS, you could replace the network-specific commands (for example, **rsh** and **rcp**) with normal UNIX system commands (for example, **sh** and **cp**).

Let's recreate the application using RFS or NFS. In this version of the application, we require the administrators of the client machine and the server machine to create the distributed file system setup shown in Figure 5.11. We will be copying files, so either RFS or NFS can be used. The setup requires the following actions:

1. The administrator of the server machine must make the **/backup** directory available to the client machine. The administrator can share the directory via RFS or NFS.

2. The administrator of the server machine must create directories under **/backup** for each user on the client machine. The administrator of the server machine must also set the permission bits on the directories so that each remote user can write into their directory.

3. The administrator of the client machine must mount the **backup** directory onto the **/rmt** directory.

Now let's create the application. To begin, we trap signals to clean up any temporary files that we create. Next, we check that the **/backup** directory on the server machine is mounted on the **/rmt** directory.

This check can be done via the **mount** command. When used with no arguments, the **mount** command displays all mount points. If the **/rmt** directory is available over NFS or RFS, the **mount** command displays the string "**read/write/remote**" with the **/rmt** entry.

```
trap 'rm -f /tmp/$$.*; exit 0' 0 1 2 3 4 5 6 7 8 10

T=`/sbin/mount | grep "^/rmt .*read/write/remote"`
if [ "$T" = "" ]
then
        echo "$0: ERROR: It seems as though the /rmt"
```

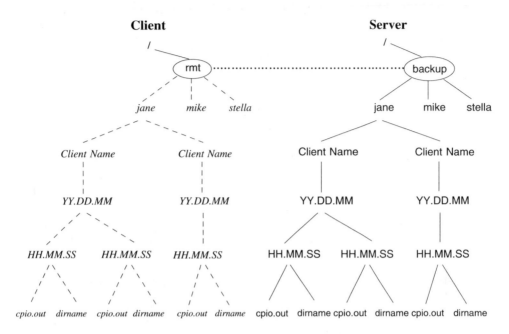

Figure 5.11   The Archive Layout

```
        echo "$0:        directory is not available"
        echo "$0:        Please consult the system"
        echo "$0:        administrator"
        exit 1
fi
```

Now that we know the remote directory is mounted, we proceed the same as in Chapter 3. We create a directory to hold a log of our actions (this log is used to restore the files later) and prompt the user for the directory to archive.

```
if [ ! -d $HOME/backup ]
then
    mkdir $HOME/backup 2>/dev/null
    if [ $? -ne 0 ]
    then
        echo "$0: ERROR: could not create the $HOME/backup"
        echo "$0:        directory.  This directory is"
```

```
        echo "$0:           necessary to log your backups"
        exit 1
    fi

fi

echo "Please enter the file or directory you want to"
echo "back up: \c"
read DIR
while [ ! -f "$DIR" -a ! -d "$DIR" ]
do
    echo "$DIR does not exist!"
    echo "Please enter the file directory you want to"
    echo "back up: \c"
    read DIR
done
```

Because we are using RFS or NFS, we do not need to ask for a server machine name. We can simply create an archive file and copy it from the local system to the remote directory. The following commands create the archive file the same as in Chapter 3.

```
FIRST_CHAR=`echo $DIR | cut -c1`
if [ "$FIRST_CHAR" != "/" ]
then
    DIR=`pwd`/$DIR
fi

(
cd /
if [ -f $DIR ]
then
    echo $DIR >/tmp/$$.bkup
else
    find $DIR -print >/tmp/$$.bkup
fi

echo "Backing up the following files:"
cat /tmp/$$.bkup
cat /tmp/$$.bkup | sed 's/^.//' | cpio -odcm >/tmp/$$.cpio
echo $DIR >/tmp/$$.dname
)
```

Now that we've created the **cpio** archive file, let's create the directory structure on the server machine. We'll get the user's name along with the current time and date, and use the **mkdir** command to create a directory on the server machine.

```
NAME=`id | cut -d'(' -f2 | cut -d')' -f1`
CLIENT=`uname -n`
DATE=`date +"%y.%m.%d"`
TIME=`date +"%H.%M.%S"`

cd /rmt
mkdir $NAME $NAME/$CLIENT \
      $NAME/$CLIENT/$DATE 2>/dev/null

mkdir $NAME/$CLIENT/$DATE/$TIME 2>/dev/null

if [ $? -ne 0 ]
then
    echo "error in creating the directory"
    echo "/rmt/$NAME/$CLIENT/$DATE/$TIME"
    exit 1
fi
```

At this point, we can transfer the archive file to the directory on the server machine. We use the **mv** command to do the transfer.

```
mv /tmp/$$.cpio \
      /rmt/$NAME/$CLIENT/$DATE/$TIME/cpio.out &&
mv /tmp/$$.dname \
      /rmt/$NAME/$CLIENT/$DATE/$TIME/dirname

if [ $? -ne 0 ]
then
    echo "error in transferring the files to"
    echo "/rmt/$NAME/$CLIENT/$DATE/$TIME"
    exit 1
fi
```

The transfer is complete. Let's record what was done so that we can restore the archive file later. The record contains the directory we backed up and the location of the archive file.

```
echo $DIR $CLIENT/$DATE/$TIME/cpio.out \
                    >>$HOME/backup/client.log

echo "Transfer complete."
echo "Files saved in cpio format in"
echo "/rmt/$NAME/$CLIENT/$DATE/$TIME/cpio.out"
exit 0
```

Restoring files is just as easy. Because we are using a distributed file system, we can modify the **restore** shell script created in Chapter 3 to use the normal UNIX commands to transfer files.

The **restore** script assumes that you archived a file or directory with our archive shell script. It asks which archive you want restored, copies the archive to the local machine, and unpackages the archive.

To begin, we'll trap signals to clean up any temporary files we create. Next, we make sure the **/rmt** directory is mounted. If it is, we prompt the user for the archive they want to restore.

```
#!/bin/ksh
trap 'rm -f /tmp/$$.*; exit 0' 0 1 2 3 4 5 6 7 8 10

T=`/sbin/mount | grep "^/rmt.*read/write/remote"`
if [ "$T" = "" ]
then
    echo "$0: ERROR: It seems the /rmt directory"
    echo "$0:          is not available.  Please consult"
    echo "$0:          the system administrator"
    exit 1
fi

echo "Please enter the name of the"
echo "file or directory you want restored: \c"
read DIR
```

Next, we check the record of archives to figure out how often the specified directory was archived. In this application, the record does not contain the name of the server machine (because our archive script simply copied the archive from one directory to another). So, we proceed exactly as in Chapter 3, except we obtain the date and time of the archive assuming the record does not contain the server name.

```
CLIENT=`uname -n`
ALL_DATES=`grep "^$DIR $CLIENT/" $HOME/backup/client.log |
            cut -d' ' -f2 | cut -d/ -f2 | sort -u 2>/dev/null`

if [ "$ALL_DATES" = "" ]
then
    echo "There is no record of archive $DIR"
    echo "Please check for the archive in the backup"
    echo "directory in your home directory on the server"
    echo "machine to which you archived."
    exit 1
fi

NUMBER_OF_BKUPS=`echo $ALL_DATES | wc -w`
if [ $NUMBER_OF_BKUPS -eq 1 ]
then
    DATE=$ALL_DATES
else
    echo
    echo "You have archived $DIR $NUMBER_OF_BKUPS times"
    echo "Please select the date of the archive you want"
    echo "restored"
    PS3="Please enter the number corresponding to the date "
    select DATE in `echo $ALL_DATES | sed 's/\./\//g'`
    do
        break
    done
    DATE=`echo $DATE | sed 's/\//./g'`
fi

ALL_TIMES=`grep "^${DIR} ${CLIENT}/${DATE}"  \
                        $HOME/backup/client.log |
            cut -d' ' -f2 | cut -d/ -f3 | sort -u 2>/dev/null`

NUMBER_PER_DAY=`echo $ALL_TIMES | wc -w`
if [ $NUMBER_PER_DAY -eq 1 ]
then
    TIME=$ALL_TIMES
else
    P_DATE=`echo $DATE | sed 's/.///'`
    echo
```

```
    echo "You have backed up $DIR $NUMBER_PER_DAY times"
    echo "on $P_DATE. Please select the time associated"
    echo "with the archive you want restored."
    PS3="Please select the time "
    select TIME in `echo $ALL_TIMES | sed 's/./:/g'`
    do
        break
    done
    TIME=`echo $TIME | sed 's/:/./g'`
fi
```

We now get the name of the user and copy the archive file from the server machine to the client machine. The copy is done via the normal UNIX **cp** command.

```
NAME=`id | cut -d'(' -f2 | cut -d')' -f1`

echo "About to restore files, please wait..."
```

**cp /rmt/$NAME/$CLIENT/$DATE/$TIME/cpio.out \
        /tmp/$$.cpio.out**

```
if [ $? -ne 0 ]
then
    echo "error occurred during transfer"
    exit 1
fi
```

Now that we have a local copy of the archive, we ask the user where they want it restored. The user may want to restore the files to a directory different from the original location.

```
echo
echo "Archive successfully restored."
echo "Please hit the return key if you want to copy the"
echo "files to their original location, or enter a new"
echo "directory to which to restore them: \c"
read NEWDIR

if [ "$NEWDIR" = "" ]
then
```

```
    NEWDIR=/
fi

while [ ! -d "$NEWDIR" ]
do
    echo "$NEWDIR does not exist!"

    echo "Please hit the return key if you want to copy the"
    echo "files to their original location, or enter a new"
    echo "directory to which to restore them: \c"
    read NEWDIR
    if [ "$NEWDIR" = "" ]
    then
        NEWDIR=/
    fi
done

(
cd $NEWDIR
echo "Restoring the following files under $NEWDIR"
cpio -idcvm </tmp/$$.cpio.out
)

exit 0
```

The **archive** and **restore** shell scripts show how to transfer files from one machine to another using RFS or NFS. RFS and NFS make remote files appear as local files, so we can transfer files using the normal UNIX file-copy commands.

Now let's create a different type of application. As stated earlier, RFS lets machines share files, devices, and named pipes. Because we can share pipes, we can create a simple remote execution application.

5.16 A Simple Remote Execution Application Using RFS

As stated earlier, RFS lets you share all types of files, including named pipes and pipes attached to files. We can use this feature to create a simple remote execution facility.

The application has two processes: a master process and a slave process. The master process creates a pipe, attaches a pipe to a file, and waits for input. The slave process writes a string containing a UNIX command into the pipe. The master process reads the string, invokes the UNIX shell to execute the command, and writes the results back into the pipe. Because RFS lets you share pipes between machines, the master process can run on a server machine and the slave process can run on a client machine!

Figure 5.12 shows how this works. We assume the administrator of the server machine has advertised the root directory, and the administrator of the client machine has mounted it onto the **/rmt** directory.

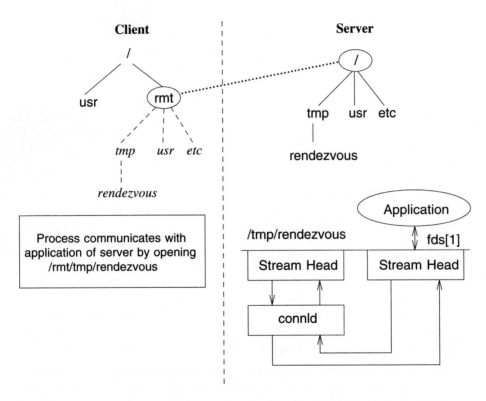

Figure 5.12 Application Setup

On the server machine, we create the master process that does the following:

1. Creates a pipe. Because we are using SVR4, the pipe is STREAMS-based.

2. Attaches one end of the pipe to the **/tmp/rendezvous** file (using the **fat-tach()** routine introduced in Chapter 2). To work correctly, the **/tmp/rendezvous** file must exist. At this point, any process that opens the **/tmp/rendezvous** file gets one end of the pipe, even if that process is running on a client machine.

3. Pushes the **connld** module onto the pipe. As described in Chapter 2, this module creates a unique pipe to any process that opens the file.

4. Waits for the slave process to open the file. Once opened, we receive a file descriptor for the new pipe created by the **connld** module.

5. Issues the **fork()** system call to create a child process. The child process reads a string from the pipe (this string specifies a UNIX command to execute). The child process issues the **popen()** library call to execute the command, reads the output of the command, and writes the output into the pipe.

On the client machine, we create the slave process that writes a string containing a command into the pipe and reads the results. In SVR4, pipes are bidirectional, so one pipe can be used for reading and writing.

Let's begin with the master process. First, because we will create a child process to execute a command, we ignore the **SIGCHLD** signal. Then, we create a pipe, attach one end of the pipe to the **/tmp/rendezvous** file, and push the **connld** module onto the attached end. The **connld** module sends a file descriptor to a new pipe each time someone opens the **/tmp/rendezvous** file.

```
#include <sys/types.h>
#include <sys/signal.h>
#include <stropts.h>
#include <stdio.h>

#define   SERVER_RENDEZVOUS "/tmp/rendezvous"

char *cmd_name;

main(argc, argv)
int argc;
char *argv[];
{
    int fds[2];                      /* file descriptors to   *
                                      * the pipe we create    */
    struct strrecvfd strrecvfd;      /* contains fd of newly  *
                                      * created pipe          */

    cmd_name = argv[0];

    (void) signal(SIGCHLD, SIG_IGN);
```

```
/*
 * First, create a STREAMS-based pipe.  This is
 * done via the normal pipe system call.
 */

if (pipe(fds) < 0) {
    fprintf(stderr, "%s: cannot create pipe\n",
                    cmd_name);
    perror("Reason:");
    exit(1);
}

/*
 * Now, attach one end of the pipe to a file.
 */

if (fattach(fds[0], SERVER_RENDEZVOUS) < 0) {
    fprintf(stderr, "%s: cannot attach pipe to file\n",
                    cmd_name);
    perror("Reason:");
    exit(1);
}

/*
 *  Push the connld module onto the named end, so
 *  any process that opens the file gets a unique
 *  pipe to us.
 */

if (ioctl(fds[0], I_PUSH, "connld") < 0) {
    fprintf(stderr, "%s: pushing connld failed\n",
                    cmd_name);
    perror("Reason:");
    exit(1);
}
```

Next, we enter a loop to read file descriptors. To do this, we issue the `ioctl()` system call with the **I_RECVFD** parameter. That sleeps waiting for someone to open the **/tmp/rendezvous** file. When the file is opened, the **connld** module creates a new pipe and sends us the file descriptor in a **strrecvfd** structure.

The **strrecvfd** structure contains three pieces of information:

---

int **fd**   the file descriptor of the new pipe;

uid_t **uid**   the user id of the process that opened the attached file (that is, the **/tmp/rendezvous** file); and

gid_t **gid**   the group id of the process that opened the attached file.

We use the information in the **strrecvfd** structure within the loop. First, we issue the **fork()** system call to create a child process. The parent process simply closes the file descriptor returned from the **ioctl()** system call and begins the loop again, waiting for another process to open the **/tmp/rendezvous** file.

The child process sets its effective user ID and effective group ID to that of the process opening the **/tmp/rendezvous** file. It then calls a subroutine to do the rest of the work.

```
while (ioctl(fds[1], I_RECVFD, &strrecvfd) == 0) {
    switch(fork()) {
      case -1:
          printf("Error: cannot fork!\n");
          perror("Reason:");
          exit(1);
      case 0:
          (void)seteuid(strrecvfd.uid);
          (void)setegid(strrecvfd.gid);
          child(strrecvfd.fd);
          exit(0);
      default:
          /*
           *  Parent simply goes back to
           *  read the next file descriptor
           */
          close(strrecvfd.fd);
          break;
    }
  }
}
```

The **child()** subroutine does the real work. Given a file descriptor to a pipe, the subroutine does the following:

1. Reads data from the pipe. This data contains the UNIX command to execute.

2. Issues the **popen()** library call to execute the command.

3. Ignores the SIGPIPE signal. SVR4 generates a SIGPIPE signal when you attempt to write data into a pipe that no other process holds open. In addition to getting the signal, the **write()** system call fails. In our case, this error condition happens if the slave process terminates unexpectedly. Because this is an unrecoverable error, we ignore the SIGPIPE signal and check the return value of the the **write()** system call. If the **write()** system call fails, we terminate the process.

4. Enters a loop that reads the output from the command and writes it into the pipe.

5. Closes the pipe after it writes all of the data.

The code follows:

```
int
child(fd)
int fd;
{
    char buf[BUFSIZ];
    FILE *fp;
    int n;

    /*
     *  Read the command from the pipe, execute it
     *  via popen, and send the results back.
     */

    if (read(fd, buf, BUFSIZ) < 0) {
        fprintf(stderr, "%s: cannot read pipe\n", cmd_name);
        perror("Reason:");
        exit(1);
    }

    if ((fp = popen(buf, "r")) == NULL) {
        fprintf(stderr, "%s: popen failed!\n", cmd_name);
        exit(1);
    }
```

```
    (void) signal(SIGPIPE, SIG_IGN);
    while ((n = fread(buf, 1, BUFSIZ, fp)) > 0) {
        if (write(fd, buf, n) < 0) {
                fprintf(stderr, "%s: cannot write into pipe\n",
                                cmd_name);
                perror("Reason:");
                exit(1);
        }
    }
    close(fd);
    exit(0);
}
```

Note that we close the pipe after we've written all data into it. This ensures that the process reading from the pipe gets an end-of-file indication when it consumes all data in the pipe.

Instead of closing the pipe, we could have sent a zero-length message to the reader to indicate the end of the data. However, special actions must be taken to do that. By default, a pipe silently ignores a request to write a message containing zero bytes.

If you want to send a zero-byte message to the process reading the pipe, you must issue an **ioctl()** system call with the **I_SWROPT** parameter. The following code illustrates this. Here, **fd** is a file descriptor into a pipe. After the **ioctl()** system call completes, writing zero bytes into the pipe sends a zero-byte message to the reader.

```
        ioctl(fd, I_SWROPT, SNDZERO);
        write(fd, "", 0);
```

Now let's look at the slave process. This process is run on the client machine and is straightforward. It does the following:

1. Takes a UNIX command as its first argument.

2. Opens the **/rmt/tmp/rendezvous** file. Note that the master process running on the server machine attached a pipe to this file. By opening this file, we get a unique pipe to the master process.

3. Checks that the file is attached to the STREAMS-based pipe by calling the **isastream()** library routine. The **isastream()** library routine fails if the specified file descriptor is not a STREAMS file.

4. Ignores the SIGPIPE signal. As mentioned earlier, SVR4 generates a SIGPIPE
    signal when you attempt to write data into a pipe that no other process holds
    open (the **write()** system call returns an error condition as well). In our case,
    that only happens if the master process terminates. Because that is an unrecover-
    able error, we ignore the signal and check the return value of the the the **write()**
    system call to figure out if something is amiss.

5. Writes the string containing a UNIX command into the pipe.

6. Reads the results of the command from the pipe and displays the results onto
    standard output.

The code follows:

```
#include <sys/types.h>
#include <fcntl.h>
#include <signal.h>
#include <stdio.h>

#define   CLIENT_RENDEZVOUS    "/rmt/tmp/rendezvous"

main(argc, argv)
int argc;
char *argv[];
{
    int fd;
    int num_bytes;
    char buf[BUFSIZ];

    if (argc != 2) {
        fprintf(stderr, "%s: usage: %s command\n",
                        argv[0], argv[0]);
        exit(1);
    }

    if ((fd = open(CLIENT_RENDEZVOUS, O_RDWR)) < 0) {
        fprintf(stderr, "%s: cannot open %s\n",
                        argv[0], CLIENT_RENDEZVOUS);
        perror("Reason");
        exit(1);
    }
```

```
/*
 *    Check that the CLIENT_RENDEZVOUS file is stream
 */

if ( !isastream(fd)) {
    fprintf(stderr, "%s: %s is not a stream\n",
                      argv[0], CLIENT_RENDEZVOUS);
    fprintf(stderr, "%s: Check that the server process
                        is running\n", argv[0]);
    exit(1);
}

(void) signal(SIGPIPE, SIG_IGN);

num_bytes = strlen(argv[1]) + 1;
if (write(fd, argv[1], num_bytes) != num_bytes) {
    fprintf(stderr, "%s: cannot write to pipe\n",
                      argv[0]);
    perror("Reason");
    exit(1);
}

while ((num_bytes = read(fd, buf, BUFSIZ)) > 0) {
    (void) write(1, buf, num_bytes);
}
exit(0);
}
```

Now that we've written the code, we can run the application. First, compile the code for the master process and run it on the server machine. After it starts, any process that opens the **/tmp/rendezvous** file gets a unique pipe into the master process.

On the client machine, compile the code for the slave process into an executable object called **rem_exec**. The **rem_exec** command accesses the **/tmp/rendezvous** file by opening the **/rmt/tmp/rendezvous** file. Because it sends a UNIX command to the master process on the server machine, we have a simple remote execution facility.

Here are some sample runs:

```
$ rem_exec  "uname -a"
farside  farside  4.0  3.0  i386  386/AT
$ rem_exec "who | sort"
john    tty02    May 10 14:12
mary    tty05    May 10 12:10
root    console  May 10 21:01
$
```

5.17 Summary

Distributed file systems provide transparent access to remote files and directories. RFS and NFS are two distributed file systems on SVR4 that let you share files without modifying applications. RFS provides full UNIX system semantics when accessing files, and NFS lets you share files with non-UNIX operating systems.

For Further Reading

1. AT&T, *UNIX System V Release 4 Network User's and Administrator's Guide*, Prentice Hall, Englewood Cliffs, NJ, 1990.

2. Bach, M., Luppi, M., Melamed, A., and Yueh, K., ''A Remote File Cache for RFS,'' *USENIX Conference Proceedings*, Summer 1987.

3. Chartok, H., ''RFS in SunOS,'' *USENIX Conference Proceedings*, Summer 1987.

4. Padovano, M., ''How NFS and RFS Compare,'' *System Integration Magazine*, December 1989.

5. Rifkin, A., Forbes, M., Hamilton, R., Sabrio, M., Shah, K., and Yueh, K., ''Remote File Sharing Architectural Overview,'' *USENIX Conference Proceedings*, Summer 1986.

6. Sandburg, R., Goldberg, D., Kleinman, S., Walsh, D., and Lyon, B., ''Design and Implementation of the Sun Network File System,'' *USENIX Conference Proceedings*, Summer 1985.

7. Sun Microsystems, Inc., ''NFS: Network File System Protocol Specification,'' *RFC 1094*, 1989.

Exercises

5.1   In a distributed file system, is state information necessary on the server machine to provide full data-cache consistency to client machines? Why or why not?

5.2   Explain why RFS does not support diskless client machines and why NFS does. What are the trade-offs to diskless client machine support?

5.3   Explain why NFS allows the client machine to mount a remote file system on a remote directory. What are the pros and cons of this capability?

5.4   What are the benefits of providing full UNIX system functionality within a distributed file system? What are the drawbacks?

5.5   Would the simple remote execution application developed in Section 5.16 be able to work over NFS? Explain.

Chapter 6

Applications Using the
Remote Procedure Call Facility

6.1   Introduction

The Remote Procedure Call (RPC) mechanism is a high-level model for client-server interactions. It lets you write C programs that follow the normal procedure call model—but, instead of invoking normal procedures, it lets you invoke procedures that run on a remote machine.

This lets you write powerful network applications. For example, suppose you wrote a procedure that took an employee's name as a parameter, searched a database containing information about all employees, and returned the entry for the specified employee. The RPC mechanism lets remote applications execute this procedure on your machine, providing an easy way to implement a remote database facility.

The RPC mechanism hides the lower-level networking details from your applications. By following the procedure call model, it lets you write and call a remote procedure just as easily as writing and calling a normal procedure.

RPC also provides an easy way to turn nonnetworked applications into networked applications. Because most applications are divided into procedures, you simply have to figure out which procedures to run on remote machines and modify the application to use the RPC mechanism. Before we show how to do this, we present an overview of RPC.

6.2   Overview of RPC

RPC lets you create distributed programs by providing a mechanism to call remote procedures. Remote procedures are similar to normal procedures. But, where a normal procedure executes on the local machine, a remote procedure executes on a remote machine.

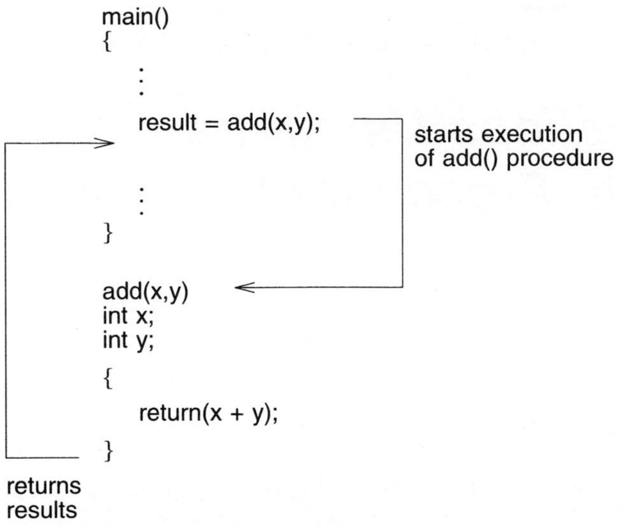

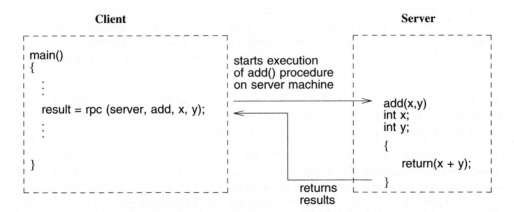

Figure 6.1   A Local Procedure Call

Figure 6.2   A Remote Procedure Call

Figures 6.1 and 6.2 illustrate this. Figure 6.1 shows an application invoking a local procedure named **add()**. This procedure takes two integers as arguments and returns their sum. The application doesn't care how the procedure does its job; it only cares that the procedure returns the correct results.

Figure 6.2 shows the RPC mechanism. Instead of invoking the local `add()` procedure, the application invokes the `add()` procedure on another machine. The application calls the procedure, specifying the arguments and the name of the server machine, and obtains the results. Again, the application doesn't really care how the `add()` procedure works. It knows that if two integers are given, the procedure returns their sum.

When Should You Use RPC?

RPC is an excellent facility to use when you want to convert an existing local application into a distributed one. Because most programs are already divided into procedures, converting them into remote procedures is a straightforward process. We'll see examples of this in Section 6.7.

You should also use the RPC mechanism when you want to distribute an application over several machines. RPC lets you use machines in the most efficient way. For example, if a machine does vector manipulation quickly and efficiently, you can execute vector-manipulation procedures on that machine.

RPC gives you an easy way to create new distributed applications. For example, suppose you wrote a local procedure that returned a linked list of users currently logged into the machine. By incorporating this procedure into the RPC mechanism, you can write applications that call the procedure remotely. This creates a distributed application that can display users logged into any machine in the network.

We can now take a closer look at client-server interactions. We begin by presenting an overview of the SVR4 RPC architecture.

RPC Architecture

The RPC architecture consists of three parts: an application on the client machine, the procedure on the server machine, and a program to resolve addresses.

The key to all RPC operations is the program that resolves addresses. On SVR4, that program is called `rpcbind` (on previous releases of the UNIX system, the program was called `portmap`).

The `rpcbind` program is a daemon process that runs on the server machine. It keeps a table that maps all available RPC procedures into their corresponding transport addresses. When an application on the client machine wants to invoke a remote procedure, it first sends a query to the `rpcbind` process on the server machine to get the transport address of the procedure.

This means that applications on the client machine must know the transport address of the `rpcbind` process on the server machine. Hence, the `rpcbind` process must attach to a well-known transport address.

Here's how it works. The `rpcbind` process is started as part of a machine's initialization sequence. When the `rpcbind` process starts, it figures out which transport providers are on the system (it uses the Network Selection routines described in Chapter 9 to do this). Then, for each transport provider, it attaches to a well-known transport address. The well-known transport address is obtained via the Name-to-Address Mapping routines, which are described in Chapter 9. For example, the well-known address of `rpcbind` over TCP/IP is the server machine's IP address combined with port number `111`.

The next element of the RPC architecture is the remote procedure. To make a procedure available over the network, you must write the procedure and use RPC facilities to encapsulate it into a program (details are given later). This program is also a daemon process that runs on the server machine. When started, it does the following:

1. Determines which transport providers are on the system.

2. Attaches itself to an arbitrary, unused address for each transport provider.

3. Sends a message to the `rpcbind` daemon through a local loopback transport provider, informing it of the addresses to which it is attached.

At this point, we have two processes running: the `rpcbind` process and the program containing the procedure. The program containing the procedure is attached to an arbitrary transport address, but that address is now known by the `rpcbind` daemon. The `rpcbind` process is on a well-known transport address.

Applications on clients machines can now call the procedure. Figure 6.3 shows the actions involved:

1. The application on the client machine specifies that it wants to call a procedure on the server machine. It selects a transport provider on the client machine, and using that transport provider, it sends a message to the `rpcbind` process on the server machine. It uses the Network Selection and Name-to-Address Mapping facility (described in Chapter 9) to select a transport provider and obtain the well-known address of the `rpcbind` process. The message contains a query for the transport address of the program containing the desired procedure.

2. The `rpcbind` process gets the message and notes on which transport provider the message arrived. It responds to the query, telling the client machine the transport address of the program containing the procedure. Because the program containing the procedure may have several transport addresses (one for each transport provider on the server machine), the `rpcbind` process returns the transport address corresponding to the transport provider over which the query arrived.

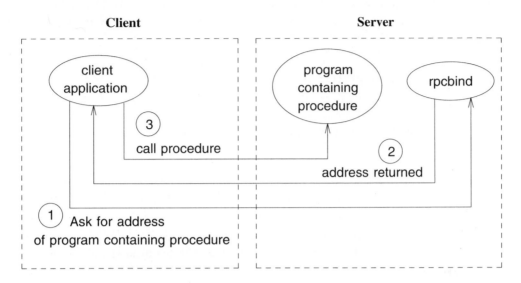

Figure 6.3   RPC Setup

3.   The application on the client machine uses the transport address to communicate
     with the program containing the procedure.

This architecture has several advantages. First, it is completely transport-independent.
The processes on the server machine make themselves available over every transport
provider, and the application on the client machine can use any transport provider to
communicate with the server machine.

Second, applications on the client machine only have to know one transport address,
that is, the transport address of the **rpcbind** process. All other addresses are
obtained by querying the **rpcbind** process.

Third, programs containing the procedures don't have to worry about getting a unique
transport address. Each time they start, they get an arbitrary transport address and tell
the **rpcbind** daemon what it is.

Now let's look at some lower-level functions. Before going into the details of how to
create applications that use the RPC facility, we have to address the problem of data
representation.

Data on the remote system may not have the same format as on the local system. If
an application on a client machine sends data to a procedure on a server machine,
differences in format may cause the remote procedure to misinterpret the data. To
solve this problem, all data passed to a remote procedure and returned by that

procedure should be encoded into a common data representation. SVR4 provides the eXternal Data Representation (XDR) package to do this. Because XDR is an integral part of the RPC mechanism, an overview of XDR is presented next.

6.3   Overview of XDR

The XDR package provides routines that applications use to encode data into a common format. This is necessary because different computers represent data differently.

The differences include the following:

1. **Data size**. The amount of storage necessary to hold data may vary from machine to machine. For example, some machines require 32 bits to hold an integer, whereas others require only 16 bits.

2. **Byte ordering**. Some machines represent data with the most significant byte as the leftmost byte, whereas others represent data with the most significant byte as the rightmost byte.

3. **Data representation**. Data types may differ from one machine to the next. For example, the logical bits of a floating-point value on one machine can be different from that on another. Even the representation of character strings may differ, because some systems represent a string as a NULL-terminated sequence of bytes, whereas others represent the string as a value indicating the length of the string followed by the string itself.

4. **Alignment**. Some machines have restrictions on address boundaries. For example, some machines align data on full-word boundaries, whereas others align data on half-word boundaries.

XDR addresses these differences by defining a common data representation. For example, XDR defines the format of an integer as a value that is 32 bits in length, represented in two's-complement notation, with the most significant byte leftmost and the least significant byte rightmost. Applications can use the XDR routines to translate the local representation of an integer into the XDR representation before sending the integer over the network.

Figure 6.4 illustrates this. Here, an application on a client machine converts the local representation of a data structure into the XDR representation. Similarly, the application on the server machine translates the XDR representation into its local representation when it receives the data.

You can use XDR to represent any type of data. However, it is essential that the sender and receiver know the format of the data being sent. For example, if the application on the client machine sends an integer, two characters, and a floating-point value, the program on the server machine must be written to receive that data structure.

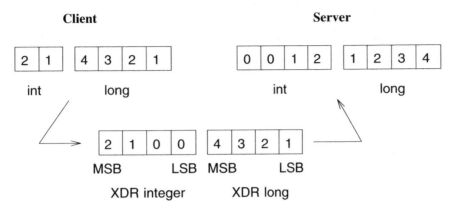

Figure 6.4   XDR Representation

Figure 6.5 shows a way to represent a linked list in XDR format. This example represents a node in the list as an integer value and a boolean value. The integer value is the data in the node, and the boolean value is **1** if a non-NULL pointer exists and another node follows.

When the application on the server machine gets the XDR data, it translates it into the local representation. In the case presented in Figure 6.5, the application on the server machine recreates the linked list by allocating space to hold a node, translating the integer in the node into the local representation, and examining the boolean value to figure out if another node exists. If another node exists, the application allocates space to hold the next node and recursively continues until it recreates the entire list. The pointer values in the resultant list will not be the same as in the original list, but the structure of the list will be the same.

In general, a data structure with pointer values is translated into XDR by transforming the pointer into a boolean value, followed by the data pointed to. A boolean value of **1** indicates a pointer exists, and a boolean value of **0** indicates the pointer has a NULL value. If the data structure had several pointers (for example, a binary tree), each pointer would be transformed into a boolean value followed by the data it points to. So, the application that receives the data can recreate the original data structure.

Common data format is not the only concern when creating RPC applications. As with any network application, security is also important. We now present an overview of RPC security issues.

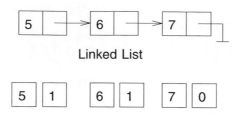

Linked List

XDR Representation

Figure 6.5   XDR Linked List

6.4   RPC Security Issues

Every RPC call and reply is authenticated. When the application on the client machine issues an RPC request, it carries information about the user executing it. When the server sends results, they carry authentication information as well.

Authentication information contains two parts: credentials and a verifier. The credentials identify the user sending the message, and the verifier proves that user's identity.

The application on the client machine and the procedure on the server machine must agree on a ''flavor'' of authentication. As shown in Figure 6.6, the RPC facility provides several flavors of authentication:

- **None**. If you use this flavor of authentication, the credentials are empty and the verifier is empty. This means the message contains no information about the user that sent it. In this case, the procedure on the server machine cannot figure out who is calling it.

- **Unix**. If you use this flavor of authentication, the credentials contain the machine name, the effective user ID of the user sending the message, and the effective group ID of the user sending the message. However, the verifier field is empty. That means the sender does not prove their identity. For example, if the client application sends a message that claims it is from user ID **107** on machine **far-side**, the application on the server machine simply has to believe it.

- **Secure**. This flavor of authentication uses cryptography for verification of the caller's identity. The credentials contain the sender's identity, and the verifier contains an encrypted token that proves the sender's identity. So, not only does the application on the server machine know the identity of the user on the client machine, it is sure that the identity is correct. Applications using this form of authentication are said to be using ''Secure RPC.'' We will see examples of this in Section 6.12.

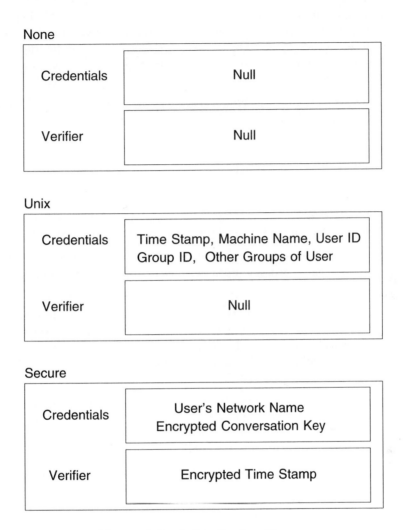

Figure 6.6   Authentication Flavors

- **Vendor-defined**. The RPC mechanism lets you create your own authentication flavor. For example, researchers at the Massachusetts Institute of Technology have developed an authentication scheme named Kerberos. Kerberos verifies a user's identity by using a three-party handshake scheme. Several vendors have implemented a Kerberos-based RPC authentication flavor.

Which authentication flavor to use depends upon your application. The simplest form of authentication is the **none** flavor. This can be used for procedures that don't care who is making the request. The **unix** and **secure** flavors give more information about the caller, but also take more time to create. We'll examine how to use each of these flavors in Section 6.12.

Now let's examine the tools available to help generate RPC programs. We begin by explaining the steps necessary in creating an RPC program.

6.5   Creating an RPC Program

To create an RPC program, you must first group a set of remote procedures into a *program*. Each program has a program number, a version number, and a list of procedures. Each procedure in the list has a procedure number associated with it.

The program number defines a set of procedures. The version number lets you extend RPC protocols, and the procedure number specifies the procedure within the program set.

Figure 6.7 shows an example. Here, we define a program with three procedures. The program is named **math**. It has program number **536870920** and version number **1** (why we chose that program number is explained shortly). The procedures within the program are sequentially numbered from **1** to **3**. Procedure **1** is called **add**, procedure **2** is called **multiply**, and procedure **3** is called **cube**.

After you've defined the procedures in the program, you must implement the procedures and use low-level RPC routines to handle the networking details. The low-level RPC routines attach an unused transport address to your program and tell the **rpcbind** process the transport address to which you've attached.

Now, if an application on the client machine wanted to call the remote procedure named **multiply**, it must first specify that it wanted to communicate with program **536870920** version **1**. Then, it specifies that it wants to call procedure **2**.

When the application on the client machine uses the RPC routines to specify that it wants to communicate with program **536870920** version **1**, the lower-level RPC routines send a message to the **rpcbind** process on the server machine to get the transport address of the remote program. After it gets the transport address, the client application uses it to call remote procedures within the program.

There are a few things to know about the version number and the program number. The version number lets you modify the programs easily. For example, it you wanted to extend the program in Figure 6.7 to add a **divide** procedure, you could define version **2** of program **536870920**. This new version would have four procedures, the original three from version **1** and the new **divide** procedure. Older applications

```
struct  intpair {
    int a;                          data structure used by procedures
    int b;
};
```

```
program name:  math
program number:  536870920
version:  1
    procedure 1:
            name:  add                          procedure
            parameter:  intpair                 definition
            return: int
    procedure 2:
            name: subtract
            parameter:   intpair
            return:  int
    procedure 3:
            name: multiply
            parameter:  intpair
            return:  int
```

Figure 6.7   Remote Procedures in a Program Specification

can still can communicate with version **1**, and newer applications can communicate with version **2**.

The program number identifies the procedure grouping. It is important that program numbers be unique. To help ensure unique numbers, Sun Microsystems, Inc., keeps track of which RPC programs correspond to which program numbers. When you create an RPC program, choose a program number based on the following:

- Program numbers **0** - **1fffffff**: Numbers in this range are reserved for existing RPC programs. Sun Microsystems administers these numbers. You should not use a number in this range when creating RPC applications, because the number may already correspond to an existing RPC program. However, if you create an RPC program that you think deserves an official number, send a description of the associated procedures to the RPC Administrator at Sun Microsystems. If approved, one of these program numbers will be assigned to your program.

- Program numbers `20000000` - `3fffffff`: Numbers in this range can be used for site-specific RPC programs. When you create an RPC program, you should use a number within this range. If you are planning to submit an RPC for an official number in the `0` through `1ffffff` range, you should still use a number in this range while debugging the program. In the example presented in Figure 6.7, we used program number `536870920` because it falls in this range (`536870920` has the hexadecimal value of `20000008`).

Each procedure within a program must specify its arguments and its return value. Within the RPC framework, each procedure takes one argument and returns one result. However, as shown in Figure 6.7, these may be structures.

So, to create an RPC program, you must do the following:

1. Define a set of procedures and group them together by specifying a program number and a version number.

2. Define exactly what each procedure does. Specify the argument to the procedure and define what the procedure returns.

3. Implement all of the procedures.

4. Create client applications that call the remote procedures.

SVR4 provides a compiler to help write programs using the RPC facility. The compiler takes a high-level specification of the remote procedures and generates the C language code that calls the lower-level RPC routines. We now look at examples of how to use this compiler to create RPC applications.

6.6   Using the RPC Compiler

The details of creating applications using the RPC mechanism can be tedious. You must use low-level RPC routines to handle network activity and write the XDR routines that convert data into and out of a common format.

Fortunately, SVR4 provides the **rpcgen** command that lets you create RPC applications easily. The **rpcgen** command is a compiler. It takes an RPC language as input and generates C code that does most of the lower-level RPC work. It also generates the XDR routines needed to convert data into and out of the XDR format.

The input to **rpcgen** is an RPC specification written in the RPC definition language (we will describe the RPC definition language shortly). From this specification, the **rpcgen** compiler generates several C files and a header file. The C files contain the source code that calls the lower-level RPC routines. The header file contains structure definitions needed by the remote procedures.

The RPC specification is in one of three files needed to create an RPC program using **rpcgen**. The three files are:

1. An RPC "**.x**" file, which contains the RPC specification written in the RPC definition language.

2. The server side "**.c**" file, which implements the remote procedures.

3. The client side "**.c**" file, which contains the application that calls the remote procedures.

To illustrate, let's create three simple procedures and transform them into remote procedures. The procedures perform arithmetic operations on integers.

6.7   A Simple RPC Example

To show how to create programs that use the RPC mechanism, let's start by writing three local procedures. The procedures are:

1. **add()**, which takes two integers and returns their sum.

2. **multiply()**, which takes two integers and returns their product.

3. **cube()**, which takes one integer and returns the cube of that integer.

The following C code implements these procedures:

```
struct intpair {
    int    a;
    int    b;
};

int
add (intpair)
struct intpair intpair;
{
    return(intpair.a + intpair.b);
}

int
multiply (intpair)
struct intpair intpair;
{
    return(intpair.a * intpair.b);
}
```

```
int
cube(base)
int base;
{
     return(base * base * base);
}
```

Now that we've written the procedures, we can create a C program that calls them:

```
#include <stdio.h>

main(argc, argv)
int argc;
char *argv[];
{
     struct intpair numbers;
     int result;

     if (argc != 3) {
          fprintf(stderr,
                    "%s: usage: %s num1 num2\n",
                    argv[0], argv[0]);
          exit(1);
     }

     numbers.a = atoi(argv[1]);
     numbers.b = atoi(argv[2]);

     result = add(numbers);
     printf("The add (%d, %d) procedure returned %d\n",
                numbers.a, numbers.b, result);

     result = multiply(numbers);
     printf("The multiply(%d, %d) procedure returned %d\n",
                numbers.a, numbers.b, result);

     result = cube(numbers.a);
     printf("The cube(%d) procedure returned %d\n",
                numbers.a, result);
     exit(0);
}
```

Now let's convert **add()**, **multiply()**, and **cube()** into remote procedures. To
do this, we must create a ''**.x**'' file that contains the information about the procedures.
The data in the ''**.x**'' file contains code written in the RPC specification language.

Using the RPC language, you specify the parameters and return values of each procedure. You also associate the procedures with a program number and a version
number. Before examining the details, let's look at the RPC definition in a file called
math.x:

```
/*
 *       math.x
 */

struct intpair {
        int a;
        int b;
};

program MATHPROG {
    version MATHVERS {
                int ADD(intpair)      = 1;
                int MULTIPLY(intpair) = 2;
                int CUBE(int)         = 3;
        } = 1;
} = 536870920;
```

This specification defines the following:

1. A program named **MATHPROG**. The program number is **536870920** and the
    version number is **1**.

2. This program has three procedures: **ADD**, **MULTIPLY**, and **CUBE**. The pro-
    cedures have procedure numbers **1**, **2**, and **3**, respectively..

3. The **ADD** and **MULTIPLY** procedures take an **intpair** as a parameter (the
    definition of the **intpair** structure is included in the specification) and return
    an **int**. The **CUBE** procedure takes an **int** as a parameter and returns an
    int. Because **int** is a standard C language type, its definition is not required.

Note that this specification defines the protocol. If you were to write an application
that called these procedures, you now know exactly what to give each procedure and
what to expect.

The program name, version name, and procedure names in this example are specified
with all capital letters. This is not required, but is a good convention to follow. The

reason is because the **rpcgen** compiler generates a C header file that associates these names to their corresponding numbers. The association is done via a sequence of **#define** statements.

After you create the **math.x** file, give it to the **rpcgen** compiler. The **rpcgen** compiler generates C code that does most of the lower-level RPC functions.

There are only two more pieces to create. You must create the C file that contains the code that implements the procedures and the C file that contains the the client program that calls the procedures. We'll write the C code for the procedures in a file called **serv.c**. The procedures are very similar to the local versions. The implementation follows:

```c
#include <rpc/rpc.h>
/* math.h is generated by rpcgen */
#include "math.h"

int *
add_1 (pair)
intpair * pair;
{
        static int result;

        result = pair->a + pair->b;
        return(&result);
}

int *
multiply_1 (pair)
intpair * pair;
{
        static int result;

        result = pair->a * pair->b;
        return(&result);
}

int *
cube_1 (base)
int * base;
{
        static int result;
        int baseval = *base;
```

```
        result = baseval * baseval * baseval;
        return(&result);
}
```

The declaration of these remote procedures differs from their local counterparts in three ways. Each procedure:

1. Appends a **_1** to its name. In general, you create the name of a remote procedure by converting the procedure name in the RPC definition to all lowercase letters, adding an underbar character, and adding the version number. In our example, we defined version **1** of **MATHPROG** to have three procedures: **ADD**, **MULTIPLY**, and **CUBE**. So, we have three procedures: **add_1()**, **multiply_1()**, and **cube_1()**.

2. Takes a pointer to its argument instead of the actual data type.

3. Returns a pointer to its results.

The next thing to do is to create the client program that calls the remote procedures. We'll create a file called **client.c** to do this. The code for this follows:

```c
#include <stdio.h>
#include <rpc/rpc.h>
#include "math.h"

main(argc, argv)
int argc;
char *argv[];
{
    CLIENT *cl;
    intpair numbers;
    int *result;

    if (argc != 4) {
        fprintf(stderr, "%s: usage: %s server num1 num2\n",
                argv[0], argv[0]);
        exit(1);
    }

    cl = clnt_create(argv[1], MATHPROG, MATHVERS, "netpath");
    if (cl == NULL) {
        clnt_pcreateerror(argv[1]);
        exit(1);
    }
```

```
numbers.a = atoi(argv[2]);
numbers.b = atoi(argv[3]);

result = add_1(&numbers, cl);
if (result == NULL) {
    clnt_perror(cl, "add_1");
    exit(1);
}
printf("The add (%d, %d) procedure returned %d\n",
        numbers.a, numbers.b, *result);

result = multiply_1(&numbers, cl);
if (result == NULL) {
    clnt_perror(cl, "multiply_1");
    exit(1);
}
printf("The multiply(%d, %d) procedure returned %d\n",
        numbers.a, numbers.b, *result);

result = cube_1(&numbers.a, cl);
if (result == NULL) {
    clnt_perror(cl, "cube_1");
    exit(1);
}
printf("The cube(%d) procedure returned %d\n",
        numbers.a, *result);

exit(0);
}
```

There are four things to note in the client side of an RPC program:

1. The application must first establish communication with the program on the server machine. It does this by calling **clnt_create()**, specifying the server name, the program number, the version number, and a transport-provider specification. In this example, the transport-provider specification is the **"net-path"** string, indicating to use any available transport provider (details of valid strings are given in Section 6.10). The **clnt_create()** routine returns a client handle that is used on all subsequent RPC calls.

2. If the **clnt_create()** call fails, the application issues the **clnt_pcreateerror()** routine to display the reason for the failure.

3. The client forms the name of the remote procedure the same way as the server did—by converting the procedure name in the RPC definition to all lowercase letters, adding an underbar character, and adding the version number. However, although the name is the same, this is a totally different routine than that used by the server side of the application. This routine takes two parameters, a pointer to the procedure argument and the client handle. The routine returns a pointer to the results.

4. If the RPC mechanism fails when trying to execute the remote procedure, the remote procedure returns a NULL value. The application issues the **clnt_perror()** routine, passing the client handle and a string, to print the reason for the error.

Now let's tie everything together. First, run the **math.x** file through the **rpcgen** compiler:

```
$ rpcgen math.x
```

This produces three files:

math.h   Contains the **#define** statements for **MATHPROG**, **MATHVERS**, **ADD**, **MULTIPLY**, and **CUBE**. It also contains the definition of the **intpair** structure. The client and server files include this file to get these definitions.

math_svc.c   Contains the C code that does the lower-level server RPC functions. This file has the code that registers the program with the **rpcbind** daemon. It also contains the code that calls **add_1()**, **multiply_1()**, and **cube_1()** when an application on the client machine invokes these procedures.

math_clnt.c Contains the C code that implements the low-level client RPC functions. It also contains the code that implements the client side of **add_1()**, **multiply_1()**, and **cube_1()**.

math_xdr.c   Contains all of the XDR routines needed to convert data into XDR format. In this example, it contains the routines to transform the **intpair** structure into XDR format.

In general, if the file given to **rpcgen** is name **any.x**, the files generated are **any.h**, **any_xdr.c**, **any_svc.c**, and **any_clnt.c**.

Now let's compile everything together. On the server machine, compile **math_svc.c**, **math_xdr.c**, and the procedures you wrote in **serv.c**:

```
$ cc -o math_server math_svc.c math_xdr.c serv.c -lnsl
```

On the client machine, compile **math_clnt.c**, **math_xdr.c**, and the program you wrote in **client.c**:

```
$ cc -o remote_math math_clnt.c math_xdr.c client.c -lnsl
```

Now let's execute the programs. On the server machine, execute the server program:

```
$ math_server &
```

When this program is executed, it finds all transport providers on the server machine. Then, for every transport provider, it attaches itself to an unused transport address. Next, it informs the **rpcbind** program that version **1** of program **536870920** is available over the attached transport address.

On the client machine, we execute the RPC program:

```
$ remote_math farside 3 12
The add (3, 12) procedure returned 15
The multiply(3, 12) procedure returned 36
The cube(3) procedure returned 27
$
```

Now let's take a closer look at the three pieces we created. We begin with the RPC definition language.

6.8   The RPC Definition Language

The RPC definition language lets you define a set of remote procedures. For each procedure in the set, it lets you specify a procedure name, the argument to the procedure, and the results of the procedure.

The RPC language source code is placed in a ''**.x**'' file. The ''**.x**'' file contains a specification of the data structures used by each procedure. It also has the definition of the program that contains the procedures.

This program definition is the most important part of the RPC specification. It has the following form:

```
program identifier {
        version_list
} = value ;
```

The `identifier` is a string that names the program, and the `value` is an unsigned integer value. You specify the value the same as in the C language, that is, you can precede it with **0x** to represent a hexadecimal value and **0** to represent an octal value.

The `version_list` is a list of definitions. It contains at least one definition of the following form:

```
version identifier {
        procedure_list
} = value ;
```

The `identifier` is a string that names the version of the program, and the `value` is an unsigned integer. Usually, you only specify one version in the program definition. However, multiple versions can be specified if needed.

Each version definition contains a list of procedures. The `procedure_list` contains at least one definition of the following form:

```
data_type procedure_name ( data_type ) = value ;
```

The `procedure_name` is a string that names the procedure, and the `value` is an unsigned integer that specifies the procedure number. The `data_type` can be any simple C data type (for example, **int, unsigned int, void,** or **char**) or a complex data type. We will describe complex data types shortly.

To summarize, consider the following program definition:

```
program TIMEINFO {
        version TIMEVERS {
                unsigned int GETTIME (void) = 1;
        } = 1;
} = 0x20000009;
```

This example defines a program named **TIMEINFO** with program number
0x20000009. The version number of the program is **1**. This program has only one
procedure (named **GETTIME**), which takes no arguments and returns an unsigned
integer. Although the procedure takes no arguments, a data type must be specified to
comply with the syntax of a procedure definition. As we will see shortly, the **void**
data type signifies that the procedure takes no arguments.

The **rpcgen** compiler generates a header file from the program definition. The
header file contains a **#define** statement that associates the program name with the
program number, the version name with the version number, and the procedure names
with the procedure numbers. It also generates a C language definition for the procedure name.

In the previous example, the **rpcgen** compiler produces a header file that contains
the following lines:

```
#define TIMEINFO ((u_long)0x20000009)
#define TIMEVERS ((u_long)1)
#define GETTIME ((u_long)1)
extern u_int *gettime_1();
```

If the procedures require complex data types, you must specify them in the ''**.x**'' file
as well. You can specify constants, structures, enumerations, unions, and type
definitions. We now present the RPC definition language syntax of these data types.

Constants

The RPC definition language lets you specify constant values. Constant values can be
used in place of an integer value. The definition follows:

```
const identifier = integer_value ;
```

This associates the `identifier` with the integer value. The **rpcgen** compiler
translates the **const** definition into a **#define** construct in the generated header
file. For example, the definition

```
const MAX_ENTRIES = 1024;
```

is translated into

```
#define MAX_ENTRIES 1024
```

Structures

Structures in the RPC definition language are defined the same as in the C programming language. The **rpcgen** compiler transfers the structure into the header file and adds a corresponding **typedef** definition. For example, the RPC definition:

```
struct intpair {
        int a;
        int b;
};
```

generates the following definition in the header file:

```
struct intpair {
        int a;
        int b;
};
typedef struct intpair intpair;
```

The **typedef** definition lets you use the type **intpair** instead of **struct intpair** when declaring variables in RPC programs.

Enumerations

As with structures, enumerations in the RPC definition are the same as in the C programming language. The **rpcgen** compiler transfers the enumeration into the header file, followed by a **typedef** for the enumeration.

For example, the following enumeration in the ''**.x**'' file:

```
enum trafficlight {
        RED = 0,
        AMBER = 1,
        GREEN = 2
};
```

is translated into

```
enum trafficlight {
        RED = 0,
        AMBER = 1,
        GREEN = 2
};
typedef enum trafficlight trafficlight;
```

Unions

Unions in the RPC definition language look very little like their C counterparts. In the C language, a union is a list of components that is conceptually overlaid in a storage area. In the RPC definition language, a union is a specification of data types based on some criteria.

To illustrate, consider a procedure that does the following:

1. Accepts a character array containing a user name as a parameter.

2. Determines if that user is currently logged onto the system. If the user is logged on, the procedure returns a character array containing the time the user logged on. If the user is not logged on, the procedure returns no data. If information about the user could not be obtained, the procedure returns an integer containing an error code.

In this example, the procedure returns one of three data types: a character array, an integer, or a void (that is, no value). Unions in the RPC definition language let you convey this information. They contain a switch that lets applications know which elements of the union should be used in which cases.

The definition of a union follows:

```
        union identifier switch ( declaration ) {
              case_list
   };
```

The `identifier` is the name of the union. The `declaration` is a simple declaration as defined by the C language (an example will follow shortly).

Based on the value of the declaration, an element of the `case_list` is used. The `case_list` is a list of statements of the following form:

```
        case value : declaration ;
```

The `case_list` can also contain an optional **default** line of the following form:

```
        default : declaration ;
```

To illustrate, consider the procedure described before that accepts a user name and returns the time of day that user logged onto the system. If the procedure is successful, it returns a character array containing the time a specified user logged on. If the user is not logged on, the procedure returns nothing (that is, a **void** value). If the information cannot be obtained, the procedure returns an integer containing an error code.

You can specify these three cases with a union definition which follows:

```
const MAX_TIME_BUF = 30;

union time_results switch (int status) {
        case 0:
                char timeval[MAX_TIME_BUF];
        case 1:
                void;
        case 2:
                int reason;
};
```

This definition describes the three possible data types returned from the procedure. The **rpcgen** compiler generates the following C data structure from this definition:

```
#define MAX_TIME_CHARS 30

struct time_results {
        int status;
        union {
                char timeval[MAX_TIME_CHARS];
                int reason;
        } time_results_u;
};
typedef struct time_results time_results;
```

When implementing an RPC program, you must use the generated structure. The RPC definition of the union is for informational purposes, defining the possible data structures the procedure can return.

Because you must use the generated data structure, there are several things to note:

1. The union component of the structure has the same name as the union identifier in the RPC definition, except it has a trailing **_u**.

2. The **void** declaration is omitted, as it is used only to inform users that no information is returned in the specified case.

3. The first element of the structure is the same as the union declaration in the RPC definition.

4. When implementing the procedure, be sure that you assign the **status** element only the values of **0**, **1**, or **2**. This is because the union definition in the RPC language only shows those values. Fill the rest of the structure according to the RPC specification:

   - If you place a **0** in the **status** field, you must assign data to the **time_results_u.timeval** array.

   - If you assign a **1** to **status**, you need not fill in any part of the union (a **1** in the **status** field says nothing is returned).

   - If you assign a **2** to **status**, you must assign a value to the **time_results_u.reason** element.

5. When the application on the client machine receives this structure from the procedure, it must first check the value of the **status** element. Based on that value, it uses the corresponding element of the union.

We will see an example of how to use unions in Section 6.11.

Type Definitions

Type definitions are the same as their C counterparts. The **rpcgen** compiler transfers type definitions into the generated header file unchanged. So, the line

```
typedef long counter_t;
```

is transferred directly into the header file.

Structures, unions, and type definitions contain declarations. These declarations can be simple C data types (such as **int** or **char**) or they can be arrays or pointers. Declarations of arrays and pointers are described next.

Declarations of Arrays

The **rpcgen** compiler lets you declare arrays within structures, unions, and typedefs. Arrays can be of fixed-length or of variable-length. Fixed-length arrays are declared in the same way as their C language counterparts. Consider the following:

```
int proc_hits[100];
```

This declares **proc_hits** to be an array of 100 integers. The **rpcgen** compiler transfers this declaration into the header file without modification.

You can also specify variable-length arrays. The maximum size of the array is enclosed in angle braces. You can omit the size to indicate that there is no maximum value. For example, consider the following declaration:

```
long x_coords<50>;
```

This declares **x_coords** to be an array of 0 to 50 long integers. Similarly, the following declaration

```
long z_coords<>;
```

declares **z_coords** to be an array of long integers. In this case, the array size can be any value that fits in an unsigned integer.

Because the C language does not support variable-length arrays, the **rpcgen** compiler translates these declarations into a C data structure. The structure has a length indicator and a pointer to the array. For example, the declaration

```
typedef long x_coords<50>;
```

is translated into

```
typedef struct {
        u_int x_coords_len;
        long *x_coords_val;
} x_coords;
```

The length indicator is an unsigned integer that is formed by appending **_len** to the declaration name. The pointer to the array is formed by appending **_val** to the declaration name.

When implementing the remote procedures, you must use the **x_coords_len** and the **x_coords_val** elements of the **x_coords** structure. When populating the structure, you must set the length of the array in the **x_coords_len** element and allocate space to store the array in the **x_coords_val** element.

Declarations of Pointers

Pointer declarations in the RPC definition language are the same as in the C language. For example, the declaration

```
int *nextp;
```

is transferred without modification into the header file generated by **rpcgen**.

Address pointers are not sent over the network, because they reference memory locations on the local machine. However, you can use pointers to structure recursive data such as linked lists and binary trees. As mentioned in Section 6.3, a pointer value is sent over the network as a boolean value followed by the data to which it points.

To illustrate, consider the following structure definition of a linked list:

```
struct linked_list {
        int value;
        struct linked_list *nextp;
};
```

When populating this structure, you allocate the space needed and fill the values of the list. When using the list as part of an RPC call, the corresponding XDR routines transform the pointers into boolean values. We present an example in Section 6.11 that illustrates how to use a linked list in an RPC program.

Strings

The RPC definition language lets you declare strings. Strings are declared as if they were variable-length arrays. For example, consider the following declaration:

```
string first_name<50>;
```

This declares **first_name** to be a string of at most 50 characters. The value in the angle brackets can be empty, specifying there is no maximum length of the string. The **rpcgen** compiler translates this into the following declaration:

```
char *first_name;
```

The declaration of the string in the ''**.x**'' file shows that the string may contain a maximum number of characters. When implementing your procedures, you must allocate space to hold the string and make sure the string length does not exceed the maximum value specified in the RPC definition.

Boolean Values

You can declare boolean values in the RPC language. For example, the following declares **waiting** as a boolean value:

```
bool waiting;
```

The **rpcgen** compiler translates this into the following:

```
bool_t waiting;
```

Because **bool_t** is not a C data type, the RPC library creates a type definition for you. You should only place the values **TRUE** or **FALSE** in a variable of this type.

Void

In a **void** declaration, a variable is not named. The declaration is simple:

```
void;
```

A declaration of this type can only appear in two places:

1. A union definition. In a union definition, it is interpreted as "no value." For example, recall the discussion on union definitions. In our example, the **time_results** union declared a **void** in case **1**. This means the union has no value if the associated condition is **1**.

2. A program definition. In a program definition, the argument or the result of a procedure can be **void**. A **void** argument means no argument is needed, and a **void** result means nothing is returned.

Opaque Data

The RPC definition language also lets you declare opaque data. Opaque data are untyped and contain an arbitrary sequence of bytes. They can be declared with a fixed or a variable length. For example, consider the following declaration:

```
opaque extra_bytes[1024];
```

This declares **extra_bytes** to be an arbitrary sequence of **1024** bytes. The **rpcgen** compiler translates this into a character array:

```
char extra_bytes[1024];
```

Variable-length opaque data are declared with angle brackets:

```
opaque more_bytes<1024>;
```

This declares **more_bytes** to be an arbitrary sequence of **0** to **1024** bytes. The **rpcgen** compiler translates this into the following structure:

```
struct {
        u_int  more_bytes_len;
        char   *more_bytes_val;
} more_bytes;
```

When your RPC application populates this structure, you must allocate space in **more_bytes.more_bytes_val** to hold the data. You must also specify the number of bytes in **more_bytes.more_bytes_len**.

Summary

The RPC definition language lets you specify the procedures in a program. It lets you specify the argument and a return value of each procedure, letting applications know what data to give each procedure and what results to expect.

Some data types in the RPC definition are different from those in the C programming language. These are meant to help users understand the nature of the data. For example, RPC unions let you specify not only the data types in the union, but also under what conditions the data types should be used. In cases like these, you must use the C structure generated by the **rpcgen** compiler when populating the data type.

The RPC definition is only one of the three pieces we had to create in an RPC program. Now let's take a closer look at the second piece, that is, the server code.

6.9   The Server Code

The **rpcgen** compiler generates most of the lower-level RPC routines needed by the server side of the application. The generated code does the following:

1. Binds to a transport address on all transport providers that exist on the machine;

2. Tells the **rpcbind** daemon the addresses to which it is bound;

3. Accepts RPC requests from client applications;

4. Translates the procedure arguments from XDR representation into the local machine representation;

5. Invokes the requested procedure;

6. Translates the procedure results into XDR format; and

7. Sends the results to the application on the client machine.

The only thing you have to do is write the procedures! The procedures you create are called in step **5** in the preceding list.

The procedure's name, argument, and return value are derived from the RPC specification in the ``**.x**'' file. Because the **rpcgen** compiler generates the code that invokes a procedure when an RPC request arrives, you must follow a set of rules when writing the procedures:

1. You must create the name of a remote procedure by converting the procedure name in the RPC definition to all lowercase letters, adding an underbar character, and adding the version number.

2.   The argument to the procedure is a pointer to the argument data type specified in the RPC definition language.

3.   The procedure must return a pointer to the data type specified in the RPC definition language.

4.   The lower-level RPC routines use the procedure's return value after the procedure ends, so a procedure must return the address of a **static** variable.

5.   If the procedure allocates memory (for example, to hold the elements of a linked list), the data must not be deallocated until all processing of the data is complete. Unfortunately, data are translated into XDR representation *after* the procedure ends. So, you must not deallocate any memory your procedure allocates until the *next* invocation of the procedure. Routines are available to do this, and an example is presented in Section 6.11.

Let's look at how a remote procedure allocates and frees memory. Suppose you define a remote procedure that returns a linked list of data. When called, the procedure uses the normal memory allocation routines (**malloc()**, **calloc()**, etc.) to populate the linked list. When the procedure ends, the lower-level RPC routines translate the list into XDR representation and send the data to the application on the client machine. However, the lower-level RPC routines do not free this memory.

This is a problem because the program supplying the procedure never exits. As mentioned earlier, the program supplying remote procedures runs continually on the server machine waiting for RPC requests. The next time someone calls a procedure, the previously allocated memory still exists.

Therefore, a procedure must deallocate previously allocated memory when it *begins*. But, because the previously allocated data are now in XDR format, the procedure must use XDR routines to free the data. We now present these XDR routines.

XDR Routines

The XDR routines are generated by the **rpcgen** compiler. The lower-level RPC routines call the XDR routines to translate data into and out of XDR representation. All translation is done outside the procedure, so you normally don't have to worry about the XDR routines when writing RPC applications.

There is one exception, however. You must use the **xdr_free()** routine to free data the procedure allocates. The **xdr_free()** routine takes a pointer to an XDR function and a data pointer. It frees the memory associated with the data pointer.

The function passed to **xdr_free()** is the XDR routine corresponding to the data type. The **rpcgen** compiler always names these functions **xdr_*any*()**, where *any* is the data type name. For example, if you defined a structure named **intpair**, the corresponding XDR routine is called **xdr_intpair()**.

To illustrate, suppose you define the following linked list structure in a "**.x**" file:

```
struct link_list {
        int data;
        struct link_list *nextp;
};
```

The **rpcgen** compiler creates a function named **xdr_link_list()** that translates this data structure into XDR format. Now, suppose you allocate memory to hold the list and place the first memory location of the list in a variable named **headp**. After the XDR routines translate the list into XDR format, you can free the entire linked list with the following call:

```
xdr_free(xdr_linked_list, headp);
```

As mentioned earlier, the lower-level RPC routines translate a procedure's results into XDR representation after the procedure ends. So, if the results contain allocated memory, you must not free the memory until the next time an application on a client machine calls the procedure. Usually, you free previously allocated memory at the beginning of the procedure and then allocate new data as needed. We will see an example of this in Section 6.11.

As a side note, the **rpcgen** compiler will not generate XDR routines if your procedures use only simple data types. The XDR routines for simple C data types already exist in the SVR4 C library.

Now let's look at the code for the client side of the application. The client side of the application calls the remote procedures that exist on server machines.

6.10 The Client Code

The **rpcgen** compiler generates most of the code for the client side of the application. You simply have to write the code that calls the remote procedures.

The first thing to do is establish communication with the program supplying the procedures. To do this, call the **clnt_create()** subroutine. The **clnt_create()** routine contacts the **rpcbind** daemon on the server machine, finds the address of the program offering the procedures, and establishes communication with that program. It takes four arguments:

1.   The name of the server machine with which you want to communicate;

2.   The program number;

3.   The version number; and

4.   A transport-provider indication.

The transport-provider indication lets you specify how to select a transport provider. Here's how it works: the `clnt_create()` routine uses the Network Selection facilities (described in Chapter 9) to find a transport provider. The Network Selection routines find all transport providers on a machine by searching the `/etc/netconfig` file. One set of Network Selection routines lets you search this file sequentially, and another set uses the **NETPATH** environment variable to direct the search (the **NETPATH** variable is a colon-separated list of transport provider names that directs the search for transport providers similar to the way the **PATH** variable directs the search for UNIX commands). Details of these routines are presented in Chapter 9.

Because the Network Selection routines let you search for a transport provider several ways, the `clnt_create()` function accepts several values for a transport-provider specification. You can specify one of the following strings:

`"netpath"`   Uses the Network Selection routines that employ the **NETPATH** environment variable. The `clnt_create()` routine uses the first transport provider it finds. The transport provider can supply either connection-oriented or connectionless service.

`"circuit_n"`   Also uses the Network Selection routines that employ the **NETPATH** environment variable. But, the `clnt_create()` routine uses the first connection-oriented transport provider it finds. It skips all connectionless transport providers.

`"datagram_n"` Uses the Network Selection routines that employ the **NETPATH** environment variable. The `clnt_create()` routine uses the first connectionless transport provider it finds. It skips all connection-oriented transport providers.

`"visible"`   Uses the Network Selection routines that search the `/etc/netconfig` sequentially. The `clnt_create()` routine uses the first visible entry in this file (a visible entry is defined in Chapter 9). The transport provider can supply either connection-oriented or connectionless service.

`"circuit_v"`   Uses the Network Selection routines that search the `/etc/netconfig` sequentially. The `clnt_create()` routine uses the first visible connection-oriented transport provider it finds. It skips all connectionless transport providers.

`"datagram_v"` Uses the Network Selection routines that search the `/etc/netconfig` sequentially. The `clnt_create()`

routine uses the first visible connectionless transport provider it finds. It skips all connection-oriented transport providers.

"tcp"   Causes `clnt_create()` to use the Transmission Control Protocol. This is provided for backward compatibility only.

"udp"   Causes `clnt_create()` to use the User Datagram Protocol.

These strings provide a lot of flexibility. However, you should use the following guidelines when specifying one these strings:

- If you want to communicate with the procedures over a virtual-circuit transport provider, specify "circuit_n". This incorporates the **NETPATH** environment variable, and hence lets users of the application direct the search for a virtual-circuit transport provider.

- If you want to communicate with the procedures over a datagram transport provider, specify "datagram_n". Again, this lets users of the application direct the search for a datagram transport provider via the **NETPATH** environment variable.

- If either a datagram transport provider or a virtual-circuit transport provider will do, specify "netpath". Most RPC application use this string.

The `clnt_create()` routine returns a ''client handle'' that you use on all subsequent calls to procedures in the requested program. The **rpcgen** compiler creates a high-level interface for each remote procedure.

The high-level interface routine has the same name as the procedure you wrote on the server machine. The name is created by converting the procedure name in the RPC definition to all lowercase letters, adding an underbar character, and adding the version number.

Although the high-level interface routine has the same name as the procedure you wrote on the server machine, it is *not* the same routine. The routine you wrote on the server machine implements the procedure. The high-level interface routine on the client machine calls the RPC functions that send network messages to the server machine.

To add to the confusion, the high-level interface routine for the client machine takes *two* parameters (the procedure you wrote on the server machine takes only one parameter). But again, you must remember that the high-level interface routine on the client machine is completely different from the procedure you wrote on the server machine.

The parameters to the high-level interface routine are the following:

1. A pointer to the procedure argument type specified in the RPC definition language.

2. The client handle returned from `clnt_create()`. The client handle contains all information needed to communicate with the server machine.

The high-level interface routine allocates space to hold the procedure results and returns a pointer to those results.

To illustrate, consider the `math.x` file presented earlier that contained the RPC definition of the `MATHPROG` program:

```
program MATHPROG {
        version MATHVERS {
                int ADD(intpair)      = 1;
                int MULTIPLY(intpair) = 2;
                int CUBE(int)         = 3;
        } = 1;
} = 536870920;
```

Here, the client application would use three interface routines: `add_1()`, `multiply_1()`, and `cube_1()`. These routines are generated by the `rpcgen` compiler and, in this example, are contained in `math_clnt.c`. Each of these routines takes a pointer to the procedure argument and a client handle returned from `clnt_create()`. Each routine does the following:

1. Translates the parameter into XDR representation.

2. Sends an RPC request to the program containing the procedures on the server machine. The request tells the remote program which procedure to invoke. All information needed to communicate with the remote program (for example, the transport address) is contained in the client handle.

3. Waits for the results. If you are using a datagram transport provider, the routine retransmits the request if it does not get a response. If several attempts fail, the routine returns an error to your application.

4. Allocates space to hold the results.

5. Reads the results from the remote procedure.

6. Translates the results from the XDR format into local representation.

7. Returns a pointer to the results.

Besides the high-level interface routines, there are four more routines that you can use: `clnt_pcreateerror()`, `clnt_perror()`, `clnt_freeres()`, and `clnt_destroy()`. We will use each of these routines in the RPC program that is created in Section 6.11. A summary follows:

`clnt_pcreateerror()`   Call this routine if `clnt_create()` fails. This routine prints the reason for failure onto standard error.

`clnt_perror()`   Call this routine if a high-level interface routine fails. This routine also prints the reason for failure onto standard error.

`clnt_freeres()`   Frees all memory the high-level interface routine allocated to hold the results of the procedure. When you are finished with the results of a procedure, call `clnt_freeres()` to deallocate the memory.

`clnt_destroy()`   Frees memory allocated by `clnt_create()` when it created the client handle. Use this routine when you are finished calling procedures in the remote program.

Now that we've seen the components, let's create an RPC application. This application lists all users currently logged into a remote machine.

6.11 A Remote Users Service

To illustrate how to put all the pieces together, let's create an RPC program that tells which users are currently logged onto a remote system.

To do this, we'll define a remote procedure called **RUSERS**. This procedure takes no parameter and returns a linked list of user names. The RPC definition of this procedure follows:

```
const MAX_NAME_SIZE = 20;

struct personinfo {
        string login_name<MAX_NAME_SIZE>;
        struct personinfo *nextp;
};

enum errorcodes {
        NO_MEMORY = 0,
        CANT_GET_INFO = 1
};

union results switch (int status) {
        case 0:
                struct personinfo *personinfop;
        default:
```

```
                    enum errorcodes reason;
};

program RUSERS_PROG {
        version RUSERS_VERS {
                results RUSERS(void) = 1;
        } = 1;
} = 0x200010f4;
```

There are several things of interest in this RPC definition:

- The program defines only one procedure. The procedure is named **RUSERS**.

- The procedure takes no argument and returns a **results** union.

- The **results** union tells us two things:

  a. If the **status** element is **0**, the procedure returns a pointer to a **per-soninfo** structure.

  b. If the **status** element is anything else, the procedure returns an enumeration that tells what went wrong.

  The client application that calls the procedure must check the **status** element in the generated structure. If it is **0**, the procedure was successful. Otherwise, the client application must check the value of the enumeration to see the reason for failure.

- The **personinfo** structure contains two elements:

  1. A string with at most **MAX_NAME** characters; and

  2. A pointer to the next element.

Now let's write the procedure. The procedure is quite simple. Because the SVR4 **who** command displays all users on the system, we invoke the **who** command via the **popen()** subroutine. It is faster to obtain this information from the **/etc/utmp** file directly, but the **popen()** routine suffices for our example.

The code follows:

```
#include <stdio.h>
#include <rpc/rpc.h>
#include "rusers.h"

results *
rusers_1(filler)
```

```
int *filler;
{
   static results results;
   personinfo     *currp;
   personinfo    **currpp;
   FILE *fp;
   char buf[BUFSIZ];

   /*
    *  Free the space we allocated the previous time this
    *  procedure was called.
    */

   xdr_free(xdr_results, &results);

   /*
    *  Get the users currently logged on by calling
    *  the popen function
    */

   if ((fp = popen("who | cut -d' ' -f1", "r")) == NULL) {
       results.status = 1;
       results.results_u.reason = CANT_GET_INFO;
       return (&results);
   }

   currpp = &results.results_u.personinfop;

   while (fgets(buf, BUFSIZ, fp) != NULL) {
      if ((currp = *currpp =
         (personinfo *)malloc(sizeof(personinfo))) == NULL){
            results.status = 1;
            results.results_u.reason = NO_MEMORY;
            return (&results);
      }
      if (strlen(buf) > MAX_NAME_SIZE) {
           buf[MAX_NAME_SIZE - 1] = '\0';
      } else {
           /*
            *  Get rid of new-line character
            */
           buf[strlen(buf) - 1] = '\0';
      }
```

```
        currp->login_name = (char *)malloc(strlen(buf));
        strcpy(currp->login_name, buf);
        currp = &(currp->nextp);
    }
    *currpp = NULL;
    results.status = 0;
    return &results;
}
```

There are several things to notice about this code:

1. Although the procedure takes no parameter, we still pass it a value. We don't have to do this, but, as we will see in the Section 6.12, authentication information may be passed as the second parameter. If authentication information is used, you must pass an unused variable as the first parameter.

2. We declare the **results** variable as **static**. This is necessary because we return a pointer to this variable.

3. We call **xdr_free()** at the beginning of the procedure, passing it a pointer to the **results** variable and a pointer to the **xdr_results()** function (the **rpcgen** compiler generates the **xdr_results()** function). This frees the data allocated in the *previous* invocation. On the first invocation, the **results** variable will have a value of **0**, and the **xdr_free()** routine returns immediately. That is another reason you must declare the **results** variable as **static**. It must retain its value on all subsequent invocations.

4. The **popen()** subroutine is called to let the **who** command figure out which users are logged on. If this fails, we set the **status** element of the **results** structure to **1**. This informs the caller that we failed the request. We set the enumeration value to **CANT_GET_INFO**.

5. We issue a while-loop, reading all users on the system. Inside the loop, we allocate space to hold an element of the linked list. We also allocate space to hold the user name. This memory is freed the next time an application calls the procedure. If we can't allocate memory, set the **status** element of the **results** structure to **1** and set the enumeration value to **NO_MEMORY**.

6. When all names are read and placed into the linked list, a pointer to the **results** structure is returned.

Now let's write the client code. This code calls **clnt_create()** to establish communication. It then calls the remote procedure and prints the list.

The code follows:

```
#include <stdio.h>
#include <rpc/rpc.h>
#include "rusers.h"

main(argc, argv)
int argc;
char *argv[];
{
    CLIENT *cl;
    results *resultp;
    struct personinfo *currp;
    int filler;
    int i;
    int error = 0;

    if (argc < 2) {
        fprintf(stderr, "%s: usage: %s server [server...]\n",
                argv[0], argv[0]);
        exit(1);
    }

    for (i = 1; argv[i]; i++) {
        printf("---------- %s -------------\n", argv[i]);
        cl = clnt_create(argv[i], RUSERS_PROG, RUSERS_VERS,
                        "netpath");
        if (cl == NULL) {
            clnt_pcreateerror(argv[i]);
            error = 1;
            continue;
        }

        resultp = rusers_1(&filler, cl);
        if (resultp == NULL) {
            clnt_perror(cl, "rusers_1");
            error = 1;
            continue;
        }

        if (resultp->status != 0) {
            printf("ERROR!\n");
            switch (resultp->results_u.reason) {
```

```
                        case NO_MEMORY:
                            printf("Server ran out of memory\n");
                            break;
                        case CANT_GET_INFO:
                            printf("Server could not get info\n");
                            break;
                    }
                    error = 1;
                    continue;
            }

            currp = resultp->results_u.personinfop;

            while (currp) {
                printf("%.20s\n", currp->login_name);
                currp = currp->nextp;
            }

            /*
             *   Free all data associated with this RPC
             */

            clnt_freeres(cl, xdr_results, resultp);
            clnt_destroy(cl);
        }

    exit(error);
}
```

Let's examine the client code:

1. The code accepts several server names as arguments and loops calling the remote procedure on each server machine.

2. The code calls **clnt_create()** within the loop. The **clnt_create()** routine returns a client handle that you use to identify the server machine.

3. If the **clnt_create()** call fails, we use the **clnt_pcreateerror()** routine to display the reason for failure.

4. We call the **rusers_1()** function, passing it the client handle. But, because the client handle is the second argument (and the RPC definition states the remote procedure takes no argument), we pass the address of an unused variable as the first argument.

The `rusers_1()` function returns a pointer to the `results` structure. The space for that structure is allocated by the lower-level RPC routines that `rusers_1()` calls.

5. If the `rusers_1()` function fails, we call `clnt_perror()` to display the reason for failure.

6. Because the RPC definition specifies the procedure returns a union, we check the `status` element of the generated structure. If this element is not `0`, we know the procedure call failed. We check the `reason` element of the `results_u` union (the `reason` element is an enumeration) and print an error message based on the enumeration value.

7. If the `status` element is `0`, we display all names in the linked list.

8. We call `clnt_freeres()` to free the data allocated in the `results` structure. We also call `clnt_destroy()` to free the client handle. We then continue the loop to call the remote procedure on the next server machine.

That's all there is to it! The `rpcgen` compiler generates the code that handles the lower-level networking routines and the XDR translation.

Now let's take a closer look at security issues. If security is a concern, you can use a stricter flavor of authentication.

6.12 Changing Authentication

As mentioned in Section 6.4, RPC supports several flavors of authentication. By default, remote procedures incorporate the **none** flavor of authentication. In the ''remote users'' application presented in Section 6.11, this is acceptable. We freely give out the names of the users currently logged into a system without caring who asked for it.

However, the **none** flavor of authentication is unacceptable for other types of applications. To illustrate, we'll create a program that provides remote file-access procedures. These procedures let applications on client machines read and write local files. In procedures like these, it is essential that we know the identity of the user on the client machine. Otherwise, we may give users from a client machine unauthorized access to local files.

We can find out the identity of the user on the client machine by incorporating a stricter flavor of authentication into the procedures. We begin by presenting the RPC definition of a program that contains remote file-access procedures:

```
/*
 *      rread.x
 */

const MAX_FILE_NAME = 64;
const MAX_DATA = 1024;

struct read_request {
        string filename<MAX_FILE_NAME>;
        int start_location;
        int how_many;
};

union read_results switch (int status) {
        case 0:
                opaque filedata<MAX_DATA>;
        default:
                void;
};

struct write_request {
        string filename<MAX_FILE_NAME>;
        int start_location;
        int how_many;
        opaque filedata<MAX_DATA>;
};

union write_results switch (int status) {
        case 0:
                int how_many;
        default:
                void;
};

program READ_PROG {
        version READ_VERS {
                read_results READ(read_request) = 1;
                write_results WRITE(write_request) = 2;
        } = 1;
} = 0x200010f5;
```

This RPC program defines two procedures: READ and WRITE. These procedures let applications on a client machine read and write files that exist on the server machine. Before looking at the security implications, let's briefly examine these procedures.

The READ procedure takes a read_request structure as an argument and returns a read_results union. The read_request structure has three values:

1. The name of the file to read (this is a string of at most 64 characters);

2. A byte offset specifying where to start reading; and

3. The number of bytes to read.

The read_results union uses the status element to indicate which part of the union to use. If the status element is 0, the union contains the requested data. Otherwise, the union contains no information. Note that the maximum number of bytes returned is 1024. Hence, applications cannot request more than 1024 bytes of data in a single RPC request.

The WRITE procedure takes a write_request structure as an argument and returns a write_results union. The write_request structure has the following four elements:

1. The name of the file to update (this is a string of at most 64 characters);

2. A byte offset specifying where to start writing;

3. The number of bytes to write; and

4. The data to write into the file.

The write_results union uses the status element to indicate which part of the union to use. If the status element is 0, the union contains the number of bytes successfully written. Otherwise, the union contains no information.

These two procedures are very useful, They let applications on client machines read and write files on a server machine. But, the procedures must validate the identity of the user making the request. They cannot let unauthorized users update files on the server machine.

As mentioned earlier, remote procedures use the **none** authentication flavor by default. This simply will not do for procedures like READ and WRITE. Stricter authentication must be used.

Let's start by looking at the **unix** authentication flavor. The **unix** authentication flavor passes the identity of the user on the client machine. To use this flavor, you have to modify the client and the server sides of the application.

Incorporating Unix Authentication

The **unix** authentication flavor incorporates the sender's effective user ID, effective group ID, machine name, and other information. To use this flavor of authentication, you have to modify the client and server sides of the application.

The client code is simple. You have to modify the **cl_auth** field of the client structure returned from **clnt_create()**. The code segment follows:

```
cl = clnt_create(argv[1], READ_PROG, READ_VERS, "netpath");
if (cl == NULL) {
    clnt_pcreateerror(argv[1]);
    exit(1);
}
if ((cl->cl_auth = authsys_create_default()) == NULL) {
    fprintf(stderr,
            "cannot create authentication information\n");
    exit(1);
}
```

Calling the **authsys_create_default()** routine causes the RPC request to carry authentication information in an **authsys_parms** structure. The **authsys_parms** structure has the following definition:

```
struct authsys_parms {
    u_long   aup_time;      /* credential creation time  */
    char    *aup_machname;  /* name of client machine    */
    uid_t    aup_uid;       /* user's effective user ID  */
    gid_t    aup_gid;       /* user's current group ID   */
    int      aup_len;       /* element length of aup_gids */
    gid_t   *aup_gids;      /* array of groups user is in */
};
```

Now let's look at the server side of the application. On the server side, you have to modify the procedures to accept the authentication information. The code generated by the **rpcgen** compiler actually passes *two* parameters to the procedures. The first is a pointer to the procedure argument, and the second is a **svc_req** structure.

The **svc_req** structure contains the authentication information (and other information) from the client machine. It has the following definition:

```
struct svc_req {
  u_long              rq_prog;       /* program number      */
  u_long              rq_vers;       /* version number      */
  u_long              rq_proc;       /* procedure number    */
  struct opaque_auth  rq_cred;       /* credential info     */
  caddr_t             rq_clntcred;   /* credentials         */
  SVCXPRT            *rq_xprt;       /* associated transport */
};
```

You must cast the **rq_clntcred** element of the **svc_req** structure into the structure corresponding to the authentication flavor. For the **unix** authentication flavor, you must cast the **rq_clntcred** element to a pointer to the **authsys_parms** structure. You can check the **rq_cred.oa_flavor** element of the **svc_req** structure to determine the authentication flavor the application on the client machine used. For the **unix** flavor, that element is set to **AUTH_SYS**.

To illustrate, let's look at the implementation of the **READ** procedure described earlier.

```
#include <sys/types.h>
#include <sys/param.h>
#include <rpc/rpc.h>
#include <fcntl.h>
#include <unistd.h>
#include "rread.h"

read_results *
read_1(request, rq)
read_request *request;
struct svc_req *rq;
{
    static read_results read_results; /* Holds results of */
                                      /* the RPC          */
    struct authunix_parms *aup;   /* Authentication info */
    uid_t uid;                    /* User ID of caller   */
    uid_t uid_orig;               /* User ID to restore  */
    gid_t gid;                    /* Group ID of caller  */
    gid_t gid_orig;               /* Group ID to restore */
    int   gid_len;                /* Number of groups    */
    gid_t *group_listp;           /* Auxiliary groups    */
    int n;                        /* Number of bytes read */
    int fd;                       /* fd of file to read  */
```

```
    char buf[MAX_DATA];                 /* buffer to hold data   */

    switch (rq->rq_cred.oa_flavor) {
      case AUTH_SYS:
            aup = (struct authunix_parms *) rq->rq_clntcred;
            uid = aup->aup_uid;
            if (uid <= 100) {
                uid = UID_NOBODY;
                gid = GID_NOBODY;
                gid_len = 0;
                group_listp = 0;
            } else {
                gid = aup->aup_gid;
                gid_len = aup->aup_len;
                group_listp = aup->aup_gids;
            }
            break;
      default:
            uid = UID_NOBODY;
            gid = GID_NOBODY;
            gid_len = 0;
            group_listp = 0;
            break;
    }

    /*
     *  If the client requested too much data, return with
     *  an error indication
     */

    if (request->how_many > MAX_DATA) {
        read_results.status = 1;
        return(&read_results);
    }

    /*
     *  Set the effective user ID, effective group ID, and
     *  group list of the user calling this routine.
     */

    uid_orig = geteuid();
    gid_orig = getegid();
```

```
if (   (setegid(gid) < 0)
    || (setgroups(gid_len, group_listp) < 0)
    || (seteuid(uid) < 0)) {
     read_results.status = 1;
     return(&read_results);
}

/*
 *  Now that the effective user ID and the effective
 *  group ID are set, perform the read operation...
 */

read_results.status = 0;

if (((fd = open(request->filename, O_RDONLY)) < 0)
   || (lseek(fd, (off_t)(request->start_location),
                                     SEEK_SET) < 0)
   || ((n = read(fd, buf, request->how_many)) < 0)) {
      read_results.status = 1;
}

/*
 *  Set your effective user and group ID back to their
 *  Original value
 */

(void) setegid(gid_orig);
(void) seteuid(uid_orig);

/*
 *  Close the file, fill in the information and return.
 */

if (fd >= 0)
    (void)close(fd);

if (read_results.status == 1) {
    return(&read_results);
}

read_results.read_results_u.filedata.filedata_len = n;
read_results.read_results_u.filedata.filedata_val = buf;
```

```
        return(&read_results);
}
```

In this procedure, the first thing we do is look at the authentication flavor. If it is **AUTH_SYS**, we extract the effective user ID, effective group ID, and group list from the **authsys_parms** structure. If the authentication flavor is not **AUTH_SYS**, we set the user ID to **UID_NOBODY** and the group ID to **GID_NOBODY**. SVR4 defines these values in **sys/param.h**, and they correspond to guest users of the system. A local user on the server machine will not have a user ID nor a group ID corresponding to those values.

We provide an extra security check if the **AUTH_SYS** flavor is used: because a user ID of **100** or less corresponds to "system users" (that is, users that own files critical to the system), we handle user IDs in this range differently. If the remote user ID is **100** or less, we change the user ID to **UID_NOBODY** and the group ID to **GID_NOBODY**. This protects critical files from malicious users.

Next, the procedure changes its effective user ID and effective group ID to the remote user. It accesses the requested file, and if successful, it returns the data. The procedure then restores its original effective user ID and effective group ID.

For the procedure to work correctly, it must be started as the superuser. Only the superuser can change its effective user ID and group ID each time an application on the client machine calls the procedure.

Unfortunately, the **unix** authentication flavor is easy to defeat. An application on the client machine could create an **authsys_parm** structure with invalid information and send the fake credentials to the server machine. Because the **unix** authentication flavor sends no proof of identity, the remote procedure could not tell it was being fooled.

The **secure** authentication flavor solves this problem by providing a verifier with the credentials. As we will see shortly, the verifier proves the identity of the user sending the RPC request. We now present an overview of this style of authentication.

Incorporating Secure Authentication

The **secure** flavor of authentication provides an encrypted verifier with a user's credentials. Applications using this authentication flavor are said to be using "Secure RPC."

Secure RPC uses public and private keys for encryption. Each user of the network is assigned a public key and private key. A user's public key, as its name implies, is known to all other users (it is in a publicly readable database). A user's private key is a secret key that only the user knows (similar to a login password). As we will see in what follows, Secure RPC uses both keys to prove a user's identity.

Unfortunately, Secure RPC will not work unless the system administrators of the client and server machines do some setup procedures. First, the administrators must assign a private and public key to every user on the system. Then, they must make sure the `keyserv` daemon is running. The `keyserv` daemon stores the private key of each user logged into a system (the low-level RPC routines query this daemon to get the private key of the user running the RPC program). Third, the administrators must ensure the time is synchronized between all machines in the network.

If the administrators do the work required to set up Secure RPC, your application can use it. Before showing how to modify your applications to use Secure RPC, we present an overview of its functionality.

Overview of Secure Authentication

Secure RPC works by authenticating a user's "network name." A network name identifies a user on a network. A network name is not machine-specific. Your network name is the same no matter what machine you are logged into.

Network names depend upon a "Secure RPC Domain." A Secure RPC Domain is a collection of machines, and every machine using Secure RPC must be a member of one. All machines in a Secure RPC Domain must have the same `/etc/password` file, ensuring a user has the same user ID on every machine in the domain.

A user's network name is created by combining the machine's operating system name, the user ID, and the Secure RPC Domain name. A period (".") separates the operating system name and the user ID, and an at-sign character ("@") separates the user ID and the Secure RPC Domain name. For example, if a set of machines running SVR4 belonged to the Secure RPC Domain named `olympus`, the user with user ID `307` would have the following network name:

`UNIX.307@olympus`

There is one exception to this convention. The `root` user of a machine (which has user ID `0`), uses the machine name for the user ID. So, the `root` user on machine `hercules` in the Secure RPC Domain named `olympus` would have the following network name:

`UNIX.hercules@olympus`

Similarly, the `root` user on machine `zeus` in the Secure RPC Domain named `olympus` would have the following network name:

`UNIX.zeus@olympus`

This lets you specify the network name of a machine by specifying the network name of the `root` user on that machine.

Secure RPC authenticates two parties: the user on the client machine that issued the RPC request and the user on the server machine that started the RPC program. Usually, the `root` user on the server machine starts the RPC program.

Before authentication can take place, the two parties must compute a "Common Key." The Common Key is known only by the two parties.

The two parties create a Common Key from their public and secret keys. As mentioned earlier, the administrator assigns each user a secret key (the secret key is similar to a password). The administrator does this via the `newkey` administrative command. This command also generates a public key for the user. It generates the public key by raising a constant value to the user's secret key. The public key is then placed in a database.

You may think you can figure out a user's secret key by examining that user's public key (after all, if you know the constant value and the public key, you can do the math `log` function to figure out the secret key). The reason you can't do that is because the constant value and the secret key are very large numbers, making the `log` operation computationally infeasible. However, you should change your secret key often to foil malicious users that try to figure out secret keys.

Given the way public keys are generated, two users can compute a Common Key. Figure 6.8 shows how this is done. To illustrate, suppose you wanted a common key between User A and User B (for example, User A would be the user issuing an RPC call and User B would be the `root` user on the server machine).

User A computes the Common Key by raising User B's public key to User A's secret key. This value is equivalent to the constant value raised to User B's secret key, raised again to User A's secret key. User B computes the Common Key by raising User A's public key to User B's secret key. This value is equivalent to the constant value raised to User A's secret key, raised again to User B's secret key. And, because raising `x` to `y` to `z` is the same as raising `x` to `z` to `y`, User A and User B compute the same values. You can generate this value correctly only if you know either User A's secret key or User B's secret key. So, the resultant value is a Common Key that only User A and User B can generate.

Now that we have a Common Key, let's look at the steps involved in the authentication. As mentioned earlier, there are two parties involved:

1. The user making the RPC request on the client machine; and

2. The user that started the RPC program on the server machine. Usually, this is the `root` user on the server machine.

Figure 6.9 shows the steps involved in Secure RPC. In this figure, a value in a small box represents encrypted data. The value under the box (that is, `K` or `CK`) represents the key used in the encryption. A user can only read the contents of the box if they know the corresponding key. The authentication procedure follows:

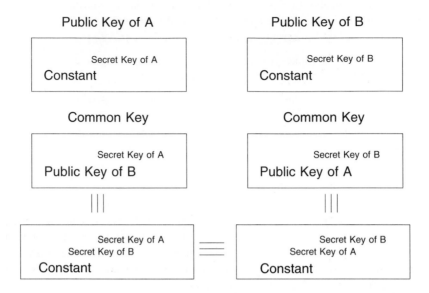

Figure 6.8 Common Keys

1. The two parties compute a Common Key. In Figure 6.9, the Common Key is represented by **K**.

2. The application on the client machine generates a random Conversation Key. In Figure 6.9, the Conversation Key is represented by **CK**.

3. The application on the client machine selects a "window" value (represented by **win** in Figure 6.9). The window represents the lifetime of the credential. We will see how it is used in step 10.

4. The application on the client machine gets the current time. This is represented by **t1** in Figure 6.9.

5. The application on the client machine creates its credentials in the following way:

   — It places the user's network name in the credentials structure.

   — It encrypts the random Conversation Key using the Common Key. The remote user is the only other person that can calculate the Common Key. So, only the remote user can decrypt the Conversation Key. The application on the client machine places the encrypted value in the credentials structure.

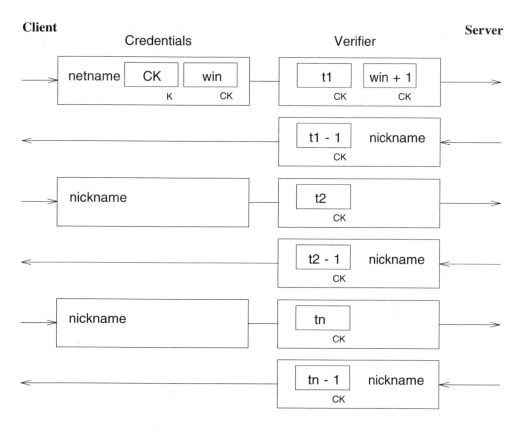

Figure 6.9 Secure RPC Authentication

— It encrypts the window value using the Conversation Key. It places the encrypted value in the credentials structure. We will see how the server uses the window value in step 10.

6. The application on the client machine then creates a verifier in the following way:

— It encrypts the current time using the Conversation Key. It places the encrypted value in the verifier structure.

— It computes the window value plus one, and encrypts the result using the Conversation Key. It places the encrypted value in the verifier structure.

7. The application on the client machine sends the credentials and the verifier to the server machine.

8. The program on the server machine reads the information. It gets the network name from the credentials and computes the Common Key between that user and itself (by "itself" we mean the effective user ID of the program on the server machine).

9. The program uses the Common Key to decrypt the Conversation Key. It uses the Conversation Key to decrypt the window value and the two other values in the verifier.

10. The program now uses the window value in the following way:

— It looks at the time stamp sent by the application on the client machine. If the time indicated by the sum of the time stamp plus the window has passed, the program rejects the request. So, the program uses the window as an indication of how long it can take for a message to arrive. This ensures the message was generated recently.

11. The program checks that the decrypted value of the "window plus one" is correct. If it is, then the user sending the message encrypted the window and the "window plus one" values correctly. This means the user sending the message knows the Conversation Key. And, because the Conversation Key is encrypted by the Common Key, the remote user must also know the Common Key. And, because the user with the network name specified in the credentials structure is the only other person that can calculate the Common Key, the remote user must be who they claim to be.

12. Once satisfied that the remote user's identity is correct, the program sends a verifier back to the client machine. The verifier contains the following:

1. A nickname that the client machine uses for all future requests between the two parties.

2. An encrypted time stamp. The time stamp is the value the application sent minus one. It is encrypted with the Conversation Key.

13. When the application on the client machine gets the verifier from the remote program, it decrypts the time stamp using the Conversation Key. If the decrypted value is the original time stamp minus one, the application knows the remote program encrypted that value correctly. That means the remote program was able to figure out the Conversation Key, and therefore it must have known the Common Key.

14. The application on the client machine and the program on the server machine use the Conversation Key to authenticate all other messages. The credentials associated with the messages from the client machine to the server machine contain the nickname. The verifier contains the current time encrypted with the Conversation Key. Again, if the time indicated by the sum of the time stamp plus the

window has passed, the program on the server machine rejects the request. The server machine's verifier is the time stamp minus one, encrypted with the Conversation Key. The application on the client machine decrypts this value to verify the program on the server machine.

The server machine keeps a local table that maps each nickname into a window and a Conversation Key. That is why the window and the Conversation Key are not sent on every request. If the server machine crashes, it loses this information. When the server machine comes back, the application on the client machine must start the authentication process over again.

As a side note, it is important to realize that the window value specifies how long it takes for a message to arrive. It does *not* specify the length of the conversation.

Although there are many steps involved, they are all done by the lower-level RPC routines. The higher-level code is easy to create.

Using Secure Authentication

Now let's write an RPC application that uses Secure RPC. As with the **unix** authentication flavor, you have to modify the client and the server sides of the application.

On the client side of the application, you have to modify the **cl_auth** field of the client structure returned from **clnt_create()**. The code segment follows:

```
char servername[MAXNETNAMELEN];

/*
 *   Assume argv[1] holds the name of the server with
 *   which we want to communicate
 */

cl = clnt_create(argv[1], READ_PROG, READ_VERS, "netpath");
if (cl == NULL) {
    clnt_pcreateerror(argv[1]);
    exit(1);
}

host2netname(servername, argv[1], NULL);

if ((cl->cl_auth = authdes_seccreate(servername, 60,
                        argv[1], NULL)) == NULL) {
    fprintf(stderr,
```

```
            "cannot create authentication information\n");
        exit(1);
}
```

The **host2netname()** routine creates the network name of the **root** user on the server machine. As mentioned earlier, we use the network name of that user because the program containing the remote procedures is usually started by **root**.

The first argument to **host2netname()** is a buffer to hold the network name of the **root** user on the server machine. The second argument is the name of the server machine (in our example, we use **argv[1]**, because it contains the server machine name). The third argument holds the Secure RPC Domain name. A NULL value directs the call to use the Secure RPC Domain name of the client machine.

If a user other than **root** starts the procedure on the server machine, the client side of the application must replace the **host2netname()** routine with the **user2netname()** routine. The code follows:

```
        user2netname (servername, uid, NULL);
```

Here, the second argument is the numeric user ID of the user that started the program containing the remote procedures.

The **authdes_seccreate()** routine creates the authentication information and handles the lower-level functions. It has the following arguments:

1. The network name of the user on the server machine. This is created with the **host2netname()** routine or the **user2netname()** routine.

2. The lifetime of the credentials. This argument specifies when the credentials will expire (this is the window value discussed earlier). Because we specified a value of **60**, the credentials will expire in **60** seconds.

3. The name of a machine with which to synchronize time. For Secure RPC to work correctly, the client machine and the server machine must agree on what time it is. In this example, we pass the server machine's name. This indicates the client machine and the server machine are both using the server machine's idea of time. If the time of day on the client machine and the server machine were completely in synch, you could use a NULL value for this argument.

4. The address of the Conversation Key to use for encryption. If this value is NULL, the RPC mechanism picks a random Conversation Key.

That is all you have to do for the client side of the application. All other processing is done by the lower-level RPC routines.

Now let's look at the server code. On the server side of the application, you must modify your procedures to accept the authentication information.

Fortunately, all of the authentication processing is done for you by the time your procedure starts. If the authentication fails, your procedure is not invoked. So, when your procedure begins, the only thing you have to do is get the name of the user making the RPC request.

To do this, you must cast the **rq_clntcred** element of the **svc_req** structure into the structure corresponding to the authentication flavor. For Secure RPC, you must cast that value into a pointer to the **authdes_cred** structure.

The **authdes_cred** structure has several elements that are used by the lower levels of RPC. From the procedure's point of view, you need only one element of this structure: the network name of the user on the client machine. That network name is contained in the **adc_fullname.name** element of the **authdes_cred** structure.

Given the network name, you must translate it into the user ID and the group ID of a local user. You do that with the **netname2user()** routine. The format of the routine follows:

---

   netname2user(netname, &uid, &gid, &gidlen, gidlist);

This routine translates a network name into the local information. It fills the user ID, the group ID, the number of groups, and the group list.

To illustrate, consider the server implementation of the **READ** procedure presented earlier. We'll rewrite this procedure to use Secure RPC. The server code follows:

```
#include <sys/types.h>
#include <sys/param.h>
#include <rpc/rpc.h>
#include <fcntl.h>
#include <unistd.h>
#include "rread.h"

#define MAX_GROUPS 50

read_results *
read_1 (request, rq)
read_request *request;
struct svc_req *rq;
{
    static read_results read_results; /* Holds results of */
```

```
                                        /* the RPC            */
struct authdes_cred *descp;     /* Authentication info  */
uid_t uid;                      /* User ID of caller    */
uid_t uid_orig;                 /* User ID to restore   */
gid_t gid;                      /* Group ID of caller   */
gid_t gid_orig;                 /* Group ID to restore  */
int    gid_len;                 /* Number of groups     */
gid_t gidlist[MAX_GROUPS];      /* Auxiliary groups     */
int n;                          /* Number of bytes read */
int fd;                         /* fd of file to read   */
char buf[MAX_DATA];             /* buffer to hold data  */

switch (rq->rq_cred.oa_flavor) {
    case AUTH_DES:
        descp = (struct authdes_cred *)rq->rq_clntcred;
        if (!netname2user(descp->adc_fullname.name, &uid,
                &gid, &gid_len, gidlist)) {
            read_results.status = 1;
            return(&read_results);
        }
        if (uid <= 100) {
            uid = UID_NOBODY;
            gid = GID_NOBODY;
            gid_len = 0;
        }
        break;
    default:
        uid = UID_NOBODY;
        gid = GID_NOBODY;
        gid_len = 0;
        break;
}


/*
 *  If the client requested too much data, return with
 *  an error indication
 */

if (request->how_many > MAX_DATA) {
    read_results.status = 1;
    return(&read_results);
}
```

```
/*
 *  Set the effective user ID, effective group ID, and
 *  group list of the user calling this routine.
 */

uid_orig = geteuid();
gid_orig = getegid();

if (   (setegid(gid) < 0)
    || (setgroups(gid_len, gidlist) < 0)
    || (seteuid(uid) < 0)) {
    read_results.status = 1;
     return(&read_results);
}

/*
 *  Now that the effective user ID and the effective
 *  group ID are set, perform the read operation...
 */

read_results.status = 0;

if (((fd = open(request->filename, O_RDONLY)) < 0)
  || (lseek(fd, (off_t)(request->start_location),
                                    SEEK_SET) < 0)
  || ((n = read(fd, buf, request->how_many)) < 0)) {
      read_results.status = 1;
}

/*
 *  Set your effective user and group ID back to their
 *  Original value
 */

(void) setegid(gid_orig);
(void) seteuid(uid_orig);

/*
 *  Close the file, fill in the information and return.
 */

if (fd >= 0)
    (void)close(fd);
```

```
    if (read_results.status == 1) {
        return(&read_results);
    }

    read_results.read_results_u.filedata.filedata_len = n;
    read_results.read_results_u.filedata.filedata_val = buf;

    return(&read_results);
}
```

In this procedure, we check the authentication flavor. If the authentication flavor is **AUTH_DES**, we use the **netname2user()** function to figure out the effective user ID, the effective group ID, and the group list from the network name. And, as done in the version that used **AUTH_SYS**, we handle user IDs from **0** to **100** differently than others. If the remote user ID is **100** or less, we change the user ID to **UID_NOBODY** and the group ID to **GID_NOBODY**.

If the authentication flavor is not **AUTH_DES**, we set the user ID to **UID_NOBODY** and the group ID to **GID_NOBODY**. After the user ID and group ID are set, the procedure changes its effective user ID and effective group ID to the remote user. It accesses the requested file, and if successful, it returns the data. The procedure then restores its original effective user ID and effective group ID.

6.13 Using SVR4 Port Monitors

There is a drawback to the RPC architecture. Recall that each set of remote procedures is compiled into a program and that program runs on the server machine waiting for requests. That means if you have many RPC programs, your system will have many processes running constantly. This consumes system resources and may slow down the server machine.

A solution is to start an RPC program on the server machine only when an application on a client machine wants to communicate with it. The RPC facility lets you do this by incorporating the help of the **listen** port monitor. As mentioned in Chapter 1, the SVR4 **listen** port monitor is a general-purpose network listener. It reads a configuration file to figure out which addresses to monitor, attaches *itself* to each address, and waits for messages to arrive. When a message arrives, the network listener starts the associated program.

Here's how you can use this with RPC. First, create the client side and the server side of the RPC application, as we described in this chapter. Then, instead of running the server side of the application on the server machine, you register the RPC program with the network listener. This must be done by the administrator of the server machine with the following command:

```
pmadm -a -p pm_tag -s name -i username -v `nlsadmin -V`   \
          -m `nlsadmin -c path -D -R prognum:versnum`
```

In this command, the **pm_tag** parameter corresponds to a transport provider (for example, `tcp`). The **name** is an arbitrary string that names the program (usually the program name you specified in the RPC program definition). The **username** specifies the effective user ID of the program when it starts (this is usually `root`). The **path** is the full path name of the executable program you created by compiling the server files. The **prognum** and **versnum** are the program number and version number, respectively, specified in the RPC program definition.

For example, the administrator can register the remote math program developed in Section 6.3 with the following command:

```
pmadm -a -p tcp -s mathprog -i root -v `nlsadmin -V`   \
   -m `nlsadmin -c /usr/sbin/math_server -D -R 536870920:1`
```

This command updates the configuration file for the network listener monitoring the Transmission Control Protocol. The command instructs the network listener to do the following:

1. The network listener attaches *itself* to an unused transport address.

2. The network listener tells the local **rpcbind** process that RPC program `536870920` version `1` is available over TCP on the address to which it is attached.

3. When an application on a client machine wants to call a procedure in program `536870920`, it does its normal operations. It contacts the **rpcbind** process on the server machine. The **rpcbind** process tells the client application the address of the requested program.

4. When the application on the client machine sends a request to the transport address, the network listener accepts the request and starts the `/usr/sbin/math_server` program.

5. The `/usr/sbin/math_server` program realizes it was started from the network listener. It performs all necessary authentication, translates procedure arguments from XDR format into local representation, invokes the request procedure, translates the procedure results into XDR format, sends the results to the client machine, and exits.

6. The network listener continues to listen for client requests.

You don't have to do anything special for this to work. The **rpcgen** compiler automatically generates the code. When the server program starts, it checks to see if a network connection already exists. If it does, the program starts the RPC protocol. If a network connection doesn't already exist, the program performs its normal operations: It binds to an unused address over all transport providers on the server machine, tells the local **rpcbind** the addresses, and runs continually waiting for messages to arrive.

6.14 Summary

The RPC mechanism provides an easy way to create distributed applications. By following the normal procedure call model, it lets you write applications that call procedures on remote machines.

The **rpcgen** compiler generates most of the lower-level RPC routines. You have to create an RPC specification in the RPC definition language, write the procedures, and write the client side of the application that calls the procedures. The **rpcgen** compiler generates the code that glues everything together.

For Further Reading

1. AT&T, *UNIX System V Release 4 Programmer's Guide: Networking Interfaces*, Prentice Hall, Englewood Cliffs, NJ, 1990.

2. Sun Microsystems, Inc., ''RPC: Remote Procedure Call, Protocol Specification, Version 2,'' *RFC 1057*, 1988.

3. Sun Microsystems, Inc., ''XDR: External Data Representation Standard,'' *RFC 1014*, 1987.

Exercises

6.1   Explain why XDR is necessary for RPC applications. Is XDR always needed? Why or why not? Suggest an alternative approach to data representation other than that provided by XDR.

6.2   Suppose a remote procedure returned a binary tree with seven elements. Show the XDR representation of this tree.

6.3   Explain the RPC authentication flavors. Describe the types of remote procedures appropriate for each flavor.

6.4   Modify the **RUSERS** program presented in Section 6.11 to return additional information about users logged into a remote system. Have it return the time a user logged in and the terminal they are using.

6.5   Create a "remote directory listing" RPC. The procedure takes the name of a directory and returns a linked list of the elements in that directory. Use the **unix** authentication flavor.

6.6   Create the **WRITE** procedure from the RPC specification given in Section 6.12. Incorporate either the **unix** or the **secure** authentication flavor.

6.7   Consider the RPC specification of **READ_PROG** in Section 6.12. Create two programs, one that calls the **READ** procedure and another that calls the **WRITE** procedure. The programs should take all information needed by the procedure as arguments. In addition, each program must take a flag that specifies whether to use the **unix** authentication flavor or the **secure** authentication flavor.

6.8   Examine the server code produced by **rpcgen**. How does the server code know whether it was started by a port monitor or by a user?

6.9   Create an RPC program that implements a remote database facility. The database should contain entries of user names and phone numbers. Create three procedures: one that adds an entry to the database, one that removes an entry from the database, and one that searches the database. The search routine should take a user name as a parameter and return a list of phone numbers for that user.

Chapter 7

Introduction to TLI

7.1   Introduction

The SVR4 Transport Level Interface (TLI) is a set of programming subroutines. They give a direct interface to a transport provider, letting you establish communication, manage a connection, and transfer data. You use the routines to create networking applications that handle lower-level networking actions.

The TLI routines are based on the functionality specified in the ISO Transport Service Specification (ISO standard 8072). By using TLI, your applications can interface with services that correspond to the transport layer of the OSI model.

The TLI routines are designed to work with any transport provider. For example, you can use TLI to interface with TCP, UDP, or OSI TP4. TLI provides routines that let you use connectionless and connection-oriented modes of service.

We present TLI in two chapters. This chapter introduces TLI by presenting an overview of TLI functionality, explaining when to use TLI and showing the details of the TLI routines. Chapter 8 explains how to use the TLI routines in networking applications and shows examples of TLI programs. We begin by presenting an overview of TLI functionality.

7.2   Overview of TLI

TLI provides a low-level "end-to-end" interface between networking applications. It has routines that let you establish communication over both connection-oriented and connectionless transport providers. As mentioned in Chapter 1, connection-oriented transport providers give reliable transmission of data between applications. All messages are guaranteed to arrive at their destination, and the sender can be sure that they arrive in the order sent. Connectionless transport providers, on the other hand, do not guarantee delivery of a message but let you address each message separately. Chapter 1 discussed the types of applications suitable for each mode of service.

By using TLI, the client side and the server side of your networking application get a ''transport endpoint,'' and you use that endpoint for all communication. A transport endpoint is your interface into the network.

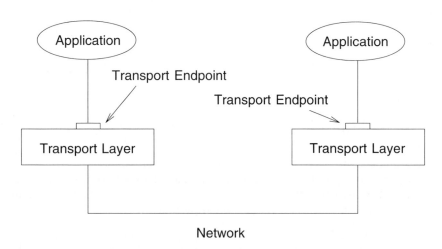

Figure 7.1   Transport Endpoints

For example, a transport endpoint over connection-oriented transport providers is like a telephone. When placing a phone call, the telephone is the end of the network. You interface directly with the telephone when communicating with another party, and you are not concerned with the details of voice transmission.

Similarly, a transport endpoint on connectionless transport provider is like a post office mailbox. When sending letters, the mailbox is the end of the network. You interface directly with the mailbox when sending and receiving letters, and you are not concerned with the details of how the letter gets to its destination.

When discussing TLI, we will also use the term ''transport user.'' A transport user is simply an application that accesses the services of a transport provider. Both the client side and the server side of an application are transport users. Transport users attach themselves to the transport provider through the transport endpoint.

Figure 7.1 shows two transport users (that is, two networking applications) communicating through their respective transport endpoints. The transport endpoint can be attached to either a connection-oriented transport provider or a connectionless transport provider. As far as the application is concerned, the transport endpoint is the ''end'' of the network. After the application sends data through the transport endpoint, it is not concerned with the details of transmission.

TLI provides routines that let you manage transport endpoints. When using a connection-oriented transport provider, TLI provides routines that let you attach a transport address to an endpoint, make a connection to another endpoint, and perform other operations. When using a connectionless transport provider, TLI lets you send and receives messages between endpoints.

When Should You Use TLI?

You should use TLI to create sophisticated applications that have full control over the transport provider. Applications using TLI can negotiate transport-provider options, manage multiple network connections simultaneously, and monitor transport-provider events.

You should also use TLI when creating applications that cannot use the Remote Procedure Call mechanism. RPC is easier to use than TLI, because it calls most of the lower-level networking routines for you. However, some networking applications do not fit into the RPC model.

For example, consider a remote-login application, which must maintain a two-way communication channel between the client machine and the server machine. The client side of the application must send commands, data, and signals to the server side of the application. The server side of the application must send command results and error information to the client side. Applications like that do not fit the procedure-call model.

Summary of TLI Routines

TLI routines let you do all the processing needed to manage a session over a transport provider. The following list summarizes the routines.

Common management routines:

`t_open()`	Creates a transport endpoint and return a file descriptor.
`t_bind()`	Assigns a transport address to an endpoint.
`t_unbind()`	Detaches a transport address from an endpoint.
`t_close()`	Destroys an endpoint.
`t_optmgmt()`	Negotiates options with a transport provider.
`t_getinfo()`	Gets transport-provider specific information.

`t_getstate()`	Gets the current state of the endpoint.
`t_sync()`	Synchronizes the application with the transport provider.
`t_alloc()`	Allocates memory for TLI structures.
`t_free()`	Frees allocated memory.
`t_error()`	Prints error messages.
`t_look()`	Gets the current event on the endpoint.

Connection-mode routines:

`t_connect()`	Connects to a remote transport user.
`t_rcvconnect()`	Receives an asynchronous notification of an accepted connection.
`t_listen()`	Listens for a connection request to arrive.
`t_accept()`	Accepts a connection request.
`t_snd()`	Sends data.
`t_rcv()`	Receives data.
`t_snddis()`	Sends a disconnect request.
`t_rcvdis()`	Receives a disconnect request.
`t_sndrel()`	Sends an orderly release request.
`t_rcvrel()`	Receives an orderly release indication.

Connectionless-mode routines:

`t_sndudata()`	Sends a datagram.
`t_rcvudata()`	Receives a datagram.
`t_rcvuderr()`	Reads information about an error in a previous datagram.

TLI routines maintain an integer global variable called `t_errno`. If a TLI routine fails, you can examine the `t_errno` variable to figure out the reason for failure.

TLI routines let you manage network communication. However, they only provide an interface to the network. Within your application, you must still handle:

1. The actions of the *application layer* of the OSI model. You must define the networking service, specify the data the service requires, and detail the service results. And, of course, you must implement the service on the server machine.

2. The actions of the *presentation layer* of the OSI Model. You must place all data in a common format to handle differences in data representation. We show ways to handle the presentation layer in Chapter 8.

3. The actions of the *session layer* of the OSI Model. Your application must manage the session by providing ''over'' and ''over and out'' synchronization messages. We show ways to handle the session layer in Chapter 8.

The TLI routines let your applications interface with the *transport layer* of the OSI model, so you do not have to worry about the details of network transmission.

As mentioned throughout the book, the client side of the application uses a transport address to locate the server side of the application. TLI is designed to work with any transport provider, so it handles transport addresses in a flexible way. We now show how applications specify transport addresses using TLI.

Transport Addresses

TLI is designed to work with any transport provider. And, because different transport providers have different address formats, TLI lets you specify any type of address.

TLI defines a generic network structure named **netbuf**, which holds all types of information, including transport addresses. It also holds data in datagrams, transport-provider option information, and other pieces of information. The **netbuf** structure definition follows:

```
struct netbuf {
    unsigned int maxlen;
    unsigned int len;
    char         *buf;
}
```

The **buf** element of the **netbuf** structure is a buffer that holds a sequence of bytes. The **len** element specifies the number of bytes in the buffer, and the **maxlen** element specifies the maximum number of bytes the buffer can hold.

When the structure contains a transport address, the **buf** element is a buffer containing the address. The **len** element specifies the number of bytes in the address, and **maxlen** is not used.

For example, the SVR4 implementation of TCP/IP represents a TCP transport address as four pieces of information:

1. A 2-byte field containing a protocol identifier. For TCP, the value is always **2**.

2. A 2-byte field containing the TCP port number of the service. We describe TCP port numbers in Chapter 3.

3. A 4-byte field containing the IP address of the machine offering service. We describe the IP address in Chapter 3.

4. An 8-byte filler. The filler value is always **0**.

If TCP/IP is used to communicate with a remote service, you must fill the **buf** field of the **netbuf** structure with the address in the above format. We will see an example in Chapter 8.

As mentioned earlier, the `netbuf` structure holds other types of data. We will see how to use the `netbuf` structure throughout the chapter.

Addresses are not the only things that TLI handles in a flexible way. Because some transport providers support logical message boundaries, TLI supports that as well. TLI lets you send a Transport Service Data Unit (TSDU), described next.

Transport Service Data Units

TLI supports the concept of a Transport Service Data Unit (TSDU). A TSDU is a unit of data that one side of your application sends to the other. The unit has a logical boundary, that is, a distinct size.

A TSDU is similar to a piece of paper with data written on it. If one side of your application sends three TSDUs, it is like sending three pieces of paper. When the receiver reads the data, it sees the data as three separate entities. The TSDUs do not have to be the same length (that is, each piece of paper can be a different size), but the transport provider may impose a maximum-size TSDU.

On a connectionless transport provider, the maximum TSDU is the maximum number of bytes you can send in a datagram. Each datagram is a separate TSDU.

On a connect-oriented transport provider, the maximum TSDU is the maximum number of bytes in a single message unit. A message unit is a piece of data that retains its message boundary across the network.

As illustrated in Figure 7.2, TSDUs on connection-oriented transport providers let you structure data easily. For example, suppose you had to create a networking application in which the client side of the application sent information about two company employees to the server side of the application. You could place the information about each employee in a separate TSDU. By doing that, the server side of the application knows where the information about one employee ends and the information about the next employee begins.

TLI routines tell the reader when the TSDU is completely read. To illustrate, suppose you send `1024` bytes of data in a single TSDU. It is possible that the TSDU is divided into smaller pieces as it travels over the network to its destination. For example, to avoid network congestion, software under the transport layer may partition the message into smaller pieces. Because of that, the reader may only find the first `25` bytes when first retrieving the TSDU. However, the TLI routines let the reader know that more of the TSDU is coming. The reader keeps reading the data until they consume the entire TSDU. We describe the details in the `t_rcv()` heading of Section 7.9.

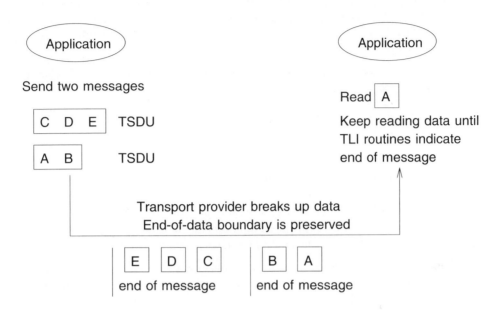

Figure 7.2   TSDUs on Connection-Oriented Transport Providers

Some connection-oriented transport providers do not support the concept of a TSDU. For example, *the Transmission Control Protocol (TCP) does not support message boundaries and therefore it does not support a TSDU.* TCP is a stream-oriented protocol, so it sends data as a stream of bytes.

For example, suppose you sent `1024` bytes of data into a TCP transport endpoint. The TCP software may divide the data into smaller pieces before delivering them to the destination. The reader may only consume the first `25` bytes, and the TLI routines will *not* let the reader know that more data are coming. That is because TCP does not support message boundaries.

We'll describe how to figure out if a transport provider supports a TSDU in Section 7.9. If you use a connection-oriented transport provider that does not support a TSDU, your application can do one of several things to compensate for the lack of message boundaries:

1.   The sender can write a special sequence of bytes to signify the end of a message. For example, you can send the `NULL` character to show the end of a string. The reader keeps reading until it reads the `NULL` character.

2. The sender can deliver a fixed-length header message that contains the length of
    the data. The reader keeps reading until it gets the entire header. When it reads
    the full header, the application examines it to figure out the length of the subse-
    quent data.

3. The sender and the receiver can agree on the length of each message. The
    reader keeps reading until it gets a full message.

Now let's look at how to use TLI routines to manage transport endpoints. We begin
by presenting the details of connection-mode service.

7.3   TLI Connection-Mode Service

Using TLI over a connection-oriented transport provider is similar to placing a telephone call. The client side of the application acts as the person doing the calling. The
server side of the application acts as the person accepting the phone call.

By using that analogy, both parties get a telephone (that is, a transport endpoint) before
communication begins. In SVR4, applications get a transport endpoint by using the
TLI routines to open a device file.

Here's how it works. Every connection-oriented transport provider in SVR4 has many
device files. As mentioned in Chapter 2, each device file has a major number and a
minor number. The major number identifies the transport provider (for example, the
Transmission Control Protocol), and the minor number identifies a unique transport
endpoint within that transport provider. In many networking environments, a transport
provider requires that each application create a unique transport endpoint to establish
communication. In that case, if your application attempts to open a device file that
another application is using, the attempt fails.

So, to get a transport endpoint, your application must use TLI routines to open a device file that is not currently used by another application. Searching for an unused device file can be tedious, so SVR4 provides clone devices (described in Chapter 2) that
expedite the search. Each transport provider has a corresponding clone device file.
Your application simply opens the clone device file. The clone device finds an unused
device file, opens it, and returns the file descriptor to your application.

Now let's look at the steps involved in setting up communication. Figure 7.3 shows
the initial setup sequence. In the server side of the application, you must:

1. Open the clone device corresponding to the transport provider using the
    `t_open()` routine. That returns a file descriptor into the transport provider.
    The file descriptor is the transport endpoint. This action is similar to getting a
    telephone.

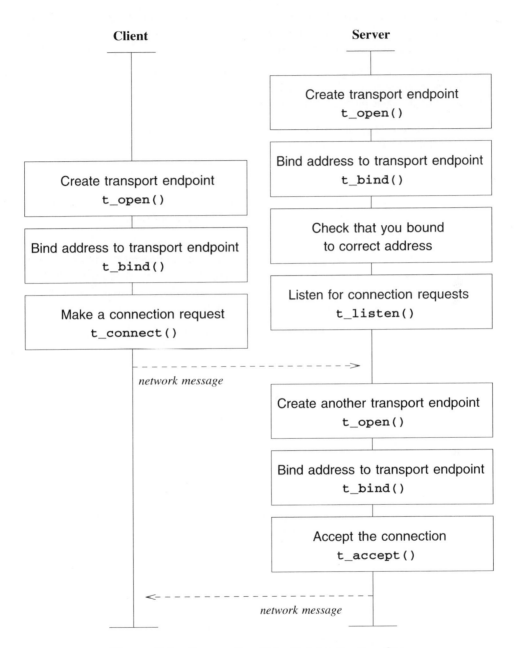

Figure 7.3   Connection-Oriented Application Setup

2. Bind a transport address to the transport endpoint using the **t_bind()** routine. This is like getting a phone number that people use to call you. The format of the transport address depends upon which transport provider you are using.

3. Check that you bound to the address you asked for. TLI routines may return an unused address if the requested address is already in use. If you did not bind to the address asked for, you have several options:

    a. Exit the application with an error indication, telling the administrator of the server machine that another application is using the address you want to use. Here, you asked for a telephone number, but were told the telephone number is already used by someone else.

    b. Use the new address, but inform everyone of your new address. In our telephone analogy, this is like changing the telephone book to reflect your new telephone number.

4. Listen for connection requests using the **t_listen()** routine. The **t_listen()** routine sleeps waiting for a connection request to arrive. This is like waiting for the phone to ring. When a connection request arrives (that is, the phone rings), the **t_listen()** routine returns.

5. When the **t_listen()** routine returns (that is, the phone is ringing), you must do the following:

    a. Get *another* transport endpoint by using the **t_open()** routine again. This gets a second telephone.

    b. Bind a transport address to the new transport endpoint using the **t_bind()** routine. This is like assigning an arbitrary telephone number to the second telephone.

    c. Accept the connection request using the **t_accept()** routine. You pass *both* transport endpoints to the **t_accept()** routine (that is, the telephone that is ringing and the new telephone). The **t_accept()** routine accepts the connection on the *second* transport endpoint. Using our telephone analogy, the **t_accept()** routine answers the ringing telephone and transfers the call to the new telephone. When **t_accept()** returns, the original transport endpoint can now wait for new calls, and the second transport endpoint is connected to the caller. Usually, the application issues the **fork()** system call when the **t_accept()** routine returns. The child process handles the new connection. The parent process issues another **t_listen()** call using the original transport endpoint and waits for the phone to ring again.

On the client side of the application, you must do the following:

1. Open the clone device corresponding to the transport provider using the
    `t_open()` routine. That returns a file descriptor into the transport provider.
    The file descriptor is the transport endpoint. This action is similar to getting a
    telephone.

2. Bind a transport address to the transport endpoint using the `t_bind()` routine.
    That is like getting a phone number. Here, you don't really care what your tele-
    phone number is, because no one is going to call. You are placing the outgoing
    call.

3. Establish a connection with the server machine using the `t_connect()` rou-
    tine. You must specify the transport address of the server side of the applica-
    tion. This is like dialing a phone and placing a phone call.

We now have a connection between two transport users. As illustrated in Figure 7.4,
data can be sent over the connection using the following routines:

1. The `t_snd()` routine is used to send data from one transport user to another.
    The `t_snd()` routine lets you send either normal data or expedited data.
    Expedited data are ''emergency data'' that should be sent as quickly as possible.
    Different transport providers handle expedited data differently. However, most
    transport providers place expedited data ahead of normal data when they get to
    the server's transport endpoint.

2. The `t_rcv()` routine is used to read data sent by the peer transport user.

After all communication is finished, we can close down the virtual circuit. There are
two ways to do this:

1. Perform an **abrupt shutdown**. This is like hanging up the phone. You do this
    in one of three ways:

    a. Exit the application.

    b. Issue the `t_close()` routine on the transport endpoint.

    c. Issue the `t_snddis()` routine to explicitly send a disconnect message.
        The `t_snddis()` routine lets you send data with the disconnection
        request if the transport provider allows. We will see how to figure out if
        the transport provider allows that in the `t_open()` heading of Section
        7.9.

    An abrupt shutdown destroys the connection and may destroy any data in transit
    (that is, any data that have not been received by the peer transport user).

2. Perform an **orderly shutdown**. This is like telling your peer ''I'm finished talk-
    ing'' and waiting for the peer to reply with ''OK, I'm also finished talking.''
    This type of shutdown is sometimes called ''orderly release.'' You use the
    `t_sndrel()` and the `t_rcvrel()` routines to perform orderly release.

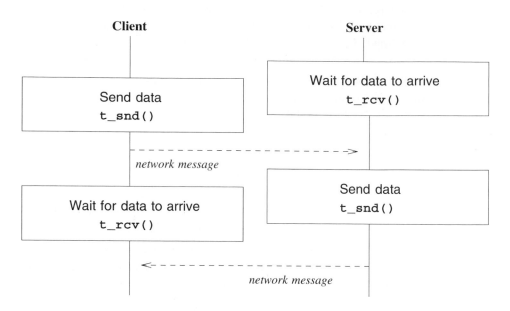

Figure 7.4 Connection-oriented Application Data Transfer

However, some transport providers do not support this feature. If a transport provider does not allow orderly release, you must use an abrupt shutdown. We will see how to figure out if a transport provider allows orderly release in the `t_open()` heading of Section 7.9.

In the actions just described, the application waited for an action to complete. For example, the `t_listen()` routine waited for a connection request to arrive and did not return until a connection request appeared. If you wait for an action to complete, your application is in the **synchronous mode**. Your application can also run in the **asynchronous mode**, in which you do not wait for an action to complete. Details of these two modes are described next.

Synchronous and Asynchronous Modes

Your application can run in one of two modes: **synchronous mode** or **asynchronous mode**. As we will see in Section 7.9, you specify the type of mode when the `t_open()` routine is issued.

In the synchronous mode, the TLI routines do not return to your application until the operation is complete (that is also called **blocking mode**). For example, if the client side of the application issues a `t_connect()` routine, that routine does not return until the connection is established. In our telephone analogy, this is like dialing a telephone and waiting for the peer to answer.

In the asynchronous mode, TLI routines return before the operation completes (that is also called **nonblocking mode**). For example, if the client side of the application issues a `t_connect()` routine in the asynchronous mode, that routine returns immediately. When the acknowledgment of the connection arrives, the client side of the application must issue a `t_rcvconnect()` to complete the connection. In our telephone analogy, this is like dialing a phone, going away to do something else, and periodically checking to see if the peer has answered.

You should use the synchronous mode if you want to wait for functions to complete. For example, suppose you issued the `t_rcv()` routine. In the synchronous mode, that routine waits for data to arrive before returning to your application. If you must have the data before you can do any other processing, then you should be in the synchronous mode.

You should use the asynchronous mode if there are other tasks to do while waiting for a TLI function to complete. For example, the `t_rcv()` routine in the asynchronous mode returns immediately if no data are available. That lets your applications do other processing and periodically poll the transport endpoint until data arrive.

Applications running in the asynchronous mode must be aware of when an event happens. For example, if the client side of the application issues the `t_connect()` routine, it must know when the acknowledgment arrives (so it can issue the `t_rcvconnect()` routine to complete the connection). Here, the event is the arrival of the connection acknowledgment. You can check if an event happened in one of two ways:

1. Use the `t_look()` routine periodically to figure out if an event occurred on a transport endpoint. We describe the possible events in the next section.

2. Set up the transport provider to send you a **SIGPOLL** signal when an event happens. You do that with the following `ioctl()` call:

    ```
    ioctl(fd, I_SETSIG, S_INPUT);
    ```

    Here, `fd` is the file descriptor into the transport endpoint. When you get the **SIGPOLL** signal, issue the `t_look()` routine to see what event occurred. We present details in Chapter 8.

TLI defines a distinct set of events that can happen on a transport endpoint. The following section details those events.

7.4 Transport Endpoint Events

There are several events that can happen to a transport endpoint on a connection-oriented transport provider. TLI gives names to those events:

T_LISTEN   A connection indication has arrived on the transport endpoint of the server side of the application.

T_CONNECT   A connection confirmation has arrived on the transport endpoint of the client side of the application.

T_DATA   Normal data have arrived on the transport endpoint.

T_EXDATA   Expedited data have arrived on the transport endpoint.

T_DISCONNECT   The other side of the application (or the transport provider itself) has shut down the connection.

T_ORDREL   An orderly release indication has arrived on the transport endpoint.

You must check for those events if you are in the asynchronous mode. As mentioned in Section 7.3, you use the **t_look()** routine to figure out which event is on the transport endpoint.

For example, suppose the client side of the application is in the asynchronous mode. It calls the **t_connect()** routine to connect to the server and then periodically checks if the **T_CONNECT** event occurs on its transport endpoint. When that event occurs, the application calls the **t_rcvconnect()** routine to complete the connection.

When an event happens, you must consume the event with a TLI routine. The following is what you do for each event:

- Consume the **T_LISTEN** event by issuing the **t_listen()** routine. This event only happens on the server side of an application.

- Consume the **T_CONNECT** event by issuing the **t_rcvconnect()** routine. This event only happens on the client side of the application.

- Consume the **T_DATA** event and the **T_EXDATA** event by issuing the **t_rcv()** routine. The client side and the server side of the application can get this event.

- Consume the **T_DISCONNECT** event by issuing the **t_rcvdis()** routine. The client side and the server side of the application can get this event.

- Consume the **T_ORDREL** event by issuing the **t_rcvrel()** routine. The client side and the server side of the application can get this event.

Even if you are in the synchronous mode, an asynchronous event can happen. For example, if you are reading data from a transport endpoint, the **T_DISCONNECT** event can happen if the peer unexpectedly terminates or closes the connection.

When an unexpected event happens, several TLI routines return an error and set the `t_errno` value to the **TLOOK** error. The **TLOOK** error tells your application to check the event on the transport endpoint. The following lists the TLI routines that can set the **TLOOK** error and the events that caused the error:

- The following routines return an error and set `t_errno` to **TLOOK** when the **T_DISCONNECT** event happens:

`t_accept()`	`t_connect()`	`t_listen()`	`t_snd()`
`t_rcv()`	`t_rcvconnect()`	`t_rcvrel()`	`t_snddis()`

- Additionally, the following routines return an error and set `t_errno` to **TLOOK** when the **T_ORDREL** event occurs:

`t_snd()`	`t_rcv()`

If one of those TLI routines returns the **TLOOK** error, you can use the `t_look()` routine to see the event that caused the error. If the event is **T_DISCONNECT**, issue the `t_rcvdis()` function to complete the abortive release. If the event is **T_ORDREL**, use the `t_rcvrel()` routine to complete the orderly release.

Because you do many operations on a transport endpoint, it is in a well-defined state at any given moment. The state tells you the valid operations that can occur. We now present the states of a transport endpoint for a connection-mode transport provider.

7.5   Connection-Mode Transport Endpoint States

TLI defines the operations that you can do on a transport endpoint based on the current state of that endpoint. The transport endpoints on the client side and the server side of an application have well-defined states.

Figure 7.5 shows the states of the transport endpoint on the client side of the application. TLI defines the states as follows:

1. The transport endpoint is in the **T_UNINIT** (uninitialized) state when no application has it opened.

2. In the **T_UNINIT** state, your application can issue the `t_open()` routine to create a file descriptor into the transport endpoint. When that routine completes, it places the transport endpoint in the **T_UNBND** (unbound) state. Although not shown in Figure 7.5, you can issue the `t_close()` routine in this state and in any subsequent state. That closes the transport endpoint and places it back into the **T_UNINIT** state.

3. You can now issue the `t_bind()` routine to attach a transport address to the transport endpoint. Upon completion, the transport endpoint is in the **T_IDLE** (idle) state. Although not shown in Figure 7.5, you can issue the `t_unbind()`

routine in the **T_IDLE** state. That places the transport endpoint back into the **T_UNBND** state.

4. In the **T_IDLE** state, you can issue the **t_connect()** routine to connect to the server side of the application. If you are in the synchronous mode, the transport endpoint is in the **T_DATAXFER** (data-transfer) state when the **t_connect()** routine completes. If you are in the asynchronous mode, the transport endpoint is in the **T_OUTCON** state when the **t_connect()** routine returns. When the connection acknowledgment arrives from the server side of the application, you issue the **t_rcvconnect()** routine to place the transport endpoint in the **T_DATAXFER** state.

5. The transport endpoint stays in the **T_DATAXFER** state while you exchange data (via the **t_snd()** and **t_rcv()** routines). Besides exchanging data, this state lets you do an abrupt or orderly shutdown.

6. If you initiate an abrupt shutdown from the **T_DATAXFER** state (via the **t_snddis()** routine) or if you receive an abrupt shutdown indication from the server side of the application (via the **t_rcvdis()** routine), the transport endpoint goes back to the **T_IDLE** state.

7. If you initiate an orderly shutdown from the **T_DATAXFER** state (via the **t_sndrel()** routine), the transport endpoint goes to the **T_OUTREL** state. You can still issue the **t_rcv()** routine to receive messages from the server side of the application in this state. Recall that an orderly release indication tells the server side of the application that you are finished sending data. However, the server side of the application can continue sending data to you.

    After you get an orderly release indication from the server side of the application (via the **t_rcvrel()** routine), the transport endpoint goes to the **T_IDLE** state. If you get an abrupt shutdown indication from the server side of the application while you are in the **T_OUTREL** state (or if you send an abrupt shutdown request), the transport endpoint goes to the **T_IDLE** state as well.

8. If you receive an orderly shutdown request from the server side of the application while the transport endpoint is in the **T_DATAXFER** state (via the **t_rcvrel()** routine), the transport endpoint goes to the **T_INREL** state. You can still issue the **t_snd()** routine to send messages to the server side of the application. An orderly release indication from the server side of the applications tells you that the server is finished sending data. However, you can still send messages to the server side of the application before sending the orderly release acknowledgment.

    After you acknowledge the orderly release (via the **t_sndrel()** routine), the transport endpoint goes to the **T_IDLE** state. An abrupt shutdown indication at the **T_OUTREL** state causes the transport endpoint to go to the **T_IDLE** state as well.

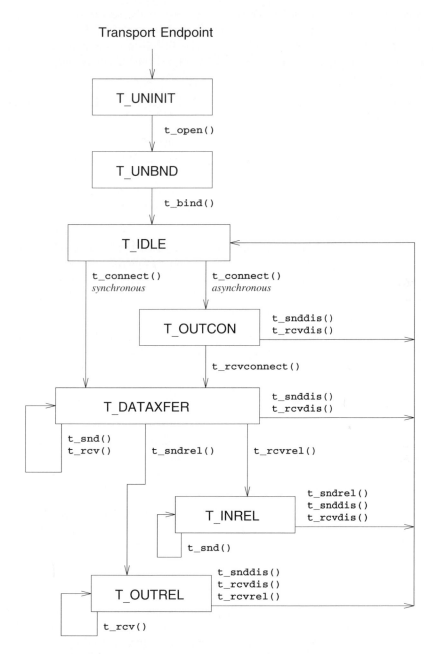

Figure 7.5   Client Transport Endpoint States

The transport endpoint states also dictate the actions of the server side of the application. Figure 7.6 shows those states. As mentioned in Section 7.3, the server side of the application has *two* transport endpoints. The first listens for connection requests, and the second accepts the connections. TLI defines the transport endpoint states on the server side of the application as follows:

1. The transport endpoint is in the **T_UNINIT** state before the server side of your application accesses it.

2. In the **T_UNINIT** state, your application issues the **t_open()** routine to create a file descriptor into the transport endpoint. When that routine completes, it places the transport endpoint in the **T_UNBND** state. As with the client side of the application, you can issue the **t_close()** routine in this state and in any subsequent state. That closes the transport endpoint and places it back into the **T_UNINIT** state.

3. In the **T_UNBND** state, you can issue the **t_bind()** routine to attach a transport address to the transport endpoint. Upon completion, the transport endpoint is in the **T_IDLE** state. Although not shown in Figure 7.6, you can issue the **t_unbind()** routine from the **T_IDLE** state. That places the transport endpoint back into the **T_UNBND** state.

4. In the **T_IDLE** state, you can issue the **t_listen()** routine to wait for incoming connections. If you are in the synchronous mode, the transport endpoint is in the **T_INCON** (incoming connection) state when the **t_listen()** routine completes. If you are in the asynchronous mode, the transport endpoint remains in the **T_IDLE** state until a connection request arrives.

5. When the transport endpoint is in the **T_INCON** state, you can accept the connection. As mentioned in Section 7.3, you must have two transport endpoints when you accept the connection. The second endpoint must be in the **T_IDLE** state (it gets to the **T_IDLE** state after you complete the **t_open()** routine and the **t_bind()** routine).

6. The **t_accept()** routine places the first transport endpoint in the **T_IDLE** state and the second transport endpoint in the **T_DATAXFER** state. You can call **t_listen()** again on the first transport endpoint.

   Although not shown in Figure 7.6, there are two other conditions that can occur when you call the **t_accept()** routine:

   • You may specify that your application wants to queue connection requests (we describe how to do that in the **t_bind()** heading of Section 7.9). In our telephone analogy, this is like having a feature that allows several calls to arrive simultaneously. Here, the first transport endpoint goes to the **T_INCON** state if another connection request has arrived. From that state, issue another **t_listen()** routine followed by the **t_accept()** routine.

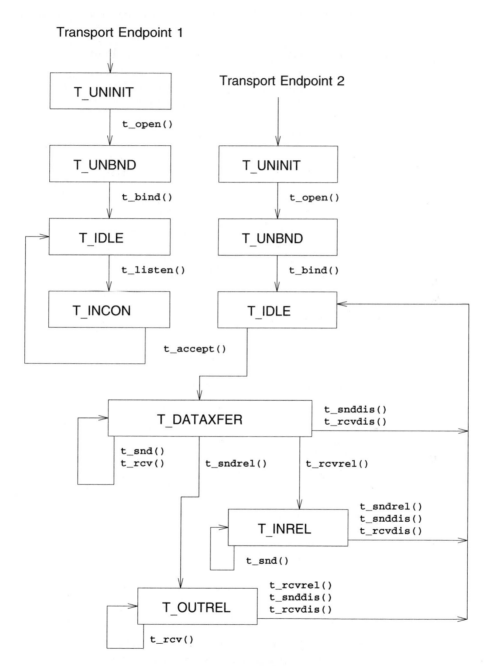

Figure 7.6   Server Transport Endpoint States

We present the details of how to handle queued connection requests in Chapter 8.

- You may accept the connection request using the same transport endpoint on which you issued the `t_listen()` routine. In our telephone analogy, this is like accepting the call on the same phone that was ringing. This puts the transport endpoint in the `T_DATAXFER` state. In that state, you cannot listen for another connection request until the connection is shut down and the transport endpoint goes into the `T_IDLE` state.

7. The second transport endpoint is now in the `T_DATAXFER` state. The valid operations in this state are the same as on the client side of the application.

Your application can issue the `t_getstate()` routine at any time to see the current state of a transport endpoint. That routine takes a file descriptor corresponding to a transport endpoint and returns an integer corresponding to the transport endpoint state.

Now let's look at how to use TLI routines with a connectionless transport provider. A connectionless transport provider lets you send and receive datagrams.

7.6   TLI Connectionless-Mode Service

Using TLI over a connectionless transport provider is very similar to sending a postal letter. The client side of the application acts as the person sending the letter. The server side of the application acts as the person receiving the letter.

Using this analogy, both parties must get a mailbox (that is, a transport endpoint) before communication can begin. In SVR4, applications get a transport endpoint by using TLI routines to open a device file.

As with connection-oriented transport providers, every connectionless transport provider in SVR4 has many device files. The major number of each device file identifies the transport provider (for example, the User Datagram Protocol), and the minor number identifies a unique transport endpoint within that transport provider. As mentioned earlier, some transport providers require that each application create a unique transport endpoint to establish communication. In that case, if your application attempts to open a device file that another application is using, the attempt fails.

Because of that, applications usually open a clone device file (described in Chapter 2) to find a device file with an unused minor number. The clone device finds an unused device file, opens it, and returns the file descriptor to your application.

Now let's look at the steps involved in setting up communication. Figure 7.7 shows the initial setup sequence. On the server side of the application, you must:

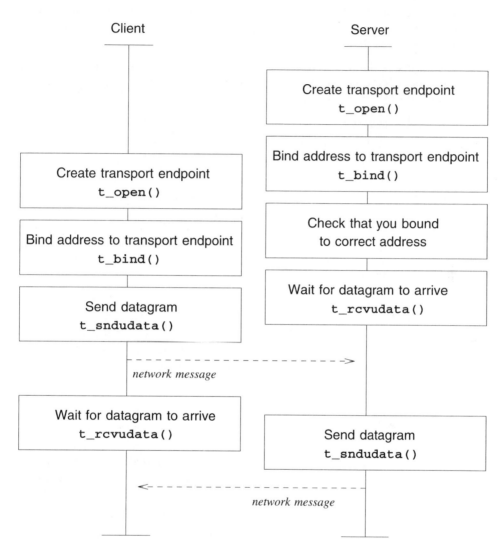

Figure 7.7   Connectionless Application Communication

1. Open the clone device corresponding to the transport provider using the
    `t_open()` routine. That returns a file descriptor into the transport provider.
    The file descriptor is the transport endpoint. This action is similar to getting the
    mailbox.

2. Attach a transport address to the transport endpoint using the `t_bind()` routine. This is like assigning a postal address to the mailbox. People use that postal address when they send you letters.

3. As with connection-oriented applications, check that you bound to the address asked for. TLI routines return an unused address if the requested address is already in use.

4. Wait for a datagram to arrive using the `t_rcvudata()` routine. This is like waiting for a letter to appear in your mailbox. When a message arrives, the `t_rcvudata()` routine returns the data and the transport address of the sender.

5. If needed, send a reply with the `t_sndudata()` routine. This is like sending a letter. You must specify the destination address when sending the datagram.

On the client side of the application, you must do the following:

1. Open the clone device corresponding to the transport provider using the `t_open()` routine. That returns a file descriptor into the transport provider. This action is like getting a mailbox.

2. Bind a transport address to the transport endpoint using the `t_bind()` routine. This is like assigning a postal address to the mailbox. Here, you don't really care what your address is. When sending a datagram, your transport address is sent with the data. So, if the server side of the application must return data, it can look at the datagram to figure out your transport address.

3. Send a message to the server side of the application using the `t_sndudata()` routine.

4. If you expect a response, issue the `t_rcvudata()` to wait for the response to arrive. However, because you are using a connectionless transport provider, *the response may never arrive!* Connectionless transport providers do not guarantee delivery. The response may not arrive because the original message was lost or because the server's response was lost.

   Therefore, you must time out and resend the request if you do not get a response after a period of time. We will see an example of how to do that in Chapter 8.

In the actions just described, the application waited for an action to complete. For example, the `t_rcvudata()` routine waited for a datagram to arrive and did not return until a datagram appeared on the transport endpoint. That type of behavior is called the **synchronous mode**. Your application can also run in the **asynchronous mode**, in which you do not wait for an action to complete. Details are described next.

Synchronous and Asynchronous Modes

As with connection-oriented applications, connectionless applications can run in either the synchronous or the asynchronous mode. As we will see in Section 7.9, you specify the type of mode when you issue the `t_open()` routine.

In the synchronous mode, TLI routines do not return to your application until the operation is complete. When using connectionless transport providers, this only applies to the `t_rcvudata()` routine. In the synchronous mode, the `t_rcvudata()` routine sleeps until a datagram arrives. In the asynchronous mode, the `t_rcvudata()` returns immediately if a datagram is not present on the transport endpoint.

Applications running in the asynchronous mode must be aware of when an event happens. For example, an event that can occur is the arrival of a datagram on the transport endpoint. You can check if an event occurs in one of two ways:

1. Use the `t_look()` routine periodically to figure out if an event occurs on a transport endpoint. We describe the events on a transport endpoint in the next section.

2. Set up the transport provider to send you a **SIGPOLL** signal when an event happens. Do this with the following `ioctl()` call:

    ```
    ioctl(fd, I_SETSIG, S_INPUT);
    ```

    Here, **fd** is the file descriptor into the transport endpoint. When you get the **SIGPOLL** signal, issue the `t_look()` routine to see what event occurred. We present details of the `t_look()` routine in Chapter 8.

TLI defines a distinct set of events that can happen on a transport endpoint into a connectionless transport provider. The following section details those events.

7.7   Connectionless-Mode Transport Endpoint Events

There are only two events that can happen to a transport endpoint into a connectionless transport provider:

T_DATA   A datagram has arrived on the transport endpoint.

T_UDERR   The system could not process a previous datagram you sent. This can happen if the destination address is invalid or some transport-provider-specific error occurs.

You consume the **T_DATA** event by issuing the `t_rcvudata()` routine. That routine returns the datagram to your application.

If the **T_UDERR** event occurs when you are in the synchronous mode, you will be notified when you try to issue the next **t_rcvudata()** routine. If the **T_UDERR** event is on the transport endpoint, the **t_rcvudata()** routine returns an error condition and sets **t_errno** to **TLOOK**.

When that happens, you must consume the event with the **t_rcvuderr()** routine. The **t_rcvuderr()** routine tells you information about the datagram that produced the event. We present the details of the **t_rcvuderr()** routine in Section 7.9.

The transport endpoint into a connectionless transport provider is in a well-defined state at any given moment. The state of the transport endpoint tells you the valid TLI operations that can occur. We now present the states of a transport endpoint into a connectionless transport provider.

7.8   Connectionless-Mode Transport Endpoint States

TLI defines the operations that can be done on a connectionless transport endpoint based on the current state of that endpoint. The states of a connectionless transport endpoint are the same for the client side and the server side of an application.

Figure 7.8 shows the states of a connectionless transport provider. The states follow:

1. The transport provider is in the **T_UNINIT** state when no application has it opened.

2. In the **T_UNINIT** state, your application can issue the **t_open()** routine to create a file descriptor into the transport endpoint. When that routine completes, it places the transport provider in the **T_UNBND** state. Although not shown in Figure 7.8, you can issue the **t_close()** routine in this state and in any subsequent state. That closes the transport endpoint and places it back into the **T_UNINIT** state.

3. In the **T_UNBND** state, you can issue the **t_bind()** routine to attach a transport address to the transport endpoint. Upon completion, the transport endpoint is in the **T_IDLE** state.

4. In the **T_IDLE** state, the transport provider can send and receive datagrams. Although not shown in Figure 7.8, you can also issue the **t_unbind()** routine in the **T_IDLE** state. That places the transport endpoint into the **T_UNBND** state.

Now let's take a closer look at the details of the TLI routines. We present the details of the routines that manage connection-oriented and connectionless transport providers.

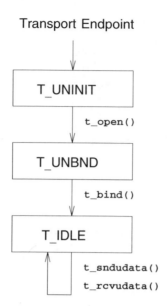

Figure 7.8 Connectionless Transport Endpoint States

7.9   Details of TLI Routines

The previous sections presented an overview of some TLI routines. Before showing an application that uses those routines, we present the details. Because the TLI routines depend upon one another, we present the routines in the order they are used in your applications.

t_open()

The **t_open()** routine is the first TLI routine you use in your application. It creates a transport endpoint and returns a file descriptor corresponding to that endpoint. You use it in the client side and the server side of your application, over both connection-oriented and connectionless transport providers.

The syntax follows:

```
#include <tiuser.h>
#include <fcntl.h>
```

```
int fd;
char *path;
int flag;
struct t_info info;

fd = t_open(path, flag, &info);
```

The `t_open()` routine returns a file descriptor that you use on all subsequent TLI routines. From an application's point of view, the file descriptor is the transport endpoint. The routine returns `-1` if it fails.

The `path` argument is a character string naming the device file corresponding to the transport provider. Usually, you specify a clone device file here. As mentioned in Chapter 2, opening a clone device file for a transport provider opens an unused device into that transport provider. If you don't specify a clone device file, your application must issue the `t_open()` routine on every device file corresponding to the transport provider, searching for an unused one.

The `flag` argument is an integer that specifies whether to create the transport endpoint in the synchronous mode or the asynchronous mode. For the synchronous mode, the flag must have the following value:

O_RDWR

To create the transport endpoint in the asynchronous mode, the flag must have the following value:

O_RDWR | O_NDELAY

or

O_RDWR | O_NONBLOCK

The third argument is a pointer to a `t_info` structure. The `t_open()` routine fills this structure with information about the transport provider. The `t_info` structure has the following form:

```
struct t_info {
      long addr;
      long options;
      long tsdu;
      long etsdu;
      long connect;
      long discon;
      long servtype;
};
```

All the fields except **servtype** contain information that you can use to allocate buffers for other TLI structures. For example, the **addr** element contains the maximum number of bytes in a transport address. You can use that when you allocate space to hold the transport address to which you want to attach. But, as we will show in what follows, you can also use the **t_alloc()** routine to allocate space for TLI structures.

The fields are defined as follows:

addr The maximum number of bytes in a transport address for the transport provider. If the value is **-1**, then there is no maximum address size. If the value is **-2**, then the transport provider does not let you use transport addresses, and you should not use the transport provider for your application.

options The maximum number of bytes needed to hold transport-provider-specific options. You set transport-specific options with the **t_optmgmt()** routine, described later in this section. If the value is **-1**, then there is no limit on the option size. If the value is **-2**, then the transport provider does not support user-settable options.

tsdu The maximum number of bytes in a Transport Service Data Unit (TSDU). As mentioned in Section 7.2, a TSDU is a piece of data that has a logical boundary. If this value is **0**, then the transport provider does not support the concept of a TSDU. However, it does let you send data without preserving data boundaries (the Transmission Control Protocol is an example of this). If the value is **-1**, then there is no limit on the TSDU size. If the value is **-2**, then the transport provider does not support the transfer of normal data.

etsdu The maximum number of bytes in an Expedited Transport Service Data Unit (ETSDU). An ETSDU is a TSDU that is marked "urgent." If the value is **0**, then the transport provider does not support the concept of a ETSDU. However, it does let you send expedited data without preserving data boundaries (again, the Transmission Control Protocol is an example of this). If the value is **-1**, then there is no limit on the ETSDU size. If the value is **-2**, then the transport provider does not support the transfer of expedited data.

connect The maximum number of bytes of data that you can send on a connection request. As we will see in the description of the **t_connect()** routine that follows, TLI lets you send user data to the server side of the application when you establish a connection. If this value is **-1**, then there is no limit on the amount of data that you can send on a connection request. If this value is **-2**, then the transport provider does not support the transfer of data on connection establishment.

discon   The maximum number of bytes of data that you can send on a discon-
          nection request. As we will see in the descriptions of the
          `t_snddis()` and `t_rcvdis()` routines that follow, TLI lets you
          send data when you tear down a connection. If this value is `-1`, then
          there is no limit on the amount of data that you can send when you tear
          down a connection. If this value is `-2`, then the transport provider does
          not support the transfer of data on connection teardown.

servtype Tells the type of service supported by the transport provider. It can
          have one of three values:

    T_COTS   The transport provider is connection-oriented but does
                 not support orderly shutdown.

    T_COTS_ORD   The transport provider is connection-oriented and sup-
                 ports orderly shutdown.

    T_CLTS   The transport provider supports connectionless service.
                 Here, `t_open()` places `-2` in the `etsdu`, con-
                 `nect` and `discon` fields of the `t_info` structure.
                 This is because a connectionless transport provider does
                 not support connection establishment and teardown, nor
                 does it support sending expedited data. The `tsdu` field
                 of the `t_info` structure contains the maximum amount
                 of data you can use in a single datagram.

You can use the information in the `t_info` structure to allocate space for data
buffers. You can also use it to figure out if you can send data on connection establishment or connection teardown.

You can specify a `NULL` value as the third argument to the `t_open()` routine. That
says you do not want the information contained in the `t_info` structure.

t_bind()

The `t_bind()` routine attaches a transport address to a transport endpoint. You use
the routine in the client side and the server side of your application. You can use it on
both connectionless and connection-oriented transport providers. It has the following
form:

```
#include <tiuser.h>

int fd;
struct t_bind *requestp;
```

```
struct t_bind *returnp;
int status;

status = t_bind(fd, requestp, returnp);
```

The three arguments to the **t_bind()** routine are the following:

1. A file descriptor corresponding to a transport endpoint (obtained from the **t_open()** routine).

2. A pointer to a structure containing the address to which you want to attach.

3. A pointer to a structure that contains the address to which you actually attached (this information is filled in by the **t_bind()** routine).

You must allocate space to hold the structures before calling the **t_bind()** routine. You can do that with the **t_alloc()** routine, described in what follows.

The second and third arguments are pointers to a **t_bind** structure. The **t_bind** structure has the following form:

```
struct t_bind {
    struct netbuf addr;
    unsigned      qlen;
}
```

The **addr** element contains a transport address. The address is a sequence of bytes in a **netbuf** structure. As described in Section 7.2, the **netbuf** structure is a TLI structure that holds information. It has three elements: **buf** (a buffer containing a sequence of bytes), **len** (the number of characters in **buf**), and **maxlen** (the maximum number of bytes **buf** can hold).

In the second argument (that is, the address to which you want to attach), the **buf** element of the **netbuf** structure contains the address. The **len** element contains the size of the address, and the **maxlen** element is not used. In the third argument (that is, the address that **t_bind()** fills in), the **maxlen** element must contain the size of the **buf** element.

As mentioned earlier, you use the **t_bind()** routine on both the server side and the client side of your application. However, you only use the **qlen** field of the **t_bind** structure on the server side. Additionally, you only use it on connection-oriented transport providers. On the client side of the application, you set **qlen** to **0**, indicating that you do not want to receive any incoming calls.

The `qlen` field specifies the maximum number of outstanding connection indications your application wants to support. An outstanding connection indication is a connection request that you have retrieved but have not accepted yet (you retrieve a connection request with the `t_listen()` routine and accept it with the `t_accept()` routine). It is like having several lights on a telephone, where each light goes on when an incoming call arrives. If you have five lights on the telephone, then you can have up to five connection requests arrive simultaneously. If every light is on (that is, the queue of incoming connection requests is full), all further connection requests may get an error. Every time you accept a call and listen for a new call, a light goes off (allowing a new connection request to arrive).

If `qlen` is 1, you have a maximum of one outstanding connection. In that case, there is only one light on the telephone. If you are not listening for connection requests, the application making the connection request may get an error. If `qlen` is n, then you can have up to n connection requests arrive simultaneously.

The `qlen` field affects the transport endpoint states. As described in Section 7.5, a transport provider can accept connection requests if the transport endpoint is in the `T_INCON` state. Normally, after you accept the connection, the transport endpoint goes to the `T_IDLE` state. You can then listen for a new connection request and accept it when it arrives.

However, if `qlen` is greater than 1, *you must retrieve all outstanding connection requests before you can accept any of them!* If you try to accept a connection request and a second connection request arrives, TLI will not let you accept the first connection request (that is, the `t_accept()` routine fails). You must issue the `t_listen()` routine to get information about the second connection request before you can accept either of the two. Going back to the telephone analogy, you must obtain information about all incoming calls before you can answer any of them.

TLI works that way so you can prioritize incoming calls. For example, you may want to listen for several connection requests and assign a priority to each. You can then accept the connections in the prioritized order (for example, you can base the priority on the client machine making the connection request). We show how to handle applications that set `qlen` greater than 1 in Chapter 8.

As a side note, the implementation of a transport provider may queue connection requests internally even if `qlen` is set to 1. However, if it does not do that, the new connection request is rejected. Going back to the telephone analogy, the new connection request is rejected because the telephone is busy. If the queue of incoming calls on the server side of the application is full, the client side of the application must retry the connection request.

For connectionless transport providers, the `qlen` field is ignored. A connectionless transport provider does not accept connections.

The **requestp** argument of the **t_bind()** routine contains the address to which you want to attach and the **qlen** value you want to use. The **t_bind()** routine tries to attach the transport endpoint to that address. However, if it can't use that address, it may attach the transport endpoint to another address. The **t_bind()** routine fills the **addr** field of the **returnp** argument with the address to which it attached. Also, if the specified **qlen** value is too high for the transport provider to handle, it may pick a new value. The **t_bind()** routine puts the new value in the **qlen** field of the **returnp** structure.

As mentioned in Section 7.3, there are several things you can do if you do not get the address you asked for. Typically, the server side of an application binds to a well-known address and the client side of the application connects to that address. In that case, the server side of the application usually exits if it doesn't get the address it asked for.

However, suppose the server side of the application publishes its address in a database and the client side of the application figures out the address by querying the database. In that case, the server side of the application may want to use the address to which it is attached, even if the address is not the one it asked for. The server side of the application would have to update the database to reflect the address to which it is attached.

If the **len** field of the **netbuf** structure in the **requestp** argument is **0**, the transport provider picks an unused address for you. You may want to do this if you don't care what the address is to which you bind. For example, the client side of an application must attach its transport endpoint to a transport address. But, because no other application is going to connect to it, the client side of the application may not care what address it gets.

Some server applications may want to attach to an arbitrary address as well. They can bind to an arbitrary address and tell a database server the address to which they bound. Recall that RPC services work that way. As explained in Chapter 6, the server side of an RPC application binds to an arbitrary, unused address and tells the **rpcbind** process the address to which it is bound. The client side of an RPC application queries the **rpcbind** process to figure out the transport address of the service.

If the **requestp** argument is **NULL**, the transport provider picks an unused address for you. Here, the **t_bind()** routine assumes the **qlen** field has the value of **0**. Because a **qlen** of **0** means the transport endpoint cannot accept any connections, you should only use a **NULL** value on the client side of the application.

You can also specify a **NULL** value for the **returnp** argument. That says you don't care to which address you are attached. You usually do not do this on the server side of the application. The server side accepts connection requests, so it must know the transport address to which it is bound. However, the client side of the application can specify a **NULL** value when it binds to an arbitrary address.

The `t_bind()` routine returns `0` on success. It returns `-1` if an error condition occurs.

t_unbind()

The `t_unbind()` routine detaches the transport endpoint from its address. You can use this on the client side and the server side of the application. It has the following form:

```
#include <tiuser.h>

int fd;
int status;

status = t_unbind(fd);
```

The file descriptor corresponds to a transport endpoint. The transport endpoint must have an address associated with it (that is, you must have previously issued the `t_bind()` routine). You can only call the routine when the transport endpoint is in the `T_IDLE` state. If you call it in any other state, the routine fails.

You should only use the `t_unbind()` routine to reuse a transport endpoint with a different transport address. The routine returns `0` on success and `-1` if an error occurs.

t_close()

The `t_close()` routine closes the transport endpoint and places it in the `T_UNINIT` state. You can call it in any transport endpoint state. It has the following form:

```
#include <tiuser.h>

int fd;
int status;

status = t_close(fd);
```

The **fd** argument is a file descriptor returned from the **t_open()** routine. The **t_close()** routine returns **-1** on error and **0** on success. You can only get an error if the file descriptor does not refer to a transport endpoint.

t_getinfo()

The **t_getinfo()** routine gets information about the transport endpoint. It gets the same information that the **t_open()** routine placed in the **t_info** structure. But, unlike the **t_open()** routine, you can call the **t_getinfo()** routine in any of the transport endpoint states.

The **t_getinfo()** routine is useful in a child process that inherited a transport endpoint (that is, a process that does not issue **t_open()** directly). It is also useful in functions that are passed a transport endpoint and want to find information about it.

The format of the routine follows:

```
#include <tiuser.h>

int fd;
struct t_info info;
int status;

status = t_getinfo(fd, &info);
```

The **fd** argument is a file descriptor returned by the **t_open()** routine. The **t_getinfo()** routine fills the **info** structure in the same way that the **t_open()** routine did (the fields of the **t_info** structure are detailed in the description of the **t_open()** routine). The **t_getinfo()** routine returns **0** on success and **-1** on failure.

t_getstate()

The **t_getstate()** routine lets you figure out the current state of the transport endpoint. As explained in Sections 7.5 and 7.8, the current state of a transport endpoint dictates the valid operations on that endpoint.

It has the following format:

```
#include <tiuser.h>

int fd;
int current_state;

current_state = t_getstate(fd);
```

The routine returns a -1 on failure. An error can occur if the transport endpoint is currently going through a state change or if the file descriptor does not refer to a valid transport endpoint.

If the return value is not -1, it is one of the following:

T_UNBND   The transport endpoint is not bound to a transport address.

T_IDLE   The transport endpoint is bound but in an idle state.

T_OUTCON   The client side of the application issued a **t_connect()** routine but the connection acknowledgment has not arrived.

T_INCON   The server side of the application has an incoming connection establishment request.

T_DATAXFER   The connection-oriented transport endpoint is in the data-transfer state.

T_OUTREL   The transport user has sent an orderly release indication and is waiting for an orderly release from its peer.

T_INREL   The transport endpoint has received an orderly release indication and the transport user has not sent an orderly release reply.

t_sync()

The **t_sync()** routine synchronizes your application with the transport endpoint. You use the routine when you have several processes manipulating the same transport endpoint.

As illustrated in Figure 7.9, you must use the **t_sync()** routine because the TLI functions are implemented in a user-level library. The library routines maintain data structures that must be kept synchronized with the data structures used in the SVR4 kernel.

For example, suppose your application created a transport endpoint via the **t_open()** routine and then created several child processes to manage that endpoint.

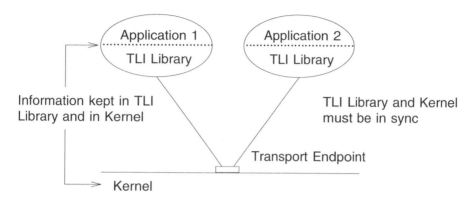

Figure 7.9   Two Applications Manipulating the Same Transport Endpoint

Because one of the child processes may change the state of the endpoint, each must issue the **t_sync()** routine to synchronize itself with the current state of the transport endpoint.

You can also use the **t_sync()** routine to initialize a transport endpoint. For example, suppose your application creates a transport endpoint and issues the **fork()** system call to create a child process. If the child process execs a new program, the new program must issue the **t_sync()** routine on the transport endpoint to initialize and synchronize itself with the current state of the transport endpoint.

The syntax of the **t_sync()** routine follows:

```
#include <tiuser.h>

int fd;
int current_state;

current_state = t_sync(fd);
```

The **fd** argument is a file descriptor into the transport endpoint. On success, the **t_sync()** returns the current state of the transport provider (that is, the same values that **t_getstate()** returns). It returns **-1** if an error occurs.

Note that if several processes are manipulating the same transport endpoint, it is possible that a process can change the transport provider's state *after* you call the **t_sync()** routine. So, if you must have several processes manipulating the same transport endpoint, you should coordinate their activities as not to change the state of the transport endpoint. Or, if a process must change the state of the transport endpoint, it should send a signal or use an interprocess communication mechanism to inform the other processes that they must call the **t_sync()** routine.

t_look()

The **t_look()** routine lets you examine the current event on a transport endpoint. Section 7.4 explained the events that can happen on transport endpoints into connection-oriented transport providers, and Section 7.7 explained the events that can happen on transport endpoints into connectionless transport providers.

If a TLI routine fails with **t_errno** set to **TLOOK**, then you can issue the **t_look()** routine to figure out what event caused the failure. If you are in the asynchronous mode, you can use the **t_look()** routine to figure out if an event occurred.

The syntax of the **t_look()** routine follows:

```
#include <tiuser.h>

int fd;
int current_event;

current_event = t_look(fd);
```

The **fd** argument is a file descriptor corresponding to a transport endpoint. The **t_look()** routine returns **-1** on failure, **0** if no event is on the transport endpoint, or one of the following values:

T_LISTEN   A connection indication has arrived on the transport endpoint in the server side of the application.

T_CONNECT   A connection confirmation has arrived on the transport endpoint in the client side of the application.

T_DATA   Normal data have arrived on the transport endpoint.

T_EXDATA   Expedited data have arrived on the transport endpoint.

T_DISCONNECT   The other side of the application has shut down the connection.

T_ORDREL   An orderly release indication has arrived on the transport endpoint.

T_UDERR   The previous datagram sent could not be processed.

You consume each event with a TLI routine. Sections 7.4 and 7.7 explain the TLI routines that consume each event.

t_connect()

The `t_connect()` routine establishes a connection. You can only use it on connection-oriented transport providers and only on the client side of the application.

The `t_connect()` routine lets the client side of the application establish a connection to the server side of the application. It also lets you send and receive data when you establish the connection.

The syntax follows:

```
#include <tiuser.h>

int fd;
int status;
struct t_call *send_infop;
struct t_call *return_infop;

status = t_connect(fd, send_infop, return_infop);
```

The `fd` argument is a file descriptor into a transport endpoint (created by the `t_open()` routine). The `send_infop` argument contains information that the transport provider needs to establish a connection. The `return_infop` argument is filled in by the `t_connect()` routine and contains information about the newly created connection.

The `send_infop` argument and the `return_infop` argument are pointers to a `t_call` structure. You must allocate space to hold the structures before calling the `t_connect()` routine (you can do that with the `t_alloc()` routine described in what follows). The `t_call` structure has the following form:

```
struct t_call {
        struct netbuf addr;
        struct netbuf opt;
        struct netbuf udata;
        int           sequence;
}
```

As described in Section 7.2, the `netbuf` structure is a TLI structure that holds information. It has three elements: `buf` (a buffer containing a sequence of bytes), `len` (the number of characters in `buf`), and `maxlen` (the maximum number of bytes `buf` can hold).

For the `send_infop` argument, the structure elements contain the following:

`addr`   Contains the transport address of the service to which you want to connect. Here, the `buf` field of the `netbuf` structure contains the address, the `len` field contains the number of bytes in the address, and the `maxlen` field is ignored.

`opt`   Contains transport-provider-specific options that you want to pass to the transport provider. For example, you can use this field on an OSI transport provider to negotiate quality-of-service parameters like the desired throughput and the allowable transit delay.

Unfortunately, using options makes your application inherently transport-provider-specific. You should not use this field unless one of the following is true:

1. Your application is intended to work over a predefined transport provider.

2. The information is obtained in a transport-independent way. For example, you can get the information from a database that maps transport-provider device names onto the options for that transport provider. We discuss that further in the description of the `t_optmgmt()` routine that follows.

If you use this field, the `buf` field of the `netbuf` structure contains the options, the `len` field contains the number of bytes in the options, and the `maxlen` field is ignored. If you do not use this field, the `len` field of the `netbuf` structure must be `0`.

`udata`   Contains data that you want to send to the service on connection establishment. For example, you may want to send the user's name or other data when you establish the connection. However, not all transport providers allow that to happen. You must examine the `connect` element of the `t_info` structure to figure out how much data you can send. You get the `t_info` information from the `t_open()` or the `t_getinfo()` routines.

If the transport provider lets you send user data on the connection establishment, then the `buf` field of the `netbuf` structure contains the data you want to send. The `len` field contains the number of bytes of data, and the `maxlen` field is ignored.

sequence   Do not use this field when making connections. It is used in the
           t_listen() and **t_accept()** routines, because they also use the
           t_call structure. The **t_listen()** and **t_accept()** routines are
           described in what follows.

The **return_infop** argument is filled in by the **t_connect()** routine and contains information about the connection. If that value is **NULL**, the **t_connect()** routine does not return any information about the connection.

If the **return_infop** argument is not **NULL**, the **t_connect()** routine uses the **maxlen** element of the **netbuf** structure to figure out the size of the associated buffers. If the **t_connect()** routine successfully establishes a connection, it fills the **t_call** structure elements with the following information:

addr   Contains the address to which you are connected. The **buf** element of
           the **netbuf** structure contains the address, and the **len** field contains
           the number of bytes in the address.

opt   Contains the transport-provider-specific options used in the connection
           establishment. The **buf** field of the **netbuf** structure contains the
           options, and the **len** field contains the number of bytes in the options.

udata   Contains data that the server may have sent on the connection acknowledgment. The server side of the application specifies the data in
           the **t_accept()** routine, described in what follows. Here, the **buf**
           field of the **netbuf** structure contains the data, and the **len** field contains the number of bytes in the data.

sequence   Not used. This field is not populated by the **t_connect()** routine.
           It is used in the **t_listen()** and the **t_accept()** routines (those
           routines also use the **t_call** structure).

If the transport endpoint is in the asynchronous mode, the **t_connect()** routine begins the connection establishment and returns without waiting for an acknowledgment. In that case, the **t_connect()** routine does not fill the **return_infop** argument and returns **-1**. However, it sets **t_errno** to **TNODATA**. That value of **t_errno** does not indicate a failure condition. It indicates that the connection is not established yet.

In all other cases, **t_connect()** returns **-1** on failure and **0** on success.

t_rcvconnect()

If your application is running in asynchronous mode, you can use the **t_rcvconnect()** routine to complete a connection request that the **t_connect()** routine started. You use it on the client side of your application, and you can only use it on connection-oriented transport providers.

When the `t_rcvconnect()` routine returns successfully, the connection to the server side of the application is complete. It has the following syntax:

```
#include <tiuser.h>

int fd;
int status;
struct t_call *return_infop;

status = t_rcvconnect(fd, return_infop);
```

The `fd` argument is a file descriptor into a transport endpoint that is in the **T_OUTCON** state. As described in Section 7.5, a transport endpoint is in the **T_OUTCON** state if you issued the `t_connect()` routine in the asynchronous mode.

The `return_infop` argument is a pointer to a `t_call` structure. You must allocate space to hold the structures before calling the `t_rcvconnect()` routine (you can do that with the `t_alloc()` routine, which is described in what follows).

The `t_rcvconnect()` routine fills the `t_call` structure with information about the newly established connection. It is filled in exactly the same way as if you had issued the `t_connect()` routine in the synchronous mode. The details of the structure elements and their meaning are given in the description of the `t_connect()` routine. And, as with the `t_connect()` routine, the `t_rcvconnect()` routine uses the **maxlen** element of the **netbuf** structure to figure out the size of the associated buffers.

You can use the `t_rcvconnect()` routine in three ways:

1. Stay in the asynchronous mode and periodically use the `t_rcvconnect()` routine to check if the connection acknowledgment arrived. If the connection acknowledgment has not arrived, the `t_rcvconnect()` routine returns `-1` and sets `t_errno` to **TNODATA**. That value of `t_errno` is not an error condition; it simply means the connection is not yet established.

2. Likewise, use the `t_look()` routine periodically to check if the connection acknowledgment arrived. When it arrives, the `t_look()` routine returns a value of **T_CONNECT**.

3. Put your application into the synchronous mode before calling the `t_rcvconnect()` routine and wait for the connection establishment to arrive. You can put your application into the synchronous mode with the following call:

    `fcntl(fd, F_SETFL, 0);`

Here, **fd** is a file descriptor into the transport endpoint. After you place your application in the synchronous mode, the **t_rcvconnect()** routine sleeps until a connection acknowledgment arrives. You can use the **fcntl()** routine to put your application into the synchronous mode at any time after you obtain a transport endpoint.

The **t_rcvconnect()** routine returns **-1** on failure and **0** on success.

t_listen()

The server side of the application issues the **t_listen()** routine to listen for incoming connection requests. It can only be used on connection-oriented transport providers.

If your application is in the synchronous mode, the **t_listen()** routine sleeps until a connection request arrives. If your application is in the asynchronous mode, the **t_listen()** routine will not sleep.

The syntax of the **t_listen()** routine follows:

```
#include <tiuser.h>

int fd;
int status;
struct t_call *connect_infop;

status = t_listen(fd, connect_infop);
```

The **fd** argument is a file descriptor of a transport endpoint. The **connect_infop** argument is a pointer to a **t_call** structure. You must allocate space to hold the **t_call** structure (you can do that with **t_alloc()** routine, which is described in what follows). The fields of the **t_call** structure are filled in by the **t_listen()** routine.

As mentioned in the description of the **t_connect()** routine, the **t_call** structure has the following form:

```
struct t_call {
    struct netbuf addr;
    struct netbuf opt;
    struct netbuf udata;
    int           sequence;
}
```

The **netbuf** structure is a TLI structure that holds information. It contains three fields: **buf** (a buffer that contains a sequence of bytes), **len** (the number of bytes of data in **buf**), and **maxlen** (the maximum number of bytes **buf** can hold). Because the **t_listen()** routine fills the elements of the **t_call** structure, you must set the value of **maxlen** in each **netbuf** structure. That lets **t_listen()** know the size of the buffer.

The **t_listen()** routine fills the fields with the following information:

addr   Contains the transport address of the client side of the application that sent the connection request. The address is in the **buf** field of the **netbuf** structure, and the size of the address is in the **len** field.

opt   Contains protocol-specific options associated with the connection request. The **buf** field of the **netbuf** structure contains the options, and the **len** field contains the number of bytes in the options.

data   Contains any data that the client side of the application sent on the connection request. The **buf** field of the **netbuf** structure contains the data, and the **len** field contains the number of bytes in the data. Applications can send data on a connection request only if the transport provider allows it. Applications can call the **t_getinfo()** routine to figure out if a transport provider lets you send data on a connection request.

sequence   Uniquely identifies the connection request. It is only useful if, when you issued the **t_bind()** routine, you set the **qlen** field of the **t_bind** structure to a value greater than **1**. As mentioned in the description of the **t_bind()** routine, the **qlen** field specifies the number of outstanding connection requests you can have. An outstanding connection request is one that arrived but has not been accepted yet.

           If you set **qlen** to a value greater than **1**, you can listen for multiple connection requests before responding to them. You can use the **sequence** field to identify each connection request. We present details of setting **qlen** to a value greater than **1** in Chapter 8.

If you are in the asynchronous mode and there is no connection request on the transport endpoint, the **t_listen()** routine returns **-1** and sets **t_errno** to **TNO-DATA**. This is not an error condition. It says that no connection request has arrived yet.

In all other cases, the **t_listen()** routine returns **-1** on failure and **0** on success.

t_accept()

The **t_accept()** routine accepts a connection. You use it on the server side of the application, and it is only valid on connection-oriented transport providers.

As mentioned in Section 7.3, accepting a connection requires two transport endpoints: the transport endpoint that listened for the connection and a second transport endpoint on which to accept the connection. When the **t_accept()** routine completes, the first transport endpoint can listen for new connections and the second transport endpoint can exchange data with the client side of the application.

The **t_accept()** routine has the following form:

```
#include <tiuser.h>

int fd;
int new_fd;
struct t_call *response_infop;
int status;

status = t_accept(fd, new_fd, response_infop);
```

The **t_accept()** routine takes three arguments:

1. The **fd** argument is a file descriptor into the transport endpoint. That transport endpoint must be in the **T_INCON** state, that is, it must have a connection request associated with it.

2. The **new_fd** argument is a second transport endpoint.

3. The **response_infop** argument is a pointer to a **t_call** structure. This structure contains information about the connection request. We described the fields of the **t_call** structure in the description of the **t_listen()** routine.

    Usually, the **response_infop** argument is the same **t_call** structure that the **t_listen()** routine filled in. Applications normally take the **t_call** structure passed to the **t_listen()** routine and give it as the third argument of the **t_accept()** routine.

There is one exception, however. In the `t_listen()` routine, the **udata** field of the **t_call** structure contained data that the client side of the application sent to you. In the `t_accept()` routine, the **udata** field of the **t_call** structure contains data that you want to send to the client side of the application on the connection acknowledgment.

For example, you may want to place authentication information or other user data in **udata** field. However, you can only do that if the transport provider allows it. You can figure out if the transport provider allows it by examining the **t_info** structure returned by `t_open()` or `t_getinfo()`. The **connect** field of that structure tells how many bytes of data you can send when issuing the `t_accept()` routine.

If you want, you can accept the connection on the same transport endpoint where the connection indication arrived (that is, you can have **fd** equal to **new_fd**). But that puts the original transport endpoint in the **T_DATAXFER** state. And, as described in Section 7.5, you cannot accept any more connection requests while the transport endpoint is in that state.

The `t_accept()` routine returns **-1** on failure and **0** on success.

t_snd()

The `t_snd()` routine sends data over connection-oriented transport providers. You can use the routine to send normal data and expedited data, and you use it on the client side and the server side of the application. It has the following syntax:

```
#include <tiuser.h>

int fd;
char *buf;
int nbytes;
int flags;
int num_bytes;

num_bytes = t_snd(fd, buf, nbytes, flags);
```

The **fd** argument is a file descriptor into the transport endpoint. The **buf** argument is a buffer containing the data you want to send, and the **nbytes** argument contains the number of bytes in the buffer.

The **flags** argument contains flags that describe information about the data. You specify the flags by logically OR-ing the following values:

T_EXPEDITED   Marks the data as expedited. As mentioned in Section 7.3, most transport providers treat expedited data specially. Upon receipt, most transport providers place expedited data ahead of normal data.

T_MORE   Says the data are only part of a Transport Service Data Unit (TSDU). As mentioned in Section 7.2, a TSDU is a logical piece of data. This flag implies that you will issue more **t_snd()** routines to complete the TSDU. The transport provider knows the TSDU is complete when you do not set the **T_MORE** bit in the **flags** argument. That lets you divide a large TSDU into smaller pieces and send each of the the smaller pieces with a separate **t_snd()** routine.

When you send data, make sure not to exceed the maximum TSDU of the transport provider. You can figure out the maximum TSDU by looking at the **t_info** structure returned from **t_open()** or **t_getinfo()**. The **tsdu** element of the **t_info** structure contains the maximum TSDU size for normal data. The **etsdu** element of that structure contains the maximum TSDU size for expedited data.

You must also remember that some transport providers do not support the concept of a TSDU. For example, the Transmission Control Protocol (TCP) does not maintain data boundaries. If you send **100** bytes over TCP in a single **t_snd()** call, the receiver may get the message as **50** bytes, followed by **10** bytes, followed by **40** bytes. Using TCP, the receiver gets no indication that you sent all **100** bytes with a single **t_snd()** routine.

As explained in Section 7.5, you can only send data if the transport endpoint is in the **T_DATAXFER** state or the **T_INREL** state. If the transport provider is in the **T_IDLE** state, *the transport provider may silently discard the data!*

The transport endpoint can go into the **T_IDLE** state if the connection was aborted and there is a pending disconnect indication that the sender has not seen yet. This can happen because *the **t_snd()** routine does not check for disconnects before sending data!* So, if you are in a loop sending large amounts of data, you will never know if or when the connection was aborted. In that case, you must use the **ioctl()** system call with the **I_SETSIG** parameter to check for incoming messages, such as a disconnect indication. Details of using the **ioctl()** system call with the **I_SETSIG** parameter are given in Chapter 8.

If the transport endpoint is in any other state (other than **T_DATAXFER**, **T_INREL**, or **T_IDLE**), the **t_snd()** routine fails.

In the synchronous mode, the **t_snd()** routine sleeps until all data are sent and returns the number of bytes sent. Normally, the number of bytes sent is the same as the **nbytes** argument.

In the asynchronous mode, the **t_snd()** fails if the data cannot be sent immediately (that can happen if the transport provider is limiting outgoing data due to flow-control restrictions). If the **t_snd()** routine can only send part of the data, it does so and returns the number of bytes sent.

The **t_snd()** routine returns **-1** on failure. Otherwise, it returns the number of bytes delivered to the transport provider.

t_rcv()

The **t_rcv()** routine reads data over connection-oriented transport providers. You use the routine to read normal data and expedited data, and you use it on the client side and the server side of your application.

The syntax follows:

```
#include <tiuser.h>

int fd;
char *buf;
int nbytes;
int flags;
int num_bytes;

num_bytes = t_rcv(fd, buf, nbytes, &flags);
```

The **fd** argument is a file descriptor into the transport endpoint. The **buf** argument is a buffer into which the **t_rcv()** routine places incoming data. The **nbytes** argument specifies the maximum number of bytes that can fit in the buffer.

The **flags** argument is a pointer to an integer. The **t_rcv()** routine populates the integer with information about the incoming data. The information corresponds to the **flags** argument of the **t_snd()** routine and can have one or both of the following bits set:

T_EXPEDITED   The data placed in the data buffer were sent as expedited data.

T_MORE   The data in the buffer are only part of a Transport Service Data Unit (TSDU). As mentioned in Section 7.2, a TSDU is a logical piece of data. This flag implies that you must issue more **t_rcv()** routines to read the rest of the TSDU. Your application knows it read the entire TSDU when the **T_MORE** bit is no longer set in the **flags** argument.

Again, you must remember that some transport providers do not support the concept of a TSDU (for example, TCP does not support message boundaries and therefore does not support TSDUs). So, when using TCP, the **T_MORE** bit is never set in the flags field of the **t_rcv()** call.

As explained in Section 7.5, you can only read data if the transport endpoint is in the **T_DATAXFER** state or the **T_OUTREL** state.

In the synchronous mode, the **t_rcv()** routine sleeps until data arrive, fills the buffer with the data, and returns the number of bytes transferred into the buffer. If the transport provider supports TSDUs, the **t_rcv()** routine will set the **T_MORE** bit in the **flags** argument if you did not get the entire TSDU.

In the asynchronous mode, the **t_rcv()** routine returns immediately if no data are available. In that case, the **t_rcv()** routine returns **-1** and sets **t_errno** to **TNODATA**. This is not really an error; it simply means no data have arrived yet.

In all other cases, the **t_rcv()** routine returns **-1** on failure. Otherwise, it returns the number of bytes it put into the buffer.

t_sndrel()

The **t_sndrel()** routine starts an orderly shutdown of an established connection. By issuing the **t_sndrel()** routine, you inform the application on the other side of the connection that you have no more data to send.

Both the client side and the server side of the application can use this routine. However, you can only use it over connection-oriented transport providers that support orderly release. You can figure out if the transport provider supports orderly release by looking at the **t_info** structure returned by **t_open()** and **t_getinfo()**. The **servtype** field of that structure is set to **T_COTS_ORD** if the transport provider supports orderly release.

The syntax of the routine follows:

```
#include <tiuser.h>

int fd;
int status;

status = t_sndrel(fd);
```

The `fd` argument is a file descriptor into the transport endpoint. After the routine is called, the transport endpoint is in the **T_OUTREL** state. As described in Section 7.5, you cannot send data in that state. However, you can still receive data.

The `t_sndrel()` routine returns **-1** on error and **0** on success.

t_rcvrel()

The `t_rcvrel()` routine reads an orderly release message that appears on a transport endpoint. After issuing the routine, you should not attempt to read any more data from the connection.

Both the client side and the server side of the application can use this routine. However, you can only use it over connection-oriented transport providers that support orderly release. Use this routine to consume the orderly release message sent by the application on the other side of the connection.

The syntax of the routine follows:

```
#include <tiuser.h>

int fd;
int status;

status = t_rcvrel(fd);
```

The `fd` argument is a file descriptor into the transport endpoint. After this routine is called, the transport endpoint is in the **T_INREL** state. As described in Section 7.5, you can continue to send data in this state. However, you cannot receive data.

The `t_rcvrel()` routine returns **-1** on error and **0** on success.

t_snddis()

You use the `t_snddis()` routine in two cases:

1. When the client side or the server side of the application wants to tear down an existing connection.

2. When the server side of the application wants to reject a connection request.

You must be careful if the `t_snddis()` routine is used to tear down an existing connection. The `t_snddis()` routine generates a disconnect indication that may destroy any data in transit (that is, any data not already received by the remote side of the application). This destructive nature means that applications must implement an orderly release protocol before tearing down a connection with the **t_snddis()** routine. For example, applications can send an "end-of-data" marker in the transferred data and have the *receiver* of the data, not the sender of the data, call the **t_snddis()** routine after it sees the end-of-data marker.

You can only use the **t_snddis()** routine on connection-oriented transport providers. It has the following form:

```
#include <tiuser.h>

int fd;
struct t_call *infop;
int status;

status = t_snddis(fd, infop);
```

The **fd** argument is a file descriptor into a transport endpoint. The **infop** argument is a pointer to a **t_call** structure.

As mentioned in several routines before, the **t_call** structure has the following definition:

```
struct t_call {
    struct netbuf  addr;
    struct netbuf  opt;
    struct netbuf  udata;
    int            sequence;
}
```

A **netbuf** structure is a TLI structure that holds information. It contains three fields: **buf** (a buffer that contains a sequence of bytes), **len** (the number of bytes of data in **buf**), and **maxlen** (the maximum number of bytes **buf** can hold).

You use the **t_call** structure differently, depending on how you are using the **t_snddis()** routine:

1. If you are using **t_snddis()** to tear down an existing connection, all fields except **udata** are ignored. The **udata** field can contain user data that your application wants to send with the disconnect request. However, the amount of user data must not exceed the limit the transport provider imposes.

You can examine the **t_info** structure returned by **t_open()** and **t_getinfo()** to see how much data can be sent on a disconnect request. The **discon** field of the **t_info** structure contains the maximum amount. The **buf** field of the **netbuf** structure contains the data, the **len** field specifies the number of bytes of data, and the **maxlen** field is ignored.

2. If you are using **t_snddis()** to reject a connection request, the **sequence** element must be the same value that the **t_listen()** routine placed in its **t_call** structure. The **addr** and **opt** fields are ignored. You can send user data if the transport provider allows it.

If the server side of the application rejects the connection request, it causes the **T_DISCONNECT** event to occur on the transport endpoint of the client side of the application. That, in turn, causes many of the client's TLI routines to fail with **t_errno** set to **TLOOK**. Section 7.4 described the TLI routines that fail when the **T_DISCONNECT** event occurs.

The **t_snddis()** routine returns **-1** on failure and **0** on success.

t_rcvdis()

The **t_rcvdis()** routine reads information about a disconnect request. You call this routine when a **T_DISCONNECT** event occurs on a transport endpoint. You can only use the **t_rcvdis()** routine on connection-oriented transport providers.

The syntax of the **t_rcvdis()** routine follows:

```
#include <tiuser.h>

int fd;
struct t_discon *infop;
int status;

status = t_rcvdis(fd, infop);
```

The **fd** argument is a file descriptor into a transport endpoint. The **infop** argument is a pointer to a **t_discon** structure. The **t_rcvdis()** routine fills in that structure. It contains information associated with the disconnect indication.

You must allocate space to hold the **t_discon** structure before calling the **t_rcvdis()** routine. You can use the **t_alloc()** routine (described in what follows) to allocate space.

The **t_discon** structure has the following elements:

```
struct t_discon {
        struct netbuf udata;
        int           reason;
        int           sequence;
}
```

As mentioned earlier, a **netbuf** structure is a TLI structure that holds information. It contains three fields: **buf** (a buffer that contains a sequence of bytes), **len** (the number of bytes of data in **buf**), and **maxlen** (the maximum number of bytes **buf** can hold). Because the **t_rcvdis()** routine fills the **t_discon** structure, the **maxlen** field of the **netbuf** structure must be set.

The **t_rcvdis()** routine populates the **t_discon** structure as follows:

udata   Contains any data that the peer sent with the disconnect request. It is only valid if the transport provider allows an application to send data on a disconnect request.

reason   This is a protocol-specific reason the disconnect happened. You should make no assumptions about this value. Most applications simply write the value into a log file (along with the associated transport provider) if an unexpected disconnect happens.

sequence   If the server side of the application issued the disconnect request, the client side of the application ignores this field. If the client side of the application issued the disconnect request, the server side of the application only uses the **sequence** field on outstanding connections (that is, connections that have arrived but have not been accepted yet). The **sequence** field identifies the outstanding connection that received the disconnect request.

The **t_rcvdis()** routine returns **0** on success and **-1** on failure.

t_sndudata()

The **t_sndudata()** routine sends a datagram over a connectionless transport provider. The server side and the client of the application can use this routine. The syntax follows:

```
#include <tiuser.h>

int fd;
struct t_unitdata *unitdatap;
int status;

status = t_sndudata(fd, unitdatap);
```

The **fd** argument is a file descriptor into a transport endpoint. The **unitdatap** argument is a pointer to a **t_unitdata** structure that contains all information needed to send a datagram. The **t_unitdata** structure has the following form:

```
struct t_unitdata {
    struct netbuf addr;
    struct netbuf opt;
    struct netbuf udata;
}
```

The **netbuf** structure is a TLI structure that holds information. It contains three fields: **buf** (a buffer that contains a sequence of bytes), **len** (the number of bytes of data in **buf**), and **maxlen** (the maximum number of bytes **buf** can hold). Each element of the **t_unitdata** structure uses the **netbuf** structure to hold different types of data.

You must allocate the **t_unitdata** structure before calling the **t_sndudata()** routine. You use the fields of the **t_unitdata** structure in the following way:

addr   Contains the transport address of the service to which you want to send the datagram. In the **netbuf** structure, **buf** contains the address, **len** specifies the length of the address, and **maxlen** is ignored.

opt   Contains transport-specific information that you want to send with the datagram. Because it is transport specific, you should not use this field except under the conditions we describe in the **t_optmgmt()** section that follows. In the **netbuf** structure, **buf** contains the options, **len** specifies the length of the options, and **maxlen** is ignored.

udata   Contains the data you want to send. In the **netbuf** structure, **buf** contains the data, **len** specifies the size of the data, and **maxlen** is ignored. You must make sure you do not exceed the maximum data size. You can figure out the maximum data size by looking at the **t_info** structure returned from **t_open()** or **t_getinfo()**. The **tsdu** element of the **t_info** structure contains the maximum data size for a datagram.

The **t_sndudata()** routine returns **0** on success and **-1** on failure. However, an indication of success does not mean the transport provider delivered the data successfully. It simply means the transport provider sent the data on their way. The datagram may be lost as it travels to its destination.

t_rcvudata()

The **t_rcvudata()** routine lets you read a datagram that another application sent to you. You use this routine on both the client side and the server side of the application. It has the following syntax:

```
#include <tiuser.h>

int fd;
int flags;
struct t_unitdata *unitdatap;
int status;

status = t_rcvudata(fd, unitdatap, &flags);
```

The **fd** argument is a file descriptor into the transport endpoint. The **unitdatap** argument is a pointer to a **t_unitdata** structure, and the **flags** argument is a pointer to an integer.

As described in the **t_sndudata()** routine, the **t_unitdata** structure has the following definition:

```
struct t_unitdata {
    struct netbuf addr;
    struct netbuf opt;
    struct netbuf udata;
}
```

The **t_rcvudata()** routine fills the **unitdatap** argument with information about the datagram. You must allocate space to hold the structure before calling the **t_rcvudata()** routine. And, because the **t_rcvudata()** routine must know the sizes of the buffers in the **netbuf** structures, you must set **maxlen** in each **netbuf** structure. You can use the **t_alloc()** routine (described in what follows) to do that. The **t_alloc()** routine allocates space and sets the **maxlen** field of the **netbuf** structures to the maximum buffer space the transport provider allows.

The `t_rcvudata()` routine fills the fields of the `t_unitdata` structure with the following information:

addr   Contains the transport address of the application that sent the datagram. In the `netbuf` structure, `buf` contains the address and `len` specifies the length of the address.

opt   Contains transport-specific options associated with the datagram. In the `netbuf` structure, `buf` contains the options and `len` specifies the length of the options.

         You usually do not use this field unless you are writing an application that uses a specific transport provider. We show an example of how to use this field in the description of the `t_optmgmt()` routine in what follows.

udata   Contains the data in the datagram. In the `netbuf` structure, `buf` contains the data and `len` contains the number of bytes in the data.

Usually, the `t_rcvudata()` routine does not place any information in the `flags` argument. However, if the `maxlen` field of the `netbuf` structure associated with the `udata` field is not large enough to hold all of the data, the `t_rcvudata()` routine sets the `flag` value to `T_MORE`.

In that case, you must issue more `t_rcvudata()` routines to get the rest of the data in the datagram. When you do that, the `addr` and `opt` elements of the `t_unitdata` structure have a length of `0`. When you read the full datagram, the `t_rcvudata()` routine sets the `flags` argument to `0`.

If you use the `t_alloc()` routine to allocate space for the `t_unitdata` structure, you don't have to check for the `T_MORE` bit. As we describe in what follows, the `t_alloc()` routine sets the `maxlen` field of the `netbuf` structure to the largest possible value the transport provider allows.

If you are in the synchronous mode, the `t_rcvudata()` routine sleeps until a datagram arrives. If you are in the asynchronous mode and a datagram has not arrived, the `t_rcvudata()` routine returns a value of `-1` immediately and sets `t_errno` to `T_NODATA`. This is not a failure condition. It is an indication that a datagram is not available. In all other cases, the `t_rcvudata()` routine returns `0` on success and `-1` on failure.

t_rcvuderr()

The `t_rcvuderr()` routine provides information about an error that occurred with a datagram you previously sent. You use this routine on the client side and server side of your application, but you can only use it on connectionless transport providers.

You should only use this routine when you get an error indication on the transport endpoint. As described in Section 7.7, you get an error indication if the **T_UDERR** event occurs. You are notified of that event when you try to issue the next **t_rcvudata()** routine. If the **T_UDERR** event is on the transport endpoint, the **t_rcvudata()** returns an error condition and sets **t_errno** to **TLOOK**. When that happens, you *must* issue the **t_rcvuderr()** routine to clear the event.

The **t_rcvuderr()** routine provides information about the datagram that produced the error. It has the following form:

```
#include <tiuser.h>

int fd;
struct t_uderr *uderrp;
int status;

status = t_rcvuderr(fd, uderrp);
```

The **fd** argument is a file descriptor into the transport endpoint. The **uderrp** argument is a pointer to a **t_uderr** structure. The **t_rcvuderr()** routine fills in that structure with information about the datagram that caused an error. It has the following elements:

```
struct t_uderr {
    struct netbuf addr;
    struct netbuf opt;
    int           error;
}
```

You must allocate the **t_uderr** structure before calling the **t_rcvuderr()** routine (you can use the **t_alloc()** routine, described in what follows, to do that).

The **netbuf** structure has three elements: a **buf** field (which holds data), a **len** field (which tells the number of bytes in **buf**), and a **maxlen** field (which contains the full size of the buffer). You must set the **maxlen** element of each **netbuf** structure so the **t_rcvuderr()** routine knows the size of the buffer (the **t_alloc()** routine sets the **maxlen** field for you).

The **t_rcvuderr()** routine populates the fields of the **t_uderr** structure with the following information:

addr   Contains the destination address of the datagram that produced the error. The **buf** field of the **netbuf** structure contains the address, and the **len** field contains the number of bytes in the address.

opt   Contains the options associated with the datagram that produced the error.
            The **buf** field of the **netbuf** structure contains the option, and the **len**
            field contains the number of bytes in the option.

error   Contains a protocol-specific error code. Your application should not try to
            interpret this value. Typically, applications write this value into a log file
            when an error occurs.

The **udatap** argument can be **NULL** if you don't want the information about the
datagram that produced the error. The **t_rcvuderr()** routine returns **0** on success
and **-1** on failure.

t_error()

If a TLI routine fails, you can use the **t_error()** routine to display the reason for
failure onto standard error. It is similar to the SVR4 **perror()** routine, but whereas
perror() displays an error message based on the **errno** variable, the
t_error() routine displays an error message based on the **t_errno** variable.

The format follows:

```
#include <tiuser.h>

char *prefix;

t_error(prefix);
```

The **t_error()** routine prints the error message onto standard error, preceded by the
string given as its argument.

t_alloc()

The **t_alloc()** routine allocates memory to hold data structures used by other TLI
routines. You specify the type of structure, and the **t_alloc()** routine gets the
memory for you. It has the following syntax:

```
#include <tiuser.h>

int fd;
int type;
int fields;
```

```
char *memoryp;

memoryp = t_alloc(fd, type, fields);
```

The **fd** argument is a file descriptor into the transport endpoint. We will explain why that is needed shortly. The **type** argument specifies the type of data structure you want to allocate. It can have one of the following values:

T_BIND   Allocates a **t_bind** structure. You use the **t_bind** structure in the **t_bind()** routine.

T_CALL   Allocates a **t_call** structure. You use the **t_call** structure in the following routines:

>   **t_connect()   t_rcvconnect()   t_listen()**
>   **t_accept()   t_snddis()**

T_OPTMGMT   Allocates a **t_optmgmt** structure. You use the **t_optmgmt** structure in the **t_optmgmt()** routine.

T_DIS   Allocates a **t_discon** structure. You use the **t_discon** structure in the **t_rcvdis()** routine.

T_UNITDATA   Allocates a **t_unitdata** structure. You use the **t_unitdata** structure in the **t_sndudata()** routine and in the **t_rcvudata()** routine.

T_UDERROR   Allocates a **t_uderr** structure. You use the **t_uderr** structure in the **t_rcvuderr()** routine.

T_INFO   Allocates a **t_info** structure. You use the **t_info** structure in the **t_open()** routine and in the **t_getinfo()** routine.

All of these structures have at least one field with a **netbuf** structure. As mentioned earlier, the **netbuf** structure contains three fields: **buf** (a buffer that holds data), **len** (the length of the data), and **maxlen** (the total length of the buffer).

You can use the **t_alloc()** routine to allocate the memory for the **buf** element of the **netbuf** structure as well. When you do that, the **t_alloc()** routine sets the **maxlen** field to the size of the allocated buffer.

That is why the **fd** argument is needed in the **t_alloc()** routine. The **t_alloc()** routine must query the transport endpoint to figure out the maximum size of each buffer. It gets the maximum size by examining the **t_info** structure that the **t_getinfo()** routine fills in.

The **fields** argument of the **t_alloc()** routine specifies the fields to allocate. It is a bitwise OR of any of the following:

T_ADDR   Allocates the buffer of the **netbuf** structure for the **addr** field of the **t_bind**, **t_call**, **t_unitdata**, or **t_uderr** structures. It fills in the **maxlen** field and allocates the **buf** field to hold **maxlen** bytes.

T_OPT   Allocates the buffer of the **netbuf** structure for the **opt** field of the **t_optmgmt**, **t_call**, **t_unitdata**, or **t_uderr** structures. It fills in the **maxlen** field and allocates the **buf** field to hold **maxlen** bytes.

T_UDATA Allocates the buffer of the **netbuf** structure for the **udata** field of the **t_call**, **t_discon**, or **t_unitdata** structures. It fills in the **maxlen** field and allocates the **buf** field to hold **maxlen** bytes.

T_ALL   Allocates the buffer of the **netbuf** structure for all fields of the associated data structures. It fills in the **maxlen** field and allocates the **buf** field to hold **maxlen** bytes.

If the transport provider says the maximum length of a field is **-1** (that is, there is no maximum value), the **t_alloc()** routine fails. If the transport provider says the maximum length of a field is **-2** (the associated data type is not supported), the **t_alloc()** routine may either fail or set the **maxlen** field to **0**. It returns **NULL** on failure. It returns a pointer to the newly allocated memory on success.

t_free()

The **t_free()** routine frees memory allocated by the **t_alloc()** routine. It has the following form:

```
#include <tiuser.h>

int type;
char *memoryp;
int status;

status = t_free(memoryp, type);
```

The **memoryp** argument is the data location returned by the **t_alloc()** routine. The **type** argument is one of the types used in **t_alloc()**. Valid values are as follows:

T_BIND   Frees a **t_bind** structure.

T_CALL   Frees a **t_call** structure.

T_OPTMGMT   Frees a **t_optmgmt** structure.

T_DIS   Frees a **t_discon** structure.

T_UNITDATA   Frees a **t_unitdata** structure.

T_UDERROR   Frees a **t_uderr** structure.

T_INFO   Frees a **t_info** structure.

The **t_free()** routine also frees the data in the **buf** field of a **netbuf** structure if it has a non-**NULL** value. The **t_free()** routine returns **0** on success and **-1** on failure.

t_optmgmt()

The **t_optmgmt()** routine lets you negotiate options with the transport provider. The client side and the server side of the application can use this routine, and it works over connection-oriented and connectionless transport providers.

Unfortunately, options are transport-provider-specific. For example, SVR4 supplies a connectionless "loopback" transport provider that two applications on the same system can use to send datagrams to one another. That transport provider supports a "user-info" option. If the server side of an application sets that option, then the connection-less loopback transport provider includes the effective user ID of the user sending a datagram. The user ID is placed in the **opt** element of the **t_unitdata** structure. By using that option, the receiver can figure out the user ID of the person sending the datagram. However, the option is only available on the loopback transport provider.

Before discussing when to use **t_optmgmt()**, let's look at its syntax:

```
#include <tiuser.h>

int fd;
struct t_optmgmt *request_optp;
struct t_optmgmt *return_optp;
int status;

status = t_optmgmt(fd, request_optp, return_optp);
```

The **fd** argument is a file descriptor into the transport endpoint. The **request_optp** and the **return_optp** are pointers to a **t_optmgmt** structure. The **t_optmgmt** structure has the following definition:

```
struct t_optmgmt {
    struct netbuf opt;
    long          flags;
}
```

As described earlier, the **netbuf** structure is a TLI structure that holds information. It has three elements: **buf** (a buffer containing a sequence of bytes), **len** (the number of characters in **buf**), and **maxlen** (the maximum number of bytes **buf** can hold).

You send information to the **t_optmgmt()** routine with the **request_optp** argument. The **t_optmgmt()** routine passes information back to you by filling in the **return_optp** argument. You must allocate memory to hold the structures before calling the **t_optmgmt()** routine. Usually, applications call the **t_alloc()** routine to allocate memory.

The **flags** field of the **t_optmgmt** structure in the **request_optp** argument specifies the action you want to perform. It can have one of the following values:

T_NEGOTIATE   Indicates you want to set options. The options are in the **opt** field of the **request_optp** argument. You set the fields of the corresponding **netbuf** structure as follows:

buf   Contains a sequence of bytes representing the options.

len   Contains the number of bytes in the options.

maxlen   Is ignored.

The transport provider attempts to set the options. However, it may not set them exactly as requested. That can happen because you specified an invalid value for an option. The transport provider fills in the **opt** element of the **return_optp** argument with the options it set. The corresponding **buf** field of the **netbuf** structure contains the options, and the **len** field contains the number of bytes in the options. Because the **t_optmgmt()** routine fills in the buffer, you must make sure the **maxlen** element of the **opt** field of the **return_optp** argument contains the size of the buffer.

T_CHECK   Lets you determine if the transport provider supports a given option. You put the option in the **opt** field of the **request_optp** argument. The **t_optmgmt()** routine fills in the **flags** field of the **return_optp** argument with one of the following values:

> **T_SUCCESS** The transport provider supports the options.
>
> **T_FAILURE** The transport provider does not support the options.
>
> Here, the **t_optmgmt()** routine does *not* fill in the **opt** field of the **return_optp** argument.

T_DEFAULT   Causes the transport provider to return its default options. The **t_optmgmt()** routine fills in the **opt** element of the **return_optp** argument with the default values. The **buf** field of the **netbuf** structure contains the options, and the **len** field contains the number of bytes in the options. And, because you are not passing information to the transport provider, the **len** field of the **opt** element in the **request_optp** argument must be **0**.

The **t_optmgmt()** routine returns **0** on success and **-1** on failure.

The **t_optmgmt()** routine is a difficult routine to use because it is transport-provider-specific. We conclude this chapter by presenting an example of how to use the **t_optmgmt()** routine.

Example of the t_optmgmt() Routine

To illustrate how to use the **t_optmgmt()** routine, let's look at the SVR4 connectionless loopback transport provider. As mentioned earlier, that transport provider supports a ''user-info'' option. This option lets the application reading a datagram get the user ID of the application that sent the datagram.

The application receiving the datagram sets the option. You set the option by populating a data structure specific to the connectionless loopback transport provider and assigning the data structure to the **opt** element of the **request_optp** argument of the **t_optmgmt()** routine.

Here's what you have to do to set the option. First, define a local structure that contains two fields:

1. a **tcl_opt_hdr** structure; and

2. a **tcl_opt_setid** structure.

Both of these structures are specific to the connectionless loopback transport provider, and they are defined in **<sys/ticlts.h>**. The **tcl_opt_hdr** structure has header information. It contains an offset to where the current information starts and an offset to where the next header information starts.

The **tcl_opt_setid** structure contains an indication to set the user-info option. It contains a ''type'' field and a ''flag'' field. To set the user-info option, you must set the type field to **TCL_OPT_SETID** and the flag to **TCL_IDFLG_UID**.

After you do that, assign the local structure to the **opt** field of the **t_optmgmt** structure. Then, set the **flags** field of the **t_optmgmt** structure to **T_NEGOTIATE**. Finally, issue the **t_optmgmt()** routine.

If you think that's complicated, you're correct. It is also very specific to the SVR4 connectionless loopback transport provider. Even if other transport providers supply a user-info option, the option will probably not be set up the same way.

After viewing the code that sets the user-info option for the connectionless loopback transport provider, we discuss ways to do these types of operations in a transport-independent way.

The following code sets the user-info option for the SVR4 connectionless transport provider. We enclose the code in a routine called **set_user_info_opt()**. The routine takes a file descriptor into the SVR4 connectionless transport provider as an argument. The code segment follows:

```
#include <sys/types.h>
#include <sys/ticlts.h>
#include <fcntl.h>
#include <stdio.h>
#include <tiuser.h>
/*
 *   The fd argument is a transport endpoint into the
 *   SVR4 connectionless loopback transport provider.
 */

set_user_info_opt (fd)
int fd;
{
   struct t_optmgmt *reqp;   /* used in t_optmgmt() */
   struct t_optmgmt *retp;   /* used in t_optmgmt() */
   int return_val = 0;       /* return of this procedure */

   struct {
       struct tcl_opt_hdr    header;
       struct tcl_opt_setid  data;
   } option_input_data, *option_return_data;

   /*
```

```
 *   Allocate space to hold the t_optmgmt structure
 *   for the request.  We set the last parameter of
 *   t_alloc() to 0.  That is because we don't want to
 *   allocate space for the opt buffer.  Instead, we will
 *   assign the opt buffer to our local
 *   ''option_input_data'' data structure
 */

reqp = (struct t_optmgmt *) t_alloc (fd, T_OPTMGMT, 0);
if (reqp == NULL) {
   return (-1);
}

/*
 *   Allocate space to hold the t_optmgmt structure
 *   for the reply.  Here, we set the last parameter of
 *   t_alloc() to T_OPT.  That is because we want
 *   to allocate space for the opt buffer of the
 *   return structure.  We could have used T_ALL as
 *   well, because the t_optmgmt structure only has one
 *   netbuf structure in it.
 */

retp = (struct t_optmgmt *) t_alloc (fd, T_OPTMGMT, T_OPT);

if (retp == NULL) {
   (void) t_free ((char *)reqp, T_OPTMGMT);
   return (-1);
}

/*
 *   Fill in the ugly transport-specific data structure
 *   with the ugly transport-specific data.
 */

option_input_data.header.hdr_thisopt_off =
                             sizeof(struct tcl_opt_hdr);
option_input_data.header.hdr_nexthdr_off = TCL_OPT_NOHDR;
option_input_data.data.setid_type= TCL_OPT_SETID;
option_input_data.data.setid_flg= TCL_IDFLG_UID;

/*
 *   Fill in the t_optmgmt structure that holds
```

```
 *   the options
 */

reqp->opt.maxlen = 0;
reqp->opt.len = sizeof (option_input_data);
reqp->opt.buf = (char *) &option_input_data;
reqp->flags = T_NEGOTIATE;

if (t_optmgmt(fd, reqp, retp) == -1) {
   /*
    *   The t_optmgmt() routine failed!
    *   Set the buffer in the request options back to 0
    *   so t_free() doesn't try to free it...
    */
   reqp->opt.buf = 0;
   (void)t_free((char *)reqp, T_OPTMGMT);
   (void)t_free((char *)retp, T_OPTMGMT);
   return (-1);
}

/*
 *   If the returned options are not the same as the
 *   options we tried to set, return an error.
 */

if ((reqp->opt.len != retp->opt.len)
 || (memcmp(reqp->opt.buf,retp->opt.buf,reqp->opt.len))){
   return_val = -1;
}

/*
 *   Now that we've set the option, we free the memory
 *   we allocated.
 *   Set the buffer in the request options back to 0 so
 *   t_free() doesn't try to free it...
 */

reqp->opt.buf = 0;
(void)t_free((char *)reqp, T_OPTMGMT);
(void)t_free((char *)retp, T_OPTMGMT);
return (return_val);
}
```

Now that we've created a routine that sets the user-info option, we'll show how to use it. Unfortunately, the code that uses the option is just as ugly as the code that sets the option.

After your application sets the user-info option, you can figure out who sent you a datagram. The connectionless loopback transport provider places the user ID in the **opt** field of the **t_unitdata** structure.

The information in the **opt** field of the **t_unitdata** structure is similar to the information in the **opt** field of the **t_optmgmt** structure. To get the user ID of the person sending the datagram, you must define a local structure containing two fields:

1. a **tcl_opt_hdr** structure; and

2. a **tcl_opt_uid** structure.

Both of these structures are specific to the connectionless loopback transport provider, and they are defined in **<sys/ticlts.h>**. The **tcl_opt_hdr** structure has header information. It tells where the current information starts and an offset to where the next header begins. Because we are only getting one piece of information (the user ID of the person sending the datagram), we ignore the **tcl_opt_hdr** structure in our example.

The **tcl_opt_uid** structure contains the information we want. It contains a "type" field and a "val" field. The transport provider sets the type field to **TCL_OPT_UID** and the val field to the user ID of the person sending the datagram.

To illustrate, we'll create a program that does the following:

1. Creates a transport endpoint into the SVR4 connectionless loopback transport provider. We do that by calling the **t_open()** routine specifying the **/dev/ticlts** device file. The **/dev/ticlts** file is the clone device file for the SVR4 connectionless loopback transport provider.

2. Calls the **t_alloc()** routine to allocate space to hold the address to which we want to bind.

3. Calls the **t_alloc()** routine again to allocate space to hold the address to which the transport provider binds us.

4. Sets the transport address in the **t_bind** structure. In the SVR4 connectionless transport provider, a transport address is an arbitrary sequence of characters. So, we set the transport address to **"example.addr"**.

5. Issues the **t_bind()** routine to bind the transport endpoint to our transport address. We also check that we are bound to the correct address.

6. Calls the **set_user_info_opt()** routine that we created earlier. That sets the user-info option.

7. Allocates space to hold a datagram by calling the **t_alloc()** routine.

8. Calls the **t_rcvudata()** routine to read a datagram. That routine sleeps waiting for a datagram to arrive.

9. When an application sends us a datagram, the **t_rcvudata()** routine returns. And, because we set the user-info option, the datagram contains the user ID of the application that sent the datagram. That application did not have to do anything unusual. Because we set the option, the transport provider automatically places the user ID in the datagram.

10. Extracts the user ID from the **opt** field of the **t_unitdata** structure. We then display the user ID of the person that sent the datagram.

The code segment follows:

```
#include <sys/types.h>
#include <sys/ticlts.h>
#include <fcntl.h>
#include <stdio.h>
#include <tiuser.h>

#define LOOPADDR "example.addr"

main(argc, argv)
int argc;
char *argv[];
{
    struct localinfo {
        struct tcl_opt_hdr header;
        struct tcl_opt_uid data;
    }  *option_datap;

    int uid;                    /* user ID of sender    */
    int addrlen;                /* used for t_bind()    */
    int flags;                  /* used in t_rcvudata() */
    int fd;                     /* transport endpoint   */
    struct t_unitdata *datap;   /* data in datagram     */
    struct t_bind *req, *ret;   /* used in binding      */

    /*
     * Create a transport endpoint into the SVR4
     * connectionless loopback transport provider.
     */
```

```
if ((fd = t_open("/dev/ticlts", O_RDWR, 0)) < 0) {
   t_error("t_open");
   exit(1);
}

/*
 *  Allocate space to hold the addresses...
 */

if ((req = (struct t_bind *)t_alloc(fd, T_BIND, T_ALL))
                                         == NULL) {
   t_error("t_alloc of request addr failed");
   exit(1);
}

if ((ret = (struct t_bind *)t_alloc(fd, T_BIND, T_ALL))
                                         == NULL) {
   t_error("t_alloc of return addr failed");
   exit(1);
}

addrlen = strlen(LOOPADDR) + 1;
req->qlen = 0;
req->addr.len = addrlen;
strncpy(req->addr.buf, LOOPADDR, addrlen);

/*
 *  Bind to the address and check that we bound correctly
 */

if (t_bind(fd, req, ret) < 0) {
   t_error("t_bind");
   exit(1);
}

if ((req->addr.len != ret->addr.len) ||
   (memcmp(req->addr.buf, ret->addr.buf, req->addr.len))){
   fprintf(stderr, "Did not bind to correct address!\n");
   exit(1);
}

/*
 *  Set the "user-info" option...
```

```
    */

    if (set_user_info_opt(fd) < 0) {
        return(-1);
    }

    /*
     *  Allocate space to hold a datagram and wait for a
     *  datagram to arrive.
     */

    if ((datap = (struct t_unitdata *)t_alloc(fd, T_UNITDATA,
                                    T_ALL)) == NULL) {
        t_error("t_alloc, ret");
        exit(1);
    }

    if (t_rcvudata(fd, datap, &flags) < 0) {
        t_error("could not read datagram!");
        exit(1);
    }

    /*
     *  Now, extract the user ID from the datagram.   The
     *  transport provider put the user ID in the opt
     *  field because we set the user-info option.
     */

    option_datap = (struct localinfo *)(datap->opt.buf);
    if (option_datap->data.uid_type != TCL_OPT_UID) {
        (void)t_free((char *)datap, T_UNITDATA);
        exit(1);
    }

    uid = option_datap->data.uid_val;

    printf("uid = %d\n", uid);
```

This code is transport-provider-specific. It's ugly, it's complicated, and it *only* works over the SVR4 connectionless loopback transport provider.

Because the t_optmgmt() routine makes your application transport-specific, you should only use it in two cases.

First, you can use `t_optmgmt()` when you are using a predefined transport provider. For example, the `rpcbind` program (detailed in Chapter 6) maintains a database that maps RPC program numbers onto transport addresses. When an RPC program binds to a transport address, it tells the `rpcbind` program what that address is. All communication between the RPC program and the `rpcbind` program is done over the connectionless loopback transport provider.

Because the `rpcbind` program talks to RPC programs using the connectionless loopback transport provider, the `rpcbind` program can set options on that transport provider. In fact, the `rpcbind` program sets the user-info option described earlier to get the user ID of the person starting the RPC program.

The second way you can use the `t_optmgmt()` routine is in a transport-independent manner. For example, you can maintain a database that maps a transport provider name onto the `t_optmgmt()` parameters for a given option.

To illustrate, consider a unique feature of some connectionless transport providers: support of a ''Transport-Level Broadcast'' option. Those transport providers define a special ''Transport-Level Broadcast Address.'' When you send a datagram to the Transport-Level Broadcast Address, the datagram goes to *all* machines in a local area network. Usually, you must set transport options to enable that functionality.

So, because different connectionless transport providers set up that functionality differently, you can maintain a database that maps a device file onto the options for that transport provider. So, when you want to enable the Transport-Level Broadcast option, you can query the database to figure out the format of the options. When the administrator adds a new transport provider, they add an entry to the database.

As we will see in Chapter 9, that is what the SVR4 Name-to-Address Mapping feature does. It maintains a separate library for each transport provider on the system. Each library contains a subroutine that does the `t_optmgmt()` functions to enable the Transport-Level Broadcast for the associated transport provider.

Your application simply calls the higher-level Name-to-Address Mapping routine, specifying the transport provider to use. That routine links in the appropriate library, and calls the corresponding subroutine. The subroutine in the library issues the TLI routines that enable the Transport-Level Broadcast. When the administrator adds a new transport provider to your system, they add a new library as well. We present the details in Chapter 9.

7.10 Summary

TLI routines are a set of low-level networking routines that give a direct interface to a transport provider. You use TLI routines to establish communication, manage a connection, and transfer data.

In this chapter, we presented an overview of TLI functionality and showed the details of TLI routines. In the next chapter, we show how to incorporate TLI routines into networking applications.

For Further Reading

1. AT&T, *UNIX System V Release 4 Programmer's Guide: Networking Interfaces*, Prentice Hall, Englewood Cliffs, NJ, 1990.

2. Stevens, R., Chapter 7, System V Transport Layer Interface, *UNIX Network Programming*, Prentice Hall, Englewood Cliffs, NJ, 1990.

Exercises

7.1 Describe the TLI routines a networking application would use over a connection-oriented transport provider. Describe the TLI routines it would use over a connectionless transport provider.

7.2 Describe the differences between synchronous TLI actions and asynchronous TLI actions. When would an application use each?

7.3 Describe Transport Service Data Units. How do TSDUs help carry out session layer services? Can your applications always use TSDUs? Why or why not?

7.4 Describe the transport endpoint states for connectionless transport providers and connection-oriented transport providers. Why are the states needed?

Chapter 8

Applications Using TLI

8.1 Introduction

In Chapter 7, we presented an overview of TLI and gave the details of TLI routines. TLI routines give a direct interface to a transport provider, letting you establish communication, manage a connection, and transfer data. And, as explained, you use the routines to create networking applications that handle lower-level networking actions.

In this chapter, we show how to use TLI routines in networking applications and show examples of TLI programs. We show how to create programs using both connection-oriented and connectionless transport providers.

As mentioned in Chapter 7, TLI routines only provide an interface to the network. Within your application, you must still handle the actions of:

1. The *application layer* of the OSI Model. You must define the networking service, specify the data the service requires, and detail the service results. And, of course, you must implement the service on the server machine.

2. The *presentation layer* of the OSI Model. You must place all data in a common format to handle differences in machine data representation.

3. The *session layer* of the OSI Model. Your application must manage the session by providing "over" and "over and out" synchronization messages.

TLI routines let applications interface with the *transport layer* of the OSI Model, so you do not have to worry about the details of network transmission.

Before showing how to use TLI routines in networking applications, let's first look at the presentation and session layers. We begin by describing the presentation layer.

8.2   The Presentation Layer

There are several ways to carry out the functionality of the presentation layer. As mentioned in Chapter 1, the presentation layer is where you convert data into a common format.

A simple common format is ASCII strings. For example, suppose you had to send three integers over the network. You can convert the three integers into an ASCII string by using the **sprintf()** routine:

```
struct local_data {
    int x;
    int y;
    int z;
};

struct local_data data;

data.x = 10234;
data.y = 9081;
data.z = 983523224;

sprintf(buf, "%d %d %d", data.x, data.y, data.z);
```

You can then send the string over the network. The receiver can use the **sscanf()** routine to convert the string back to three integers. The result is three integers in the local representation.

A drawback of converting all data into ASCII strings is the increased message size. For example, the previous code creates the following string:

"10234 9081 983523224"

There is a total of 21 characters in that string (including the terminating **NULL** character). As the values of the integers increase, so does the length of the character string.

A better common format is the eXternal Data Representation (XDR) format. As described in Chapter 6, the XDR format defines a common format for all data types. For example, XDR defines the format of an integer as a 4-byte value, represented in two's-complement notation, with the most significant byte leftmost. You can use XDR routines to convert data into the XDR format before sending them over the network.

Fortunately, you don't have to write the XDR routines yourself. You can generate them automatically by using the **rpcgen** compiler. As described in Chapter 6, the **rpcgen** compiler generates a C file that contains XDR routines.

Normally, the **rpcgen** compiler takes an RPC specification in a ''**.x**'' file. The RPC specification contains data declarations and program declarations. However, you can omit the program declarations and create an RPC specification that only contains data declarations. If you do that, the **rpcgen** compiler generates the XDR routines to translate the data declarations into the XDR format.

That gives an easy way to generate the XDR routines. To illustrate, suppose you wanted to generate the XDR routine to convert a data structure containing three integers into the XDR format. To do that, you would create a file named **def.x** that contained the structure definition:

```
/*
 *  def.x
 */

struct local_data {
    int x;
    int y;
    int z;
};
```

Those are the only lines in the file. Next, run the **rpcgen** compiler, giving it the ''**.x**'' file as input:

```
$ rpcgen def.x
```

There is no RPC program declaration in the ''**.x**'' file, so the **rpcgen** compiler produces only two files: **def.h** and **def_xdr.c**. The **def_xdr.c** file contains the routine to convert the data structure into the XDR format. The **def.h** file contains the structure definition. To summarize, if you give a file named *foo*.**x** to the **rpcgen** compiler, it generates *foo*.**h** and *foo_xdr*.**c**.

In our example, the **def_xdr.c** file contains the XDR routine named **xdr_local_data()**. That routine translates our **local_data** data structure into and out of the XDR format. The **rpcgen** complier always names XDR routines that way. If the structure tag is *any*, the **rpcgen** compiler generates an XDR routine named **xdr_any()**.

The XDR routine generated by **rpcgen** takes two arguments. The first is a pointer to an **XDR** structure, and the second is a pointer to the data structure you defined. The **XDR** structure is used internally by the XDR routines, so you should not modify it within your application. We show how to use the XDR routine shortly.

Before calling the XDR routine, you must initialize the **XDR** structure. You do that by calling the **xdrmem_create()** routine, which takes four arguments:

1. A pointer to an **XDR** structure.

2. A pointer to a buffer. The **xdrmem_create()** routine associates the buffer with the **XDR** structure. When you pass the **XDR** structure to the XDR routine, the XDR routine uses the buffer to encode and decode data. If you are encoding data, the XDR routine puts the encoded data in the buffer. If you are decoding data, the XDR routine reads the encoded data from the buffer.

3. The size of the buffer.

4. An indication of the format direction. The **xdrmem_create()** routine puts the indication of the direction in the **XDR** structure. So, when you pass the **XDR** structure to the XDR routine, the XDR routine knows whether to encode or decode the data. The value is **XDR_ENCODE** if you are encoding data and **XDR_DECODE** if you are decoding data.

To illustrate, consider the **def.x** file presented earlier. That file defines a data structure named **local_data** containing three integers. If you run the **def.x** file through the **rpcgen** compiler, you get two files: **def.h** and **def_xdr.c**. The **def_xdr.c** file contains the code for the **xdr_local_data()** routine.

To encode data, you must first initialize an **XDR** structure with the **xdrmem_create()** routine. You must give the routine a pointer to an **XDR** structure, a buffer, the size of the buffer, and the **XDR_ENCODE** value. The size of the buffer must be large enough to hold the XDR representation of the data. Because you are encoding three integers (and each XDR integer is 4 bytes), you must allocate at least 12 bytes for the buffer. Next, you call the **xdr_local_data()** routine, which was generated by the **rpcgen** compiler.

So, let's create a function named **encode_data()** that encodes the **local_data** structure into the XDR format. The function takes a pointer to a **local_data** structure and returns a pointer to a buffer containing the XDR representation of the structure. The code follows:

```
#include <stdio.h>
#include <rpc/rpc.h>
#include "def.h"
#define MAX_BUF 12

char *
encode_data(datap)
struct local_data *datap;
{
```

```
    XDR xdrs;   /* XDR structure for xdrmem_create() */
    char *buf; /* buffer to hold encoded data          */

    if ((buf = (char *)malloc(MAX_BUF)) == NULL) {
        return(NULL);
    }

    xdrmem_create(&xdrs, buf, MAX_BUF, XDR_ENCODE);

    if (xdr_local_data(&xdrs, datap) == FALSE) {
        free(buf);
        buf = NULL;
    }
    return(buf);
}
```

After you encode the data, send the resultant buffer over the network. When your peer application reads the data, it decodes the data into its local data format.

Now let's create a function named **decode_data()** that decodes the XDR representation into the local data format. To decode data, you must initialize an **XDR** structure with the **xdrmem_create()** routine. However, this time we set the second argument to a buffer containing the encoded data. We also set the fourth argument to the **XDR_DECODE** value.

Next, call the **xdr_local_data()** routine. Because we initialized the **XDR** structure with **XDR_DECODE**, the **xdr_local_data()** routine decodes the data from the XDR format into local representation.

We pass the **decode_data()** function a buffer containing the XDR format of the **local_data** structure. It returns a pointer to a **local_data** structure. The code follows:

```
#include <stdio.h>
#include <rpc/rpc.h>
#include "def.h"
#define MAX_BUF 12

struct local_data *
decode_data(buf)
char *buf;
{
    XDR xdrs;                       /* XDR structure          */
```

```
    struct local_data *datap; /* local representation */

    if ((datap =
      (struct local_data *)malloc(sizeof(struct local_data)))
                                                == NULL){
            return(NULL);
    }

    xdrmem_create(&xdrs, buf, MAX_BUF, XDR_DECODE);

    if (xdr_local_data(&xdrs, datap) == FALSE) {
            free(datap);
            datap = NULL;
    }

    return(datap);
}
```

The SVR4 C library contains the XDR routines to convert simple C data types into XDR format. For example, the C library contains:

- The **xdr_int()** routine, which converts an integer into the XDR format.

- The **xdr_short()** routine, which converts a short integer into the XDR format.

- The **xdr_char()** routine, which converts a character into the XDR format.

- The XDR routines for all other simple C data types. The routines are named **xdr_*type*()**, where *type* is a simple C data type.

The **encode_data()** and **decode_data()** routines we created let us convert data into and out of XDR representation. That lets us send data across the network in a common format, completing the functions of the presentation layer. Now let's look at how we can manage the session layer.

8.3   The Session Layer

The session layer is where you synchronize dialogue. You must create "over" messages and "over and out" messages that let the client and server sides of your application know when a complete message arrives.

SVR4 provides no routines to help manage the session layer. However, you can use some TLI primitives to do the work.

One way to synchronize data is to use a Transport Service Data Unit (TSDU) for each message. As described in Chapter 7, a TSDU is a unit of data that maintains its boundary. If you send each piece of data in a TSDU, the receiver knows when the data end.

Unfortunately, some connection-oriented transport providers do not support TSDUs. Most notably, the Transmission Control Protocol (TCP) does not support them.

If that is the case, you must send a distinct message to indicate the end of the data. Usually, you can send a **NULL** byte or a unique byte sequence to indicate the end of a message. Or, as mentioned in Chapter 7, you can also do one of the following:

1. You can send a fixed-length header message that contains the length of the data. When the receiver reads the full header, it examines the header to figure out the length of the data and keeps reading until it consumes the entire message.

2. The sender and the receiver can send fixed-length messages. For example, you can enclose all data in 512-byte messages. In that way, the receiver keeps reading until it consumes the entire 512-byte message.

After you've sent all data on a connection-oriented transport provider, you can send an orderly release message. That tells the receiver you are finished sending data (that is, it is like sending a ''over and out'' message).

But, not all transport protocols support orderly release messages. Most notably, the OSI transport protocols do not support them. In that case, you can do one of several things to indicate that you are finished sending data:

1. Decide upon a unique sequence of bytes that signifies the end of the session. When you have finished sending all of the data, send that sequence of bytes. When the reader gets that sequence, it knows you will not send any more data.

2. Do an abrupt shutdown. That tears down the connection. However, as mentioned in the **t_snddis()** section in Chapter 7, you must do some handshaking with this approach. Sending a disconnect request may distroy data in transit (that is, data sent prior to the disconnect request that may not yet have reached the remote application).

Now let's create two simple networking applications using TLI routines. The first uses a connection-oriented transport provider, and the second uses a connectionless transport provider.

8.4   A Simple Connection-Oriented Application

Let's create a simple connection-oriented application that shows how to use TLI routines. For our example, we'll write the C code that is specific to the Transmission

Control Protocol (TCP). Our transport-specific application is for illustration purposes only. After we see the transport-specific parts, we'll explain how to make applications transport-independent.

The application carries out a "person query" protocol. The following defines the action we'll do at each of the upper three layers of the OSI Model:

1. The **application layer** implements the protocol. The client side of the application sends a user name to the server side of the application. The server side reads the user name and determines if the user is currently logged onto the system. If the user is logged on, the server returns the "**y**" character. If the user is not logged on, the server returns the "**n**" character. After reading the response, the client side of the application can send another user name to the server. The loop continues until the client side of the application has no more user names to send.

2. The **presentation layer** formats the data. In our application, we only use ASCII characters. However, if we had to send other data types, we could use the methods presented in Section 8.2.

3. The **session layer** synchronizes dialogue. Because we are using the Transmission Control Protocol, we cannot use TSDUs to synchronize dialogue. TCP does not support message boundaries. So, in our application, the client side of the application sends a byte with the **0** value to indicate the end of a user name. Because the response is a single character (a "**y**" or an "**n**"), the client side of the application knows it has the entire response when it reads the single byte.

   As mentioned earlier, the client side of the application can repeat the process many times. So, when we are finished sending user names, we send an orderly release indication and wait for an orderly release reply. That lets the server side of the application know we have finished sending user names.

   Therefore, the "over" indication is when we send a **0** byte, and the "over and out" indication is when we send the orderly release indication.

We begin by presenting the server side of the application.

The Server Code

The following code carries out the server side of the application. Because we are using TCP/IP, we define a TCP port number. For this example, we simply hard code the value in the application.

```
#include <tiuser.h>
#include <stropts.h>
```

```
#include <stdio.h>
#include <fcntl.h>
#include <signal.h>
#include <sys/types.h>
#include <sys/socket.h>
#include <netinet/in.h>
#include <netdb.h>

extern int t_errno;

#define SERV_PORT 5134

main()
{
    int listen_fd;      /* file descriptor into transport */
    int recfd;          /* fd on which to to accept       */
    struct t_bind *req; /* address to which to bind       */
    struct t_bind *ret; /* actual address that was bound  */
    struct t_call *call; /* used to listen for connection */
    struct sockaddr_in myaddr; /* holds the address of    */
                               /* this service            */
```

To begin, we call the **t_open()** routine to create a transport endpoint. Our application is specific to TCP, so we specify the **/dev/tcp** file. That file is a clone device corresponding to the TCP transport provider. As described in Chapter 2, opening a clone device file causes the clone device to find an unused device into the transport provider, open it, and return the corresponding file descriptor.

We also set the the third argument of the **t_open()** routine to **NULL**. We do that because we don't need any transport-provider information.

We then have to bind a transport address to the transport endpoint. But, before we can do that, we must allocate space to hold the **t_bind** structures needed for the **t_bind()** routine.

We need two **t_bind** structures. The first structure contains the transport address to which we want to bind. The second holds the transport address to which we actually bound. The second address will be filled in by the **t_bind()** routine.

So, we call the **t_alloc()** routine to allocate the space. The second parameter is **T_BIND** (specifying we want a **t_bind** structure), and the third argument is **T_ALL** (specifying we want to allocate space for the **buf** element of the **netbuf** structure corresponding to the **addr** field). As mentioned in Chapter 7, the **t_alloc()** routine queries the transport provider to figure out the maximum size of the buffers.

```
if ((listen_fd = t_open ("/dev/tcp", O_RDWR, NULL)) < 0) {
   t_error ("t_open failed");
   exit(1);
}

/*
 *   Get space to hold the address to which you
 *   want to bind
 */

if ((req = (struct t_bind *) t_alloc (listen_fd, T_BIND,
                               T_ALL)) == NULL) {
   t_error ("t_alloc failed");
   exit(1);
}

/*
 *   Get space to hold the address o which
 *   you actually bound
 */

if ((ret = (struct t_bind *) t_alloc (listen_fd, T_BIND,
                               T_ALL)) == NULL) {
   t_error ("t_alloc failed");
   exit(1);
}
```

Now that we have the space to hold the address, we can bind the transport address to the transport endpoint. Because we are using the TCP transport provider, we construct a TCP-specific address.

As mentioned in Chapter 7, the SVR4 implementation of TCP/IP structures a TCP address as four pieces of information:

1. A 2-byte field containing a protocol identifier. For TCP/IP, this always contains a value of **2**.

2. A 2-byte field containing the TCP port number of the service.

3. A 4-byte field containing the IP address of the machine offering service.

4. An 8-byte filler. This is always **0**.

SVR4 provides the **sockaddr_in** structure that formats a TCP address. It has the following fields:

```
struct sockaddr_in {
    u_short          sin_family;
    u_short          sin_port;
    struct  in_addr  sin_addr;
    char             sin_zero[8];
};
```

The **sin_addr** field is an **in_addr** structure. This structure is a union that lets you access the 4-byte IP address as four separate bytes, as two short integers, or a single long integer.

In the following code segment, we set the **sin_family** field to **AF_INET** (a defined value of **2**), the **sin_port** field to the port number defined at the beginning of the application, and the **sin_addr** field to **INADDR_ANY**. The **INADDR_ANY** value is the special IP address **0.0.0.0**. As explained in Chapter 3, that address binds all IP addresses on the machine to the transport endpoint.

Note that we create the TCP transport address by assigning numeric values to the port number field and IP address field of the **sockaddr_in** structure. That poses a problem if our machine does not have the data representation assumed by the TCP/IP protocols. The IP protocols assume all addresses are in a "network representation." If we bind to an address that is not in the correct data format, the transport-provider functions may fail.

To solve that problem, you must put the IP address and port number in the network representation. You use the following TCP/IP specific routines to do the conversion:

1. Use the **htons()** routine to convert a short integer (for example, the port number) into the network representation.

2. Use the **htonl()** routine to convert a long integer (for example, the IP address) into the network representation.

The **htons()** routine and the **htonl()** routine are TCP/IP specific. As we will see in Chapter 9, SVR4 provides the Name-to-Address Mapping routines. These routines obtain addresses in a transport-independent way. The addresses returned from the Name-to-Address Mapping routines are already converted into the correct format.

After we structure the IP address in the **sockaddr_in** structure, we copy it into the **netbuf** structure associated with the **addr** field of the **t_bind** structure. We also set the **qlen** field to **1**, meaning that we can retrieve only one connection request at a time.

You should only set the **qlen** field to a value greater than **1** in a TLI application if
you need to process several incoming calls simultaneously. For example, you should
set **qlen** to a value greater than **1** if you want to impose some level of priority on
the incoming calls.

Most applications should *not* set **qlen** to a value greater than **1**, because it imposes
more complexity on the server side of the application. If **qlen** is greater than **1**, you
must retrieve any and all connection requests before you can successfully accept any of
them! And, even if **qlen** *is* set to **1**, the transport provider can still queue up incoming calls without passing them to the transport user. We present the details of how to
handle a **qlen** greater than **1** in Section 8.5.

After we issue the **t_bind()** routine, we check that the address to which we bound
was the address requested. If not, we issue an error message and exit the application.

```
/*
 *  Set qlen to 1 and fill in the address.
 */

req->qlen = 1;
req->addr.len = sizeof(struct sockaddr_in);

memset((void *)&myaddr, 0, sizeof(struct sockaddr_in));
myaddr.sin_family = AF_INET;
myaddr.sin_addr.s_addr = htonl(INADDR_ANY);
myaddr.sin_port = htons(SERV_PORT);

(void)memcpy(req->addr.buf, &myaddr,
                            sizeof(struct sockaddr_in));

/*
 *  Bind to the address the service will be offered
 *  over.
 */

if (t_bind(listen_fd, req, ret) < 0) {
  t_error("t_bind failed");
  exit(1);
}

/*
 *  Make sure the address you got was the one you wanted!
 */
```

```
if ((req->addr.len != ret->addr.len) ||
  (memcmp(req->addr.buf, ret->addr.buf, req->addr.len))){
  fprintf(stderr, "Did not bind to correct address!\n");
  exit(1);
}
```

Now that we have a transport address bound to our transport endpoint, we can listen for connection requests. In the following code segment, we do the following:

1. Use the **t_alloc()** routine to allocate space to hold a **t_call** structure. We use the **t_call** structure when listening for connection requests. When a connection request arrives, the **t_listen()** routine fills the **t_call** structure with the address of the application making the connection request, the transport options, data sent on the connection request, and a sequence number that identifies the connection request.

   In our example, we do not use any transport options, so we do not use the **opt** field of the **t_call** structure. And, because TCP does not allow the sending of data on a connection request, we also do not use the **udata** field of the **t_call** structure.

2. Loop continuously. Within the loop, we wait for connection requests. When a connection request arrives, we accept it and create a child process to carry out the protocol. Specifically, we do the following:

   a. Issue the **t_listen()** routine, passing it the **t_call** structure and the file descriptor into the transport endpoint.

   b. When the **t_listen()** routine returns, we have a connection request pending on the transport endpoint. So, we call the **t_open()** routine to create a second transport endpoint, which is used to accept the connection.

   c. Call **t_bind()** to bind an arbitrary transport address to the second transport endpoint. We specify that we want an arbitrary address by passing a **NULL** value as the second parameter. And, because we don't care what address is obtained, we pass a **NULL** value as the third parameter as well.

   d. Call the **t_accept()** routine to accept the connection. We pass it the original transport endpoint, the second transport endpoint, and the **t_call** structure filled by the **t_listen()** routine.

   e. Check the return value of the **t_accept()** routine. If the routine failed, we check if it set the **t_errno** variable to **TLOOK**. As explained in Chapter 7, the **t_accept()** routine sets the **t_errno** variable to **TLOOK** if we received a disconnect event on the transport endpoint while trying to accept the connection. If **t_errno** is set to **TLOOK**, we issue the **t_rcvdis()** routine to clear the disconnect event and continue the loop to accept the next connection request.

f. If the **t_accept()** routine fails for any other reason, something is wrong with the transport endpoint. We print the reason for failure and exit the application.

g. If the **t_accept()** routine succeeds, then the second transport endpoint is connected to the client side of the application, and the first transport endpoint is back in the **T_IDLE** state.

We then issue the **fork()** system call to create a child process. The child process closes the first transport endpoint and calls a subroutine to implement the protocol. The parent process closes the second transport endpoint and continues the loop, listening for the next connection request on the original transport endpoint.

The code follows:

```
if ((call = (struct t_call *) t_alloc (listen_fd, T_CALL,
                                 T_ALL)) == NULL) {
    t_error ("could not allocate space for t_call!");
    exit(1);
}
/*
 *  Loop continuously, listening for connection requests,
 *  accepting the call, and performing the service.
 */

while (1) {
    if (t_listen (listen_fd, call) < 0) {
        t_error ("could not listen!");
        exit(1);
    }

    if ((recfd = t_open ("/dev/tcp", O_RDWR, NULL)) < 0) {
        t_error ("could not open device!");
        exit(1);
    }

    if (t_bind (recfd, NULL, NULL) < 0) {
        t_error ("bind for responding failed!");
        exit(1);
    }
```

```
    if (t_accept (listen_fd, recfd, call) < 0) {

        /*
         *  Did it fail because the client disconnected?
         *  t_errno is set to TLOOK if it did.
         */

        if (t_errno == TLOOK) {
            if (t_rcvdis (listen_fd, NULL) < 0) {
                t_error ("could not disconnect");
                exit(1);
            }
            (void) t_close (recfd);
            continue;
        } else {
            t_error ("could not accept call");
            exit(1);
        }
    }
    switch (fork()) {
        case -1:
            perror("fork failed!\n");
            exit(1);

        default: /* parent */

            t_close (recfd);
            break;

        case 0:  /* child */

            t_close (listen_fd);

            /*
             *  The child_actions() routine exits
             *  when it completes
             */
            child_actions(recfd);
        }
    }
}
```

Now, we create the **child_actions()** routine to carry out the protocol. It takes one argument—the transport endpoint that has the established connection. We do the following:

1. Loop, calling a local subroutine (named **perform_actions()**) to carry out our protocol. As we will see shortly, that subroutine reads a user name, figures out if that user is logged onto the system, and sends a response to the client side of the application. It returns **1** if it carried out the protocol correctly. It returns **0** if an error occurs. It also returns **0** if the client side of the application sends an orderly release message (indicating it is finished sending user names). So, we continue the loop until the subroutine returns **0**.

2. When we break out of the loop, check if an orderly release event is on the transport endpoint. If it is, we read the orderly release message and send back an orderly release message. That handshake completes our session layer functions.

3. If an orderly release event is not on the transport endpoint, then the **perform_actions()** routine encountered an error. In that case, we exit the child process.

```
int
child_actions (resfd)
int resfd;
{
    while (perform_actions(resfd))
                ;

    /*
     *  Did we exit the above loop because the orderly
     *  release happened?  If so, accept the orderly
     *  release and send an acknowledgment.
     */

    if (t_look (resfd) == T_ORDREL) {
        if (t_rcvrel (resfd) < 0) {
            t_error ("t_rcvrel failed!");
            exit(1);
        }
        if (t_sndrel (resfd) < 0) {
            t_error ("t_sndrel failed!");
            exit(1);
        }
        exit(0);
    }
}
```

```
        exit(1);
}
```

The **perform_actions()** routine does the real work. We do the following:

1. Use the **t_rcv()** routine to read the user name from the transport endpoint. However, because TCP does not preserve message boundaries, we continue reading until we see the **0** byte. The **0** byte indicates the end of the string.

2. Return a **0** if the **t_rcv()** routine fails, Remember that the **t_rcv()** routine fails if an orderly release indication arrives. In that case, it is not an error. The client side of the application simply told us it is through sending user names.

3. If the **t_rcv()** routine succeeds, we have a user name. We figure out if the user is logged into the system, and send a **y** or an **n** to the client side of the application.

    We call the **popen()** routine to figure out if a user is logged onto the system. We could have done that more efficiently by searching the **/etc/utmp** file directly, but the **popen()** routine suffices for our example.

The code follows:

```
int
perform_actions(conn_fd)
int conn_fd;
{
    int done;        /* indicates all data are read        */
    int where;       /* points to where we are in buffer   */
    int nbytes;      /* the number of bytes read           */
    int flags = 0;   /* info returned from t_rcv()         */
    char reply;      /* a 'y' or 'n' to reply to client    */
    char buf[BUFSIZ];   /* buffer to hold the name         */

    char cmd[BUFSIZ];      /* used to figure out if the    */
    char junkbuf[BUFSIZ];  /* specified user is logged     */
    FILE *fp;              /* onto the system              */

    /*
     * Read the user name from the client.
     * The flags argument would contain information like
     * whether the data was "expedited", but it is ignored
     * in this example.
     */
```

```
    done = 0;
    where = 0;
    do {
        if ((BUFSIZ - where) == 0) {
            return(0);
        }
        if ((nbytes = t_rcv(conn_fd, &buf[where],
                     BUFSIZ - where, &flags)) < 0) {
            return(0);
        }
        where += nbytes;
        if (buf[where - 1] == '\0') {
            done = 1;
        }
    } while (!done);

    /*
     *  Determine if the user is logged on...
     */

    sprintf(cmd, "who | grep '^%s '", buf);
    if ((fp = popen(cmd, "r")) == NULL
     || fgets(junkbuf, BUFSIZ, fp) == NULL) {
        reply = 'n';
    } else {
        reply = 'y';
    }

    /*
     *  Send a "y" or an "n" to the client.
     *  The last argument is 0, specifying that no
     *  flags are sent.
     */

    if (t_snd(conn_fd, &reply, 1, 0) < 0) {
        t_error("t_snd failed!");
        return(0);
    }
    return(1);
}
```

Now let's look at the client side of the application. As with the server side, the client side is specific to the Transmission Control Protocol (TCP).

The client side of the application establishes a connection to the server side. It sends a user name and reads the response. It continues sending a user name and reading a response until it has no more names to send. It informs the server that it is finished sending names by sending an orderly release message.

The Client Code

The following code carries out the client side of the application. The client side takes user names as parameters. For each user name specified on the command line, it sends the name to the server side of the application, reads a response to figure out if that user is logged onto the server machine, and displays the response.

Because we are using TCP/IP, we use the TCP port number to which the server side of the application is attached. For this example, we simply hard code that value in the application.

```
#include <stdio.h>
#include <tiuser.h>
#include <fcntl.h>
#include <sys/types.h>
#include <sys/socket.h>
#include <netinet/in.h>
#include <netdb.h>
#define SERV_PORT 5134
struct hostent *gethostbyname();

main(argc, argv)
int argc;
char **argv;
{
  int fd;                      /* fd into transport provider */
  int flags = 0;               /* used to receive info       */
  int i;                       /* indexes through user names */
  char buf[BUFSIZ];            /* holds message from server  */
  struct t_call *sndcall;      /* used to call server        */
  struct hostent *hp;          /* holds IP address of server */
  struct sockaddr_in myaddr;   /* address that client uses   */
  struct sockaddr_in servaddr; /* the server's full addr     */
```

To begin, we check that at least one user name is given to the application. Next, we do the following:

1. Create a transport endpoint into the TCP transport provider. We do that by issuing the **t_open()** routine, specifying the **/dev/tcp** device file.

2. Bind to an arbitrary transport address. We are on the client side of the application, so we don't care what address we get. No application is going to connect to us, so no application needs to know our address. We issue the **t_bind()** routine, specifying a **NULL** pointer as the requested address and a **NULL** pointer as the returned address.

```
/*
 *  Check for proper usage.
 */

if (argc < 3) {
    fprintf(stderr,
            "Usage: %s server username [username...]\n",
            argv[0]);
    exit(1);
}

/*
 *  Create the transport endpoint.
 */

if ((fd = t_open("/dev/tcp", O_RDWR, NULL)) < 0) {
    t_error("t_open failed!");
    exit(1);
}

/*
 *  Bind to an arbitrary return address.
 */

if (t_bind(fd, NULL, NULL) < 0) {
    t_error("t_bind failed!");
    exit(1);
}
```

Now, we are ready to make the connection to the server machine. First, we call the **t_alloc()** routine to allocate memory to hold the **t_call** structure. We use the **t_call** structure in the **t_connect()** routine.

The only field of the **t_call** structure that we use is the **addr** field. We are not setting any protocol-specific options, so we do not use the **opt** field. And, because TCP does not support sending data on a connection request, we do not use the **udata** field.

We populate the **addr** field with the transport address to which we want to connect. As mentioned earlier, the SVR4 implementation of TCP/IP structures a TCP address into four fields: a 2-byte field containing a protocol identifier, a 2-byte field containing the TCP port number of the service, a 4-byte field containing the IP address of the machine offering service, and an 8-byte filler. So, as with the server side of the application, we use the **sockaddr_in** structure to format the TCP transport address. We fill the fields of the **sockaddr_in** structure as follows:

1. Fill the entire structure with **0** values. That places a **0** in the 8-byte filler area at the end of the structure.

2. Assign the value **AF_INET** to the **sin_family** field (SVR4 defines **AF_INET** as **2**). That places the required value of **2** in the first two bytes of the TCP address.

3. Place the server's port number in the **sin_port** field. As with the server side of the application, we convert that value into network representation by calling the **htons()** routine.

4. Figure out the IP address of the server machine. We do that by calling the **gethostbyname()** routine. The **gethostbyname()** routine is a TCP/IP-specific routine that returns a list of IP addresses for a given machine. The addresses are in network representation, so we don't have to call the **htonl()** routine to convert them ourselves.

   The **gethostbyname()** routine returns a list of IP addresses for a given machine because, as explained in Chapter 3, a single machine can have several IP addresses. Unfortunately, SVR4 provides no routines that figure out whether one address is better than another. So, we simply copy the first address in the list into the **sin_addr** field.

After we create the TCP/IP address, we copy the **sockaddr_in** structure into the **addr** field of the **t_call** structure. We then issue the **t_connect()** routine. The code follows:

```
/*
 *   Get memory to hold call structure, copy in
 *   the server's address, and connect to the service.
 */
if ((sndcall = (struct t_call *) t_alloc (fd, T_CALL,
                              T_ADDR)) == NULL) {
```

```
            t_error("t_alloc failed!");
            exit(1);
        }

        sndcall->addr.len = sizeof(struct sockaddr_in);
        memset((void *)&servaddr, 0, sizeof(struct sockaddr_in));
        servaddr.sin_family = AF_INET;
        servaddr.sin_port = htons(SERV_PORT);

        hp = gethostbyname(argv[1]);
        if (hp == 0) {
            fprintf(stderr, "could not obtain address of %s\n",
                    argv[1]);
            return (-1);
        }

        (void)memcpy((caddr_t)&servaddr.sin_addr,
                    hp->h_addr_list[0], hp->h_length);

        (void)memcpy(sndcall->addr.buf, &servaddr,
                                            sizeof(servaddr));

        if (t_connect(fd, sndcall, NULL) < 0) {
            t_error("t_connect failed!");
            exit(1);
        }
```

Now that there is an established connection, we can carry out the protocol. We loop through all of the user names given as parameters. Within the loop, we do the following actions:

1. Send the user name to the server machine via the **t_snd()** routine. We make sure to send the **0** byte at the end of the name, because the server side of our application uses that to figure out where the name ends.

   We are not sending expedited data, so the fourth argument to the **t_snd()** routine is **0**.

2. Issue the **t_rcv()** routine to read the response from the server machine. The response is a single byte (a "**y**" or an "**n**" character), so we get the entire message with a single **t_rcv()** call. The **t_rcv()** routine sleeps until the message arrives.

When we complete the loop, we send an orderly release message by calling the
t_sndrel() routine. That lets the server side of the application know we are
finished sending user names. We then issue the **t_rcvrel()** routine, which sleeps
waiting for the orderly release indication from the server.

The code follows:

```
/*
 *  Send each user name, and read the response.
 *  The user names start at argv[2].
 */

for (i = 2; i < argc; i++) {
    if (t_snd(fd, argv[i], strlen(argv[i])+1, 0) == -1) {
        t_error("t_snd failed!\n");
        exit(1);
    }

    /*
     *  We must pass the address of a flags integer to the
     *  t_rcv() routine, even though we do not use it in
     *  our application.
     */

    if (t_rcv(fd, buf, 1, &flags) == -1) {
        t_error("t_rcv failed!\n");
        exit(1);
    }

    if (buf[0] == 'y') {
        printf("%s is logged on server\n", argv[i]);
    } else {
        printf("%s is not logged on server\n", argv[i]);
    }
}

/*
 *  Perform the orderly release...
 */
if (t_sndrel(fd) < 0) {
    t_error("t_sndrel failed!\n");
    exit(1);
}
```

```
/*
 *  Wait for server to respond with an orderly release.
 */

(void) t_rcvrel(fd);

exit(0);
}
```

Now that we've seen how to use TLI for connection-oriented transport providers, let's look at an application that uses TLI routines for connectionless transport providers.

8.5 A Simple Connectionless-Mode Application

Now let's create a simple application that illustrates how to use TLI routines over a connectionless transport provider. For this example, we'll write the C code that is specific to the User Datagram Protocol (UDP). A transport-specific application like this is for illustration purposes only. We'll explain how to make applications transport-independent in Section 8.6.

Our application carries out the same "person query" protocol implemented in the connection-oriented application. The following defines the action we'll do at each of the upper three layers of the OSI model:

1. The **application layer** implements the protocol. The client side of the application sends a datagram containing a user name to the server side of the application. The server side reads the user name and figures out if the user is currently logged onto the system. If the user is logged on, the server returns a datagram containing the "**y**" character. If the user is not logged on, the server returns a datagram containing the "**n**" character.

2. The **presentation layer** formats the data. In our application, we only use ASCII characters. However, if we had to send other data types, we could use the methods presented in Section 8.2.

3. The **session layer** synchronizes dialogue. Because we are using the User Datagram Protocol, each datagram contains a complete message. So, we coordinate dialogue by incorporating a complete message in a single datagram.

We begin by presenting the server side of the application.

The Server Code

The following code carries out the server side of the application. Because we are using UDP, we define a UDP port number. For this example, we simply hard code the value in the application.

```
#include <tiuser.h>
#include <stropts.h>
#include <stdio.h>
#include <fcntl.h>
#include <signal.h>
#include <sys/types.h>
#include <sys/socket.h>
#include <netinet/in.h>
#include <netdb.h>

extern int t_errno;

#define SERV_PORT 5134

main()
{
    int dg_fd;              /* file descriptor into transport */
    struct t_bind *req;     /* requested addr to which to bind*/
    struct t_bind *ret;     /* actual address that was bound  */
    int flags;              /* holds info when reading        */
    struct t_unitdata *datap;  /* the actual datagram         */
    struct sockaddr_in myaddr; /* address of server           */

    char cmd[BUFSIZ];       /* used to figure out if the      */
    char junkbuf[BUFSIZ];   /* specified user is logged       */
    FILE *fp;               /* onto the system                */
```

To begin, we create a transport endpoint into the User Datagram Protocol. We call the **t_open()** routine, passing it the clone device file for UDP. Because our application is specific to UDP, we don't need the information in the **t_info** structure. So, the third argument to the **t_open()** routine is **NULL**.

Next, we bind to our transport address. We do that as follows:

1. Call the **t_alloc()** routine to allocate space to hold the address to which we want to attach.

2. Call the **t_alloc()** routine again to allocate space to hold the address to which we actually bind.

3. Construct our transport address. As mentioned earlier, the SVR4 implementation of TCP/IP formats a transport address as a 2-byte family name, a 2-byte port number, a 4-byte IP address, and an 8-byte filler. And, as we did in the connection-oriented version of the application, we place that information in the **sockaddr_in** structure. We construct the address as follows:

    a. Fill the structure with **0** values. That places a **0** in the 8-byte filler area at the end of the structure.

    b. Assign the **AF_INET** value to the **sin_family** field. That places the required value of **2** in the first two bytes.

    c. Place our port number in the **sin_port** field. As in the connection-oriented version of the application, we convert that value to network representation by calling the TCP/IP-specific **htons()** routine.

    d. Set the **sin_addr** field to **INADDR_ANY**. The **INADDR_ANY** value is the special IP address **0.0.0.0**. As explained in Chapter 3, that says we want to bind to all IP addresses on the machine. We convert the **INADDR_ANY** value to network representation by calling the **htonl()** routine.

4. Copy the address into the **addr** field of the **t_bind** structure, and call the **t_bind()** routine to bind the transport address to the transport endpoint. Next, check that the address to which we bound to was the address requested.

The code follows:

```
if ((dg_fd = t_open ("/dev/udp", O_RDWR, NULL)) < 0) {
    t_error ("t_open failed");
    exit(1);
}

/*
 *  Get space to hold the address to which you want
 *  to bind.
 */

if ((req = (struct t_bind *) t_alloc (dg_fd, T_BIND,
                                   T_ALL)) == NULL) {

    t_error ("t_alloc failed");
    exit(1);
}
```

```
/*
 *  Get space to hold the address to which you
 *  actually bind.
 */

if ((ret = (struct t_bind *) t_alloc(dg_fd, T_BIND,
                                      T_ALL)) == NULL) {
    t_error("t_alloc failed");
    exit(1);
}

/*
 *  Set qlen to 0 because qlen has no meaning for
 *  connectionless transport providers.
 */

req->qlen = 0;
req->addr.len = sizeof(struct sockaddr_in);

memset((void *)&myaddr, 0, sizeof(struct sockaddr_in));
myaddr.sin_family = AF_INET;
myaddr.sin_port = htons(SERV_PORT);
myaddr.sin_addr.s_addr = htonl(INADDR_ANY);

(void)memcpy(req->addr.buf, &myaddr,
                            sizeof(struct sockaddr_in));

/*
 *  Bind to the address the service will be offered
 *  over.
 */

if (t_bind(dg_fd, req, ret) < 0) {
    t_error("t_bind failed");
    exit(1);
}

/*
 *  Make sure the address you got was the one you wanted!
 */

if ((req->addr.len != ret->addr.len) ||
    (memcmp(req->addr.buf, ret->addr.buf, req->addr.len))){
```

```
        fprintf(stderr, "Did not bind to correct address!\n");
        exit(1);
    }
```

Now that we've bound to a transport address, we're ready to read datagrams. We do the following:

1. Call the **t_alloc()** routine to allocate a **t_unitdata** structure. We use one structure for both receiving and sending datagrams.

2. Loop forever, processing datagrams. Within the loop, we do the following:

   a. Issue the **t_rcvudata()** routine to read a datagram. That routine sleeps until a datagram arrives. When that happens, the **t_rcvudata()** routine fills the **t_unitdata** structure with information about the datagram. The **addr** field contains the source address of the application that sent the datagram, the **opt** field identifies protocol-specific options (there are none in this application), and the **udata** field contains the data.

   The **flags** argument of **t_rcvudata()** must point to an integer value. The **t_rcvudata()** routine sets it to **T_MORE** if the **udata** element of the **t_unitdata** structure was not large enough to hold all of the data.

   In that case, you would have to issue another **t_rcvudata()** routine to get the rest of the datagram. However, in our example, we allocated space to hold the **t_unitdata** structure by calling the **t_alloc()** routine with the **T_ALL** flag. That allocated space to hold the maximum datagram the transport provider allows. So, there is no need to check for the **T_MORE** flag.

   If the **t_rcvudata()** routine fails, we check if the failure was due to a **T_UDERR** event. As mentioned in Chapter 7, we get the **T_UDERR** event if the system could not process a previous datagram we sent (we send datagrams in this loop in step c, which follows). The **T_UDERR** event on the transport endpoint causes the **t_rcvudata()** routine to fail and set the **t_errno** variable to **TLOOK** (the **T_UDERR** event is the only event that causes **t_errno** to be set to **TLOOK** in the **t_rcvudata()** routine). So, as mentioned in Chapter 7, we *must* consume that event by calling the **t_rcvuderr()** routine.

   The reason we may get the **T_UDERR** event is protocol-specific. It does not necessarily indicate whether the transport provider delivered the previously sent datagram (connectionless transport providers do not guarantee delivery). As explained in Chapter 7, the **t_rcvuderr()** routine returns information about the datagram that produced the event. However, in this example, we don't examine that information because we will code the client side of the application to resend the request if it does not get a response. So, if we get the **T_UDERR** event, we simply clear the event with the **t_rcvuderr()** routine and continue reading datagrams.

b. Figure out if the user is logged into the machine. Depending upon the results, we place a "**y**" or an "**n**" in the **udata** field of the **t_unitdata** structure.

c. Issue the **t_sndudata()** routine to send the results back to the application that sent us the datagram. Here, the **addr** field of the **t_unitdata** structure contains the destination address. And, because we are using the same structure used with the **t_rcvudata()** routine, the destination address is already filled in. The **t_rcvudata()** routine filled in the **addr** field with the address of the application that sent the datagram.

The code follows:

```
if ((datap = (struct t_unitdata *) t_alloc (dg_fd,
                            T_UNITDATA, T_ALL)) == NULL) {
    t_error ("could not allocate space for t_unitdata!");
    exit(1);
}

/*
 *  Loop continuously, processing datagrams.
 */

while (1) {
    if (t_rcvudata (dg_fd, datap, &flags) < 0) {
        /*
         *  If the t_rcvudata() routine fails, check if the
         *  reason was because an error occurred on a
         *  previous datagram we sent (t_errno is set to
         *  TLOOK if that is the case).  If that's so,
         *  clear the error event with t_rcvuderr().
         */
        if (t_errno == TLOOK) {
            if (t_rcvuderr (dg_fd, NULL) < 0) {
                t_error ("could not clear error event!");
            }
        } else {
            t_error ("could not read datagram!");
```

```
        }
        continue;
    }

    sprintf(cmd, "who | grep '^%s '", datap->udata.buf);
    if ((fp = popen(cmd, "r")) == NULL
     || fgets(junkbuf, BUFSIZ, fp) == NULL) {
        strcpy(datap->udata.buf, "n");
    } else {
        strcpy(datap->udata.buf, "y");
    }
    datap->udata.len = 1;
    if (t_sndudata(dg_fd, datap) < 0) {
        t_error("could not send datagram!");
        continue;
    }
    }
}
}
```

Now let's look at the client side of the application. As with the server side, the client side is specific to the User Datagram Protocol.

The client side of the application sends a datagram containing a user name. It then waits for the response. And, because a connectionless transport provider is being used, we resend the request if we do not get the response after a period of time.

The Client Code

The following code carries out the client side of the application. The client side takes a single user name as a parameter. It constructs a datagram containing the user name, sends the datagram to the server side of the application, and reads a response to see if that user is logged onto the server machine.

The code also resends the datagram if it does not get a response. We will not get a response if one of the following happens:

1. The datagram we send to the server side of the application is lost.

2. The datagram containing the response is lost.

To begin, we declare the variables we need. Also, because we are using UDP, we specify the UDP port number to which the server is attached. For this example, we hard code that value in the application. We also hard code the number of times we resend the request before giving up. In our example, we set the number of tries to 20.

```
#include <stdio.h>
#include <tiuser.h>
#include <fcntl.h>
#include <sys/types.h>
#include <sys/socket.h>
#include <netinet/in.h>
#include <netdb.h>
#include <signal.h>

#define NUM_TRIES    20
int timed_out;

#define SERV_PORT 5134
struct hostent *gethostbyname();

main(argc, argv)
int argc;
char **argv;
{
    int fd;                    /* fd into transport provider */
    int flags = 0;             /* used to receive into       */
    char buf[BUFSIZ];          /* holds message from server  */
    struct t_unitdata *datap;/* used to call server        */
    int tries = NUM_TRIES;     /* number of tries to send    */
    int got_it = 0;            /* determines datagram receipt*/
    struct hostent *hp;        /* holds IP address of server */
    struct sockaddr_in myaddr;/* address that client uses   */
    struct sockaddr_in servaddr; /* the server's full addr */
    void handler();            /* handles time-out signals   */


    /*
     *  Check for proper usage
     */

    if (argc != 3) {
        fprintf(stderr,"Usage: %s host username\n", argv[0]);
        exit(2);
    }
```

The first thing we do is obtain a transport endpoint. We do that by calling the **t_open()** routine. We are using the User Datagram Protocol, so we specify the **/dev/udp** clone device file.

Next, we bind an arbitrary transport address to the transport endpoint. We do not care what address we get, because UDP sends our address with the datagram. So, the server side of the application gets our address when it receives the datagram. The server side of the application sends the response to the transport address that originated the message.

```
/*
 *  Open the transport provider.
 */

if ((fd = t_open ("/dev/udp", O_RDWR, NULL)) < 0) {
   t_error ("t_open failed!");
   exit(1);
}

/*
 *  Bind to an arbitrary return address.
 */

if (t_bind (fd, NULL, NULL) < 0) {
   t_error ("t_bind failed!");
   exit(1);
}
```

Now we create the datagram. First, we allocate the **t_unitdata** structure by calling the **t_alloc()** routine.

Next, we check that the user name given as a parameter can fit in a single datagram. We do that by checking the **maxlen** field of the **udata** element of the **t_unitdata** structure against the number of bytes in the user name. If the user name is too large, we exit the application.

If the user name fits in the datagram, we copy it into the **udata** field of the **t_unitdata** structure. Then, we populate the **addr** field with the transport address to which we want to send the datagram. As mentioned earlier, the SVR4 implementation of TCP/IP structures a UDP address as a 2-byte field containing a protocol identifier, a 2-byte field containing the UDP port number of the service, a 4-byte field containing the IP address of the machine offering service, and an 8-byte filler. So, as we did in the server side of the application, we use the **sockaddr_in** structure to

format the UDP transport address.   We fill the fields of the **sockaddr_in** structure
as follows:

1. Fill the structure with **0** values. That places a **0** in the 8-byte filler area at the
    end of the structure.

2. Assign the **AF_INET** value to the **sin_family** field. That places the
    required value of **2** in the first two bytes.

3. Place the server's port number in the **sin_port** field. As with the server side
    of the application, we convert the port number into network representation by
    calling the **htons()** routine.

4. Figure out the IP address of the server machine in the same way we did in the
    connection-oriented version of the application, that is, we call the **gethost-
    byname()** routine. That routine is a TCP/IP-specific routine that returns a list
    of IP addresses for a given machine. The addresses are in network representa-
    tion, so we don't have to call the **htonl()** routine to convert them ourselves.
    We copy the first address in the list into the **sin_addr** field.

After we create the UDP address, we copy the **sockaddr_in** structure into the
addr field of the **t_unitdata** structure. The code follows:

```
/*
 *  Get memory to hold the datagram.
 */

if ((datap = (struct t_unitdata *)t_alloc(fd, T_UNITDATA,
                                 T_ALL)) == NULL) {
    t_error("t_alloc failed!");
    exit(1);
}

/*
 *  Fill in the server's address and the data.
 */
if (datap->udata.maxlen < (strlen(argv[2]) + 1)) {
    fprintf(stderr, "The user name %s is too large\n",
                    argv[2]);
    exit(1);
}

datap->udata.len = strlen(argv[2]) + 1;
strcpy(datap->udata.buf, argv[2]);
```

```
datap->addr.len = sizeof(struct sockaddr_in);
memset((void *)&servaddr, 0, sizeof(struct sockaddr_in));
servaddr.sin_family = AF_INET;
servaddr.sin_port = htons(SERV_PORT);

hp = gethostbyname(argv[1]);
if (hp == 0) {
    fprintf(stderr, "could not obtain address of %s\n",
        argv[1]);
    return (-1);
}

(void)memcpy((caddr_t)&servaddr.sin_addr,
            hp->h_addr_list[0], hp->h_length);

(void)memcpy(datap->addr.buf, &servaddr,
                                sizeof(servaddr));
```

We're now ready to send the datagram. A connectionless transport provider does not guarantee delivery, so we make 20 attempts to get the information needed.

The following code loops 20 times. Within each iteration of the loop, we do the following actions:

1. Send the datagram to the server side of the application.

2. Call the **t_rcvudata()** routine to read the reply. The **t_rcvudata()** routine sleeps until the reply arrives.

    However, because we are using a connectionless transport provider, *the reply may never arrive!* So, we set an alarm to wake up the **t_rcvudata()** routine after **15** seconds. We do that with the following:

    a. Set a variable named **timed_out** to **0**.

    b. Set a signal handler for the **SIGALRM** signal. When we get the **SIGALRM** signal, we call the **handler()** routine. The **handler()** routine simply sets the **timed_out** variable to **1**.

    c. Set an alarm to generate the **SIGALRM** signal in **15** seconds.

    Here's what we've set up. After **15** seconds, we will get the **SIGALRM** signal. That causes the **handler()** routine to execute, which sets the **timed_out** variable to **1**. It also causes the **t_rcvudata()** routine to return with an error condition.

So, if the **t_rcvudata()** routine succeeds, we got our response. We turn off the alarm, set the **gotit** variable to **1** to indicate we got a response, and exit the loop.

If the **t_rcvudata()** routine fails, we check if the failure was because the alarm went off. If it was, then we didn't get a response in **15** seconds. So, we continue the loop, resend the datagram, reset the alarm to send us a signal in **15** seconds, and sleep again waiting for the response.

We also check if the **t_rcvudata()** routine failed because we got the **T_UDERR** event. As explained in Chapter 7, we get the **T_UDERR** event if the system could not process a previously sent datagram. The **T_UDERR** event on the transport endpoint causes the **t_rcvudata()** routine to fail and set the **t_errno** variable to **TLOOK**. And, as mentioned in Chapter 7, we *must* consume that event by calling the **t_rcvuderr()** routine. So, if the **t_rcvudata()** routine fails and the **t_errno** variable is set to **TLOOK**, we call the **t_rcvuderr()** routine to clear the event and continue the loop to resend the datagram. If the **t_rcvudata()** routine failed for any other reason, we exit the application.

3. Check the value of the **gotit** variable after the loop ends. If it is **0**, then we know we tried to get a response 20 times without success. Otherwise, we display the results to the user.

The code follows:

```
while (tries --) {
    if (t_sndudata(fd, datap) == -1) {
        t_error("t_sndudata failed!");
        exit(1);
    }

    /*
     *   Allow 15 seconds for the response to arrive.
     */
    timed_out = 0;
    sigset(SIGALRM, handler);
    alarm(15);

    if (t_rcvudata(fd, datap, &flags) == 0) {
        alarm(0);
        got_it = 1;
        break;
    }
```

```
        /*
         *  We now know the t_rcvudata() routine failed.
         *  Check if we timed out.  If we did, we continue
         *  the loop and resend the request.
         */

        if (timed_out) {
            printf("Server not responding, retrying...\n");
            continue;
        }

        /*
         *  If the t_rcvudata() routine fails, check if the
         *  reason was because an error occurred on a previous
         *  datagram we sent (t_errno is set to TLOOK if that is
         *  the case).  If that's so, clear the error event
         *  with the t_rcvuderr() routine.
         */

        if (t_errno == TLOOK) {
            if (t_rcvuderr(dg_fd, NULL) < 0) {
                t_error("could not clear error event!");
                exit(1);
            }
            continue;
        }

        t_error("t_rcvudata failed!");
        exit(1);
    }

    if (!got_it) {
        printf("failed %d times, exiting\n", NUM_TRIES);
        exit(1);
    }

    if (datap->udata.buf[0] == 'y')
        printf("%s is logged on server\n", argv[2]);
    else
        printf("%s is not logged on server\n", argv[2]);

    exit(0);
}
```

```
void
handler()
{
    timed_out = 1;
}
```

There is one other thing to note about our algorithm. In our example, we only send one user name to the server side of the application and exit the application when we get a result. If we were sending several users names, we would have to modify our algorithm to account for multiple responses to the same query.

Here's what can happen if the client side of the application sends several different user names to the server side of the application:

1. We send the first user name to the server side of the application and wait for a response.

2. Let's say the response takes 20 seconds to arrive. According to our algorithm, our timer expires in 15 seconds and we resend the user name (which, if successfully delivered to the server side of the application, will generate a second response). In 5 more seconds, the response to the *first* query arrives. We print the response and then send the second user name.

3. Now, the client side of the application is waiting for a response to the second user name. However, when it gets a response, the datagram only contains a "**y**" or an "**n**" character. The client side of the application does not know whether the response is to the second sending of the first user name or the response to the second user name!

To solve the problem, you can have the server side of the application send the user name along with the "**y**" or "**n**" character. In that way, the client side of the application can disregard the message if it is not to the current user name it asked about. Another solution is to send a sequence number in the request and response messages and have the client side of the application disregard any duplicate responses.

The applications presented earlier are transport-specific. The connection-oriented application uses the Transmission Control Protocol, and the connectionless application uses the User Datagram Protocol. In Section 8.6, we look at ways to make your applications transport-independent.

However, before doing that, we take a look at the queue length of incoming connections. In Section 8.3, we created an application that set the **qlen** field of the **t_bind** structure to **1** when binding a transport address to a transport endpoint. That meant the server side of the application could only have one outstanding connection indication. If you set that field to a value greater than **1**, you must code the applications differently. We now present the details of setting the **qlen** field to a value greater than **1**.

8.6 Applications With qlen Greater Than 1

The **qlen** field of the **t_bind** structure specifies the maximum number of outstanding connection indications your application wants to support. An outstanding connection indication is a connection request that you have retrieved by calling the **t_listen()** routine but have not accepted yet. If **qlen** is *n*, your application can have up to *n* outstanding connection indications.

As mentioned in Chapter 7, having a **qlen** of *n* is like having several lights on a telephone, where each light goes on when an incoming call arrives. If **qlen** is **5**, then you have five lights on the telephone. Therefore, you can have up to five connection requests arrive simultaneously. If every light is on (that is, the queue of incoming connection requests is full), the client side of the application making a new connection request may get an error. Every time you accept a call and listen for a new call, a light goes off, allowing a new connection request to arrive.

However, if **qlen** is greater than **1**, *you must retrieve all outstanding connection requests by calling the **t_listen()** routine before you can accept any of them!* If you try to accept a connection request and a second connection request arrives, TLI will not let you accept the first connection request (that is, the **t_accept()** routine fails). Going back to the telephone analogy, you must obtain information about all incoming calls before any can be answered.

There is an advantage and a drawback to this approach. The advantage is that you can prioritize incoming calls. For example, you may want to listen for several connection requests and assign a priority to each. You can then accept the connections in the prioritized order (because the **t_listen()** routine reports the address of the caller, you can base the priority on the client machine making the connection request). Therefore, if you get a call from your boss, your peer, and the CEO of your company simultaneously, you can accept the call from the CEO first (or last, depending upon your priority).

The drawback, of course, is that you must find out information about all outstanding connection requests before any can be accepted. So, if you issue the **t_listen()** routine to retrieve a call and see that it is from the CEO of your company, you must still retrieve all outstanding connection indications before you can accept the CEO's call.

To illustrate how to handle a queue length greater than **1**, let's rewrite the server code presented in Section 8.3. However, instead of using the Transmission Control Protocol, we'll use the SVR4 Connection-Oriented Loopback protocol. In that way, we will also show that the TLI routines are the same for any transport provider.

In the code that follows, we set the **qlen** field to **5**. That means we can have up to five connection requests arrive simultaneously. And, as mentioned earlier, we must issue the **t_listen()** routine on any and all pending connection requests before we can accept any of them.

To do that, we must maintain an array of five **t_call** structures, where each identifies a pending connection request. To begin, we do what we did in Section 8.3:

1. Call the **t_open()** routine to create a transport endpoint. In this example, we create a transport endpoint into the SVR4 Connection-Oriented Loopback transport provider. We do that by opening the **/dev/ticots** file. This file is a clone device corresponding to that transport provider.

2. Bind a transport address to the transport endpoint. So, we first call the **t_alloc()** routine to allocate space to hold the **t_bind** structures needed for the **t_bind()** routine.

3. In the SVR4 Connection-Oriented Loopback transport provider, an address is a sequence of bytes. In our application, we use the string **example.addr** as the server's address. So, we copy the address into the **netbuf** structure associated with the **addr** field of the **t_bind** structure. We also set the **qlen** field to **5**, meaning that we can retrieve up to five connection requests simultaneously.

4. Call the **t_bind()** routine to bind the transport address to our transport endpoint. After issuing the **t_bind()** routine, we check that the address to which we bound was the address requested. If not, we issue an error message and exit the application.

We can now start listening for connection requests and accepting them. To do that, we use the following algorithm:

```
         make all entries in the t_call array empty;
loop 1:  for ever {
             x = first empty slot in t_call array;
             listen for a connection request;
             when one arrives, put t_call information in slot x;
loop 2:      for all nonempty entries in the t_call array {
                 try to accept the connection request;
                 if accept failed because a new connection request arrived {
                     break out of loop 2 to receive new connection in loop 1;
                 }
                 if accept failed because a disconnect arrived {
                     get the information about the disconnect;
                     look for the t_call associated with the disconnect;
                     free that t_call structure and remove it from array;
                 }
                 if accept succeeded {
                     free that t_call structure and remove it from array;
                     start child process to implement protocol;
                 }
```

```
    }   end loop 2;
} end loop 1;
```

As seen in this algorithm, we use an outer loop and an inner loop. The outer loop receives incoming connection requests by calling the **t_listen()** routine, and the inner loop accepts the connection requests by calling the **t_accept()** routine. If in the inner loop we encounter an error when trying to accept a connection request because a new connection request arrived, we continue the outer loop to receive the new connection. The next time we enter the inner loop, we try to accept all of the connection requests received. Specifically, we do the following in the outer loop:

1. Look for an empty slot in the array of **t_call** structures. We know there must be at least one slot available for the following reasons:

   a. The first time we enter the loop, all of the slots are empty.

   b. We return to the outer loop if the **t_accept()** routine succeeds. If that is the case, we free the **t_call** structure and therefore have a free slot.

   c. We return to the outer loop if the **t_accept()** failed because we have a new connection indication. And, because the number of slots in the array is the same as the maximum number of incoming connection indications, an incoming connection means a slot must be available.

2. Allocate a **t_call** structure by calling the **t_alloc()** routine.

3. Call the **t_listen()** routine to receive a connection indication. If no connection indications are present, the **t_listen()** routine sleeps waiting for one to arrive.

4. Enter the inner loop to accept the connection when the **t_listen()** routine returns. The inner loop scans the array of **t_call** structures, and for each structure in the array, we do the following:

   a. Get a second transport endpoint and bind an arbitrary address to it. We do that with the **t_open()** and the **t_bind()** routines.

   b. Issue the **t_accept()** routine to try to accept the connection. If the **t_accept()** routine fails with **t_errno** set to **TLOOK**, we know that the failure occurred because a disconnect occurred or a new connection indication arrived.

   If the failure was because a disconnect indication arrived, we issue the **t_rcvdis()** routine to find the information about the associated connection indication. We then scan the array of connection indications and free the one that had the disconnect. The **sequence** field of the **t_call** structure is used to identify the associated connect indication.

    c. If the failure was because a new connection indication arrived, we set a flag that causes us to break out of the inner loop. Now, when we return to the outer loop, the `t_listen()` routine will return immediately, because a connection indication is present. The next time we enter the inner loop, we will have two connection indications to accept (the original one and the new one).

    d. If the `t_accept()` routine succeeds, free the `t_call` structure and create a child to implement the protocol.

       Note that before we enter the inner loop, we have an array of incoming connection indications. So, before entering the inner loop, you could reorder the connection requests based on a priority. Usually, applications base the priority on the machine making the connection request. However, if the transport provider supports options that let you pass other information (such as a user ID) on the connection request, you can use that as well.

  5. The rest of the application is the same as the version presented in Section 8.3.

The code follows:

```
#include <tiuser.h>
#include <stropts.h>
#include <stdio.h>
#include <fcntl.h>
#include <signal.h>
#include <sys/types.h>
#include <sys/socket.h>
#include <netinet/in.h>
#include <netdb.h>

extern int t_errno;

#define LOOPADDR "example.addr"


#define SERV_PORT 5134
#define MAX_CONN   50

struct t_call *call[MAX_CONN];

main()
{
   int listen_fd;        /* file descriptor into transport */
```

```
int recfd;              /* fd on which to accept        */
struct t_bind *req;   /* requested addr to which to bind*/
struct t_bind *ret;   /* actual address that was bound  */
int i, j, curr_call; /* index counters                 */
int new_listen;         /* flag for new connection       */
struct t_discon *discon;   /* holds disconnect info    */
struct sockaddr_in myaddr; /* holds the address of     */
                           /* this service             */

if ((listen_fd = t_open("/dev/ticots", O_RDWR, NULL))
                                                < 0) {
   t_error("t_open failed");
   exit(1);
}

/*
 *   Get space to hold the address to which
 *   you want to bind.
 */

if ((req = (struct t_bind *)t_alloc(listen_fd, T_BIND,
                        T_ALL)) == NULL) {
   t_error("t_alloc failed");
   exit(1);
}

/*
 *   Get space to hold the address to which
 *   you actually bind.
 */

if ((ret = (struct t_bind *)t_alloc(listen_fd, T_BIND,
                        T_ALL)) == NULL) {
   t_error("t_alloc failed");
   exit(1);
}
/*
 *   Set qlen to MAX_CONN to signify that we will let up
 *   to MAX_CONN more connection requests to arrive
 *   simultaneously.
 */

req->qlen = MAX_CONN;
```

```
req->addr.len = strlen(LOOPADDR) + 1;
strncpy(req->addr.buf, LOOPADDR, strlen(LOOPADDR) + 1);

/*
 *  Bind to the address to which the service will
 *  be offered.
 */

if (t_bind(listen_fd, req, ret) < 0) {
   t_error("t_bind failed");
   exit(1);
}

/*
 *  Make sure the address you got was the one you wanted!
 */

if ((req->addr.len != ret->addr.len) ||
  (memcmp(req->addr.buf, ret->addr.buf, req->addr.len))){
   fprintf(stderr, "Did not bind to correct address!\n");
   exit(1);
}

/*
 *  Loop continuously, listening for connection requests,
 *  accepting the call, and performing the service.
 */

while (1) {
   /*
    *  First, find an unused connection slot.
    */

   for (curr_call=0; curr_call < MAX_CONN; curr_call++) {
      if (call[curr_call] == NULL) {
         break;
      }
   }

   /*
    *  Allocate space to hold the t_call structure, and
    *  listen for incoming calls.  The t_listen() routine
    *  sleeps until a call arrives (it returns
```

```
 *   immediately if a call is already present).
 */

if ((call[curr_call] =
     (struct t_call *) t_alloc (listen_fd, T_CALL,
                               T_ALL)) == NULL) {
   t_error ("could not allocate space for t_call!");
   exit(1);
}

if (t_listen (listen_fd, call[curr_call]) < 0) {
   t_error ("could not listen!");
   exit(1);
}

/*
 *  Now that we have received a call, let's try to
 *  accept it.  The t_accept will fail if another call
 *  arrives.   In that case, we return to the loop to
 *  receive the new call.  So, at this point, we may
 *  have several calls waiting to be accepted.
 *  Therefore, we loop through all call structures and
 *  accept all of them.
 */

for (i = 0; i < MAX_CONN; i++) {
   if (call[i] == NULL) {
      continue;
   }

   if ((recfd = t_open ("/dev/ticots", O_RDWR, NULL))
                                                 < 0) {
      t_error ("could not open device!");
      exit(1);
   }

   if (t_bind (recfd, NULL, NULL) < 0) {
      t_error ("bind for responding failed!");
      exit(1);
   }

   new_listen = 0;
   if (t_accept (listen_fd, recfd, call[i]) < 0) {
```

```
if (t_errno != TLOOK) {
    t_error("t_accept failed");
    exit(1);
} else {
    /*
     *  Figure out why t_accept() failed.
     */

    switch (t_look(listen_fd)) {

    case T_DISCONNECT:

        /*
         *  A disconnect happened on one of the
         *  incoming calls.
         */
        if ((discon = (struct t_discon *)
            t_alloc(listen_fd, T_DIS, T_ALL))
                                    == NULL) {
            t_error("t_alloc failed");
            exit(1);
        }
        if (t_rcvdis(listen_fd, discon) <0) {
            t_error("could not disconnect");
            exit(1);
        }

        /*
         *  Figure out which call disconnected.
         */

        for (j = 0; j < MAX_CONN; j++) {
            if (discon->sequence ==
                            call[j]->sequence) {
                t_free(call[j], T_CALL);
                call[j] = NULL;
                break;
            }
        }
        t_free(discon, T_DIS);
        break;

    case T_LISTEN:
```

```
                    new_listen = 1;
                    break;

                default:

                    t_error("t_accept failed");
                    exit(1);
            }
        }

        /*
         *  If t_accept() failed because a new
         *  connection indication arrived, break
         *  the for loop.  That causes us to go back
         *  to the while loop and call t_listen()
         *  again.  Otherwise, we failed because we got
         *  a disconnect.  Because we've cleared that,
         *  continue the for loop to try to accept the
         *  next connection.
         */

        if (new_listen) {
            break;
        } else {
            continue;
        }
    }

    /*
     *  At this point, we have an accepted connection.
     *  So, we free the call structure and implement
     *  the protocol.
     */

    t_free(call[i], T_CALL);
    call[i] = NULL;

    switch (fork()) {
        case -1:
            perror("fork failed!\n");
            exit(1);

        default: /* parent */
```

```
            t_close(recfd);
            break;

        case 0:  /* child */

            t_close(listen_fd);

            /*
             *   The child_actions() routine exits
             *   when it completes.
             */
            child_actions(recfd);
        }
    }
  }
}
```

As you can see, setting **qlen** to a value greater than **1** complicates the server side of the application. Only do so if you must prioritize incoming calls. And, as mentioned previously, an implementation of a transport provider may queue connection requests internally even if **qlen** is set to **1**. Remember that **qlen** is the number of simultaneous connection requests that *your application* wants to process, and is independent of the number of connection requests the transport provider is able or willing to queue up.

Now let's look at other ways to create TLI applications. In Sections 8.3 and 8.4, we created applications that were specific to the Transmission Control Protocol and the User Datagram Protocol. We now look at ways to make applications transport-independent.

8.7   Making Applications Transport Independent

Most TLI operations in the applications created in Sections 8.3 and 8.4 work the same on any transport provider. There are only three transport-dependent things we did in those applications:

1. We hardcoded the clone device file associated with the transport provider when we called the **t_open()** routine.

2. We hardcoded the transport address information directly into the application.

3. In the connection-oriented application, we used the orderly release feature. Some transport providers do not allow orderly release.

If we created an application that did not do these actions, we would have an application that would work over any transport provider. That would let your application work without modification on any transport provider that is integrated into your machine.

Fortunately, the SVR4 Network Selection and Name-to-Address Mapping features let you eliminate the first two transport-dependent actions in this list. As we see in Chapter 9, the Network Selection routines tell you the transport providers that exist on the system and return information about each. For example, the information includes the following:

1. The name of the transport provider.

2. The name of the clone device file that you should use in the **t_open()** routine to create a transport endpoint into the transport provider.

3. An indication of whether the transport provider supports orderly release.

The Name-to-Address Mapping routines provide a way to get transport addresses at execution time, freeing your application from having to specify it explicitly. You give the Name-to-Address Mapping routines the name of the server machine and the service to which you want to talk, and they return a **netbuf** structure containing the transport address. We show the details of the Name-to-Address Mapping routines and the Network Selection routines in Chapter 9.

Here are some other things to consider if you want to write transport-independent applications:

1. Do not use the orderly release feature in your applications, because some transport providers so not support it. You should only use it if you want to limit applications to only use transport providers that support orderly release. As we will see in Chapter 9, you can use the Network Selection feature to look for a transport provider on your machine that supports orderly release.

2. Always use the **t_alloc()** routine to allocate memory for TLI data structures. If you don't, you must check the **t_info** structure returned by **t_open()** and **t_getinfo()** routines. The **t_info** structure contains limits on data size.

3. Do not send a message of **0** bytes. Some transport providers do not support zero-length messages.

4. Do not assume a connection-oriented transport provider supports TSDUs. Some transport providers do not support message boundaries, so they do not set the **T_MORE** flag when you send and receive data. So, carry out your own session-layer functions and do not rely on message boundaries.

5. Do not transmit data on connection teardown unless you know that the transport provider supports it. It is safest not to use that feature at all. However, you can code your application to send data on connection teardown if the information that `t_getinfo()` returns indicates that the transport provider supports it.

6. Avoid using the `t_optmgmt()` routine unless you can use it in a transport-independent way. For example, Chapter 9 shows how the Name-to-Address Mapping routines use the `t_optmgmt()` routine to set a "Transport-Level Broadcast" feature available on some datagram transport providers.

    The Name-to-Address Mapping routines set up the Transport-Level Broadcast feature in a transport-independent way. Instead of calling the `t_optmgmt()` routine directly, the Name-to-Address Mapping routines maintain a library for each transport provider on your machine and link in the appropriate library to do the work. Details are given in Chapter 9.

7. Do not interpret the reason code in the `t_discon` structure or the error code in the `t_uderr` structure. Those values are transport-specific. You can display those values in a log file, but you should not attach any meaning to them.

We'll present a transport-independent application in Section 8.9. First, we'll discuss some other tools that can be used in TLI applications. We begin by presenting the tools that let you poll multiple transport endpoints simultaneously.

8.8   Polling Multiple Transport Endpoints

Many networking applications need to monitor several transport endpoints simultaneously. For example, suppose your machine had several transport providers. The server side of an application may want to create several transport endpoints (one for each transport provider on the system) and wait for messages to arrive over any of the transport endpoints.

The `poll()` system call allows that. The `poll()` system call lets you specify a list of file descriptors to monitor. When you issue the system call, it sleeps waiting for an event to occur on any of the file descriptors. When an event occurs (for example, data have arrived), the `poll()` system call returns.

As shown in Figure 8.1, you can use the `poll()` system call on any file descriptor, not just on file descriptors corresponding to transport endpoints. So, you can create applications that wait for data to arrive on any STREAMS device.

That simplifies many kinds of applications. For example, suppose you created an application that had to monitor several transport endpoints and the master side of a pseudo-terminal device (as mentioned in Chapter 1, a pseudo-terminal is a master/slave pair that emulates a true terminal device). Because there is a file descriptor into each

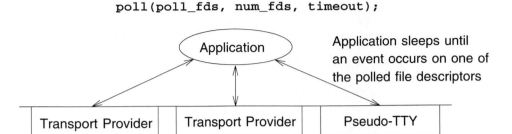

Figure 8.1   Polling Multiple File Descriptors

of the transport endpoints and into the master side of the pseudo-terminal device, you could use the **poll()** system call to figure out when data arrived on any of the file descriptors.

Let's take a closer look at the **poll()** system call. It has the following format:

```
#include <stropts.h>
#include <poll.h>

struct pollfd *fds;
size_t        nfds;
int           timeout;
int           num_selected;

num_selected = poll(fds, nfds, timeout);
```

The **fds** argument is an array of **pollfd** structures (described in what follows). The **nfds** argument is the number of elements in the array, and the **timeout** argument specifies how long to wait before returning to your application. If the time-out value is **0**, the **poll()** system call returns immediately. If the time-out value is **INFTIM**, the **poll()** system call assumes an infinite time-out period. SVR4 defines **INFTIM** as **-1**.

The **poll()** system call returns when a monitored event occurs on a file descriptor or when **timeout** milliseconds have passed. It returns the number of file descriptors that have an event pending.

The **pollfd** structure contains the file descriptor to monitor and a specification of the events for which to look. It has the following form:

```
struct pollfd {
    int     fd;
    short events;
    short revents;
};
```

The `fd` field is the file descriptor to monitor. It does not have to be a transport end-point. It can be any open file descriptor.

The `events` field indicates the event for which you want to wait. You specify the event by logically OR-ing the following values:

POLLIN   Wait until data are available on the file descriptor. For STREAMS-based devices, it means you want to wait until any message other than a high-priority message arrives. In SVR4, all transport providers are STREAMS-based.

As explained in Chapter 2, STREAMS defines three types of messages: **normal messages**, **priority messages**, and **high-priority messages**. They have the following characteristics:

a. Normal messages are not urgent. They are processed in a first in, first out basis.

b. Priority messages are more urgent than normal messages, but are not extremely urgent. Each priority message is in a "priority band" that defines the importance of the message. The higher the priority band, the more urgent the message. The STREAMS mechanism places higher-priority messages ahead of lower-priority messages. Priority messages can be in bands `0` through `255`. Normal messages are always in priority band `0`.

c. High-priority messages are extremely urgent. The STREAMS mechanism always places those messages ahead of normal messages and priority messages.

The `POLLIN` flag says you want to sleep until a normal message or a priority message arrives on the given file descriptor. The `poll()` routine will not wake up if a high-priority message arrives.

POLLRDNORM Wait until you can read **normal data** from the file descriptor without blocking. As mentioned earlier, normal data are in priority band `0`. This value is only valid for file descriptors into STREAMS devices.

POLLRDBAND   Wait until you can read **priority data** in band 1 through 255 from the file descriptor without blocking. This value is only valid for file descriptors into STREAMS devices.

POLLPRI   Wait until you can read **high-priority data** from the file descriptor without blocking. As mentioned earlier, high-priority data are marked ''extremely urgent.'' This value is also only valid for file descriptors into STREAMS devices.

POLLOUT   Wait until you can write normal data or priority data without blocking. For example, flow-control restrictions of some transport providers might cause you to sleep when you try to write data. You can use the **POLLOUT** flag to figure out if the transport provider is ready to accept data.

POLLRWNORM   This flag is exactly the same as **POLLOUT**.

POLLWRBAND   Indicates that you want to wait until you can write a priority message in a priority band greater than 0 without blocking. This value is only valid for file descriptors into STREAMS devices.

POLLMSG   Wait until a message containing the **SIGPOLL** signal arrives on the stream head. Many transport providers send that message when they want to get the attention of an application. As we will see shortly, that message causes the STREAMS mechanism to send your application the **SIGPOLL** signal if you issued the **ioctl()** routine with the **I_SETSIG** and **S_MSG** parameters. This value is only valid for file descriptors into STREAMS devices.

Most networking applications specify **POLLIN** in the events field. That lets you know when normal and priority messages arrive.

The **poll()** system call looks at the events in each of the **pollfd** structures and sleeps waiting for one or more of the events to occur. When the **poll()** system call returns, it shows which events occurred on each file descriptor. It does that by filling in the **revents** field of the **pollfd** structure.

The **revents** field of the **pollfd** structure contains a logical OR of each event that occurred. The events are the same as specified in the **events** field. For example, if you specified the **POLLIN** event in the **events** field, the **revents** field will contain **POLLIN** when you can read data from the associated file descriptor.

The **poll()** system call may logically OR three other values into the **revents** field. The values are the following:

POLLERR   A fatal error has occurred in a STREAMS module or in the device driver.

POLLHUP   A "hangup" condition occurred on the stream. This means you can't send any more messages downstream.

POLLNVAL   The file descriptor is invalid. That can only occur if the file descriptor does not refer to an open file or device.

The `poll()` system call also returns if the specified time out occurs. The time-out value is in milliseconds. If your system does not have milliseconds timing available, the `poll()` system calls rounds up the time-out value to the nearest legal value.

The `poll()` system call returns the number of file descriptors that have events pending. It returns `-1` if an error occurs. We will show an example of the `poll()` system call in Section 8.10.

The `poll()` system call is synchronous, that is, it sleeps waiting for an event to occur. SVR4 lets you determine if an event happens in the asynchronous mode as well. You do that by using the `ioctl()` routine with the `I_SETSIG` parameter.

If you issue the `ioctl()` system call with the `I_SETSIG` parameter, you will get a `SIGPOLL` signal when an event occurs on a stream. Usually, you issue the following code:

```
ioctl(fd, I_SETSIG, S_INPUT);
```

The `fd` argument is a file descriptor into a stream. The routine causes the stream to send your application the `SIGPOLL` signal when a message arrives on the stream head. The only time you don't get the `SIGPOLL` signal is if a high-priority message arrives.

You can also specify that you want the `SIGPOLL` signal when a more specific event occurs on a stream. Besides `S_INPUT`, you can specify the third argument to the `ioctl()` with the `I_SETSIG` parameter by logically ORing the following values:

S_RDNORM   Specifies that you want the `SIGPOLL` signal when a normal message arrives on the stream head. As mentioned earlier, a normal message is a message with priority band `0`.

S_RDBAND   Specifies that you want the `SIGPOLL` signal when a priority message in a priority band between `1` and `255` arrives.

S_HIPRI   Specifies that you want the `SIGPOLL` signal when a high-priority message arrives.

S_OUTPUT   Specifies that you want the `SIGPOLL` signal when you can send data without blocking. You normally use this when the stream is full and not accepting any more data.

S_WRNORM   This is the same as the **S_OUTPUT** value.

S_WRBAND   Specifies that you want the **SIGPOLL** signal when you can send a priority message in a band between **1** and **255** without blocking.

S_MSG   Specifies that you want the **SIGPOLL** signal when a message containing the **SIGPOLL** signal arrives on the stream head. As mentioned earlier, transport providers send that message when they want to get the attention of an application.

S_ERROR   Specifies that you want the **SIGPOLL** signal when a fatal error occurs on a module or the device driver on the stream.

S_HANGUP   Specifies that you want the **SIGPOLL** signal when a hangup condition occurs on the stream. A hangup condition means you can't send any more messages downstream.

S_BANDURG   Specifies that you want the **SIGURG** signal instead of the **SIGPOLL** signal when a priority message arrives. You can only use this flag with the **S_RDBAND** flag.

Polling transport endpoints and setting up notification of asynchronous events lets you create powerful networking applications. You can monitor several streams simultaneously or do other processing while waiting for messages to arrive.

SVR4 provides another feature that helps create networking applications. The feature lets you use the **read()** and **write()** system calls within networking applications and is described next.

8.9 A Read/Write Interface

Usually, you use the **t_snd()** and **t_rcv()** routines to send and receive data over a connection-oriented transport provider. SVR4 provides a way to use the **read()** and **write()** system calls instead.

There are several reasons why you would want to use **read()** and **write()** instead of **t_rcv()** and **t_snd()**:

1. Your application may want to establish a connection and then call **exec()** to execute another program. The program you execute might be using **read()** and **write()** for I/O.

2. You may want to create a subroutine that establishes a connection and returns the file descriptor associated with the transport endpoint. Here, you may want a **read()** and **write()** interface to the transport endpoint. In that way, the application calling the subroutine would not have to know the TLI routines.

As mentioned earlier, all transport providers in SVR4 are implemented using the STREAMS mechanism. As part of that mechanism, SVR4 provides the `tirdwr` module, which lets you interface with a transport provider using the `read()` and `write()` systems calls.

As illustrated in Figure 8.2, you can push the `tirdwr` module onto a stream. Once pushed, you use the `read()` and `write()` systems calls instead of the `t_rcv()` and `t_snd()` routines.

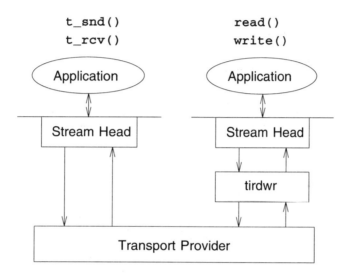

Figure 8.2   A Read/Write Interface

There are some restrictions when using the `tirdwr` module:

1. You can push the `tirdwr` module only onto a stream associated with a transport provider.

2. You can push the `tirdwr` module only if the transport endpoint is in the **T_DATAXFER** state.

3. After you push the module, you cannot use any of the TLI routines. If you issue a TLI routine, it generates an error condition that causes all subsequent systems calls to the stream to fail.

4. The `tirdwr` module only lets you process normal messages. If the remote side of the connection sends a high-priority message, the `tirdwr` module generates an error when you issue the `read()` system call. In addition, all subsequent system calls to the stream will fail.

5. If the other side of the connection sends an orderly release indication, the
    `tirdwr` module throws it away and returns `0` for all subsequent `read()` sys-
    tem calls. A `0` is the end-of-file indication.

6. If the other side of the connection sends an abrupt shutdown indication, the
    `tirdwr` module generates a hangup condition. All subsequent `write()` sys-
    tem calls fail. You can read all remaining data, but after you consume the data,
    the `tirdwr` module returns `0` for all subsequent `read()` systems calls.

7. If you try to write a `0` byte message, the `tirdwr` module discards it. So,
    although you may be able to send a `0` byte message to the other side of the con-
    nection using the `t_snd()` routine, you cannot do it with the `write()` sys-
    tem call.

8. If you pop the `tirdwr` module from the stream, it aborts the connection.

If you want to abort the connection when using the `tirdwr` module, call the
`close()` system call. This call on a transport provider with the `tirdwr` module
has the following semantics:

1. If the `tirdwr` module saw an orderly release message from the other side of
    the connection, it sends back an orderly release message.

2. If the `tirdwr` module saw a disconnect message from the other side of the
    connection, it does no special processing.

3. In all other cases, the `tirdwr` module sends a disconnect message to the other
    side of the connection.

It is not necessary that both sides of the connection use the `tirdwr` module. One
side of the connection can push the `tirdwr` module and use the `read()` and
`write()` system calls, and the other side can continue to use the `t_snd()` and
`t_rcv()` routines.

Now that we've seen some of the routines that help write TLI applications, let's create
a transport-independent application. The details of the application are presented next.

8.10 A Transport-Independent Application: rpopen()

To illustrate TLI routines, let's create a transport-independent application. As mentioned earlier, a transport-independent application can work over any transport provider
that exists on the system, provided that transport provider has the necessary mode of
service (that is, connection-oriented or connectionless). Such applications also work
over any new transport providers without modification. In this section, we'll create an
application that works over any connection-oriented transport provider.

Our application provides a subroutine that lets users execute commands on remote systems. We will name the subroutine **rpopen()** and model it after the SVR4 **popen()** routine.

The **rpopen()** routine works like the SVR4 **popen()** routine. But whereas the **popen()** routine creates a communication path to a command on the local system, the **rpopen()** routine creates a communication path to a command on a specified remote system.

We'll define the format of the **rpopen()** routine as follows:

```
int   fd;
char  *servername;
char  *command;
char  *type;

fd = rpopen(servername, command, type);
```

The **servername** is the name of a server machine and the **command** is a shell command line. The **type** is an I/O mode, either "**r**" for reading or "**w**" for writing. The **rpopen()** routine makes a network connection to the specified server machine, executes the command on that server machine, and creates a communication path between the calling program and the specified command.

The **rpopen()** routine returns a file descriptor. If the I/O mode is **w**, you can use the file descriptor to write to the standard input of the command. If the I/O mode is **r**, you can use the file descriptor to read the standard output of the command. It returns a value of **-1** on failure.

To maintain security, the **rpopen()** routine only works if you have an account on the server machine. When you call **rpopen()**, it prompts for your user name and password on the server machine and sends that information to the server side of the application. The server side of the application continues only if a correct password is specified.

Figure 8.3 illustrates the application-layer protocol of the **rpopen()** routine. The protocol consists of the following steps:

1.   The **rpopen()** routine sends a user name to the server side of the application.

2.   The **rpopen()** routine sends the user's password.

3.   The server side of the applications checks whether the password is correct. If it is, the server side sends the **y** character to the **rpopen()** routine. If the password is not correct, it sends the **n** character.

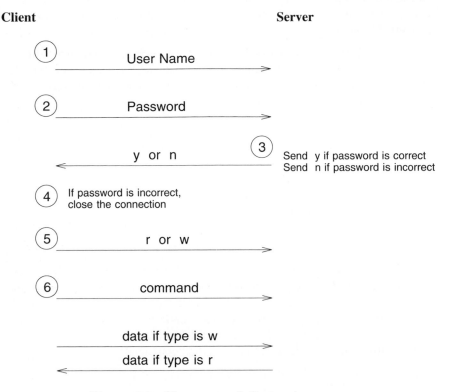

Figure 8.3 The rpopen() Protocol

4. If the password was not correct, the client side of the application shuts down the connection after it reads the **n** character. No further processing is done.

5. If the password was correct, the **rpopen()** routine sends a type specification to the server side of the application. The type specification is the **w** character or the **r** character and corresponds to the value given as the third argument to the **rpopen()** routine.

6. The **rpopen()** routine sends the command line to the server machine.

If the type specification is **w**, the application that called **rpopen()** sends data to the server side of the application. The server side of the application passes the data as the standard input of the specified command. If the type specification is **r**, the server side of the application sends the standard output of the command across the connection.

Now let's define the presentation and session layers of our application. The presentation layer places all data into a common format. In our application, we only send and receive ASCII characters in the six steps of the protocol. Therefore, we don't need any special presentation-layer processing. However, if we had to send data types other than ASCII characters, we could use the methods presented in Section 8.2.

Note that after the protocol completes, data exchange continues. If the type specification is **w**, the application that called **rpopen()** sends data to the server side of the application. If the type specification is **r**, the server side of the application sends data to the client side. Unfortunately, we do not know the nature of this data. The application calling **rpopen()** can specify any command, and therefore it can send or receive any type of data. Because we do not know the format of the data being exchanged, we can do no presentation-layer processing on that data. That means the remote command may misinterpret binary data that the client side of the applications sends to it, and the client side of the application may misinterpret binary data that the remote command sends.

In our session layer, we must synchronize dialogue. We are writing the application to work over any transport provider, so we cannot use TSDUs to synchronize dialogue. As mentioned earlier, some transport providers do not support TSDUs. So, we do the following:

1. The client side of the application sends a byte with the **0** value to show the end of the user name, password, and command.

2. When the protocol specifies that you pass a single byte (that is, a **y** or an **n** as a response to the authentication and an **r** or a **w** for the type specification), the sender does *not* write a trailing **0** byte. It sends a single character.

After the protocol completes, data exchange begins. However, we now have a problem: How does the receiver know when the sender is finished sending data? As mentioned earlier, the sender *cannot* signify the end of data by doing an abortive release via the **t_snddis()** routine. That routine generates a disconnection indication, which in turn may destroy any data in transit (that is, data that are not already received by the remote side of the application).

We have other options that the sender can use to tell the receiver it has completed data transfer:

1. Send an orderly release message. That is the cleanest solution. Unfortunately, not all transport providers support orderly release (most notably, OSI transport providers do not support it). If we used it, we would limit the transport providers over which our application could work.

2. Transmit a unique sequence of bytes to indicate the end of the data. Unfortunately, that would complicate our application. Because our application sends arbitrary data across the communication path, we would have to take special care

that the end-of-data sequence of bytes did not occur in the data stream. If it did, the receiver would incorrectly interpret that sequence as the end of the data.

A solution to this problem would be to modify the data stream if it had the end-of-data sequence in it. For example, suppose we chose the end-of-data marker to be the ''|'' character. Before the sender transmits data, it would have to check whether the ''|'' character appeared in the data. If it did, the sender could modify the data to have *two* ''|'' characters for every one in the original data stream. So, when the reader receives the data, it would translate two ''|'' characters into one and realize that it is not the end-of-data marker. And, if the reader sees a single ''|'' character, it would interpret that as the end-of-data marker.

3. Prefix all data with a length indicator. The length indicator would tell the number of bytes of data that followed. In that way, the receiver could first read the length indicator, then the data, then another length indicator, and then more data. When the sender finishes sending data, it can send a length indicator of **0**. And, of course, the length indicator must be in a common data format.

The first solution would greatly simplify the application, because no extra processing must be done on the data. In fact, the client side of the application could push the **tirdwr** module and give a read/write interface to the user that called the **rpopen()** function. As mentioned in Section 8.9, the **tirdwr** module returns a value of **0** to all **read()** requests when it sees an orderly release indication. And, because **0** is the end-of-data indication, that lets the **read()** system call behave properly when the server side of the application finishes sending data. But, as mentioned earlier, the orderly release indication is not available on some transport providers. So, we will not use that solution. Such is the price for transport independence.

The second solution is overly complicated for our application. The server side and the client side of the application would have to modify the data stream. Additionally, the client side of the application must recognize the end-of-data sequence marker even if were split across two separate read requests.

So, we will implement the third solution in our application. To simplify things, we will define a message unit as a 4-byte value followed by data. The 4-byte value is an ASCII representation of an integer, and that integer specifies the amount of data to follow. For example, if we sent five bytes of data, we would prefix the data with the string ''**0005**''. Similarly, if we send 1017 bytes of data, we would prefix the data with the ''**1017**'' string. The limitation, of course, is that we can only send at most 9999 bytes of data at a time. However, the ASCII representation ensures a common presentation-layer format of the integer. When we have sent all of the data, we send a 4-byte ASCII string of zeros (that is, the ''**0000**'' string). That tells the receiver we have no more data to send.

Therefore, we define three more functions in this application to transfer data. They have the following definitions:

```
int    fd;
char *buf;
int    len;

int
rpread(fd, buf, len);

int
rpwrite(fd, buf, len);

void
rpclose(fd);
```

The `rpread()` routine reads data from the remote command. The `fd` argument is a file descriptor obtained from the `rpopen()` routine, the `buf` argument is a data buffer into which you want to read, and the `len` argument specifies the number of bytes you want to read. It returns the number of bytes read or a value of `0` when you have consumed all data from the server side of the application. It returns a `-1` if an error occurs.

The `rpwrite()` routine writes data to the remote command. The `fd` argument is a file descriptor obtained from the `rpopen()` routine, the `buf` argument is a buffer that contains the data you want to write, and the `len` argument specifies the number of bytes in the buffer. It returns the number of bytes written. It returns a `-1` if an error occurs.

The `rpclose()` routine closes the connection. The `fd` argument is a file descriptor obtained from the `rpopen()` routine.

Now let's create the `rpopen()` application. The `rpopen()` application must be transport-independent. So, we must not hard code transport-specific information like device file names and transport addresses. Instead of hard coding that information, we use the Network Selection and Name-to-Address Mapping routines to obtain the information dynamically.

As we see in Chapter 9, the Network Selection routines figure out which transport providers exist on the system. They return information about each transport provider, such as the clone device file associated with the transport provider, whether the transport provider is connection-oriented or connectionless, and other information. The Name-to-Address Mapping routines figure out the addresses of a service. They return a list of `netbuf` structures containing addresses that you can use for communication.

In our application, we create a routine named **get_addrs()** that returns the needed information. The **get_addrs()** routine uses the Network Selection and Name-to-Address Mapping routines to generate a list of transport-provider information.

We defer writing the **get_addrs()** routine until Chapter 9, where we present the details of the Network Selection and Name-to-Address Mapping routines. However, we present the actions of the routine now so we can use it in our application.

Our **get_addrs()** routine has the following syntax:

```
char *hostname;
char *service_name;
struct tpinfo *tpinfop;

tpinfop = get_addrs(hostname, service_name);
```

The **get_addrs()** routine takes two parameters. The first is the name of the server machine, and the second is the name of the service. In the **rpopen()** application, the name of the service is **rpopen**.

The **get_addrs()** routine returns a linked list of information that we need to establish communication. We define a local structure named **tpinfo** that holds the needed information. We'll define the structure in a file named **tpinfo.h**, which has the following contents:

```
/*
 *   tpinfo.h
 */

#include <netconfig.h>
#include <netdir.h>

struct tpinfo {
    char                 *device;
    struct nd_addrlist *nd_addrlistp;
    struct tpinfo        *nextp;
};

struct tpinfo *get_addrs();
```

Our **get_addrs()** routine allocates a **tpinfo** structure for each transport provider that we can use for communication. The **device** field points to the name of the clone device file associated with the transport provider. The **nd_addrlistp** field points to a **nd_addrlist** structure. That structure contains a list of transport addresses you can use to connect to the service on the specified host.

The **nd_addrlist** structure is a part of the SVR4 Name-to-Address Mapping facility and is detailed in Chapter 9. It has two elements:

n_cnt   Contains the number of addresses for the specified service.

n_addrs   Points to an array of **netbuf** structures that contain the addresses you can use to connect to the service. As mentioned in Chapter 7, a **netbuf** structure is a TLI structure that contains a transport address.

Our **get_addrs()** routine does the following:

1.   Finds all transport providers on the system.

2.   If a transport provider is connection-oriented, it does the following:

    a.   Finds the transport addresses of the given service on the specified server name. In our application, it finds the addresses of the **rpopen** service on the given server machine. Note that the transport provider may supply several transport addresses to a service (as explained in Chapter 3, the Transmission Control Protocol may do that).

    b.   If a transport address exists, the **get_addrs()** routine allocates a **tpinfo** structure. It fills the **tpinfo** structure with the device associated with the transport provider and the addresses of the service.

To illustrate, suppose we call our **get_addrs()** routine as follows:

---

tpinfop = get_addrs("farside", "rpopen");

Figure 8.4 shows a possible result of that call. Here, we had two connection-oriented transport providers on our system that can be used to connect to the **rpopen** service on machine **farside**. On the first transport provider, we can use one of two transport addresses to make the connection. On the second transport provider, we can use one transport address.

Both the client side of the application and the server side of the application use our **get_addrs()** routine. On the client side, we call **get_addrs()** to find:

1.   The name of the clone device file to use.

2.   The transport addresses we can use to connect to the service.

On the server side of the application, we call **get_addrs()** to figure out all of the addresses to which we should attach. For example, if the **get_addrs()** routine

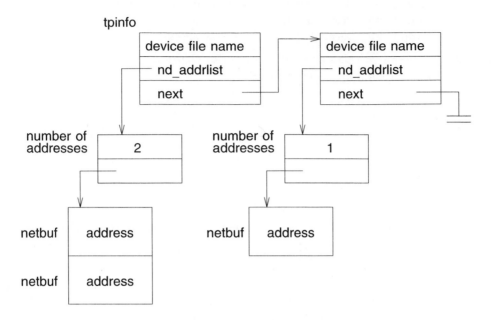

Figure 8.4   The Result of `get_addrs()`

returned the structure in Figure 8.4, the server side of the application would create three transport endpoints:

1. The first transport endpoint would be into the first transport provider, bound to the first transport address.

2. The second transport endpoint would be into the first transport provider, bound to the second transport address.

3. The third transport endpoint would be into the second transport provider, bound to the first transport address.

After the server side of the application binds to each transport endpoint, it can receive connection requests on every transport provider to which it bound.

There is one more thing to consider when using the **`get_addrs()`** routine on the server machine. Some transport providers provide a unique address to represent "this machine." For example, the TCP/IP protocol suite allows a machine to have several IP addresses. Because an application can bind only one address to a transport endpoint, TCP uses the special address of **`0.0.0.0`** to mean "all addresses for this machine." So, even if the server machine had several IP addresses, it would only need one transport endpoint. The server side of the application would bind the `0.0.0.0` address to that endpoint.

So, to specify that we want the information for "this machine," we pass a **NULL** argument as the server name in the **get_addrs()** routine. In that way, the **get_addrs()** routine knows to obtain a special address if one exists for the transport provider.

For example, suppose the server machine named **farside** had three IP addresses. The client side of out application would call **get_addrs()** in the following way:

```
tpinfo = get_addrs("farside", "rpopen");
```

That would return a **tpinfo** structure with three transport addresses for the TCP transport provider. The client side of the application could use any of the three addresses to establish a connection to **farside**.

However, the server side of the application would call **get_addrs()** in the following way:

```
tpinfo = get_addrs(NULL, "rpopen");
```

Here, the **get_addrs()** routine would return a single transport address for the TCP transport provider containing the IP address of `0.0.0.0`. So, the server side of the application needs only one transport endpoint instead of three.

As mentioned earlier, we defer the writing of the **get_addrs()** routine until Chapter 9, when we present the details of the Network Selection and Name-to-Address Mapping routines. We now present the C code for the server side of the **rpopen()** application.

The Server Code

The following code carries out the server side of the application. We call the **get_addrs()** routine to obtain information about every transport provider on the system. We create transport endpoints for each transport provider and issue the **poll()** system call to monitor each transport endpoint. When a connection indication arrives, we carry out the protocol.

By doing that, we make service available over every transport provider on the system. And, because we are relying on **get_addrs()** to get the information needed, we do not hard code device names or transport addresses.

Specifically, we do the following actions:

1. Call the **get_addrs()** routine, giving it a **NULL** server name and the **"rpo-pen"** service name. The **get_addrs()** routine returns a list of **tpinfo** structures, where each structure corresponds to a transport provider on the system. Each **tpinfo** structure contains the name of a device file and a list of transport addresses for the **rpopen** service.

2. Figure out the number of transport endpoints needed. We do that by counting the number of transport addresses for each transport provider.

3. Allocate memory to hold two arrays:

    a. The first is an array of **pollfd** structures. As mentioned in Section 8.8, the **pollfd** structure contains information needed by the **poll()** system call. Each **pollfd** structure will contain information about a transport endpoint. We will use the **poll()** routine to monitor all transport endpoints simultaneously.

    b. The second is an array of device file names. The device file in array element **n** corresponds to the **pollfd** structure in element **n** of the first array.

    We use the second array when accepting connections. As mentioned in Chapter 7, the **t_accept()** routine takes *two* transport endpoints—a transport endpoint that has a connection request and a transport endpoint on which to accept the connection. We must create a second transport endpoint to accept the connection, so we must know the device file to use in the **t_open()** routine. So, because the **pollfd** structure does not have the device file name, we obtain it from the second array.

4. Set the current **pollfd** structure to the first **pollfd** structure in the array. We then loop through the **tpinfo** structures. For each transport address in a **tpinfo** structure, we do the following:

    a. Create a transport endpoint using the device file in the **tpinfo** structure. We assign the transport endpoint to the current **pollfd** structure and increment the current **pollfd** structure to the next element in the array.

    b. Bind the transport address to the transport endpoint.

    c. Check that the address to which we bound was the address wanted.

    d. Store the device file name in the second array. So, the device file name in element **n** of the device file array corresponds to the transport endpoint in element **n** of the **pollfd** array.

5. Enter an infinite loop that waits for connection requests to arrive. We issue the **poll()** system call, passing the **pollfd** array, the number of elements in the array, and an infinite time-out indication.

When an event occurs on a transport endpoint, we search through the **pollfd** array looking for transport endpoints that have events posted. When we find one, we call a subroutine to accept the connection and carry out the **rpopen()** protocol. We pass the file descriptor that has the event posted and the device file associated with the transport endpoint to the subroutine.

The code follows:

```
#include <tiuser.h>
#include <stropts.h>
#include <stdio.h>
#include <fcntl.h>
#include <signal.h>
#include <sys/types.h>
#include <sys/poll.h>
#include <shadow.h>
#include <pwd.h>
#include "tpinfo.h"

extern int t_errno;

void process_it();

#define MAX_DATA    9999
#define HDR_SIZE    4

#define BSIZE  MAX_DATA + HDR_SIZE

main()
{
    struct t_bind *req;  /* address to which to bind      */
    struct t_bind *ret;  /* actual address that was bound */

    struct pollfd  *pollfdp;        /* holds all endpoints */
    struct pollfd  *curr_pollfdp;   /* traverses pollfdp    */

    char      **devicepp;      /* array of device names      */
    char    **curr_devicepp;  /* traverses devicepp         */
    struct tpinfo  *tpinfop; /* return value of get_addrs()*/

    struct tpinfo  *curr_tpinfop;    /* traverses tpinfop   */

    int    num_addrs;  /* number of address for a provider */
```

```
int    num_fd;      /* number of endpoints to use      */
int    fd;          /* holds current endpoint          */
int    i;           /* loop index                      */

/*
 *  Get all addresses and transport providers on the
 *  system...
 */

if ((tpinfop = get_addrs(NULL, "rpopen")) == NULL) {
   fprintf(stderr,
          "There are no addresses for this service!\n");
       exit(1);
}
/*
 *  Count the number of transport endpoints we'll need.
 */

curr_tpinfop = tpinfop;
num_fd = 0;
while (curr_tpinfop) {
   num_fd += curr_tpinfop->nd_addrlistp->n_cnt;
   curr_tpinfop = curr_tpinfop->nextp;
}
/*
 *  Allocate space to hold the information about
 *  each transport endpoint.
 */

if ((pollfdp =
 (struct pollfd *)malloc(num_fd * sizeof(struct pollfd)))
                                         == NULL) {
       fprintf(stderr,
          "Cannot allocate space for file descriptors\n");
       exit(1);
}

if ((devicepp =
   (char **)malloc(num_fd * sizeof(char *))) == NULL) {
       fprintf(stderr,
             "Cannot allocate space for device names\n");
       exit(1);
}
```

```
/*
 *  Create a bound transport endpoint for each address
 *  returned from get_addrs(), fill in the pollfd
 *  structure for each endpoint, and store the name
 *  of each device file.
 */

curr_pollfdp = pollfdp;
curr_devicepp = devicepp;
curr_tpinfop = tpinfop;
while (curr_tpinfop) {
    num_addrs = curr_tpinfop->nd_addrlistp->n_cnt;
    while (num_addrs --) {
        if ((curr_pollfdp->fd= t_open(curr_tpinfop->device,
                                    O_RDWR, NULL)) < 0) {
            t_error("t_open failed");
            exit(1);
        }
        curr_pollfdp->events = POLLIN;
        *curr_devicepp = curr_tpinfop->device;
        fd = curr_pollfdp->fd;

        if ((req = (struct t_bind *) t_alloc(fd, T_BIND,
                                        0)) == NULL) {
            t_error("t_alloc failed");
            exit(1);
        }

        if ((ret = (struct t_bind *) t_alloc(fd, T_BIND,
                                        T_ALL)) == NULL) {
            t_error("t_alloc failed");
            exit(1);
        }

        req->qlen = 1;
        req->addr= *(curr_tpinfop->nd_addrlistp->n_addrs);

        /*
         *  Bind to the address over which the service
         *  will be offered.
         */

        if (t_bind(fd, req, ret) < 0) {
```

```
                t_error("t_bind failed");
                exit(1);
            }

            /*
             *  Make sure the address you got was the one
             *  you wanted!
             */

            if ((req->addr.len != ret->addr.len) ||
                (memcmp(req->addr.buf, ret->addr.buf,
                                            req->addr.len))) {
                fprintf(stderr,
                        "Did not bind to correct address!\n");
                exit(1);
            }
            curr_pollfdp++;
            curr_devicepp++;
            curr_tpinfop->nd_addrlistp->n_addrs++;
        }
        curr_tpinfop = curr_tpinfop->nextp;
    }

    /*
     * Loop forever, polling for events.  When an event
     * occurs, find the transport endpoint and call
     * the process_it() routine to implement the protocol.
     */

    while (1) {
        if (poll(pollfdp, num_fd, -1) < 0) {
            perror("poll failed!");
            exit(1);
        }

        curr_pollfdp = pollfdp;
        curr_devicepp = devicepp;
        for (i = 0; i < num_fd; i++) {
            switch(curr_pollfdp->revents) {
                case 0:
                    break;
                case POLLIN:
                    process_it(curr_pollfdp->fd, *curr_devicepp);
```

```
                    break;
                default:
                    perror("poll returned an error");
                    exit(1);
            }
            curr_pollfdp ++;
            curr_devicepp ++;
        }
    }
}
```

Now that we have a transport endpoint with an event on it, we do the following:

1. Call the **t_look()** routine to find the event on the transport endpoint.

2. If the event is **T_DISCONNECT**, then the application making the connection request has suddenly closed the connection. So, we call the **t_rcvdis()** routine to clear the event and return to continue our loop.

3. If the event is **T_LISTEN**, then we have a connection request on the transport endpoint. In that case, we do the following:

    a. Allocate a **t_call** structure by calling the **t_alloc()** routine. We use the **t_call** structure in the **t_listen()** routine.

    b. Call the **t_listen()** routine to put the transport endpoint in the **T_INCON** state. A connection request is already on the transport endpoint, so the **t_listen()** routine returns immediately.

    c. Call the **t_open()** routine to create a second transport endpoint. We use that endpoint to accept the connection.

    d. Call the **t_bind()** routine to bind an arbitrary transport address to the second transport endpoint.

    e. Call the **t_accept()** routine to accept the connection. If the **t_accept()** routine fails, we check if it failed because a disconnect event occurred on the transport endpoint (that can happen if the client side of the application aborted the connection request). If that is the case, we issue the **t_rcvdis()** routine to clear the event and return to the loop that waits for connection requests.

4. Create a child process to carry out the **rpopen()** protocol after we establish the connection.

The code follows:

```
void
process_it(fd, device)
int fd;
char *device;
{
    struct t_call *call;   /* holds connection info     */
    int recfd;             /* endpoint on which to accept */

    switch (t_look(fd)) {
        case T_DISCONNECT:
            if (t_rcvdis(fd, NULL) < 0) {
                t_error("t_rcvdis");
            }
            return;

        default:
            return;

        case T_LISTEN:
            if ((call = (struct t_call *)t_alloc(fd,
                            T_CALL, T_ALL)) == NULL) {
                t_error("could not get space for t_call!");
                exit(1);
            }
            if (t_listen(fd, call) < 0) {
                t_error("could not listen!");
                exit(1);
            }

            if ((recfd =
                    t_open(device, O_RDWR, NULL)) < 0) {
                t_error("could not open device!");
                exit(1);
            }

            if (t_bind(recfd, NULL, NULL) < 0) {
                t_error("bind for responding failed!");
                exit(1);
            }

            if (t_accept(fd, recfd, call) < 0) {
```

```
            /*
             * Did it fail because client disconnected?
             * t_errno is set to TLOOK if it did.
             */

            if (t_errno == TLOOK) {
                if (t_rcvdis(fd, NULL) < 0) {
                    t_error("could not disconnect");
                    exit(1);
                }
                (void) t_close(recfd);
                return;
            } else {
                t_error("could not accept call");
                exit(1);
            }
        }

        switch (fork()) {
            case -1:
                perror("fork failed!\n");
                exit(1);

            default: /* parent */

                (void)t_close(recfd);
                break;

            case 0:   /* child */

                (void)t_close(fd);

                /*
                 *  The child_actions() routine exits
                 *  when it completes.
                 */
                child_actions(recfd);
        }
    }
}
```

Now that there is an established connection, we can implement the protocol. We do the following:

1. Read the user name. We continue reading until we see the **0** character. Note that we place the user name into a buffer containing **BUFSIZ** bytes. Therefore, if we don't see the **0** character after reading **BUFSIZ** bytes, we exit the child process.

2. Read the password. Again, we continue reading until we see the **0** character and exit if we don't get it after reading **BUFSIZ** bytes.

3. Check the user name and password. If the password is valid, we send a **y** character to the other side of the connection. If the password is invalid, we send an **n** character to the other side of the application.

4. As defined by the protocol, the client side of the application disconnects the connection if it reads the **n** character. The server side of the connection can't do the disconnect, because it sent the **n** character and the disconnect may destroy data in transit. When the client side of the application reads the **n** character, it knows no more data will be transferred, making it safe to abort the connection. So, the server side of the application simply issues the **t_rcv()** routine, which will return (with an error indication) when the disconnect happens. We then exit the child process. If we sent the **y** character to the client side of the application, we continue the application.

5. Set the real user ID and the real group ID to that of the specified user. We are in a child process, so we change the IDs for this connection only. Also, to work properly, the application must have enough authority to change its user ID. That means the application must be started by the superuser. If we can set the user ID and group ID correctly, we continue with the protocol.

6. Read the type (that is, a **w** or an **r**) from the client side of the application.

7. Read the command. We continue reading until we see the **0** character. If we don't see the **0** character after **BUFSIZ** bytes, we exit the child process.

8. If the type is **r**, we issue the **popen()** routine for reading. We read the data from the **popen()** routine and send it over the transport endpoint to the client side of the application. And, as discussed earlier, we precede the data with a 4-byte ASCII string containing the length. We continue until we read an end-of-file indication from the **popen()** routine.

   When we read the end-of-file indication from the **popen()** routine, we send a message containing a 4-byte ASCII string of ''**0000**''. That informs the client side of the application that we are finished sending data. When the client side reads that message, it shuts down the connection. So, we issue the **t_rcv()** routine, which returns (with an error condition) when the disconnect occurs.

Again, when creating networking applications, must make sure that the receiver of the data, not the sender, tears down the connection after all data are read. Tearing down a connection may distroy data in transit.

We must also do one more step when sending data to the client side of the application. As mentioned in the `t_snd()` section in Section 7.9, the `t_snd()` routine does not check for disconnects before sending data. And, because we are in a loop sending large amounts of data, we will never know if or when the client side of the application unexpectedly aborts the connection.

So, to solve the problem, we call the `ioctl()` system call with the `I_SETSIG` parameter. As explained in Section 8.8, that generates a **SIGPOLL** signal when a message appears on the transport endpoint. And, because our protocol does not expect any messages to arrive on the transport endpoint when we are sending data to the client side of the application, a message that appears on the transport endpoint must be a disconnect indication. So, we set up a signal handler to catch the **SIGPOLL** signal and call the `hangup()` routine if that signal occurs. The `hangup()` routine prints an error message and exits the child process.

When we are finished sending data, we turn off the signal generation with the `ioctl()` system call. We turn it off *before* sending our last message containing a 4-byte ASCII string of ``0000''. We do that because we expect a disconnect indication to arrive after we send the end-of-data message (remember that the client disconnects after it reads the end-of-data message). Here, the disconnect indication is not an error.

9. If the type is **w**, we issue the `popen()` routine for writing. Then, we do the following:

   a. Read the length indicator and continue reading until we receive the entire four bytes.

   b. Transform the length indicator into local representation.

   c. If the length indicator is **0**, then we know the client side of the application is finished sending data. At that point, we issue the `t_snddis()` routine to tear down the connection. Notice that in this case, we are the receiver of the data, so it is safe for us to abort the connection after reading all the data.

   d. If the length indicator is not **0**, we continue reading the data until we read the amount specified by the length indicator.

   e. Write the data into the pipe created with the `popen()` routine.

The code follows:

```
int
child_actions(conn_fd)
int conn_fd;
{
    int done;              /* indicates all data are read   */
    int where;             /* where we are in buffer        */
    int nbytes;            /* the number of bytes read      */
    int length;            /* the length indicator          */
    int flags = 0;         /* info returned from t_rcv()    */
    FILE *fp;              /* file pointer into popen()     */
    char *response;        /* used for authentication       */
    struct spwd *spent;    /* used for authentication       */
    struct passwd *pwent;  /* holds user information        */
    char type;             /* "r" or "w" from client        */
    char name[BSIZE];      /* user name from client         */
    char passwd[BSIZE];    /* password from client          */
    char command[BSIZE];   /* command to give popen()       */
    char buff[BSIZE];      /* holds data from popen()       */
    char sendbuff[BSIZE];  /* hold data we send to client   */
    void hangup();         /* signal handler for disconnect */

    /*
     *  Read the user's name.
     */

    done = 0;
    where = 0;
    do {
        if ((BSIZE - where) == 0) {
            exit(1);
        }
        if ((nbytes = t_rcv(conn_fd, &name[where],
                            BSIZE - where, &flags)) < 0) {
            t_error("t_rcv of user name failed!");
            exit(1);
        }
        where += nbytes;
        if (name[where - 1] == '\0') {
            done = 1;
        }
    } while (!done);
```

```
/*
 * Read the user's password...
 */

done = 0;
where = 0;
do {
    if ((BSIZE - where) == 0) {
        exit(1);
    }
    if ((nbytes = t_rcv(conn_fd, &passwd[where],
                        BSIZE - where, &flags)) < 0) {
        t_error("t_rcv of password failed!");
        exit(1);
    }
    where += nbytes;
    if (passwd[where - 1] == '\0') {
        done = 1;
    }
} while (!done);

response = "y";
if ((pwent = getpwnam(name)) == NULL
    || (spent = getspnam(name)) == NULL
    || strcmp(crypt(passwd, spent->sp_pwdp), spent->sp_pwdp)
                                                       != 0) {
    response = "n";
}

if (t_snd(conn_fd, response, 1, 0) < 0) {
    t_error("t_snd of password response failed!");
    exit(1);
}

/*
 *  If we sent an "n" character, wait for the client
 *  side of the application to disconnect.  The t_rcv()
 *  routine returns (with an error) when the disconnect
 *  occurs.
 */

if (strcmp(response, "n") == 0) {
    (void) t_rcv(conn_fd, &type, 1, &flags);
```

```
        exit(0);
}

/*
 *   Set the user ID and group ID to the specified
 *   user...
 */

if (setuid(pwent->pw_uid) < 0
   || setgid(pwent->pw_gid) < 0) {
      exit(1);
}

/*
 *   Read a w or an r.
 */

if (t_rcv(conn_fd, &type, 1, &flags) < 0) {
   t_error("t_rcv of type failed!");
   exit(1);
}

/*
 *   Read the command
 */

done = 0;
where = 0;
do {
   if ((BSIZE - where) == 0) {
      exit(1);
   }
   if ((nbytes = t_rcv(conn_fd, &command[where],
                        BSIZE - where, &flags)) < 0) {
      t_error("t_rcv of command failed!");
      exit(1);
   }
   where += nbytes;
   if (command[where - 1] == '\0') {
      done = 1;
   }
} while (!done);
```

```
if (type == 'r') {
  if ((fp = popen(command, "r")) == NULL) {
     exit(1);
  }

  /*
   * Read from the popen() call, put in the data length,
   * and send the message to the client.
   * Before doing that, set up the transport endpoint to
   * generate a SIGPOLL signal if a message appears.
   * Because we do not expect any messages, we know a
   * message is a disconnect indication.
   */

  signal(SIGPOLL, hangup);
  if (ioctl(conn_fd, I_SETSIG, S_INPUT) < 0) {
     perror("can't set S_INPUT");
     exit(1);
  }

  /*
   * Check if the disconnect arrived before we set
   * the signal catcher
   */

  if (t_look(conn_fd) != 0) {
     fprintf(stderr, "Unexpected disconnect detected\n");
     exit(1);
  }

  while ((nbytes = fread(buff, 1, BSIZE, fp)) != NULL){
     sprintf(sendbuff, "%.4d", nbytes);
     memcpy(sendbuff + HDR_SIZE, buff, nbytes);
     if (t_snd(conn_fd, sendbuff, nbytes + HDR_SIZE, 0) < 0) {
        t_error("t_snd of data failed!");
        exit(1);
     }
  }

  if (ioctl(conn_fd, I_SETSIG, 0) < 0) {
     perror("can't turn off S_INPUT");
     exit(1);
  }
```

```
        /*
         *  Send the "0000" string to indicate end-of-data and
         *  wait for the client side to disconnect.
         */

    pclose(fp);
    if (t_snd(conn_fd, "0000", HDR_SIZE, 0) != HDR_SIZE) {
        t_error("t_snd of 0 failed!");
        exit(1);
    }
    (void)t_rcv(conn_fd, &type, 1, &flags);
    exit(0);
} else {
    if ((fp = popen(command, "w")) == NULL) {
        exit(1);
    }
    for (;;) {
        /*
         *  Get the first 4 bytes (which contain
         *  the length indicator).
         */

        where = 0;
        do {
            if ((nbytes = t_rcv(conn_fd, &buff[where],
                            HDR_SIZE - where, &flags)) < 0) {
                t_error("t_rcv of command failed!");
                exit(1);
            }
            where += nbytes;
        } while (where < HDR_SIZE);

        (void)sscanf(buff, "%4d", &length);

        /*
         *  Check if this packet is the end-of-data marker.
         *  If it is, send the disconnect request to close the
         *  connection.
         */

        if (length == 0) {
            (void)t_snddis(conn_fd, NULL);
            pclose(fp);
```

```
            exit(0);
        }

        /*
         *   Because we are not at the end-of-data marker,
         *   read the data in this packet and write
         *   them to the pipe.
         */

        where = 0;
        do {
            if ((nbytes = t_rcv(conn_fd, &buff[where],
                                length - where, &flags)) < 0) {
                t_error("t_rcv of command failed!");
                exit(1);
            }
            where += nbytes;
        } while (where < length);

        if (fwrite(buff, 1, length, fp) != length) {
            exit(1);
        }
    }
  }
}

void
hangup()
{
    fprintf(stderr, "Unexpected disconnect detected\n");
    exit(1);
}
```

Now let's look at the client side of the application. The client side implements the
rpopen() routine.

The Client Code

The following code implements the client side of the application. We start with the
implementation of the **rpopen()** routine.

To begin, we check that the type specification is a **"w"** or an **"r"**. If not, we return a **-1** value. Otherwise, we set a static global variable to either **READ** or **WRITE**, depending upon the mode specified by the user. We use that variable in the **rpread()**, **rpwrite()**, and **rpclose()** routines, which are described in what follows. And, as we will discuss, those routines also use other static variables that maintain the state of the reads and writes.

Having global static variables imposes a restriction—an application can only have one instance of **rpopen()** active within a process. That means a process must close the connection with the **rpclose()** routine before it can issue a second **rpopen()** routine. We will live with this restriction in our example; eliminating the restriction requires more code and does not use any networking routines. For example, one way to eliminate the restriction is to have the **rpopen()** routine maintain a list of active connections. Each element in the list can contain the mode of the connection (that is, an indication of either **READ** or **WRITE**), the current data the application collected from the server, and all of the other information our application keeps in static global variables. The **rpopen()** routine can return a handle that identifies an element in the list, and the **rpread()**, **rpwrite()**, and **rpclose()** routines can take that handle as an argument.

Now, to continue with the **rpopen()** routine, we call our **get_addrs()** routine. As mentioned earlier, the **get_addrs()** routine returns a list of **tpinfo** structures. The **tpinfo** structure contains information about how to connect to the server side of the application.

The code follows:

```
#include <stdio.h>
#include <tiuser.h>
#include <fcntl.h>
#include <sys/types.h>
#include <netdb.h>
#include <stropts.h>
#include "tpinfo.h"

#define READ 1
#define WRITE 2

#define MAX_DATA  9999
#define HDR_SIZE  4

#define BSIZE MAX_DATA + HDR_SIZE

static int mode;                /* holds r or w indication  */
```

```
static int amount_in_buffer; /* amt in server buffer      */

int
rpopen(host, command, type)
char *host;
char *command;
char *type;
{
   int fd;                 /* holds the transport endpoint   */
   int nbytes;             /* used to read user name         */
   int flags = 0;          /* info returned from t_rcv()     */
   int got_connection;     /* 1 if connection is established */
   int num_addrs;          /* num of address for a provider  */
   char buf[BUFSIZ];       /* generic buffer to hold data    */
   char prompt[BUFSIZ];    /* holds password prompt          */

   struct t_call *sndcall;      /* used in t_connect()       */
   struct tpinfo *tpinfop;      /* return from get_addrs()*/
   struct tpinfo *curr_tpinfop; /* traverses tpinfop         */

   if ((strcmp(type, "r") != 0)
    && (strcmp(type, "w") != 0)) {
      return(-1);
   }

   if (strcmp(type, "r") == 0) {
      mode = READ;
   } else {
      mode = WRITE;
   }

   /*
    *  Get the address and transport providers to use.
    */

   if ((tpinfop = get_addrs(host, "rpopen")) == NULL) {
      fprintf(stderr,
              "There are no addresses for this service!\n");
      return(-1);
   }
```

Now that we have a list of transport providers and transport addresses, we attempt to connect to the server side of the application. We do the following:

1. Loop through each **tpinfo** structure. A **tpinfo** structure contains the name of a device file for a transport provider and a list of addresses to use for that transport provider.

2. Within the loop, we do the following:

   a. Create a transport endpoint into the transport provider by calling the **t_open()** routine. We give the **t_open()** routine the device file contained in the current **tpinfo** structure. Note that we don't know what transport provider we are using. But, because we are transport-independent, we don't care.

   b. Bind an arbitrary transport address to the transport endpoint.

   c. Allocate memory to hold a **t_call** structure. We will use the **t_call** structure when attempting to make the connection.

   d. Create another loop to go through all of the transport addresses in the current **tpinfo** structure. We do the following in the loop:

      • Attempt to make a connection to the current transport address.

      • If we succeed, we set the **got_connection** flag and break out of the loop. Otherwise, we continue the loop.

   e. If we established a connection in step d, we break out of the outer loop.

3. After the outer loop completes, we check the **got_connection** flag to figure out if we have a connection to the server side of the application. If we do, we continue with the **rpopen()** routine.

   If we do not have a connection, we call the **free_addrs()** routine and a return a **-1** value to the caller. The **free_addrs()** routine frees the memory allocated by the **get_addrs()** routine. We present the code to the **free_addrs()** and **get_addrs()** routines in Chapter 9.

The code follows:

```
got_connection = 0;
curr_tpinfop = tpinfop;
for (curr_tpinfop = tpinfop; curr_tpinfop;
                    curr_tpinfop = curr_tpinfop->nextp) {
    if ((fd = t_open(curr_tpinfop->device,
                                O_RDWR, NULL)) < 0) {
        continue;
```

```
    }

    /*
     *  Bind to an arbitrary return address.
     */

    if (t_bind(fd, NULL, NULL) < 0) {
        (void)t_close(fd);
        continue;
    }

    /*
     *  Get memory to hold call structure, copy in
     *  the server's address, and connect to the service.
     */

    if ((sndcall = (struct t_call *)t_alloc(fd,
                                T_CALL, 0)) == NULL) {
        (void)t_close(fd);
        continue;
    }

    /*
     *  Try to connect to the server by looping
     *  through all of the transport addresses.
     */

    num_addrs = curr_tpinfop->nd_addrlistp->n_cnt;
    while (num_addrs --) {
        sndcall->addr = *(tpinfop->nd_addrlistp->n_addrs);

        if (t_connect(fd, sndcall, NULL) == 0) {
            got_connection = 1;
            break;
        }
        curr_tpinfop->nd_addrlistp->n_addrs++;
    }

    if (got_connection) {
        break;
    }
    sndcall->addr.buf = 0;
    t_free(sndcall, T_CALL);
```

```
    (void) t_close(fd);
    curr_tpinfop = curr_tpinfop->nextp;
}

free_addrs(tpinfop);
sndcall->addr.buf = 0;
t_free(sndcall, T_CALL);

if (!got_connection) {
    (void) t_close(fd);
    return(-1);
}
```

Now that we have a connection, carry out the protocol. We do the following:

1. Prompt the user for his or her user name on the server machine and send the name to the server side of the application.

2. Prompt the user for his or her password on the server machine and send the password to the server side of the application.

3. Read a **y** or an **n** from the server side of the application. If we read the **n** character, then the password validation failed on the server side. So, we send a disconnect request to the server, close the transport endpoint, and return a **-1** value to the caller.

4. If the authentication passed, send the type specification to the server side of the application.

5. Send the command string to the server side of the application. That completes the application-layer protocol.

The code follows:

```
/*
 *   Read the user name, strip the newline at the
 *   end of the string, and send the name to the
 *   server side of the application.
 */

printf("Please enter your user name of %s:\n", host);
if ((nbytes = read(0, buf, BUFSIZ)) < 0) {
    (void) t_close(fd);
    return(-1);
}
```

```
buf[strlen(buf) - 1] = '\0';
if (t_snd(fd, buf, strlen(buf) + 1, 0) == -1) {
    (void)t_close(fd);
    return(-1);
}

/*
 *  Prompt for the password and send it to the
 *  server side of the application.
 */

sprintf(prompt,
            "Please enter your password on %s:\n", host);
strcpy(buf, getpass(prompt));
if (t_snd(fd, buf, strlen(buf) + 1, 0) == -1) {
    (void)t_close(fd);
    return(-1);
}

/*
 *  Read the results of the password validation.
 */

if (t_rcv(fd, buf, 1, &flags) == -1) {
    (void)t_close(fd);
    return(-1);
}
if (buf[0] == 'n') {
    fprintf(stderr, "Login Incorrect\n");
    (void)t_snddis(fd, NULL);
    (void)t_close(fd);
    return(-1);
}

/*
 *  Send the type.
 */

buf[0] = *type;
if (t_snd(fd, buf, 1, 0) == -1) {
    (void)t_close(fd);
    return(-1);
}
```

```
/*
 *   Send the command.
 */

if (t_snd (fd, command, strlen(command) + 1, 0) == -1) {
    (void) t_close (fd);
    return(-1);
}

    return(fd);
}
```

Now let's look at the other three routines needed to complete the client side of the application: **rpread()**, **rpwrite()**, and **rpclose()**. We begin with the **rpread()** routine.

The **rpread()** routine takes three arguments: a file descriptor returned from **rpopen()**, a buffer, and a length. The length specifies how many bytes to read into the buffer. The user may ask for a lesser amount of data than the server side of the application sends, so we maintain an internal buffer that holds data sent by the server.

So, in the **rpread()** code, we do the following:

1. Check that the **rpopen()** routine was called with the ''**r**'' parameter. If not, we return an error.

2. Loop, getting data from the server side of the application. Within the loop, we do the following:

    a. Check if our internal buffer has enough data to satisfy the request. If it does, we copy the data into the user buffer, modify local variables to specify the next piece of unread data in the internal buffer, and break out of the loop.

    b. If there is not enough data in our internal buffer to satisfy the request but there are some data in the internal buffer, we copy all data in the internal buffer into the user's buffer.

    c. Call the **t_rcv()** routine to get data from the server side of the application. As defined by the protocol, the server side of the application precedes the data with a 4-byte string that contains the number of bytes it is sending. So, we read the first four bytes of data.

    d. Translate that 4-byte string into an integer and loop again, calling the **t_rcv()** routine to consume all of the data the server side of the application sends. We place that data into our internal buffer.

After the loop ends, we return the number of bytes we placed into the user's buffer.

The code follows:

```
int
rpread(fd, buf, len)
int fd;
char *buf;
int len;
{
   static char from_server[BSIZE];  /* holds server data */
   static int start_of_data = 0;    /* where data start  */

   int nbytes;          /* used to read user name       */
   int flags = 0;       /* info returned from t_rcv()   */
   int amount_to_get;   /* how much more data to read   */
   int user_start;      /* current offset in user buffer */
   int where;           /* used to get data from server  */

   if (mode == WRITE) {
      return(-1);
   }

   user_start = 0;
   amount_to_get = len;
   while (amount_to_get) {
      /*
       *  The amount_in_buffer variable is a global
       *  variable initially set to 0.  If there are enough
       *  residual data from previous call to satisfy
       *  this request, fill the user buffer and break out
       *  of the loop.
       */
      if (amount_in_buffer >= amount_to_get) {
         memcpy(&buf[user_start],
                 &from_server[start_of_data], amount_to_get);
         start_of_data += amount_to_get;
         amount_in_buffer -= amount_to_get;
         break;
      }
```

```
/*
 *  Copy any residual data from previous call into the
 *  user buffer.
 */

if (amount_in_buffer) {
    memcpy(&buf[user_start],
           &from_server[start_of_data], amount_in_buffer);
    amount_to_get -= amount_in_buffer;
    user_start += amount_in_buffer;
    amount_in_buffer = 0;
}

/*
 *  Get the first 4 bytes (which contain
 *  the length indicator).  If we fail (because the
 *  connection was closed), return the amount we
 *  already put into the buffer.
 */

start_of_data = 0;
where = 0;
do {
    if ((nbytes = t_rcv(fd, &from_server[where],
                        HDR_SIZE - where, &flags)) < 0) {
        return(len - amount_to_get);
    }
    where += nbytes;
} while (where < HDR_SIZE);

(void)sscanf(from_server, "%4d", &amount_in_buffer);

/*
 *   Check if this packet is the end-of-data marker.
 *   If it is, send the disconnect request to close the
 *   connection.
 */

if (amount_in_buffer == 0) {
    (void)t_snddis(fd, NULL);
    (void)t_close(fd);
    return(len - amount_to_get);
}
```

```
    /*
     *  Because we are not at the end-of-data marker,
     *  read the data in this packet and put them into
     *  our buffer.
     */

    where = 0;
    do {
        if ((nbytes = t_rcv(fd, &from_server[where],
                    amount_in_buffer - where, &flags)) < 0) {
            (void)t_close(fd);
            amount_in_buffer = where;
            break;
        }
        where += nbytes;
    } while (where < amount_in_buffer);
    }
    return(user_start + amount_to_get);
}
```

Now let's write the **rpwrite()** routine, which simply creates a message and sends it to the server. Specifically, we do the following:

1. Check that the **rpopen()** routine was called with the ''**w**'' parameter. If not, we return an error.

2. Check if the user is sending more than 9999 bytes of data. If so, we split the data into smaller packets. We do that because we only have four bytes to hold the string that contains the length.

3. Construct the message by translating the length into a 4-byte string, and send that string followed by the data to the server side of the application.

As mentioned earlier, the **t_snd()** routine does not check for disconnects before sending data. That means the **t_snd()** routine will *not* fail if the server side of the application aborts the connection. On the server side, we solved the problem by using the **ioctl()** routine with the **I_SETSIG** parameter. That generated a **SIGPOLL** signal when a message arrived on the transport endpoint.

That solution is not correct here. It would generate the **SIGPOLL** signal within the caller's process, potentially interrupting other routines. So, instead, we will call the **t_look()** routine before sending the data. If a we received a disconnect indication, the **t_look()** routine returns a **T_DISCONNECT** value. If that is the case, the **rpwrite()** routine returns an error condition to the user.

The code follows:

```
int
rpwrite(fd, buf, len)
int fd;
char *buf;
int len;
{
    char sendbuff[BSIZE]; /* buffer to send to server     */
    int amount;           /* amount of data to send        */
    int num_sent = 0;     /* amount of data sent           */

    if (mode == READ) {
        return(-1);
    }
    while (len) {
        amount = len;
        if (amount > MAX_DATA) {
            amount = MAX_DATA;
        }
        sprintf(sendbuff, "%.4d", amount);
        memcpy(sendbuff + HDR_SIZE, buf, amount);

        if (t_look(fd) == T_DISCONNECT) {
            fprintf(stderr, "disconnect occurred!\n");
            return(-1);
        }

        if (t_snd(fd, sendbuff, amount + HDR_SIZE, 0) < 0) {
            break;
        }
        len -= amount;
        num_sent += amount;
    }
    return(num_sent);
}
```

Finally, let's create the **rpclose()** routine. In the **rpclose()** routine, we do the following:

1. If the **rpopen()** routine was called with the ''**r**'' parameter, we simply reset our pointers to our internal buffer used in the **rpread()** routine and close the

transport endpoint. We already sent the disconnect to the server side of the application when we read the message with the **0000** length. And, even if the user closes the connection early (that is, before we saw the message with the **0000** length), the **t_close()** routine will break the connection.

2. If the **rpopen()** routine was called with the "**w**" parameter, we do the following actions:

   a. Send a message with a length of **0000**. That tells the server side of the application that we are finished sending data. That causes the server to abort the connection.

   b. Issue the **t_rcv()** routine, which returns (with an error condition) when the disconnect arrives.

   c. Call **t_close()** on the transport endpoint.

The code follows:

```
void
rpclose(fd)
int fd;
{
    int flags = 0;          /* info returned from t_rcv()      */

    if (mode == 0) {
        return;
    }
    if (mode == READ) {
        amount_in_buffer = 0;
    } else {
        /*
         *  Send the "0000" string to indicate the end of the
         *  data and wait for the server side to disconnect.
         */
        if (t_snd(fd, "0000", HDR_SIZE, 0) != HDR_SIZE) {
            t_error("t_snd of 0 failed!");
            mode = 0;
            (void) t_close(fd);
            return;
        }
        (void) t_rcv(fd, &mode, 1, &flags);
        exit(0);
    }
```

```
    mode = 0;
    (void) t_close(fd);
}
```

The **rpopen()** routines are not specific to any transport provider, so they work over any connection-oriented transport provider without modification. The server side of the application calls the **get_addrs()** routine to figure out all of the connection-oriented transport providers on the system and makes itself available over every one of them. The **rpopen()** routine on the client machine uses the information returned by the **get_addrs()** routine to make the connection. It neither knows nor cares which transport provider it uses.

The key to the transport-independent feature is our **get_addrs()** routine. That routine uses the SVR4 Network Selection and Name-to-Address Mapping routines. We present the code to the **get_addrs()** routine in Chapter 9.

As we wind down our discussion of TLI, we present another SVR4 feature. As mentioned in Chapter 1, SVR4 provides several port monitors that manage transport endpoints on behalf of your application. One of the port monitors is the SVR4 **listen** port monitor (also called the SVR4 "listener"), which simplifies networking applications. We now present an overview of the SVR4 **listen** port monitor.

8.11 Using the SVR4 Listen Port Monitor

SVR4 provides the **listen** port monitor to help write networking applications. The **listen** port monitor is a process that manages a transport endpoint for you. SVR4 provides a separate **listen** process for every connection-oriented transport provider on the system.

As we saw throughout the chapter, the job of the server side of a networking application is tedious. It must create a transport endpoint, bind a transport address to the transport endpoint, and if the transport endpoint is over a connection-oriented transport provider, it must wait for connection requests and accept the connection.

The **listen** port monitor can help. It does most of the TLI operations for you. Unfortunately, it only works over connection-oriented transport providers. But, if your application uses a connection-oriented transport provider, the **listen** port monitor can simplify the server side of your application.

For the **listen** process to work with your application, the administrator of the server machine must register the server side of your application with the SVR4 listener. The administrator specifies the following:

1. The transport provider to use.

2. The path name to your application.

3. The transport address associated with the application.

After the administrator registers your application, the **listen** port monitor manages a transport endpoint for you. As shown in Figure 8.5, the **listen** port monitor does the following:

1. Issues the **t_open()** routine to create a transport endpoint into the transport provider that the administrator specified.

2. Issues the **t_bind()** routine to bind the transport address that the administrator specified to the transport endpoint.

3. Polls the transport endpoint waiting for incoming connection requests and issues the **t_listen()** request when a connection request arrives.

4. After it issues the **t_listen()** routine, the port monitor creates a second transport endpoint and issues the **t_accept()** routine to accept the connection.

5. After it accepts the connection, it issues the **fork()** system call to create a child process. The parent continues to listen for the next connection request. The child process calls the **dup()** system call to duplicate the connected transport endpoint onto file descriptors **0**, **1**, and **2**. The child then calls **exec()** to start the server side of the application.

6. When the server side of the application starts, it has a connection to the client side of the application! It does not have to call the TLI connection-establishment routines and can immediately start issuing the **t_snd()** and **t_rcv()** routines. When you complete your application-layer protocol, simply exit the application. When another connection request arrives, the **listen** process starts the application again.

There are several advantages to using the **listen** process:

1. The server side of your application runs only when a connection request arrives. That reduces the number of processes on the server machine.

2. The server side of your application is much simpler. You don't have to do the connection management routines yourself. When your application starts, you have an established connection.

When the administrator registers your application with the **listen** port monitor, he or she can specify a list of STREAMS modules to push on the stream. After the **listen** process accepts a connection, it pushes the specified modules on the connected transport endpoint before starting your application.

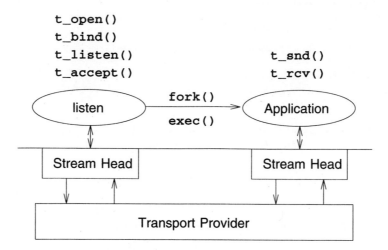

Figure 8.5   The Network Listener

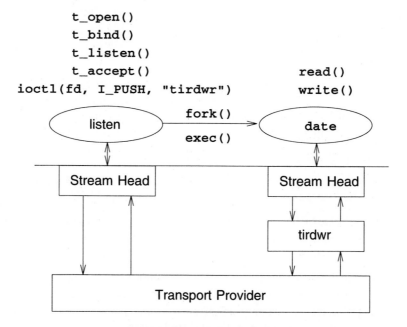

Figure 8.6   Pushing tirdwr

So, as illustrated in Figure 8.6, the `listen` process can push the `tirdwr` module onto the stream before it starts an application. Therefore, any application that issues `read()` and `write()` system calls to file descriptors `0`, `1`, and `2` can become a networking application.

In Figure 8.6, the administrator specified the SVR4 `date` command as the server side of the application. The administrator chose an arbitrary transport address and told the `listen` port monitor to associate that address with the `date` command.

That turns the `date` command into a networking application! When an application on a client machine connects to the transport address that the administrator specified, the `listen` process accepts the connection, pushes the `tirdwr` module, and invokes the `date` command. The `date` command writes the current time and date to file descriptor `0`, sending the data to the application on the client machine.

8.12 Summary

TLI routines are a set of low-level networking routines that give a direct interface to a transport provider. TLI routines are used to establish communication, manage a connection, and transfer data.

In TLI applications, you must implement the functions of the presentation layer and the session layer of the OSI Model. The presentation layer places data in a common format, and the session layer synchronizes dialogue.

TLI provides routines to manage connection-oriented and connectionless transport providers. They are designed to be transport-independent. Common routines can be used over any transport provider.

For Further Reading

1. AT&T, *UNIX System V Release 4 Programmer's Guide: Networking Interfaces*, Prentice Hall, Englewood Cliffs, NJ, 1990.

2. Stevens, R., Chapter 7, System V Transport Layer Interface, *UNIX Network Programming*, Prentice Hall, Englewood Cliffs, NJ, 1990.

Exercises

8.1   Create a program that uses XDR routines to translate a data structure into XDR format. The data structure must contain two long integers, a character, and two short integers.

8.2   Create an application that carries out a user-info service. The client side of the application sends a user name to the server side of the application. The server side of the application returns the user ID of that user, or a **-1** if the user does not exist on the system. Make sure to account for differences in data representation.

8.3   What special steps must an application take when sending data with the **t_snd()** routine? Why are these steps necessary?

8.4   Explain what steps the server side of an application must take if it sets the **qlen** field of the **t_bind** structure to a value greater than **1**. Why are these steps necessary? What are the advantages and disadvantages of setting **qlen** to a value greater than **1**?

8.5   Explain why the receiver of data, not the sender of data, must issue the disconnect request to tear down a connection.

8.6   Explain the difference between orderly shutdown and abrupt shutdown. Should an application rely of an orderly shutdown feature? Explain.

8.7   Rewrite the server side of the application presented in Section 8.4, but have the application set the **qlen** field to **5**. Does this application benefit from having **qlen** set to **5**?

Chapter 9

Network Selection and
Name-to-Address Mapping

9.1 Introduction

You have two problems when writing applications with TLI: figuring out which transport providers exist on the system and obtaining the address of a service over a given transport provider.

The Network Selection mechanism and Name-to-Address Mapping facility solve these problems. The Network Selection mechanism provides routines that let you find out which transport providers exist on the system, tell whether a transport provider supplies virtual-circuit or datagram service, show which device file to use to access the transport provider, and furnish other useful data.

The Name-to-Address Mapping facility lets your application get the addresses of network services in a transport-independent manner. It provides routines that figure out the addresses of network services on a machine over a specified transport provider.

In this chapter, we show how to use the the Network Selection and Name-to-Address Mapping routines. We begin with an overview of the facilities.

9.2 Overview

The Network Selection and Name-to-Address Mapping routines help create transport-independent applications. The Network Selection routines let you figure out which transport providers exist on your system and provide information about each transport provider. After you choose a transport provider, you can use the Name-to-Address Mapping routines to translate a service name into its transport address.

Previous to SVR4, you had to code transport-specific information into networking applications. For example, if you wrote an application that used TCP/IP, you had to use TCP/IP-specific routines to translate names into addresses. As shown in Figure

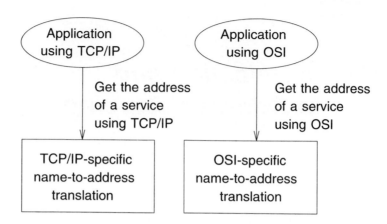

Figure 9.1   Transport-Specific Applications

9.1, embedding that information into an application makes it inherently transport-dependent.

The Network Selection and Name-to-Address Mapping routines provide a way to get transport-provider information at execution time. That frees your application from having to specify it explicitly. Figure 9.2 shows an application using Network Selection and Name-to-Address Mapping.

Both the client side and the server side of an application can use the facilities. The client side would use the Network Selection routines to choose a transport provider. It would then use the Name-to-Address Mapping routines to figure out the address of the service over the selected transport provider.

The server side of the application would use the Network Selection routines to select *all* of the transport providers on the system. Then, for each transport provider, it would create a transport endpoint, use the Name-to-Address Mapping routines to find its own transport address, and bind that address to the transport endpoint. That makes the server side of the application available over all transport providers on the machine.

The Network Selection and Name-to-Address facilities are simple and easy to use. They extract information about transport providers from a configuration file and provide routines that make it easy for applications to get the specific information needed. They are modeled after the UNIX system password-manipulation subroutines—**setpwent()**, **getpwent()**, and **endpwent()**. Just as those routines obtain user information from the **/etc/password** file, the Network Selection and Name-to-Address Mapping routines obtain their information by consulting the **/etc/netconfig** file.

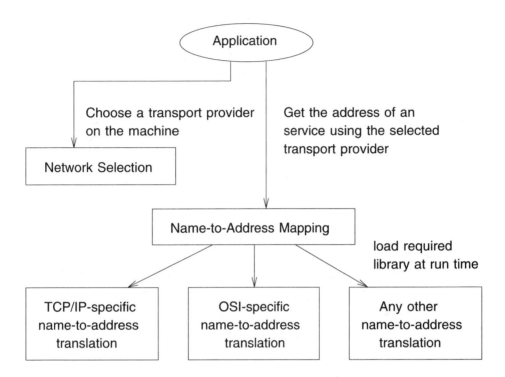

Figure 9.2   Network Selection and Name-to-Address Mapping

The `/etc/netconfig` file is a central network-configuration file controlled by the administrator of the system. It lists all the transport providers on the machine and describes their characteristics. Because it is the key to the operations of the Network Selection and Name-to-Address Mapping routines, we present a general overview of the file.

9.3   The Network-Configuration File

The `/etc/netconfig` file contains information about the transport providers on your machine in the following seven fields:

1. **Name** of the transport provider. The name is a string that locally identifies the transport provider. It has no meaning outside of the machine.

2. **Semantics** of the transport provider. Allowable values are `tpi_clts`, which signifies the transport provider is connectionless, `tpi_cots`, which signifies that it is connection-oriented, and `tpi_cots_ord`, which signifies that it is connection-oriented and supports orderly release. Applications that require characteristics like virtual-circuit establishment can use the semantics field to figure out if the transport provider has the necessary characteristics.

   This field can also contain `tpi_raw`, which signifies that the entry describes a lower-level protocol like the Internet Control Message Protocol (ICMP). Entries with `tpi_raw` are used by the SVR4 socket interface, described in Chapter 10. They are also used by transport-specific applications that must find information about the lower-level protocol (such as the device file associated with the lower-level protocol). We will revisit entries of this type in Chapter 10.

3. **Flag** field, which specifies whether the entry is considered "visible." Generally speaking, a transport provider is always visible, unless the entry describes an experimental provider that the administrator does not want applications to use or the entry describes a lower-level protocol. As we will see in Section 9.4, the basic Network Selection routines return only information about visible entries.

4. **"Protocol family"** name of the transport provider. The protocol family field contains a name that groups providers according to address formats. Common values are `inet` (specifying the protocol is of the Internet family) and `osinet` (specifying an Open System Interconnection network).

5. **Well-known protocol name** of the transport provider, such as `tcp` or `udp`. Applications that depend on characteristics of a certain provider can use this field to figure out if that provider exists on the machine.

6. **Device file** to open when accessing the transport provider.

7. **Dynamic shared libraries** that contain the Name-to-Address Mapping routines for the transport provider. The libraries are dynamic in the sense that they can be linked into an application while the application is running (the SVR4 object file format, the Extendible and Linking Format, provides that ability). Each `/etc/netconfig` entry must have at least one Name-to-Address library associated with it, but may have several. Section 9.6 explains how the Name-to-Address Mapping routines use the libraries.

Example of the /etc/netconfig File

Table 9.1 shows an example of the `/etc/netconfig` file. It shows seven transport providers on the machine:

tcpip	tpi_cots_ord	v	inet	tcp	/dev/tcp	/usr/lib/tcpip.so, \
						/usr/lib/resolv.so
udpip	tpi_clts	v	inet	udp	/dev/udp	/usr/lib/tcpip.so, \
						/usr/lib/resolv.so
xns	tpi_cots_ord	v	ns	spp	/dev/spp	/usr/lib/xnsaddr.so
osi_tp4	tpi_cots	v	osinet	-	/dev/tp4	/usr/lib/straddr.so
local	tpi_cots	-	loopback	-	/dev/loop	/usr/lib/localaddr.so
rawip	tpi_raw	-	inet	-	/dev/rawip	/usr/lib/tcpip.so, \
						/usr/lib/resolv.so
icmp	tpi_raw	-	inet	icmp	/dev/icmp	/usr/lib/tcpip.so, \
						/usr/lib/resolv.so

Table 9.1   Example of the /etc/netconfig File

- A transport provider named **tcpip** provides connection-oriented service and supports orderly release. The name **tcpip** is chosen by the administrator to locally identify the provider. The **v** in the third field shows that the transport provider is visible to applications. The fourth and fifth fields show it is of protocol family **inet** and has the well-known name of **tcp**. That name informs applications that the entry describes the Transmission Control Protocol; applications that want to use TCP-specific features will use the information in this entry. The sixth field shows that you can access the transport provider through the **/dev/tcp** device file. The last field shows two dynamic shared libraries: **/usr/lib/tcpip.so** and **/usr/lib/resolv.so** (the ''**.so**'' suffix is the SVR4 convention for naming libraries that can be linked into an application while it is running). These libraries are used by the Name-to-Address Mapping routines, described in Section 9.6.

- A second provider named **udpip** provides connectionless service. It is visible to applications, is of the protocol family **inet**, and has the well-known name **udp**. That name informs your application that the entry describes the User Datagram Protocol. It is accessible through the **/dev/udp** device file and uses the same libraries as the **tcpip** entry.

- A third transport provider named **xns** provides connection-oriented service with orderly release. It is of the protocol family **ns** and has the well-known name of **spp**. That name lets your application know the entry represents the Xerox Networking System Sequenced Packet Protocol. It has one library for obtaining addresses.

- A fourth transport provider named **osi_tp4** provides connection-oriented service, is visible to applications, is of the protocol family **osinet**, has no well-known name, and has one library for obtaining addresses.

- A fifth transport provider named `local` provides connection-oriented service. It is not visible to applications, signifying that it is an experimental transport provider that the administrator does not want applications to use. Applications that want to use the entry (for example, applications that specifically want to test the transport provider) must use the routines described in Section 9.5. The transport provider is of the protocol family `loopback`, has no well-known name, and has one library that obtains addresses.

- A sixth entry named `rawip` corresponds to a lower-level protocol. It is not visible to applications, is of the protocol family `inet`, and has no well-known name. It is accessible through the `/dev/rawip` device file and uses the same libraries as the `tcpip` entry. Applications that want to use this entry (for example, applications that specifically want to use the lower-level protocol) must use the routines described in Section 9.5.

- A final entry named `icmp` corresponds to a lower-level protocol. It is not visible to applications, is of the protocol family `inet`, and has the well-known name `icmp`. That name lets an application know that the entry represents the Internet Control Message Protocol. It is accessible through the `/dev/icmp` device file and uses the same libraries as the `tcpip` entry. As with any nonvisible entry, applications that want to access this entry must use the routines described in Section 9.5.

Now that we've seen what the configuration file looks like, we can examine the Network Selection routines. The Network Selection routines let you retrieve the entries in the `/etc/netconfig` file and use the information within your application.

9.4   Network Selection

The Network Selection mechanism provides the functionality that its name implies— the ability to select a network that fits your application's needs. It provides routines that loop through the `/etc/netconfig` file. You can examine each entry to figure out if it describes a transport provider that you can use. For example, if your application requires a connectionless transport provider, you can use the Network Selection routines to loop through the `/etc/netconfig` file until you find one.

The Network Selection routines format each entry in the `/etc/netconfig` file into a `netconfig` structure, which has the following components:

```
struct netconfig {

char            *nc_netid;      /* local name of provider   */

unsigned long   nc_semantics;  /* a value specifying       *
                                * connectionless,          *
                                * connection-oriented, or  *
                                * connection-oriented with *
                                * orderly release          */

unsigned long   nc_flag;       /* flags, currently visible *
                                * or not                   */

char            *nc_protofmly; /* protocol family name     */

char            *nc_proto;     /* well-known name          */

char            *nc_device;    /* full path name to device */

unsigned long   nc_nlookups;   /* the number of libraries  *
                                * for address resolution   */

char            **nc_lookups;  /* an array of the full     *
                                * path names of address    *
                                * lookup libraries         */
}
```

The structure elements correspond to the fields of **/etc/netconfig**, with the following exceptions:

- The **nc_semantics** element has the **NC_TPI_COTS**, **NC_TPI_COTS_ORD**, **NC_TPI_CLTS**, or **NC_TPI_RAW** bits set, depending upon whether the second field of **/etc/netconfig** is **tpi_cots**, **tpi_cots_ord**, **tpi_clts**, or **tpi_raw**, respectively.

- The **nc_flag** element has the **NC_VISIBLE** bit set if a **v** is specified in the third field of the **/etc/netconfig** entry.

- The **nc_nlookups** element contains the number of libraries in the last field of the **/etc/netconfig** entry.

Your application can use as much of the information it needs. Most applications only care about the semantics of the transport provider, for example, whether the transport provider is connection-oriented or connectionless. Applications that require semantics of a particular protocol or protocol family can consult the **nc_proto** or **nc_protofmly** elements to figure out if the entry corresponds to the required protocol or protocol family.

Now let's look at the Network Selection routines themselves. Let's suppose that an application needs a connection-oriented transport provider. The following C code uses the Network Selection routines to loop through all visible entries of the **/etc/netconfig** file, looking for any connection-oriented transport provider on the system. The Network Selection routines are presented in bold type:

```
void *handlep;                   /* handle used internally  */
struct netconfig *netconfigp; /* info about provider       */

/*
 *   Initialize the Network Selection routines.
 */

if ((handlep = setnetpath()) == NULL) {
    nc_perror(argv[0]);
    exit(1);
}

/*
 *   Loop through all visible entries in /etc/netconfig
 *   looking for a connection-oriented transport provider.
 */

while ((netconfigp = getnetpath(handlep)) != NULL) {
    /*
     *   At this point, netconfigp points to a netconfig
     *   structure that describes an entry in /etc/netconfig.
     *   Check if it is connection-oriented (or connection-
     *   oriented with orderly release).  If it is, call
     *   doit() (a routine written within this application)
     *   that performs the TLI operations for the transport
     *   provider and implements the application.
     */

    if (netconfigp->nc_semantics == NC_TPI_COTS ||
        netconfigp->nc_semantics == NC_TPI_COTS_ORD) {
            printf("Attempting to use %s\n",
                    netconfigp->nc_netid);
```

```
            if (doit(netconfigp) == SUCCESS) {
                printf("Application succeeded\n");
                break;
            }
            printf("Application failed using %s\n",
                    netconfigp->nc_netid);
        }
    }

endnetconfig(handlep);
```

This code sits at the beginning of your application. It loops through all entries in the `/etc/netconfig` file, looking for a connection-oriented transport provider on your machine.

The `setnetpath()` call initializes the routines and returns a handle used by the `getnetpath()` routine to index into the `/etc/netconfig` file. If the `setnetpath()` routine fails, the **nc_perror()** call prints the reason for failure, preceded by the string given as an argument, onto standard error.

The `getnetpath()` call returns, in the order in which they appear, each visible entry in the `/etc/netconfig` file (a visible entry is one that contains a **v** in the third field). It returns a **NULL** value when no more entries exist. The resultant **netconfigp** variable points to a **netconfig** structure, giving access to the device name, the semantics, and all other information associated with the transport provider.

The **endnetconfig()** routine frees all memory allocated by `setnetpath()` and `getnetpath()`. Once called, the data pointed to by **netconfigp** are deallocated and no longer accessible.

The `doit()` routine is not a part of network selection; it simply shows where you would do the real work. You would write the `doit()` routine and have it perform the TLI operations needed to establish communication and implement the application. As mentioned earlier, you use the Network Selection routines to loop through the `/etc/netconfig` file looking for a transport provider that your application can use. Once you find a transport provider that suits your needs, continue with the application. The previous code assumes the `doit()` routine returns **SUCCESS** if it completed successfully using the current transport provider. If not, the code loops to the next transport provider and calls `doit()` again.

You use the handle returned by `setnetpath()` to identify an instance of the loop. For example, if you called the `setnetpath()` routine again within the loop, it would return a different handle and not affect the outer loop. The handle should not be modified by your application; it is used internally by `getnetpath()` to find the next transport provider to return.

Modifying the Loop

Users manipulate the loop by setting the **NETPATH** environment variable to a colon-separated list of transport-provider names (the transport-provider name is the string specified in the first field of the **/etc/netconfig** file).

For example, a user can set **NETPATH** to the following in the shell environment:

NETPATH=osi_tp4:tcpip:xns

Here, the **getnetpath()** loop would first return the entry corresponding to **osi_tp4**, then the entry corresponding to **tcpip**, and finally the entry corresponding to **xns**. If the user does not set **NETPATH** in the environment, the loop would return all visible entries in the order they appear in the **/etc/netconfig** file.

The **NETPATH** environment variable allows users to define the order in which the client side of an application attempts to establish communication with a service. If the server side of the application uses the **getnetpath()** loop to make itself available on all transport providers, the **NETPATH** variable lets you specify the transport providers that will handle the service.

9.5   More Network Selection Routines

If desired, your application can ignore the **NETPATH** variable and loop through all entries in **/etc/netconfig** file, including the entries not marked "visible". Normally, you would not want to do that unless you had an application that must access all transport providers, such as maintenance and statistics-gathering applications. The following C code illustrates the Network Selection routines you would use:

```
void *handlep;                    /* handle used internally   */
struct netconfig *netconfigp; /* info about provider      */

/*
 *   Initialize the Network Selection routines.
 */

if ((handlep = setnetconfig()) == NULL) {
    nc_perror(argv[0]);
    exit(1);
}
```

```
/*
 *  Loop through all entries in /etc/netconfig looking for
 *  a connection-oriented transport provider.  With this
 *  loop, the NETPATH variable is ignored and all entries
 *  are retrieved.
 */

while ((netconfigp = getnetconfig(handlep)) != NULL) {
    /*
     *  At this point, netconfigp points to a netconfig
     *  structure that describes an entry in /etc/netconfig.
     *  Check if it is connection-oriented (or connection-
     *  oriented with orderly release).  If it is, call
     *  doit() to perform the TLI operations for the
     *  transport provider and implement the application.
     */

    if (netconfigp->nc_semantics == NC_TPI_COTS ||
        netconfigp->nc_semantics == NC_TPI_COTS_ORD) {
        printf("Attempting to use %s\n",
                netconfigp->nc_netid);
        if (doit(netconfigp) == SUCCESS) {
            printf("Application succeeded\n");
            break;
        }
        printf("Application failed using %s\n",
                netconfigp->nc_netid);
    }
}

endnetconfig(handlep);
```

The **setnetconfig()** and **getnetconfig()** routines work in the same way as
setnetpath() and **getnetpath()**, except:

- the **NETPATH** environment variable is completely ignored; and

- all entries in **/etc/netconfig** are accessed, even those that are not marked
  "visible."

If you wanted to obtain information about a single, named transport provider, you
could use the **getnetconfigent()** routine:

```
struct netconfig *netconfigp; /* information about provider */
char *name;                   /* name of the provider       */

name = "local";
if ((netconfigp = getnetconfigent(name)) == NULL) {
        nc_perror(argv[0]);
        exit(1);
}

/*
 *      Perform action with transport provider "local",
 *      and then call freenetconfigent() when done.
 */

doit(netconfigp);

freenetconfigent(netconfigp);
```

The **name** parameter of **getnetconfigent()** contains a string that corresponds to the first field of the **/etc/netconfig** file. If you wanted an entry corresponding to a specific transport provider (even one that was not visible), you could get it by using the **getnetconfigent()** routine. The **freenetconfigent()** routine frees the memory allocated by the **getnetconfigent()** routine.

In general, applications should use the **setnetpath()** and **getnetpath()** routines, because they incorporate the **NETPATH** environment variable. That variable lets a user direct the loop. As mentioned earlier, the other routines are available for applications that must access all transport providers, such as maintenance and statistics-gathering applications.

Now that we have seen the routines to select a transport provider, we can take the next step: finding the address of a network service over the selected transport provider. Those operations are done with the Name-to-Address Mapping routines.

9.6   Name-to-Address Mapping Routines

The Name-to-Address Mapping routines find the transport addresses of services on specified machines. They work hand in hand with the Network Selection routines. Once you have a transport provider selected, you pass the following information to the Name-to-Address Mapping routines:

1. The **netconfig** structure associated with the transport provider.

2. The server machine name.

3. The service name.

The Name-to-Address Mapping routines return a list of addresses that your application can use to communicate with the service over the specified transport provider.

Let's look at an example. The following C code shows how to get the address of the **database** service on machine **frodo** over the transport provider named **tcpip**. The Name-to-Address Mapping routines are in bold type:

```
struct nd_hostserv nd_hostserv;     /* host/service name   */
struct netconfig *netconfigp;       /* info about provider */
struct nd_addrlist *nd_addrlistp;   /* addresses returned  */

/*
 *    The netconfigp variable must first be initialized.
 *    For this example, we can simply call getnetconfigent().
 */

if ((netconfigp = getnetconfigent("tcpip")) == NULL) {
      nc_perror("No information about tcpip");
      exit(1);
}
nd_hostserv.h_host = "frodo";
nd_hostserv.h_serv = "database";

if (netdir_getbyname(netconfigp, &nd_hostserv,
    &nd_addrlistp) != 0) {
      netdir_perror(argv[0]);
      printf("Cannot determine the address!\n");
      exit(1);
}
```

The **netdir_getbyname()** routine obtains a list of addresses your application can use to communicate with a service. You specify the service in the **nd_hostserv** structure, and you specify the transport provider in the **netconfigp** variable. The **netconfigp** variable must be initialized by the Network Selection routines. The resultant addresses are pointed to by **nd_addrlistp**. You can use the addresses in TLI routines.

The `netdir_getbyname()` routine returns zero on success and nonzero on failure. It allocates and populates the space needed to store the addresses. If the routine fails, the `netdir_perror()` call prints the reason for failure onto standard error.

The `nd_hostserv` structure used by `netdir_getbyname()` contains the name of the server machine and the name of the service:

```
struct nd_hostserv {
    char *h_host;    /* name of the server */
    char *h_serv;    /* name of the requested service */
};
```

The `nd_addrlist` structure allocated by the `netdir_getbyname()` routine contains a list of addresses for the given host and service:

```
struct nd_addrlist {
    int             n_cnt;    /* the number of addresses for
                                 the service */
    struct netbuf *n_addrs;  /* pointer to array of addrs */
};
```

The `n_addrs` element of the `nd_addrlist` structure points to an array of TLI `netbuf` structures. As described in Chapters 7 and 8, a TLI `netbuf` structure contains a transport address. The `n_cnt` element specifies the number of `netbuf` structures in the array.

How It Works

The `netdir_getbyname()` routine works as follows:

1. It dynamically links the libraries specified in the `nc_lookups` field of the `netconfig` structure into your application.

2. Each of those libraries contains a routine called `_netdir_getbyname()`. The `_netdir_getbyname()` routine contains transport-specific code that does the real work.

3. The `netdir_getbyname()` routine calls the transport-specific routine. That shields applications from the details of getting addresses over the specified transport provider.

For example, Table 9.1 shows two libraries associated with the `tcpip` entry of `/etc/netconfig`: `/usr/lib/tcpip.so` and `/usr/lib/resolv.so`. The first library contains a version of `_netdir_getbyname()` that tries to get an address by consulting the `/etc/hosts` and `/etc/services` files. The second library contains a version of `_netdir_getbyname()` that attempts to get an address by querying the TCP/IP Domain Name Server. The higher layer `netdir_getbyname()` routine links in the first library and calls the version of the `_netdir_getbyname()` routine there. If an address is not returned, the higher-layer `netdir_getbyname()` routine links in the second library and calls that version of `_netdir_getbyname()`. If an address is still not found, an error is returned to your application.

When a new transport provider is added to the system, it must supply a dynamic shared library containing a version of `_netdir_getbyname()` that obtains addresses for the transport provider.

When you create a new service, the network administrator must update the transport-specific databases with the address of the service. For example, suppose you create a **printer** service. If your installation runs a TCP/IP network, the network administrator must update the `/etc/services` file or update the TCP/IP Domain Name Server to reflect the port number of the service. After the administrator does that, the transport-specific version of `_netdir_getbyname()` for TCP/IP can get the transport address.

Example: Determining Addresses

To illustrate how to use the Network Selection and Name-to-Address Mapping routines, let's write a program that figures out how many addresses a service has. We do the following:

1. Accept two parameters: the name of a server and the name of a service.

2. Use the Network Selection routines to loop through all transport providers on the system.

3. For each transport provider, use the Name-to-Address Mapping routines to figure out the transport addresses of the given service on the specified server machine. We print the number of addresses found.

The following C code implements the program. All routines that are related to the Network Selection and Name-to-Address Mapping routines are in bold type:

```
#include <stdio.h>
#include <netconfig.h>
```

```
#include <netdir.h>
#include <tiuser.h>

main(argc, argv)
int argc;
char *argv[];
{
    void *handlep;                        /* routine handle  */
    struct netconfig *netconfigp;    /* provider info    */
    struct nd_hostserv nd_hostserv;   /* host/serv. name */
    struct nd_addrlist *nd_addrlistp; /* addrs returned   */
    int num_addresses;                /* number of addrs */

    if (argc != 3) {
        fprintf(stderr,
                "%s: usage: %s server_name service_name\n",
                argv[0], argv[0]);
        exit(1);
    }

    /*
     *  Initialize the Network Selection routines.
     */

    if ((handlep = setnetpath()) == NULL) {
        nc_perror(argv[0]);
        exit(1);
    }

    /*
     *  Set up the information for the Name-to-Address
     *  Mapping routines.
     */

    nd_hostserv.h_host = argv[1];
    nd_hostserv.h_serv = argv[2];

    /*
     *  Loop through all visible transport providers
     *  on the system.
     */

    while ((netconfigp = getnetpath(handlep)) != NULL) {
```

```
        printf("For transport %s", netconfigp->nc_netid);

        switch(netconfigp->nc_semantics) {
            case NC_TPI_COTS:
            case NC_TPI_COTS_ORD:
                printf("(connection-oriented):");
                break;
            case NC_TPI_CLTS:
                printf("(connectionless):");
                break;
            default:
                printf("(unknown!):");
        }

        /*
         * Get the address of the service for the
         * current transport provider.
         */

        if (netdir_getbyname(netconfigp,
                &nd_hostserv, &nd_addrlistp) != 0) {
            num_addresses = 0;
        } else {
            num_addresses = nd_addrlistp->n_cnt;
        }

        printf(" %d address%s found\n", num_addresses,
                num_addresses == 1? "" : "es");
    }
    endnetconfig(handlep);
}
```

The program uses the Network Selection routines to loop through the transport providers on the system, and for each transport provider calls **netdir_getbyname()** to obtain the transport addresses of the service. It then displays the number of addresses found. You can use the addresses in TLI routines to establish communication with the specified service.

Here are some sample runs that display the number of addresses for the **printer** service on machine **farside**:

```
$ a.out farside printer
For transport tcpip (connection-oriented): 2 addresses found
For transport udpip (connectionless): 2 addresses found
For transport xns (connection-oriented): 0 addresses found
For transport osi_tp4 (connection-oriented): 1 address found
$
$ NETPATH=xns:tcpip
$ export NETPATH
$ a.out farside printer
For transport xns (connection-oriented): 0 addresses found
For transport tcpip (connection-oriented): 2 addresses found
$
```

Special Values for Host Name

Instead of specifying a host name, the **h_host** field of the **nd_hostserv** structure can have three special values:

- **HOST_ANY** denotes that the address of the service on any host is acceptable.

- **HOST_BROADCAST** returns a ''broadcast address'' for the service, if a broadcast address is supported by the specified transport provider.

- **HOST_SELF** returns the address of the service on the local machine.

You use the **HOST_ANY** value when your application doesn't care which machine provides the service. For example, if an installation offers a network ''news'' service that is replicated on several hosts, an application may not care which server it uses.

You use the **HOST_BROADCAST** value on transport providers that support a ''broadcast address.'' A broadcast address is one that corresponds to all machines on a local area network. For example, the UDP protocol uses the special address of **255.255.255.255** to mean ''all machines on every network attached to my machine.'' So, if your application wants to broadcast information to a service on every machine in a local area network, you specify a server name of **HOST_BROADCAST**.

You use the **HOST_SELF** value when your application wants to figure out its *own* address. The **HOST_SELF** value is needed because some transport providers have a special address to mean ''this machine.'' For example, a machine using the TCP/IP protocol suite can have several IP addresses (details were presented in Chapter 3). Because an application can bind a transport endpoint to only one address, TCP/IP provides the special address of **0.0.0.0** to mean ''all addresses for this machine.''

To illustrate, suppose an application on machine **frodo** used the following code:

```
/*
 *   Assume netcfp points to the entry for tcp
 */

nd_hostserv.h_host = "frodo";
nd_hostserv.h_serv = "database";

netdir_getbyname(netcfp, &nd_hostserv, &nd_addrlistp);
```

If **frodo** had several IP addresses, the **netdir_getbyname()** routine would return *all* of the addresses for the **database** service on **frodo**. If you were using that information to bind an address to transport endpoint, you would have to create a unique transport endpoint for each address. That means you would have to monitor several transport endpoints, making your application overly complicated.

However, suppose an application on machine **frodo** used the **HOST_SELF** value for the host name:

```
/*
 *   Assume netcfp points to the entry for tcp
 */

nd_hostserv.h_host = HOST_SELF;
nd_hostserv.h_serv = "database";

netdir_getbyname(netcfp, &nd_hostserv, &nd_addrlistp);
```

Here, the **netdir_getbyname()** routine would return only *one* address: the TCP/IP special address of **0.0.0.0** (with the appropriate TCP port for the **database** service). So, even though machine **frodo** has several IP addresses, you can create a single transport endpoint and bind the address returned by the **netdir_getbyname()** routine to it. The TCP/IP protocols interpret the **0.0.0.0** address to mean all IP addresses on the machine.

9.7   Miscellaneous Name-to-Address Mapping Routines

There are several other Name-to-Address Mapping routines. Each works similarly to
netdir_getbyname()—each takes a pointer to a netconfig structure, links in the
libraries associated with it, and calls a transport-specific version of the routine to perform the work. The routines are presented next.

netdir_getbyaddr()

The **netdir_getbyaddr()** routine performs the inverse function of the
netdir_getbyname() routine. You give it an address in a TLI **netbuf** structure
and it returns a list of machine names and services that correspond to that address.
Normally, only one machine name and one service name exist for a given transport
address. However, if a machine name or the service name has an alias, the
netdir_getbyaddr() routine puts the alias in the list as well.

To illustrate, we'll create a function called **print_name()**, which prints the host
and service names corresponding to a transport address. It takes two parameters: a
pointer to a **netconfig** structure containing transport-provider information and a
pointer to a TLI **netbuf** structure containing the transport address.

```
int
print_name(netconfigp, netbufp)
struct netconfig *netconfigp;
struct netbuf *netbufp;
{
    struct nd_hostservlist *nd_hostlistp;
    struct nd_hostserv     *nd_hostservp;
    int i;

    if (netdir_getbyaddr(netconfigp, netbufp,
        &nd_hostlistp) != 0) {
        printf("Cannot determine the host names!\n");
        netdir_perror(argv[0]);
        return(FAILURE);
    }

    printf("There are %d names:\n", nd_hostlistp->h_cnt);
    nd_hostservp = nd_hostlistp->h_hostservs;
    for (i = 0; i < nd_hostlistp->h_cnt; i++) {
        printf("--- host: %s\n", nd_hostservp->h_host);
        printf("--- service: %s\n", nd_hostservp->h_serv);
```

```
            nd_hostservp++;
      }
   return(SUCCESS);
}
```

The **netdir_getbyaddr()** routine allocates and populates the **nd_hostservlist** structure, which has the following format:

```
struct nd_hostservlist {
   int                    h_cnt;        /* number of hosts for
                                           the specified address */
   struct nd_hostserv *h_hostservs;    /* pointer to an array of
                                           host/service names  */
};
```

The **h_hostservs** field points to an array of **nd_hostserv** structures, each containing a host name and a service name. The **nd_hostserv** structure was presented in Section 9.6. The **h_cnt** field contains the number of elements of the array.

taddr2uaddr()

The **taddr2uaddr()** routine translates a TLI address into a "universal address." A universal address is a global, ASCII representation of the TLI address. You can use universal addresses when printing the address or when your application must pass an address from one machine to another. Because the internal representation of an address may be different between machines, the universal representation of the address assures correct interpretation.

The syntax follows:

```
char *
taddr2uaddr(netconfigp, netbufp)
struct netconfig *netconfigp;
struct netbuf *netbuf;
```

The routine returns a **NULL** value if it fails. Otherwise, the routine returns the universal address.

To illustrate the **taddr2uaddr()** routine, we'll create a code segment that prints the addresses of the **database** service on machine **frodo** over the transport provider **tcpip**. The following C code displays the addresses two ways: as a hexadecimal representation of the TLI **netbuf** structure and as a universal address.

```
struct nd_hostserv nd_hostserv;    /* host/service name   */
struct nd_addrlist *nd_addrlistp;  /* list of addresses   */
struct netconfig *netcfp;          /* has provider info   */
struct netbuf *netbufp;            /* contains one address */
char *u_name;                      /* holds universal addr */
int i,j;                           /* index counters      */

/*
 *   The netcfp variable must first be initialized.
 *   For this example, we can simply call
 *   getnetconfigent(), giving it the name in the
 *   first field of the /etc/netconfig file for TCP/IP.
 */

if ((netcfp = getnetconfigent("tcpip")) == NULL) {
        nc_perror("No information about tcpip");
        exit(1);
}

nd_hostserv.h_host = "frodo";
nd_hostserv.h_serv = "database";

if (netdir_getbyname(netcfp, &nd_hostserv,
                                &nd_addrlistp) != 0) {
        netdir_perror("No addresses found");
        exit(1);
}


netbufp = nd_addrlistp->n_addrs;

printf("Found %d address%s:\n", nd_addrlistp->n_cnt);
                nd_addrlistp->n_cnt == 1? "" : "es");

for (i = 0; i < nd_addrlistp->n_cnt; i++) {
    /*
     * Print out the TLI address in hex format.
     */
    printf("TLI address:       ");
```

```
for (j = 0; j < netbufp->len; j++) {
    printf("%.2x", netbufp->buf[j]);
}
printf("\n");

/*
 *  Print out the Universal address.
 */

printf("Universal address: ");
if ((u_name = taddr2uaddr(netcfp, netbufp)) == NULL)
        u_name = "unknown";
printf("%s\n", u_name);

netbufp++;
}
```

Let's look at what this code segment prints. On SVR4, the address in a TLI **netbuf** structure for a TCP/IP service has four pieces of information:

1. A 2-byte field containing a protocol identifier. For TCP/IP, it always contains the value **2**.

2. A 2-byte field containing the TCP port number of the service. The port number was described in Chapter 3.

3. A 4-byte field containing the IP address of the machine offering service. The IP address was also described in Chapter 3.

4. An 8-byte filler. The filler value is always **0**.

On *all* systems, the universal address for a TCP/IP service is an ASCII string containing six integers separated by dots. It has the following form:

a1.a2.a3.a4.p1.p2

Here, **a1** through **a4** are the decimal representations of the 4-byte IP address. The **a1** value is the first byte and the **a4** value is the last byte. The **p1** and **p2** values are the decimal representations of the 2-byte port number. The **p1** value is the first byte and the **p2** value is the second byte.

So, if incorporated into a program, the previous code segment would produce the following on SVR4:

```
Found 1 address:
TLI address:        0002144fc00b32110000000000000000
Universal address:  192.11.50.17.20.79
```

Here's how the TLI address relates to the universal address:

1. The first two bytes of the TLI address (that is, the protocol identifier) contain **00** and **02**. These bytes are not included in the universal address.

2. The next two bytes (that is, the TCP port number) contain **14** and **4f**. These hexadecimal values are translated into decimal representation (that is, **20** and **79**), and placed in the **p1** position and the **p2** position of the universal address, respectively.

3. The next four bytes (that is, the IP address) contain **c0**, **0b**, **32**, and **11**. These hexadecimal values are translated into decimal representation (that is, **192**, **11**, **50**, and **17**) and placed in the **a1** through the **a4** positions of the universal address, respectively.

4. The last eight bytes (that is, the filler) contain zeros. These bytes are not included in the universal address.

If you wanted to send an address to another application, you should send the universal representation of the address. In that way, the receiver can translate the address into local representation.

uaddr2taddr()

The **uaddr2taddr()** routine translates a universal address into a TLI address. If an application sends a universal address, you can use the **uaddr2taddr()** routine to translate it into the local representation. The syntax follows:

```
struct netbuf *
uaddr2taddr (netconfigp, uaddr)
struct netconfig *netconfigp;
char *uaddr;
```

If successful, the routine returns a pointer to a TLI **netbuf** structure that contains the local representation of the address. It returns a **NULL** value on failure.

netdir_free()

The **netdir_free()** routine frees memory allocated by the **netdir_getbyaddr()** routine and the **netdir_getbyname()** routine. The syntax follows:

```
void
netdir_free(datap, type)
char *datap;
int    type;
```

The **datap** argument points to a data structure allocated by the **netdir_getbyaddr()** routine or by the **netdir_getbyname()** routine. The **type** argument is one of the following:

- **ND_HOSTSERVLIST** if the **datap** argument points to a **nd_hostservlist** that **netdir_getbyaddr()** allocates; or

- **ND_ADDRLIST** if the **datap** argument points to a **nd_addrlist** that **netdir_getbyname()** allocates.

netdir_options()

The **netdir_options()** routine handles miscellaneous transport-provider actions. It takes four arguments:

1. A pointer to a **netconfig** structure.

2. An integer that specifies an action.

3. A file descriptor.

4. A pointer to extra information.

It returns zero on success and nonzero on failure. If the transport provider specified in the **netconfig** structure does not support the action, a failure condition is returned.

The general syntax follows:

```
int
netdir_options(netcfp, action, fd, extrap)
struct netconfig *netcfp;
int             action;
int             fd;
char            *extrap;
```

An application can specify one of four actions:

- **ND_SET_BROADCAST**, which does all the TLI management operations needed to set up the transport provider for broadcast support.

- **ND_SET_RESERVEDPORT**, which binds the application to a "reserved port," if that concept is supported.

- **ND_CHECK_RESERVEDPORT**, which checks to see if a port is a reserved port.

- **ND_MERGEADDR**, which takes a sender's address and a receiver's address and returns an optimal address the sender can use to talk to the receiver.

Each of these actions allows applications to perform transport-specific operations in a transport-independent manner. When you call the **netdir_options()** routine, the following happens:

1. The routine links in the transport-specific library associated with the given transport provider.

2. Each library contains a routine named **_netdir_options()**. That routine contains the transport-specific code needed to implement the action.

3. The **netdir_options()** routine calls the **_netdir_options()** to do the work.

In your application, you simply call the higher-level **netdir_options()** routine. In that way, you do not have to be concerned with the transport-specific details of the action.

We describe each action in the following sections.

netdir_options(): ND_SET_BROADCAST

The **ND_SET_BROADCAST** action sets up the transport provider for broadcast support. As mentioned earlier, some connectionless transport providers support a "transport-level broadcast" feature that lets you send messages to all machines in a network (for example, UDP supports this feature). Before you can use this feature, you must do some transport-specific setup.

The **ND_SET_BROADCAST** action does the TLI management operations needed to set up the transport provider for broadcast support. It takes a file descriptor returned by the **t_open()** routine (described in Chapter 7). A transport address must be bound to the file descriptor. The **extrap** argument is not used.

To illustrate, consider the following code, which searches for a connectionless transport provider, sets it up for broadcast, and gets the broadcast address of a ''library'' service:

```
/*
 *    Search through the transport providers on the system.
 */

if ((handlep = setnetpath()) == NULL) {
    nc_perror(argv[0]);
    exit(1);
}

while ((netconfigp = getnetpath(handlep)) != NULL) {

    /*
     *  Only check for connectionless transports.
     */

    if (netconfigp->nc_semantics == NC_TPI_CLTS) {

        /*
         *  Attempt to open the device and bind to an
         *  endpoint.  If either of the operations fails,
         *  continue the loop to get the next transport
         *  provider.
         */

        if ((fd = t_open(netconfigp->nc_device, O_RDWR,
                        NULL)) == -1) {
            continue;
        }
        if (t_bind(fd, (struct t_bind *)NULL,
                (struct t_bind *)NULL) == -1) {
            (void) t_close(fd);
            continue;
        }

        /*
```

```
                     * Do protocol-specific negotiating for broadcast.
                     * netdir_options returns 0 on success, nonzero
                     * on failure.
                     */

                    if (netdir_options(netconfigp,
                                    ND_SET_BROADCAST, fd, NULL) == 0) {
                        break;
                    }
                    (void) t_close(fd);
            }
    }

    if (netconfigp == NULL) {
        fprintf(stderr, "could not find a connectionless
                            transport that supports broadcast\n");
        exit(1);
    }

    nd_hostserv.h_host = HOST_BROADCAST;
    nd_hostserv.h_serv = "library";

    if (netdir_getbyname(netcfp, &nd_hostserv,
                                        &nd_addrlistp) != 0) {
            netdir_perror("No addresses found");
            exit(1);
    }


    endnetconfig(handlep);
```

This code loops through all transport providers on the system, and for each transport
provider, does the following:

1. Checks if it provides connectionless service. If it does, we call **t_open()** to
   create a transport endpoint.

2. Binds an arbitrary, unused transport address to the transport endpoint.

3. Calls **netdir_options()** to set up the transport provider for broadcast support. As mentioned earlier, the **netdir_options()** routine links in a
   transport-specific version of the routine to do the work.

4. Breaks out of the loop if the **netdir_options()** routine succeeds. Otherwise, it continues the loop and tries the next transport provider.

After the loop ends, we check the value of `netconfigp`. If that value is `NULL`, then we never broke out of the loop. Because that means the `netdir_options()` routine was never successful, we print an error message and exit the application.

Otherwise, we call the `netdir_getbyname()` routine to get the broadcast address of the "library" service. Note that we used the `HOST_BROADCAST` value as a host name. After the address is obtained, you can use it to send a datagram to the "library" service on all machines in the local area network.

netdir_options(): ND_SET_RESERVEDPORT

The `ND_SET_RESERVEDPORT` action binds a transport endpoint to a "reserved port." It only succeeds on transport providers that support the concept of a reserved port.

For example, as described in Chapter 3, the SVR4 implementation of TCP/IP uses TCP and UDP port numbers less than `1024` as "reserved ports." They are reserved in the sense that only a privileged user can bind one of them to a transport endpoint.

The `ND_SET_RESERVEDPORT` option takes a file descriptor returned by the `t_open()` routine, which must be unbound. The `extrap` argument points to a `netbuf` structure. If the pointer to the `netbuf` structure is `NULL`, the transport-specific version of `_netdir_options()` binds the file descriptor to an address corresponding to `HOST_SELF` with a reserved port. If the pointer to the `netbuf` structure is non-`NULL`, the routine attempts to bind to a reserved port with the address specified in the `netbuf` structure.

netdir_options(): ND_CHECK_RESERVEDPORT

The `ND_CHECK_RESERVEDPORT` option checks if a port is reserved. The routine does not use the file-descriptor argument. The `extrap` argument points to a `netbuf` structure. The routine returns zero if the address in the `netbuf` structure corresponds to a reserved port, and nonzero otherwise.

netdir_options(): ND_MERGEADDR

The `ND_MERGEADDR` option is used in applications that want to transform a locally meaningful address into an address that the client side of an application can use to establish communication.

The file-descriptor argument is not used, and the `extrap` argument points to a `mergeaddr` structure. The `mergeaddr` structure has the following components:

```
struct mergeaddr {
    char *s_uaddr;   /* the local universal address */
    char *c_uaddr;   /* remote universal address */
    char *m_uaddr;   /* merged universal address */
};
```

The **s_uaddr** element is the universal address corresponding to a locally meaningful transport address. The **c_uaddr** element is the universal address of an application on a client machine. The **m_uaddr** element is populated by the **netdir_options()** routine and contains the universal address that the client application can use to communicate with the service associated with the **s_uaddr** address.

To clarify, consider the **rpcbind** process used by the RPC facility. As explained in Chapter 6, the **rpcbind** process maintains a database that maps an RPC program number and version number into a transport address. When an application on a client machine wants to call an RPC program, it sends a query to the **rpcbind** process on the server machine, requesting the transport address of that program.

When the **rpcbind** process receives the query, it sends back the transport address of the requested RPC program. But, before it does that, it uses the **ND_MERGEADDR** option to translate the transport address into an address that the application on the client machine can use.

Here's why it must do that. As mentioned earlier, some transport providers have a special address to mean "this machine." For example, TCP/IP uses the special address of **0.0.0.0** to mean "all addresses for this machine." When an RPC program creates a transport endpoint using TCP/IP, it binds an address of the form **0.0.0.0** to the transport endpoint. Unfortunately, that address is meaningless to a client machine. So, the **rpcbind** process cannot send it as the answer to a query. Instead, it must use the **ND_MERGEADDR** option to figure out the correct address to send. The **rpcbind** process knows the transport address of the application that sent the query (the TLI routines told it that) and the transport address of the RPC program. So, it has everything it needs to call the **ND_MERGEADDR** option.

To illustrate the **ND_MERGEADDR** option, we'll create a function called **merge_addr()**. It takes two arguments: the universal address from a client application and the universal address corresponding to a locally meaningful transport address. It returns the universal address that the client application can use to communicate with the local application:

```
char *
merge_addr(client_uaddr, server_uaddr)
char *client_uaddr;
char *server_uaddr;
{
    struct mergeaddr ma;

    ma.c_uaddr = client_uaddr;
    ma.s_uaddr = server_uaddr;
    if (netdir_options(netconfigp, ND_MERGEADDR, 0,
                    (char *)&ma)) {
        fprintf(stderr, "could not get merged address\n");
        return (NULL);
    }
    return (ma.m_uaddr);
}
```

After calling **netdir_options()**, the **ma.m_uaddr** variable contains an address that the application on the client machine can use to communicate with the application on the server machine.

9.8   Putting It All Together

Both the server side and the client side of an application can use the Network Selection and Name-to-Address Mapping routines to free themselves from transport-provider-specific actions.

For example, the server side of your application can make itself available on all transport providers. As you loop through all transport providers using the Network Selection routines, you do the following:

1. Obtain the address of the service you are providing by calling the **netdir_getbyname()** routine. Specify the name of the service and the **HOST_SELF** value as the machine name.

2. Do the following for each address returned by the **netdir_getbyname()** routine:

    a. Create a transport endpoint with the **t_open()** routine.

    b. Call the **t_bind()** routine to bind the address to the transport endpoint.

After creating the transport endpoints, you can call the **poll()** system call to wait for messages. When a connection request comes in on a virtual-circuit transport provider, you can accept the request with the **t_listen()** and **t_accept()** routines. When a datagram arrives over a connectionless transport provider, you can read the messages with the **t_rcvudata()** routine.

The client side of your application does similar actions. You loop through the transport providers and do the following:

1. Get the address of the service by calling the **netdir_getbyname()** routine, specifying the service name and server machine name.

2. Create a transport endpoint with the **t_open()** routine. You then call the **t_bind()** routine to bind an arbitrary, unused transport address to the transport endpoint.

3. If you are using a virtual-circuit transport provider, call the **t_connect()** routine to try to connect to the address returned by **netdir_getbyname()**. If you are using a datagram transport provider, call the **t_sndudata()** routine to send a datagram to the address.

By using Network Selection and Name-to-Address Mapping routines, you free the application from the transport-specific details of selecting a transport provider and finding a transport address. We conclude the chapter by completing the **rpopen()** application developed in Chapter 8.

9.9 Completing the rpopen() Function

To sum up the Network Selection and Name-to-Address Mapping routines, consider the **rpopen()** routine developed in Chapter 8. In that application, we defined the **tpinfo** structure and put the definition in **tpinfo.h**:

```
/*
 *    tpinfo.h
 */
#include <netconfig.h>
#include <netdir.h>

struct tpinfo {
    char                *device;
    struct nd_addrlist  *nd_addrlistp;
    struct tpinfo       *nextp;
};
struct tpinfo *get_addrs();
```

In creating the application, we deferred the writing of two routines: the **get_addrs()** routine, which allocated and populated the **tpinfo** structure, and the **free_addrs()** routine, which freed the memory allocated by the **get_addrs()** routine.

The following completes the **rpopen()** application by presenting the C code for those routines. In the **get_addrs()** routine, we do the following:

1. Call the **setnetpath()** to initialize the Network Selection routines.

2. Set up the **nd_hostserv** structure to contain the host and service names. To do that, we check the host name given as the first argument. If the host name has a **NULL** value, we set the **h_host** field of the **nd_hostserv** structure to **HOST_SELF**. As described in Chapter 8, we use the **NULL** host name in the **get_addrs()** routine to mean ''this machine.''

3. Loop through the transport providers and create the list of **tpinfo** structures. We do the following within the loop:

    a. Check the semantics of the current transport provider. If it is connection-oriented or connection-oriented with orderly release, we call the **netdir_getbyname()** routine to get the addresses of the service. If the address is obtained successfully, we set the **got_it** flag.

    b. If the **got_it** flag is set, allocate a **tpinfo** structure, fill it in, and add it to the end of the list. Note that we copy the device name into the **tpinfo** structure instead of simply assigning the pointer value. We have to do that because the **endnetconfig()** routine will free all memory in the **netconfig** structure.

4. Call **endnetconfig()** to free the memory allocated by the Network Selection routines. Then, return the list of **tpinfo** structures to the caller.

The code for the **free_addrs()** routine follows the **getaddrs()** routine. The **free_addrs()** routine frees the memory that the **get_addrs()** routine allocated. It also calls the **netdir_free()** routine to free the **nd_addrlist** structure that the **netdir_getbyname()** routine allocated.

The code follows:

```
#include <netconfig.h>
#include <netdir.h>
#include <tiuser.h>
#include <stdio.h>
#include "tpinfo.h"

struct tpinfo *
```

```
get_addrs(host, service)
char *host;
char *service;
{
   void *handlep;                      /* handle to routines*/
   struct netconfig *netconfigp;       /* provider info     */
   struct nd_hostserv nd_hostserv;     /* host/service name */
   struct nd_addrlist *nd_addrlistp;   /* list of addrs     */
   struct tpinfo *headp;               /* start of tpinfo list */
   struct tpinfo *currp;               /* traverses tpinfo list */
   struct tpinfo **currpp;             /* traverses tpinfo list */
   int got_it;                         /* indicates we found a  */
                                       /* transport provider    */

   if ((handlep = setnetpath()) == NULL) {
      nc_perror("get_addr");
      return(NULL);
   }

   /*
    *  Use the host name and service name given
    *  as an argument.
    */
   if (host == NULL) {
      nd_hostserv.h_host = HOST_SELF;
   } else {
      nd_hostserv.h_host = host;
   }
   nd_hostserv.h_serv = service;

   headp = NULL;
   currpp = &headp;

   while ((netconfigp = getnetpath(handlep)) != NULL) {
      /*
       *  We only want a connection-oriented transport
       *  provider here.
       */
      got_it = 0;
      switch (netconfigp->nc_semantics) {
         case NC_TPI_COTS_ORD:
         case NC_TPI_COTS:
            if (netdir_getbyname(netconfigp, &nd_hostserv,
```

```
                                         &nd_addrlistp) == 0) {
                got_it = 1;
                break;
            }
        default:
            break;
    }

    if (got_it) {
        if ((currp = *currpp = (struct tpinfo *)
                malloc(sizeof(struct tpinfo))) == NULL) {
            fprintf(stderr, "Cannot allocate space\n");
            return(NULL);
        }
        /*
         *  Allocate space to hold the device name because
         *  endnetconfig() deallocates memory of netconfigp.
         */
        if ((currp->device = (char *)malloc(
              strlen(netconfigp->nc_device) + 1)) == NULL) {
            fprintf(stderr, "Cannot allocate space\n");
            return(NULL);
        }
        strcpy(currp->device, netconfigp->nc_device);

        currp->nd_addrlistp = nd_addrlistp;
        currpp = &(currp->nextp);
    }
  }
  *currpp = NULL;
  endnetconfig(handlep);
  return(headp);
}

free_addrs(tpinfop)
struct tpinfo *tpinfop;
{
    struct tpinfo *savep;

    while (tpinfop) {
        free(tpinfop->device);
        netdir_free((char *)tpinfop->nd_addrlistp,
                      ND_ADDRLIST);
```

```
        savep = tpinfop;
        tpinfop = tpinfop->nextp;
        free(savep);
    }
}
```

9.10 Summary

The Network Selection and Name-to-Address Mapping routines let you obtain information about the transport providers on the machine and let you obtain addresses of services in a transport-independent manner. Using these routines, you free the application from transport-specific functionality. If a transport provider on the machine is replaced over time, your applications run without change.

For Further Reading

1. AT&T, *UNIX System V Release 4 Programmer's Guide: Networking Interfaces*, Prentice Hall, Englewood Cliffs, NJ, 1990.

Exercises

9.1   Write a program that prints out information about all of the transport providers on your system. The information should include the type of service (that is, datagram or virtual circuit) of each transport provider.

9.2   Explain why the **netdir_getbyname()** routine accepts a name of **HOST_SELF**. When should **HOST_SELF** be used?

9.3   Explain how a client side of an application uses the Network Selection and Name-to-Address Mapping routines and how the server side of an application uses them.

9.4   Write a program that displays addresses. The program should take a server machine name, a service name, and a transport-provider name as arguments. The output should be the universal addresses of the service over the specified transport provider.

Chapter 10

Applications Using Sockets

10.1 Introduction

The socket interface is a set of programming subroutines that forms an interprocess communication facility. The routines are used to create a communication channel between applications on the local system and between applications on remote systems. You use the socket routines when you want to create applications that handle the lower-level communication details.

Socket routines are similar in functionality to TLI routines. They let you establish communication, manage a connection, and transfer data. And, like TLI, they let you use connectionless and connection-oriented transport providers.

Socket routines have been around much longer than TLI routines. They were introduced in 1981 as an integral part of the Berkeley Software Distribution (BSD) 4.2 UNIX system. There is a large base of applications that use the socket interface.

The SVR4 socket interface is an implementation of the BSD socket interface. From an application's point of view, it is the same as its BSD counterpart. However, the BSD implementation uses system calls and kernel support. The SVR4 implementation uses library routines that transform the socket calls into the STREAMS interface.

This chapter explains how to use socket routines in networking applications. Before presenting the details of sockets, we present an overview of its functionality.

10.2 Overview of Sockets

A socket is one endpoint in a two-way communication channel. You use the socket routines to create the communication channel, and you use the channel to send data between applications. You can create a communication channel that supplies either virtual-circuit service or datagram service.

449

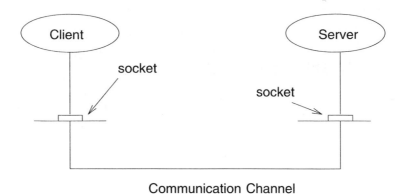

Communication Channel

Figure 10.1 Sockets

Figure 10.1 shows two applications using sockets. As far as your application is concerned, the socket is the end of the channel. When you create the socket, the socket routines return a file descriptor used when accessing the endpoint.

Using the analogies presented in Chapter 7, you can think of a communication channel that supplies virtual-circuit service as a telephone line and the socket as the telephone. Just as humans see the telephone as the end of a telephone connection, applications see the socket as the end of a virtual-circuit communication channel.

Similarly, you can think of a communication channel that supplies datagram service as the postal system and the socket as the mailbox. Where humans use the mailbox to send messages via the postal system to another mailbox, applications use the socket to send messages over a datagram communication channel to another socket.

When creating the communication channel, you specify the transport provider to be used. For example, you can use TCP, UDP, XNS, or any other transport provider.

Before we explain how to specify the transport provider to be used, we must point out some special characteristics of sockets:

- A socket has no device file associated with it. That is different from TLI. In TLI, you used the **t_open()** routine to create a transport endpoint. In that routine, you specify the device file corresponding to the transport provider.

  With sockets, you create a socket by calling the **socket()** routine. In that routine, you specify the type of communication channel to be used. As we describe in Section 10.5, you name the channel symbolically. The **socket()** routine returns a file descriptor that you use to reference one end of the communication channel.

- The socket exists as long as a process holds a file descriptor into it. When no process holds the file descriptor open, the socket goes away.

- The `socket()` routine returns a file descriptor that has the semantics of a file descriptor into a character device. You can issue `read()`, `write()`, and `ioctl()` system calls on the file descriptor.

- You can create a single socket or a pair of sockets. If you create a pair of sockets, the operating system automatically establishes a communication channel between them. If you create a single socket, you must use other socket routines to establish a communication channel to another socket. We will see how to do that in Sections 10.3 and 10.4. The application holding the socket to which you attach can be on the same system or on a remote system.

The socket interface gives six basic functions. You can:

1. **Create a socket**. You do that by calling the `socket()` routine, specifying the type of communication channel to be used. You specify the communication channel by specifying the following:

    - The *address family* of the communication channel. In the sockets framework, all transport protocols in an address family have the same address format. For example, TCP and UDP use the same form of address, so they are in the same address family.

    - The *type of service* of the communication channel. Here, you specify the semantics of communication. For example, you can specify that you want a communication channel that supplies either datagram service or virtual-circuit service.

    - The *protocol* to use for the given address family and type of service. For example, some address families have more than one transport protocol that supports the given type of service. So, the socket interface lets you specify the protocol to be used.

2. **Bind an address** to a socket. This is also called ''naming a socket.'' The format of the address depends on the address family of the socket. You must bind an address to the socket before you can transfer data. If you are using a virtual-circuit communication channel, naming the socket is like assigning a telephone number to a telephone. If you are using a datagram communication channel, naming the socket is like giving a postal address to a mailbox.

3. **Connect to another socket**. You do that by specifying the address of a remote socket. After connecting to another socket, you complete the communication channel. All data you give to the socket are sent to the socket to which you connected.

If the communication channel uses a virtual-circuit transport provider, connecting to a socket establishes the circuit. From the telephone analogy, connecting to a socket is like dialing a telephone number and waiting for an answer.

You can also connect to another socket if a communication channel that supplies datagram service is being used. However, in that case, you do not establish a true connection. Instead, the operating system maintains an association between your socket and the remote address. Whenever you write data into your socket, the operating system sends a datagram to the socket to which you connected. From the mailbox analogy, connecting a socket to address *X* is like putting a sign on the mailbox that says, ''all messages I place in this mailbox are delivered to address *X*, even if I don't put a destination address on the message.''

If you are using a communication channel that supports virtual-circuit service, you must connect to a remote socket before transferring data. If you are using a communication channel that supports datagram service, you do not have to connect to a remote socket. However, if you don't connect to a remote socket, you must specify the destination address on each datagram sent.

4. **Accept a socket connection**. You only do this on the server side of the application, and only when a communication channel that supplies virtual-circuit service is used. When a remote application wants to connect to your socket, you must accept the connection. If you don't, the virtual circuit is not established. From the telephone analogy, this is like answering the telephone.

5. **Transfer data**. The socket interface provides several routines to transfer data. For example, you can use the following routines on connected sockets:

   - The **read()** and **write()** system calls.

   - The **send()** and **recv()** routines. These routines provide more functionality than the **read()** and **write()** system calls. Using **send()** and **recv()**, you can send and receive expedited data, peek at incoming data, and do other operations. As mentioned in Chapter 7, expedited data are ''emergency data'' that you want delivered ahead of normal data.

   You can use the following routines on connected or unconnected sockets:

   - The **sendto()** and the **recvfrom()** routines. These routines do all of the functions of the **send()** and **recv()** routines, but they also let you specify the address of the peer socket. You usually use these routines with a communication channel that supplies datagram service.

   - The **sendmsg()** and the **recvmsg()** routines. These routines provide the most functionality. You can send data from multiple memory buffers, read data into disjoint memory buffers, and transfer protocol-specific information. We present the details of all data-transfer routines in Section 10.5.

6. **Shut down socket operations**. After you shut down the socket, you prohibit all further data transfer.

When Should You Use Sockets?

As mentioned earlier, the socket interface is similar to TLI. The socket routines let you create a communication channel, manage a connection, and send and receive data. They let you create networking applications that handle the lower-level communication details.

However, SVR4 provides the socket interface for backward compatibility with BSD applications. Your new networking applications should use TLI instead of sockets for the following reasons:

1. The TLI routines let you create transport-independent applications easier than the sockets interface. Using TLI, you can use the Network Selection and Name-to-Address Mapping facilities, making your applications completely transport-independent. Although the socket interface lets you create a communication channel that uses any transport provider, it does not have routines that let you select a transport provider or get addresses in a transport-independent way.

2. The TLI interface is endorsed by X/Open, an international group of companies that define a common application environment for UNIX systems.

3. The TLI design parallels the OSI Transport Service Definition, so it easily supports all of the functionality of the OSI protocols.

Still, you should use the socket routines in two cases:

1. If you are planning to port your new networking application to a system that does not have TLI. Practically every version of the UNIX system supports sockets. So, using the socket interface eases the porting effort to those systems.

2. If you are porting an existing application to SVR4. SVR4 supplies the sockets interface for that very reason. The SVR4 implementation of sockets is functionally equivalent to the BSD socket implementation.

Summary of Socket Routines

Socket routines let you do all the processing needed to manage a session over a transport provider. The following list summarizes the socket routines.

Routines that create a socket:

`socket()`	Creates a socket and returns a file descriptor.
`socketpair()`	Creates two sockets, connects them, and returns two file descriptors corresponding to the sockets.

Routine that names a socket:

`bind()`	Names a socket, that is, assigns a transport address to a socket.

Routine that connects to a socket:

`connect()`	Connects to a remote socket.

Routines that accept a connection:

`listen()`	Puts the socket into the "listen state."
`accept()`	Waits for a connection request to arrive and accepts a connection request.

Routines that transfer data:

`send()`	Sends a message over a connected socket.
`sendto()`	Sends a message, but specifies the name of the socket to which to send.
`sendmsg()`	Sends a message, specifies the name of the socket to which to send, and sends specially interpreted data.
`recv()`	Receives a messages.
`recvfrom()`	Receives a message and includes the name of the peer socket.
`recvmsg()`	Receives a message, includes the name of the peer socket, and receives specially interpreted data.

Routine that shuts down a socket:

`shutdown()`	Shuts down the socket and stops all further read and write operations.

Miscellaneous socket routines:

`getsockname()`	Returns the name of the socket.
`getpeername()`	Returns the name of the peer socket.
`setsockopt()`	Sets various socket options.
`getsockopt()`	Reports current socket options.

As mentioned earlier, the socket routines let you manage network communication. However, like TLI, they only provide an interface to the network. Within your application, you must still handle:

1. The *application layer* of the OSI Model. You must define the networking service, specify the data the service requires, and detail service results.

2. The *presentation layer* of the OSI Model. You must place all data in a common format to handle differences in machine-data representation. Chapter 8 described routines that can be used to perform presentation layer operations.

3. The *session layer* of the OSI Model. Your application must manage the session by providing ''over'' and ''over and out'' synchronization messages.

The socket routines let your applications interface with the *transport layer* of the OSI Model, so you do not have to worry about the details of network transmission.

Now let's look at some of the details of socket operations. As mentioned in Chapter 8, the client side of an application uses a transport address to locate the server side of the application. A socket is designed to work with any transport provider, so the socket interface handles transport addresses in a flexible way. We now show how applications specify transport addresses using sockets.

Transport Addresses

The socket interface works with any transport provider. And, because different transport providers have different addresses, the socket interface lets you specify any type of address.

Using the socket routines, you specify an address when doing the following:

1. Binding a transport address to a socket.

2. Connecting to a socket.

3. Sending datagrams.

The socket routines that do these actions take at least two arguments: a pointer to a buffer containing a transport address and the number of bytes in the buffer. In that way, the socket routines make no assumptions about the structure or the format of a transport address.

SVR4 provides data structures that you can use to format transport addresses. It uses the same structures as BSD systems, so you do not have to modify your BSD applications when porting them to SVR4.

For example, the BSD implementation of TCP/IP represents an address as a 16-byte value. For compatibility reasons, SVR4 uses the same convention. SVR4 structures a TCP/IP address in a BSD `sockaddr_in` structure, which has the following definition:

```
struct sockaddr_in {
    u_short             sin_family;
    u_short             sin_port;
    struct  in_addr sin_addr;
    char                sin_zero[8];
};
```

The fields of the **sockaddr_in** structure have the following values:

1. The **sin_family** field contains a protocol identifier. For TCP/IP, this is always **AF_INET**, which has a value of **2**.

2. The **sin_port** field contains the port number of the service. The port number was described in Chapter 3.

3. The **sin_addr** field contains the IP address of the machine offering service. The IP address was also described in Chapter 3.

    The **sin_addr** field is an **in_addr** structure. That structure is a union that lets you access the 4-byte IP address as four separate bytes, as two short integers, or as a single long integer. It has the following definition:

```
struct in_addr {
  union {
      struct { u_char s_b1, s_b2, s_b3, s_b4; } S_un_b;
      struct { u_short s_w1, s_w2; } S_un_w;
      u_long S_addr;
  } S_un;

#define s_addr S_un.S_addr;

};
```

4. The **sin_zero** field is unused. This value is always **0**.

The **sockaddr_in** structure contains the **sin_family** and **sin_zero** fields for compatibility with BSD systems. In BSD systems, the kernel implementation of networking protocols used a 16-byte **sockaddr** structure to hold addresses. The first two bytes held an address family, and the next 14 bytes held the address. The **sockaddr** structure has the following definition:

```
struct sockaddr {
        u_short  sa_family;
        char     sa_data[14];
};
```

In the **sockaddr** structure, the **sa_family** field holds the address family associated with the address, and the **sa_data** field holds the address. The BSD kernel used the **sockaddr** structure in routing tables, interface addresses, and other kernel-specific tables. If there were several transport providers in a BSD system, the **sa_family** field of the **sockaddr** structure would associate the address buffer with the transport provider.

That is why the TCP/IP **sockaddr_in** structure has the **sin_family** field. And, because there are only six bytes in a TCP/IP address (and the BSD kernel tables use a 14-byte area to hold addresses), the **sin_zero** field of the **sockaddr_in** structure provides the remaining eight bytes.

In BSD systems, a protocol could use an address of greater than 14 bytes if the kernel implementation of that protocol did not use the kernel routing tables that imposed the 14-byte limitation.

For example, the BSD implementation of a ''loopback'' transport provider does not use the routing tables, so it supports addresses larger than 14 bytes. You can only use the loopback transport provider between processes on the same system, and you use a transport-specific data structure (that is, the **sockaddr_un** structure) to hold addresses for that transport provider.

The SVR4 socket interface is compatible with the BSD system, so applications on SVR4 also use the **sockaddr_un** structure when using sockets to create a communication channel using the SVR4 loopback transport provider. The **sockaddr_un** structure has the following definition:

```
struct sockaddr_un {
        u_short          sun_family;
        char             sun_path[108];
};
```

The fields of the **sockaddr_un** structure have the following values:

1. The **sun_family** field contains the protocol identifier. For the loopback transport provider, this is always **AF_UNIX**, which has a value of **1**.

2. The **sun_path** holds the address. Here, the address is a UNIX file name. If the file exists, the address is in use. If the file does not exist, then the address is not in use and an application can bind that address to a socket.

We will see examples of how to use the address structures throughout the chapter when we create applications that use the socket interface. We conclude this section by describing the socket implementation in SVR4.

Socket Implementation in SVR4

Although the SVR4 socket interface is compatible with the BSD socket interface, the implementation is different. In BSD systems, the socket routines are system calls that interface directly with the UNIX kernel. In SVR4, the socket routines are in a user-level library. The library routines use the STREAMS framework to carry out the socket functionality.

The implementation maps communication channels into device files. As mentioned earlier, a socket has no device file associated with it. With sockets, you specify the type of communication channel to be used. As we describe in Section 10.5, you name the channel symbolically. However, in SVR4, applications access transport provider by opening a device file. So, the implementation of the **socket()** library routine uses the SVR4 Network Selection routines to find a device file associated with the requested communication channel. Details of Network Selection routines were presented in Chapter 9.

The implementation also uses a STREAMS module named **sockmod**, which helps supply socket semantics. The **socket()** routine opens the device file it found via the Network Selection routines and pushes the **sockmod** module onto the stream. Figure 10.2 shows the state of the application after it calls the **socket()** routine.

As we will see in Section 10.5, the **socket()** routine also lets you access lower-level protocols, such as the Internet Control Message protocol (ICMP). In SVR4, applications access these lower-level protocols in the same way as any other protocol, that is, by opening a device file. And, because the **socket()** library routine uses the SVR4 Network Selection routines to find a device file to use, the **/etc/netconfig** file must contain an entry for the lower-level protocols (as explained in Chapter 9, the Network Selection routines get all information from the **/etc/netconfig** file). That is why the **/etc/netconfig** file can have the **tpi_raw** element of the semantics field. An entry with the **tpi_raw** semantic means the entry describes a lower-level protocol.

The socket routines are in a user-level library, so you must use the **-lsocket** flag when compiling your applications. That links the socket routines into your application. And, because the socket routines use the Network Selection routines, you must also

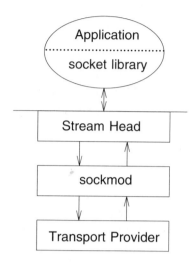

Figure 10.2   Socket Implementation in SVR4

use the -lnsl flag when compiling applications. That links the Network Selection routines into your application. And, if you use any other BSD routines, you must use the -lucb flag as well. That links in the BSD compatibility library. As a side note, some vendors put the ucb library in the /usr/ucblib directory on SVR4. You should ask the administrator to link that into the /usr/lib directory if it is not already there.

Now let's look at how to use the socket routines to manage a communication channel. We begin by presenting the details of how to use the socket routines over communication channels that supply virtual-circuit service.

10.3 Sockets Using Virtual-Circuit Service

Using sockets over a communication channel that supplies virtual-circuit service is similar to using TLI connection-mode service routines. It is like placing a telephone call. The client side of the application acts as the person doing the calling. The server side of the application acts as the person accepting the phone call.

By using this analogy, both parties get a telephone (that is, a socket) before communication begins. In SVR4, applications get a socket by using the socket() routine. Figure 10.3 shows the initial setup sequence. On the server side of the application, you must do the following:

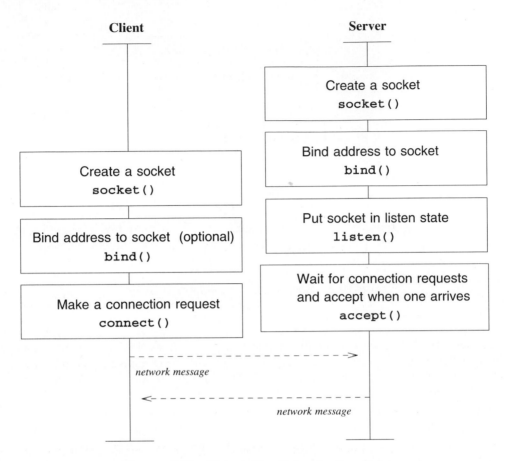

Figure 10.3 Virtual-Circuit Application Setup

1. Create a socket. You do that by issuing the **socket()** routine, specifying the address family, transport protocol, and an indication that you want to use virtual-circuit service. The **socket()** routine returns a file descriptor corresponding to the socket. This action is like obtaining the telephone.

2. Bind a transport address to the socket using the **bind()** routine. This is like getting a phone number that people use to call you. The format of the transport address depends upon which transport provider you are using.

3. Place the socket in the "listen state." You do that by calling the **listen()** routine. Unlike the TLI **t_listen()** routine, the **listen()** routine does not sleep. Instead, it marks the socket as able to accept connections and returns immediately. This is like plugging the telephone into a telephone jack.

4. Wait for a connection request to arrive. You do that by issuing the `accept()` routine. This routine sleeps and returns when a connection request arrives on the socket. This is like waiting for the phone to ring. When a connection request arrives (that is, the phone rings), the `accept()` routine returns.

   The `accept()` routine returns a new socket that contains the connection. From the telephone analogy, the `accept()` routine answers the ringing telephone, transfers the call to the new telephone, and returns the new telephone. The original socket can then wait for new calls.

   Usually, the application issues the `fork()` system call when the `accept()` routine returns. The child process handles the new connection. The parent process issues another `accept()` call and waits for the phone to ring again.

On the client side of the application, you must do the following:

1. Create a socket using the `socket()` routine. As with the server side of the application, you must specify the address family, transport protocol, and an indication that you want to use virtual-circuit service. This returns a file descriptor corresponding to the socket. This action is like getting a telephone.

2. Bind an arbitrary transport address to the socket using the `bind()` routine. This is like getting a phone number. Here, you don't really care what your telephone number is, because no one is going to call (you are placing the outgoing call).

   When using sockets, this step is optional. If you do not bind an address to the socket, SVR4 binds it automatically when you connect to the server side of the application.

3. Establish a connection with the server machine by calling the `connect()` routine. You must specify the transport address of the server side of the application. This is like dialing a phone and placing a phone call.

At this point, there is a connection between two sockets. As illustrated in Figure 10.4, you can send data over the connection using with the following routines:

1. Use the `write()` system call to send data from one socket to another. Or, if desired, use any of the following routines:

   a. The `send()` routine, which lets you send either normal data or expedited data. As mentioned in Chapter 7, expedited data are "emergency data" that you want to send as quickly as possible. Different transport providers handle expedited data differently. However, most transport providers place expedited data ahead of normal data when they get to the server's socket.

   b. The `sendmsg()` routine. You use the `sendmsg()` when you want to write data from different memory locations as a single unit and when you

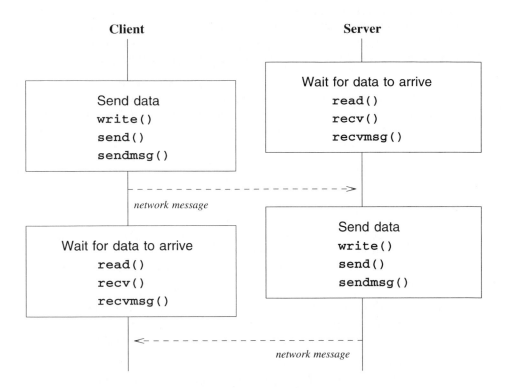

Figure 10.4 Virtual-Circuit Application Data Transfer

want to send file descriptors to another application running on the same machine. We present the details of all data-transfer routines in Section 10.5.

   c. Although not recommended, you can use the **sendto()** routine. This routine is exactly like the **send()** routine, except that you can specify the destination address. However, because the socket is connected, the destination address is ignored. Because it provides no more functionality than the **send()** routine, you should always use the **send()** routine instead of the **sendto()** routine when you use virtual-circuit transport providers.

2. Use the **read()** routine to read data. Or, if desired, you can use any of the following routines:

   a. The **recv()** routine, which is similar to the **write()** system call, but it also lets you read expedited data. It also lets you ''peek'' at data.

When you peek at data, you read them without consuming them from the input queue.

b.   The `recvfrom()` routine, which provides the functionality of the `recv()` routine, but it also returns the address of the application that sent the data. Most applications do not use this routine over virtual-circuit transport providers, because you can get the address of the connected socket when you accept the connection. You usually use the `recvfrom()` routine over datagram transport providers, because every datagram may come from a different source.

c.   The `recvmsg()` routine, which lets you read data sent via the `sendmsg()` routine. It allows reading data into different memory locations and allows receiving file descriptors from peer applications. We present the details of all data-transfer routines in Section 10.5.

After all communication is finished, you can close down the virtual circuit. There are three ways to do this:

1.   Exit the application.

2.   Issue the `close()` system call on the socket. This system call attempts to send any undelivered data.

3.   Issue the `shutdown()` routine, which provides more control over the socket. For example, you can stop incoming data, outgoing data, or both. We present the details of the `shutdown()` routine in Section 10.5.

In the actions just described, the application waited for an action to complete. For example, the `accept()` routine waited for a connection request to arrive and did not return until a connection request appeared. If you wait for an action to complete, your application is in the **synchronous mode**. Your application can also run in the **asynchronous mode**, where you do not wait for an action to complete. We now present the details of these two modes.

Synchronous and Asynchronous Modes

Your application can run in one of two modes: the **synchronous mode** or the **asynchronous mode**. By default, you are in the synchronous mode.

In the synchronous mode, the socket routines do not return to your application until the operation is complete (this is also called the **blocking mode**). For example, if the server side of the application issues an `accept()` routine, that routine does not return until a connection request arrives. In the asynchronous mode, the socket routines return immediately, even if the operation is not finished (this is also called the **nonblocking mode**).

As mentioned in Chapter 7, you should use the synchronous mode if you want to wait for functions to complete. For example, suppose you issued the **read()** system call. In the synchronous mode, this system call waits for data to arrive before returning to your application. If you must have the data before you can do any other processing, then you should be in the synchronous mode.

You should use the asynchronous mode if there are other tasks to do while waiting for a socket routine to complete. For example, the **read()** routine in the asynchronous mode returns immediately if no data are available. That lets your application do other processing while waiting for data to arrive.

By default, your application runs in the synchronous mode. To run in the asynchronous mode, you must first create a socket and then set the **FNDELAY** flag associated with the socket file descriptor. You do that by issuing the following **fcntl()** system call:

```
fcntl(fd, F_SETFL, FNDELAY);
```

Here, the **fd** argument is a file descriptor that refers to a socket. After issuing the **fcntl()** system call, the socket is in the asynchronous mode.

If you want to put the socket back in the synchronous mode, turn off the **FNDELAY** flag. You can do that with the following code:

```
int flags;

flags = fcntl(fd, F_GETFL, 0);
fcntl(fd, F_SETFL, flags & ~FNDELAY);
```

In this code segment, the **fd** argument is a file descriptor associated with a socket. The first **fcntl()** routine gets the flags associated with the socket, and the second **fcntl()** routine turns off the **FNDELAY** flag.

If your application is running in the asynchronous mode, you may want to be told when data arrive. You can check if data arrive in one of two ways:

1. Issue the **read()** routine periodically to figure out if data have arrived on the socket.

2. Set up the socket to send you a **SIGIO** signal when normal data arrive and the **SIGURG** signal when expedited data arrive. We explain how to do that in Section 10.8.

Now let's look at the socket routines using a communication channel that supplies datagram service.

10.4 Sockets Using Datagram Service

Using sockets over a communication channel that supplies datagram service is similar to sending a postal letter. The client side of the application acts as the person sending the letter. The server side of the application acts as the person receiving the letter.

By using this analogy, both parties must get a mailbox (that is, a socket) before communication can begin. Figure 10.5 shows the initial setup sequence. On the server side of the application, you must do the following:

1. Create a socket by calling the **socket()** routine. This returns a file descriptor into the socket. This action is like getting a mailbox.

2. Attach a transport address to the socket using the **bind()** routine. This is like assigning a postal address to the mailbox. Applications use that address when they send you datagrams.

3. Wait for a datagram to arrive using the **recvfrom()** routine. This is like waiting for a letter to appear in your mailbox. When a message arrives, the **recvfrom()** routine returns the data and the transport address of the sender.

4. Send a reply with the **sendto()** routine, if needed. This is like sending a letter. You must specify the destination address when sending the datagram.

On the client side of the application, you must do the following:

1. Create a socket using the **socket()** routine. This returns a file descriptor into the transport provider. This action is like getting a mailbox.

2. Optionally bind an arbitrary transport address to the socket using the **bind()** routine. This is like assigning a postal address to the mailbox. Here, you don't really care what your address is. When you send a datagram, your transport address is sent with the data. So, if the server side of the application must reply to your message, it can look at the datagram to figure out your transport address.

   If you do not bind a transport address to the socket, SVR4 does it automatically when you send a datagram.

3. Optionally connect to the server side of the application by calling the **connect()** routine. Here, the **connect()** routine does not make an actual connection. Instead, it associates your socket with a destination address. When you issue subsequent **send()** and **write()** routines to send datagrams, the system attaches the destination address to each datagram.

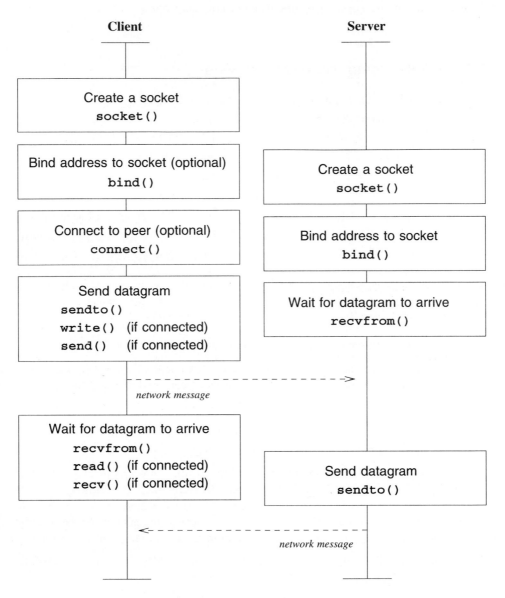

Figure 10.5 Datagram Application Communication

4. Send a message to the server side of the application using the **sendto()** rou-
    tine. This routine requires the address of the socket to which you want to send

the datagram. However, if you issued the **connect()** routine to connect to a remote socket, you can send datagrams by using the **write()** system call or the **send()** routine.

Also, although not shown in Figure 10.5, you can use the **sendmsg()** routine if you are using the connectionless loopback transport provider. As we will see in Section 10.5, this routine lets you send file descriptors to another application.

5. If you expect a response, issue the **recvfrom()** to wait for the response to arrive. If you connected to the remote socket, you can issue the **recv()** routine or the **read()** system call as well.

    And, although not shown in Figure 10.5, you can use the **recvmsg()** routine to read datagrams. We show how to use the **recvmsg()** routine in Section 10.5.

    Unfortunately, because you are using a datagram transport provider, *the response may never arrive*. Datagram transport providers do not guarantee delivery. The response may not arrive because the original message was lost or because the server's response was lost. Therefore, you must time out and resend the request if you do not get a response after a period of time. We will see an example of how to do that in Section 10.7.

In the actions described, the application waited for an action to complete. For example, the **recvfrom()** routine waited for a datagram to arrive and did not return until a datagram appeared on the socket. This type of behavior is called the **synchronous mode**. Your application can also run in the **asynchronous mode**, where you do not wait for an action to complete. Details are described next.

Synchronous and Asynchronous Modes

Applications using datagram communication channels can run in either the synchronous or the asynchronous mode. In the synchronous mode, socket routines do not return to your application until the operation is complete. In the asynchronous mode, socket routines return immediately.

When using datagram communication channels, the synchronous mode only applies when reading datagrams. In the synchronous mode, the **recvfrom()** routine, the **recvmsg()** routine, the **recv()** routine, and the **read()** system call all sleep until a datagram arrives. In the asynchronous mode, those routines return immediately if no datagram exists on the socket.

By default, your application is in the synchronous mode. To run in the asynchronous mode, you must create a socket and turn on the **FNDELAY** flag. You do that by issuing the same **fcntl()** system call as was done with sockets over a virtual-circuit transport provider:

```
fcntl(fd, F_SETFL, FNDELAY);
```

The **fd** argument is a file descriptor that refers to a socket. After issuing the **fcntl()** system call, the socket is in the asynchronous mode. You can put the socket back in the synchronous mode by turning off the **FNDELAY** flag, as described in Section 10.3.

Now let's take a closer look at the details of the socket routines. We present the details of the routines to create and manage communication channels that use both virtual-circuit and datagram transport providers.

10.5 Details of Socket Routines

The previous sections presented an overview of some socket routines. Before showing an application that uses those routines, we present the details.

socket()

The **socket()** routine is used to create a socket. The **socket()** routine creates an unbound, unconnected socket and returns a file descriptor corresponding to that socket. You use it in the client side and the server side of your application.

The syntax follows:

```
#include <sys/types.h>
#include <sys/socket.h>

int domain;
int type;
int protocol;
int fd;

fd = socket(domain, type, protocol);
```

The **socket()** routine returns a file descriptor that you use on all subsequent socket calls. From an application's point of view, the file descriptor is the end of a communication channel. The routine returns **-1** if an error occurs.

The **domain** argument is an integer that represents a protocol family of the communication channel you want to use. A protocol family is a group of transport providers that have the same address formats. For example, TCP and UDP have the same address formats, so they are in the same protocol family. Common values for this argument are as follows:

AF_INET   The TCP/IP protocol suite. As explained in Chapter 3, the TCP/IP protocol suite provides the Transmission Control Protocol (TCP) and the User Datagram Protocol (UDP).

AF_UNIX   A local communication channel. In SVR4, this value creates a communication channel using the SVR4 loopback transport provider. The loopback transport provider can only be used between applications on the same system.

AF_NS   The Xerox Network Systems (XNS) protocols. As mentioned in Chapter 1, the XNS protocols contain several transport providers, the most prominent being the Sequenced Packet Protocol (SPP).

After specifying the protocol family you want to use, you must specify the type of service desired. The **type** argument contains that specification. For example, you can specify virtual-circuit or datagram service. Common values for the **type** argument are:

SOCK_STREAM   A transport provider that supplies virtual-circuit service.

SOCK_DGRAM   A transport provider that supplies datagram service.

SOCK_RAW   A protocol under the transport layer. For example, the **SOCK_RAW** type in the **AF_INET** family can access the Internet Protocol (IP) or the Internet Control Message Protocol (ICMP) directly. IP and ICMP were described in Chapter 3.

SOCK_SEQPACKET   A transport provider that supplies virtual-circuit service and maintains message boundaries.

SOCK_RDM   A datagram transport provider that allows reliably delivered messages.

After specifying a protocol family and a type of service, you must specify a particular protocol to be used. The **protocol** argument of the **socket()** routine contains that specification. Usually, there is only one protocol for a given family and type of service. In that case, you can specify **0** for the **protocol** argument. However, if multiple protocols exist for a given family and type of service, you must specify the protocol to be used.

To illustrate, suppose you wanted a socket that used the TCP transport provider for its communication channel. TCP is a member of the TCP/IP protocol family. To use that protocol family, you specify **AF_INET** as the first argument to the **socket()** routine. And, because TCP provides virtual circuit service, you specify **SOCK_STREAM** as the second argument. And, because TCP is the *only* transport provider in the TCP/IP protocol suite that provides virtual circuit service, the **protocol** argument of the **socket()** routine is **0** (if desired, you could specify the protocol explicitly by using the **IPPROTO_TCP** value). So, to create a socket that uses TCP, you would issue the following **socket()** routine:

```
fd = socket(AF_INET, SOCK_STREAM, 0);
```

Now, suppose you wanted a socket that used the UDP transport provider for the communication channel. UDP is also a member of the TCP/IP protocol family, and it supplies datagram service. So, the first argument to the **socket()** routine is **AF_INET**, and the second argument is **SOCK_DGRAM**. In addition, UDP is the *only* transport provider in the TCP/IP protocol suite that provides datagram service. So, the **protocol** argument of the **socket()** routine is **0** as well. To create a socket that uses UDP, you would do the following:

```
fd = socket(AF_INET, SOCK_DGRAM, 0);
```

Using the protocols under the transport layer is another story. If you wanted to create a socket that accessed the lower layers of the TCP/IP protocol suite, you would use the **SOCK_RAW** type. In that case, SVR4 lets you access several lower-level protocols, including IP and ICMP. To create a socket that accesses IP directly, you would specify **IPPROTO_RAW** as the protocol:

```
fd = socket(AF_INET, SOCK_RAW, IPPROTO_RAW);
```

Similarly, you would specify the **IPPROTO_ICMP** value if you wanted to access the ICMP protocol:

```
fd = socket(AF_INET, SOCK_RAW, IPPROTO_ICMP);
```

As mentioned in Section 10.2, the SVR4 implementation of the **socket()** routine routine uses the SVR4 Network Selection routines. If an application uses the **SOCK_RAW** type, the **socket()** routine uses the Network Selection routines to find an entry with the **NC_TPI_RAW** bit in the semantics field. An entry with that bit in the semantics field means the entry describes a lower-level protocol.

Most applications do not use the **SOCK_RAW** type. It is usually used by maintenance applications and administrative applications that must access the lower-layer protocols directly. For example, the SVR4 **ping** command uses the ICMP protocol to send an ''are you alive?'' message to another machine. Because it interfaces with the ICMP protocol, it creates a socket of type **SOCK_RAW**.

Now let's look at the **SOCK_SEQPACKET** type. Remember that TCP does not support message boundaries. TCP sends data as a stream of bytes, and it does not mark where one message ends and another begins. So, the **SOCK_SEQPACKET** type in the **AF_INET** family does not exist. If you called the **socket()** routine with **AF_INET** and **SOCK_SEQPACKET** as the first two arguments, the **socket()** routine would return with an error condition.

However, the Sequenced Packet Protocol (SPP) of the Xerox Network Systems protocols does support message boundaries. So, if you called the **socket()** routine giving it as arguments **AF_NS**, **SOCK_SEQPACKET**, and **0**, it would return a socket into the SPP transport provider. Also, because SPP supplies virtual-circuit service, you can get a socket into the SPP transport provider by specifying **AF_NS**, **SOCK_STREAM**, and **0** as the arguments to the **socket()** routine.

The base SVR4 system does not contain XNS protocols. However, it does support the socket interface to the **AF_INET** and the **AF_UNIX** families. The following table shows what protocols you get for the **type** and **protocol** for the **AF_INET** and **AF_UNIX** protocol families:

Family	Type	Protocol	Result
AF_INET	SOCK_STREAM	0	The Transmission Control Protocol (TCP)
AF_INET	SOCK_STREAM	IPPROTO_TCP	The Transmission Control Protocol (TCP)
AF_INET	SOCK_DGRAM	0	The User Datagram Protocol (UDP)
AF_INET	SOCK_DGRAM	IPPROTO_UDP	The User Datagram Protocol (UDP)
AF_INET	SOCK_RAW	IPPROTO_ICMP	The Internet Control Message Protocol (ICMP)
AF_INET	SOCK_RAW	IPPROTO_RAW	The Internet Protocol (IP)
AF_INET	SOCK_SEQPACKET	*Any*	*Invalid*
AF_INET	SOCK_RDM	*Any*	*Invalid*
AF_UNIX	SOCK_STREAM	0	The connection-oriented loopback transport provider

AF_UNIX	SOCK_DGRAM	0	The connectionless loopback transport provider
AF_UNIX	SOCK_RAW	*Any*	*Invalid*
AF_UNIX	SOCK_SEQPACKET	*Any*	*Invalid*
AF_UNIX	SOCK_RDM	*Any*	*Invalid*

socketpair()

The `socketpair()` routine creates two sockets, connects them, and returns the corresponding file descriptors. The result is the same as creating an SVR4 pipe. You have a two-way communication channel that can be used within your application.

The `socketpair()` routine has the following syntax:

```
#include <sys/types.h>
#include <sys/socket.h>

int domain;
int type;
int protocol;
int status;
int fd_array[2];

status = socketpair(domain, type, protocol, fd_array);
```

The **domain**, **type**, and **protocol** arguments are the same as in the **socket()** routine. They indicate the protocol family, type of service, and protocol to use for the communication channel. However, where the **socket()** routine returns a file descriptor into an unconnected, unbound socket, the **socketpair()** routine returns two sockets that are connected to one another. The **socketpair()** routine puts the file descriptors corresponding to the sockets into the **fd_array** argument. If successful, the routine returns the number of sockets it created (that is, **2**). The routine returns **-1** if an error occurs.

In SVR4, you can only use the **socketpair()** routine in the **AF_UNIX** domain. The routine returns an error if you specify any other domain. If you use the **SOCK_DGRAM** type, the **socketpair()** routine creates a communication channel using the SVR4 connectionless loopback transport provider. If you use the **SOCK_STREAM** type, the **socketpair()** routine creates a communication channel using one of the SVR4 connection-oriented loopback transport providers. SVR4 has two connection-oriented loopback transport providers: `ticots`, which supplies connection-oriented service, and `ticotsord`, which supplies connection-oriented service with orderly release. The `socketpair()` routine uses the first one that the Network Selection routines return.

bind()

The `bind()` routine lets you name a socket, that is, it lets you attach a transport address to a socket. It has the following format:

```
#include <sys/types.h>
#include <sys/socket.h>

int fd;
struct sockaddr *addressp;
int addrlen;
int status;

status = bind(fd, addressp, addrlen);
```

The `fd` argument is a file descriptor corresponding to a socket. The `addressp` argument points to a transport address, and the `addrlen` argument contains the number of bytes in the address. The `bind()` routine associates the transport address with the socket and returns `0` on success or `-1` on failure.

The format of the address depends upon the communication channel associated with the socket. For example, if you created the socket in the `AF_INET` domain, the address must be a TCP/IP address in a `sockaddr_in` structure. If you created the socket in the `AF_UNIX` domain, the address must be a loopback transport address in a `sockaddr_un` structure.

There is one thing to note about addresses in the `AF_UNIX` domain. In BSD systems, the `AF_UNIX` domain corresponded to loopback transport providers that used UNIX file names as addresses. When you bound a socket to an address, you used a UNIX file name as that address. If the file existed, then the address was already in use. If the file did not exist, the address was available.

The SVR4 implementation of the `AF_UNIX` domain, on the other hand, uses the SVR4 loopback transport providers. These transport providers use a character string as an address. The character string has nothing to do with UNIX file names.

However, to provide compatibility with BSD systems, the SVR4 `bind()` routine artificially imposes the BSD semantics on `AF_UNIX` addresses. So, when using the

bind() routine to bind an address in the **AF_UNIX** domain to a socket, you must specify a file name as the address. If the file exists, the **bind()** routine returns an error. Otherwise, it creates the file and uses the file name as the address.

connect()

The **connect()** routine connects to another socket. You use it on the client side of your application. It has the following syntax:

```
#include <sys/types.h>
#include <sys/socket.h>

int fd;
struct sockaddr *addressp;
int addrlen;
int status;

status = connect(fd, addressp, addrlen);
```

The **fd** argument is a file descriptor into a socket. The **addressp** argument specifies the address of the socket to which you want to connect, and the **addrlen** argument contains the number of bytes in the address.

The format of the address is specific to the communication channel. For example, if the communication channel is in the **AF_INET** domain, use the **sockaddr_in** structure to hold the address. If the communication channel is in the **AF_UNIX** domain, use the **sockaddr_un** structure. The **sockaddr_in** and **sockaddr_un** structures are described in Section 10.2.

If you are using a virtual-circuit transport provider, the **connect()** routine sends a connection request to the remote socket. In that case, it behaves like the TLI **t_connect()** routine.

You can also use the **connect()** routine on datagram transport providers. As mentioned earlier, doing so simply associates the destination address with your socket. The system puts that address on all subsequent datagrams sent into the communication channel.

Usually, the client side of the application binds to an address before issuing the **connect()** routine. However, that is not required. If the client side of the application issues the **connect()** routine on an unbound socket, the **connect()** routine binds an arbitrary address to the socket. The **connect()** routine returns **0** on success and **-1** on failure.

listen()

The `listen()` routine prepares a socket to accept connections. You can only use it on sockets that use a virtual-circuit communication channel. You must use it on the server side of the application before you can accept any connection requests from the client side of the application.

The `listen()` routine has the following syntax:

```
        int fd;
        int qlen;
        int status;

        status = listen(fd, qlen);
```

The `fd` argument is a file descriptor corresponding to a socket. The socket must be of type **SOCK_STREAM** or **SOCK_SEQPACKET**.

The `qlen` argument specifies the length of the queue of connection requests. When a connection request arrives, it is placed on this queue. When you accept a connection with the `accept()` routine (described in what follows), you remove the request from the queue.

This value is different from the `qlen` value used in TLI routines. In TLI routines, the `qlen` value specifies the maximum number of outstanding connection indications your application wants to support. As explained in Chapters 7 and 8, if you had `qlen` greater than **1** in the TLI routines, you must get information about all outstanding connection indications before you can accept any of them.

That is not the case with the socket routines. No special processing is needed if you set `qlen` greater than **1**. Your server code is the same no matter what value of `qlen` is set.

Unlike the TLI `t_listen()` routine, the `listen()` routine does not sleep waiting for connection requests to arrive. It simply sets up the connection queue and returns to your application. It returns **0** on success and **-1** on failure.

accept()

The server side of your application issues the `accept()` routine to accept incoming connection requests. It is only valid on virtual-circuit transport providers.

If your application is in the synchronous mode, the `accept()` routine sleeps until a connection request arrives. If your application is in the asynchronous mode, the `accept()` routine will not sleep and returns with an error if no connection request exists.

The syntax of the `accept()` routine follows:

```
#include <sys/types.h>
#include <sys/socket.h>

int fd;
struct sockaddr *addressp;
int addrlen;
int newfd;

newfd = accept(fd, addressp, &addrlen);
```

The `fd` argument is a socket that is of type **SOCK_STREAM** or **SOCK_SEQPACKET**. The socket must be bound to an address, and you must have previously issued the `listen()` routine on the socket.

If you are in the synchronous mode, the `accept()` routine waits for a connection request to arrive. When a connection request arrives, the `accept()` routine creates a new socket, accepts the connection on the new socket, and returns a file descriptor corresponding to the new socket. You use the new socket on all subsequent communication with the client side of the application. The original socket can be used to accept more connection requests.

The `accept()` routine fills the address of the caller into the `addressp` argument. You must allocate a buffer to hold the address and pass a pointer to that buffer. You must also put the number of bytes in the buffer into the `addrlen` argument. Upon successful completion, the `accept()` routine modifies the `addrlen` argument to contain the actual length of the address.

If you are in the asynchronous mode and there are no connection requests queued, the `accept()` routine returns `-1` and sets `errno` to **EWOULDBLOCK**. That is not an error condition. It says that no connection request has arrived yet. In all other cases, the `accept()` routine returns `-1` on failure. On success, it returns a new socket that is connected to the application that made the connection request.

send()

The `send()` routine is used to send data over a communication channel. You use it on both the client side and the server side of your application. The `send()` routine can be used over both virtual-circuit and datagram communication channels. However, if you use a datagram transport provider, you must issue the `connect()` routine to establish the address of the peer socket.

The `send()` routine is similar to the `write()` system call.   In fact, you can use the `write()` system call instead of the `send()` routine.   However, as we show in what follows, the `send()` routine lets you do more operations than the `write()` system call.

The syntax of the `send()` routine follows:

```
#include <sys/types.h>
#include <sys/socket.h>

int fd;
char *buff;
int len;
int flags;
int numsent;

numsent = send(fd, buff, len, flags);
```

The `fd` argument is a file descriptor that refers to a socket, the `buff` argument is a character buffer containing data, and the `len` argument is the number of bytes in the data buffer.

The `flags` argument is what differentiates the `send()` routine from the `write()` system call.   If the flag argument is `0`, the `send()` routine behaves exactly as the `write()` system call.   If it is not `0`, it can be a logical OR of the following values:

`MSG_OOB`   The data in the buffer are "out-of-band" (that is, expedited) data. Expedited data are "emergency data" that you want to deliver as quickly as possible.   Different transport providers handle expedited data differently (in fact, some transport providers do not support expedited data at all).   However, most transport providers place expedited data ahead of normal data when they arrive at the remote socket.   You can only send expedited data on virtual-circuit transport providers.

`MSG_DONTROUTE`   The data should bypass the kernel routing facilities.   This value is usually used only by administrative and routing applications.

The `send()` routine returns `-1` on failure.   Otherwise, it returns the number of bytes it gave to the transport provider.

sendto()

The **sendto()** routine is exactly like the **send()** routine, except you can specify the destination address of the socket to which you want to send the data. It is used primarily on unconnected sockets. You can use it on a connected socket, but the system ignores the destination address specified in the **sendto()** routine (instead, it uses the address to which you are connected).

The syntax follows:

```
#include <sys/types.h>
#include <sys/socket.h>

int fd;
char *buff;
int len;
int flags;
struct sockaddr *addressp;
int addrlen;
int numsent;

numsent = sendto(fd, buff, len, flags, addressp, addrlen);
```

The **fd** argument is a file descriptor into a socket, the **buff** argument contains the data you want to send, and the **len** argument contains the number of bytes in the data.

The **flags** argument contains the same values as the **send()** routine (that is, **MSG_OOB** and **MSG_DONTROUTE**). However, if you have a socket that uses a datagram transport provider, you cannot use the **MSG_OOB** value. Datagram transport providers do not support expedited data.

The **addressp** argument holds the address of the socket to which you want to send the data, and the **addrlen** argument contains the number of bytes in the address. The format of the address depends upon the communication channel associated with the socket. Section 10.2 presented some examples of addresses. For example, if you created the socket in the **AF_INET** domain, the address must be a TCP/IP address.

You must use the **sendto()** routine if a datagram transport provider is being used and you want to send datagrams to several different sockets. Because you specify the destination address on every message, the **sendto()** routine lets you vary the destination on every datagram.

As with the **send()** routine, the **sendto()** routine returns **-1** on failure. Otherwise, it returns the number of bytes it gave to the transport provider.

sendmsg()

The **sendmsg()** routine lets you do everything the **sendto()** routine does, but it also lets you format data easily and send specially interpreted data. You can use it to send data over virtual-circuit or datagram transport providers.

The format of the **sendmsg()** routine follows:

```
#include <sys/types.h>
#include <sys/socket.h>

int fd;
struct msghdr *msgp;
int flags;
int numsent;

numsent = sendmsg(fd, msgp, flags);
```

The **fd** argument is a file descriptor corresponding to a socket. The **msgp** argument is a pointer to a message structure that contains data and other information (we describe that structure in what follows). The **flags** argument contains the same values as the **send()** and **sendto()** routines (that is, **MSG_OOB** and **MSG_DONTROUTE**). However, if you have a socket that uses a datagram transport provider, you cannot use the **MSG_OOB** value. Datagram transport providers do not support expedited data.

The **msgp** argument contains the data you want to send. It is a pointer to a **msghdr** structure, which has the following definition:

```
struct msghdr {
    caddr_t         msg_name;
    int             msg_namelen;
    struct iovec   *msg_iov;
    int             msg_iovlen;
    caddr_t         msg_accrights;
    int             msg_accrightslen;
};
```

The **msg_name** field contains the destination address of the socket to which you want
to send the message, and the **msg_namelen** field contains the number of bytes in the
address. If your socket is connected, those fields are ignored. As mentioned earlier,
the format of the address depends upon the communication channel associated with the
socket.

The **msg_iov** field points to an array of **iovec** structures that contain the message
data, and the **msg_iovlen** field contains the number of structures in the array. The
iovec structure has the following definition:

```
struct iovec {
    caddr_t    iov_base;
    int        iov_len;
};
```

The array of **iovec** structures let you take data from different memory buffers and
send them as a contiguous unit. For example, suppose you wanted to send a message
to a remote application that contained the name of a company and the names of three
employees in that company. The **sendmsg()** routine lets you send four buffers containing that information as a single message. You do not have to copy the four buffers
into a contiguous data buffer. If the routine fails, it returns **-1**. Otherwise, it returns
the number of bytes it sent into the communication channel. We show an example of
how to use the **sendmsg()** routine after we detail the rest of the socket routines.

recv()

The **recv()** routine reads data from a connected socket. It is used on both the client
side and the server side of your application.

The **recv()** routine is similar to the **read()** system call. In fact, you can use the
read() system call instead of the **recv()** routine. However, the **recv()** routine
lets you read expedited data and lets you peek at the data on the socket without reading them.

The syntax of the **recv()** routine follows:

```
#include <sys/types.h>
#include <sys/socket.h>

int fd;
char *buff;
int len;
int flags;
int numread;

numread = recv(fd, buff, len, flags);
```

The **fd** argument is a file descriptor that refers to a socket, the **buff** argument is a character buffer, and the **len** argument is the size of the buffer. The **recv()** routine reads data from the socket and places the data in the buffer.

The **flags** argument is what differentiates the **recv()** routine from the **read()** system call. If the flag argument is **0**, the **recv()** routine behaves exactly as the **read()** system call. If it is not **0**, it can be a logical OR of the following values:

MSG_OOB   Reads "out-of-band" (that is, expedited) data, not normal data. Expedited data are "emergency data" that the remote side of the application sends. Usually, you only use this flag if expedited data are present on the socket. As we will see in Section 10.8, you can have the system send a SIGURG signal when expedited data arrive.

MSG_PEEK   Puts the data in the data buffer, but it does not consume the data from the socket. So, the next read operation will get the same data.

If you are in the synchronous mode, the **recv()** routine waits for data to arrive. If you are in the asynchronous mode and data are not present on the socket, the **recv()** routine returns **-1** and sets **errno** to **EWOULDBLOCK**. That is not an error condition. It simply means no data are available yet. Section 10.8 explains how to configure your application to get a **SIGIO** signal when normal data arrive and a **SIGURG** signal when expedited data arrive.

The **recv()** routine returns **-1** on failure. Otherwise, it returns the number of bytes it put into the buffer.

recvfrom()

The **recvfrom()** routine is exactly like the **recv()** routine, except the kernel includes the address of the socket that sent the data. It is usually used on sockets that use a datagram transport provider.

The syntax follows:

```
#include <sys/types.h>
#include <sys/socket.h>

int fd;
char *buff;
int len;
int flags;
struct sockaddr *addressp;
int addrlen;
int nread;

nread = recvfrom(fd, buff, len, flags, addressp, &addrlen);
```

The **fd** argument is a file descriptor into a socket, the **buff** argument points to a data buffer, and the **len** argument contains the number of bytes in the buffer.

The **flags** argument contains the same values as the **recv()** routine (that is, **MSG_OOB** and **MSG_PEEK**). However, if you have a socket that uses a datagram transport provider, you cannot use the **MSG_OOB** value. Datagram transport providers do not support expedited data.

The **recvfrom()** routine populates the **addressp** argument with the address of the socket that sent the data. You must allocate a buffer to hold the address, and you must put the size of the buffer in the **addrlen** argument. After the **recvfrom()** routine fills the **addressp** argument with the address of the socket that sent the data, it resets the **addrlen** argument to contain the number of bytes in the address.

The **recvfrom()** routine can be used on both virtual-circuit and datagram transport providers. However, it is most useful on unconnected sockets in datagram transport providers. In that case, you can figure out who sent the data when you read them.

If you are in the synchronous mode, the **recvfrom()** routine waits for data to arrive. If you are in the asynchronous mode and no data are present on the socket, the **recvfrom()** routine returns **-1** and sets **errno** to **EWOULDBLOCK**. That is not an error condition. It simply means no data are available yet. Section 10.8 explains how to configure your application to get a **SIGIO** signal when normal data arrive and a **SIGURG** signal when expedited data arrive.

The **recvfrom()** routine returns **-1** on failure. Otherwise, it returns the number of bytes it put into the data buffer.

recvmsg()

The **recvmsg()** routine lets you read a message that an application sent with the
sendmsg() routine. The format follows:

```
#include <sys/types.h>
#include <sys/socket.h>

int fd;
struct msghdr *msgp;
int flags;
int numread;

numread = recvmsg(fd, msgp, flags);
```

The **fd** argument is a file descriptor that corresponds to a socket, and the **flags**
argument contains the same values as the **recv()** routine (that is, **MSG_OOB** and
MSG_PEEK). However, if you have a socket that uses a datagram transport provider,
you cannot use the **MSG_OOB** value, because datagram transport providers do not
support expedited data. The **recvmsg()** routine returns the number of bytes it reads
or **-1** if an error occurs.

The **recvmsg()** routine fills the **msgp** argument with the message the peer application sent via the **sendmsg()** routine. The **msgp** argument points to a **msghdr**
structure, which has the following definition:

```
struct msghdr {
    caddr_t          msg_name;
    int              msg_namelen;
    struct iovec *msg_iov;
    int              msg_iovlen;
    caddr_t          msg_accrights;
    int              msg_accrightslen;
};
```

The **msg_name** field and the **msg_namelen** field let you get the address of the
socket that sent the message. If the **msg_name** field is nonzero, it must point to a
data buffer that your application allocates. The **msg_namelen** field contains the
number of bytes in the buffer. The **recvmsg()** routine fills the buffer with the
address of the sender and resets the **msg_namelen** field to the number of bytes in
the address. If the **msg_name** field is zero, the **recvmsg()** routine does not fill in
the sender's address.

The **msg_iov** field points to an array of **iovec** structures, and the **recvmsg()** routine fills the **iovec** structures with the data sent via the **sendmsg()** routine. The **msg_iovlen** field contains the number of structures in the array. The **iovec** structure has the following definition:

```
struct iovec {
    caddr_t    iov_base;
    int        iov_len;
};
```

The **iov_base** field points to a data buffer, and the **iov_len** field contains the number of bytes in the buffer. Before calling the **recvmsg()** routine, you must allocate space for each **iov_base** buffer and set the **iov_len** accordingly. That lets you read a single message into different areas of memory. If the routine fails, it returns **-1**. Otherwise, it returns the number of bytes it received. We show an example of how to use the **recvmsg()** routine in what follows.

shutdown()

The **shutdown()** routine lets you shut down a socket and stop all further reads and writes across the communication channel. It is used on both the client and server side of the application over virtual-circuit and datagram communication channels.

The syntax follows:

```
int fd;
int action;
int status;

status = shutdown(fd, action);
```

The **fd** argument is a file descriptor corresponding to a socket. The **action** argument can have one of three values:

0   Disallows all future read operations on the socket.

1   Disallows all future write operations on the socket.

2   Disallows all future read and write operations on the socket.

The **shutdown()** routine returns **0** on success and **-1** on failure.

getsockname()

The `getsockname()` routine lets you figure out the address to which a socket is bound. It has the following syntax:

```
        int fd;
        struct sockaddr *addrp;
        int addrlen;
        int status;

        status = getsockname(fd, addrp, &addrlen);
```

The `fd` argument is a file descriptor corresponding to a socket. The `addrp` argument points to a memory buffer, and the `addrlen` points to an integer that has the number of bytes in the buffer.

The `getsockname()` routine fills the memory location to which `addrp` points with the address to which the socket is bound. Then, it modifies the `addrlen` argument to contain the actual number of bytes in the address.

The `getsockname()` returns `0` on success and `-1` on failure.

getpeername()

The `getpeername()` routine lets you figure out the address of the socket that is connected to your socket. It can be used on both the client side and the server side of your application.

It has the following syntax:

```
        int fd;
        struct sockaddr *addrp;
        int addrlen;
        int status;

        status = getpeername(fd, addrp, &addrlen);
```

The `fd` argument is a file descriptor corresponding to a socket. The `addrp` argument points to a memory buffer, and the `addrlen` points to an integer that has the number of bytes in the buffer.

The **getpeername()** routine fills the memory location to which **addrp** points with the address of the socket to which the given socket is connected. It then modifies the **addrlen** argument to contain the number of bytes in the address.

The **getpeername()** returns **0** on success and **-1** on failure.

setsockopt()

The **setsockopt()** routine lets you set options on the communication channel. For example, you can turn on debugging information, set up a transport provider for broadcast support, and do other operations.

The socket interface defines options at different levels of the communication channel. For example, if you are using the TCP/IP protocols for your communication channel, you can set options at the socket level, at the TCP level, and at the IP level.

Figure 10.6 shows the levels that have options in a TCP/IP communication channel. At the socket level, you can set options that modify input and output buffers and do other operations. At the TCP level, you can set an option that bypasses TCP buffering algorithms. And, at the IP level, you can set IP header options.

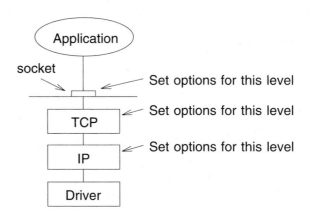

Figure 10.6   Socket Options

The format of the **setsockopt()** routine follows:

```
int fd;
int level;
int optname;
char *optvalp;
int optlen;
int status;

status = setsockopt(fd, level, optname, optvalp, optlen);
```

The **fd** argument is a file descriptor into a socket. The **level** argument indicates the level to which the option applies, and the **optname** argument indicates the option you want to do. The **optvalp** points to a buffer containing information needed by the option, and the **optlen** argument contains the number of bytes in that buffer.

The **level** argument can have several values, depending upon the transport provider of the communication channel. For example, possible values include the following:

SOL_SOCKET   Set an option at the socket level.

IPPROTO_TCP   Set an option at the TCP level. It is only valid on communication channels that use the TCP/IP protocol suite.

IPPROTO_IP   Set an option at the IP level. It is only valid on communication channels that use the TCP/IP protocol suite.

Other transport providers use different values to indicate different levels. For example, if you were using the Xerox Networking System Sequenced Packet Protocol, you could specify a level of **NSPROTO_SPP** to set options for that transport provider.

The lower-level options are specific to the underlying transport provider. However, the socket-level options are common to all transport providers. At the **SOL_SOCKET** level, the **optname** can be one of the following:

SO_BROADCAST   Sets up the communication channel for broadcast support. As mentioned earlier, some datagram transport providers support a "transport-level broadcast" facility that lets you send messages to all machines in a network. This option sets up that facility if the transport provider supports it.

Here, **optvalp** points to an integer, and **optlen** is the size of an integer. If the integer has a nonzero value, the option turns on broadcast support. If the integer is zero, the option turns off broadcast support.

SO_DEBUG   Causes the SVR4 kernel to maintain debugging information asso-
                    ciated with the communication channel. It is usually only used by
                    debugging applications. Here, **optvalp** points to an integer,
                    and **optlen** is the size of an integer. If the integer has a
                    nonzero value, the option turns on debugging support. If the
                    integer is zero, the option turns off debugging support.

SO_DONTROUTE   Causes data to bypass the kernel routing facilities. It is usually
                    used only by administrative and routing applications. You can
                    also apply this option to individual messages by setting the
                    MSG_DONTROUTE flag on the **send()** routine, the **sendto()**
                    routine, and the **sendmsg()** routine.

                    Here, **optvalp** points to an integer, and **optlen** is the size of
                    an integer. A nonzero value in the integer turns the option on,
                    and a value of zero turns the option off.

SO_KEEPALIVE   Tries to detect if a virtual circuit breaks, even if the transport pro-
                    vider does not support broken-circuit detection.

                    For example, suppose you issue a **read()** system call and wait
                    for data to arrive at the socket. If the peer machine crashes, you
                    may not get an indication that the virtual circuit no longer exists.
                    Some transport providers report a broken virtual circuit only when
                    you try to transmit data (for example, the TCP protocol works that
                    way). So, because your application is waiting for data and not
                    transmitting any, it will never get an indication of the broken
                    socket.

                    The **SO_KEEPALIVE** option solves that problem by telling the
                    underlying transport protocol to periodically send a packet over
                    the virtual-circuit connection. It is like sending an ''are you still
                    there?'' message. If the transport provider determines that the
                    application on the other side of the connection no longer exists, it
                    causes the **read()** system call to return with an error.

                    Here, **optvalp** points to an integer, and **optlen** is the size of
                    an integer. If the integer has a nonzero value, the option enables
                    the sending of ''are you there?'' messages. If the integer is zero,
                    it turns off the option. However, not all transport providers sup-
                    port this option. It is intended primarily for use with the TCP
                    protocol.

SO_LINGER   Lets you specify what to do with unsent data when you close a
                    socket. When you send data over a virtual circuit, flow-control
                    restrictions of the transport provider may keep the data queued on

the socket. By default, the system destroys queued data when you close a socket.

By setting the `SO_LINGER` option, you can cause the `close()` system call to block until the system can send the data or until a specified amount of time elapses. In this option, `optvalp` points to a `linger` structure, and `optlen` is the size of that structure. The `linger` structure has the following definition:

```
struct linger {
    int l_onoff;
    int l_linger;
};
```

If the `l_onoff` field is zero, the system does the default actions—it destroys all unsent data. If the `l_onoff` field is nonzero, then the system uses the `l_linger` field as the number of seconds to wait while trying to send the remaining data.

SO_OOBINLINE Causes expedited data to be treated as normal data when they arrives at the socket. If this option is in effect, the system does not place expedited data ahead of normal data. Expedited data are treated exactly like normal data, and you can read them without specifying the `MSG_OOB` flag on the `recv()`, `recvfrom()`, and `recvmsg()` routines. In this option, `optvalp` points to an integer, and `optlen` is the size of an integer. If the integer has a nonzero value, the system places expedited data with normal data. If the integer is zero, the system performs the default processing on expedited data.

SO_RCVBUF Lets you modify the input buffer size associated with a socket. You may want to increase the buffer size for communication channels that have high data volume, or lower it to decrease the amount of backlogged incoming data.

Here, `optvalp` points to an integer, and `optlen` is the size of an integer. The integer contains the size to which you want to set the socket input buffer.

SO_REUSEADDR Lets you bind to a TCP/IP address that is used by another process on the system. The TCP/IP protocols define a connection by a four-tuple of information: a local IP address, a local IP port, a remote IP address, and a remote IP port. Two applications on the same system can have the same local IP address and local IP port, as long as they are connected to different services.

By default, you cannot bind to a port number if it is already used by another application. However, if you know you are going to connect to a different service (and therefore create a unique four-tuple), binding to a port number that is used by another application does no harm. However, you must set this option in order for the bind to succeed.

Here, `optvalp` points to an integer, and `optlen` is the size of an integer. If the integer has a nonzero value, the option lets you bind to a port number that used by another application. If the integer is zero, you cannot bind to a port number that another application is using.

SO_SNDBUF   Lets you modify the output buffer associated with a socket. You may want to increase the buffer size for communication channels that have high data volume or lower it to decrease the amount of backlogged outgoing data.

Here, `optvalp` points to an integer, and `optlen` is the size of an integer. The integer contains the size to which you want to set the socket output buffer.

The `setsockopt()` routine returns `0` on success, and `-1` on failure.

getsockopt()

The `getsockopt()` routine lets you examine options that are set on the communication channel. It lets you view options at various levels.

The `getsockopt()` routine has the following form:

```
int fd;
int level;
int optname;
char *optvalp;
int optlen;
int status;

status = getsockopt(fd, level, optname, optvalp, &optlen);
```

The `fd` argument is a file descriptor into a socket. The `level` argument indicates the level associated with the option, and the `optname` argument indicates the option you want to query. The `optvalp` points to a buffer, and the `optlen` argument points to an integer that contains the number of bytes in the buffer. The **get-sockopt()** routine fills the buffer with the option information and resets the **optlen** argument to reflect the actual size of the option.

The **level** argument and the **optname** argument can have the same values as in the **setsockopt()** routine. Additionally, in the **SOL_SOCKET** level, the optname can have one of the following:

SO_TYPE   Returns the type of the socket. As mentioned in the description of the **socket()** routine earlier, the type of the socket specifies the type of service of the communication channel, such as **SOCK_STREAM** or **SOCK_DGRAM**.

Here, **optvalp** points to an integer, and **optlen** is the size of an integer. The option puts the socket type into the integer.

SO_ERROR   Returns any pending error on the socket and clears the error status. Here, **optvalp** points to an integer, and **optlen** is the size of an integer. The option puts the error indication into the integer.

The **getsockopt()** routine returns **0** on success and **-1** on failure. Upon success, it fills the buffer pointed to by the **optvalp** argument with the current value of the specified option.

Example of sendmsg() and recvmsg()

Socket routines are straightforward. They let you establish communication, manage a connection, and transfer data. However, the **sendmsg()** and **recvmsg()** routines tend to be harder to use than the other data-transfer socket routines, because they provide the most functionality. So, we conclude this section with an example of how to use the **sendmsg()** and **recvmsg()** routines in applications.

To illustrate how to use the **sendmsg()** routine, we'll create a routine called **send_names()**. This routine puts data into a **msghdr** structure and sends the message to the peer application. It returns **-1** on failure and the number of bytes sent on success. It takes the following arguments:

1. A file descriptor corresponding to a socket. The socket must be connected to a peer application.

2. A buffer containing a company name.

3. Three buffers containing employee names.

4. The size of each of the four buffers.

We first present the code and then explain what it does. The code follows:

```
#include <sys/types.h>
#include <sys/socket.h>

int
send_names(fd, company, emp1, emp2, emp3, bufsiz)
int fd;
char *company;
char *emp1;
char *emp2;
char *emp3;
{
    struct msghdr msg;
    struct iovec  iov_array[4];

    iov_array[0].iov_base = company;
    iov_array[0].iov_len  = bufsiz;

    iov_array[1].iov_base = emp1;
    iov_array[1].iov_len  = bufsiz;

    iov_array[2].iov_base = emp2;
    iov_array[2].iov_len  = bufsiz;

    iov_array[3].iov_base = emp3;
    iov_array[3].iov_len  = bufsiz;

    /*
     *  Fill in the io vector in the message.
     */

    msg.msg_iov    = iov_array;
    msg.msg_iovlen = 4;

    /*
     *  Set the "name" field to 0 because the socket is
     *  connected.  If the socket were not connected,
     *  we would place the destination address here.
     */

    msg.msg_name    = (caddr_t)0;
    msg.msg_namelen = 0;
```

```
/*
 *  We are not passing access rights in this example,
 *  so set them to 0.
 */

msg.msg_accrights    = (caddr_t)0;
msg.msg_accrightslen = 0;

/*
 *  Send the message to the peer application.
 */

return(sendmsg(fd, &msg, 0));
}
```

In this code, we define an array of four **iovec** structures. We set the **iov_base** field of each **iovec** structure to one of the data buffers passed into the routine. We also set the **iov_len** field of each **iovec** structure to a given size. We did not set it to the length of the string in the **iov_base** field. We did that because the application reading the data must specify the size of each buffer before it calls the **recvmsg()** routine. Later in this section, we present the code that reads the data.

After we initialize each **iovec** structure, we assign the array to the **msg_iov** field of the **msghdr** structure. We also set the **msg_iovlen** field to **4**, because there are four **iovec** structures in the array. Then, we call the **sendmsg()** routine to send the data. That routine send all four data buffers as a single message.

There are two other members of the **msghdr** structure that we have not yet described: **msg_accrights** and **msg_accrightslen**. These fields let you pass specially interpreted data across the communication channel. In the **AF_UNIX** domain, they let you pass open file descriptors to unrelated processes.

As mentioned in Chapter 2, passing a file descriptor from one process to another is a powerful feature. Applications in SVR4 can pass file descriptors through a pipe by using the **ioctl()** system call with the **I_SENDFD** parameter. The **sendmsg()** routine provides the same functionality by letting you pass file descriptors through an **AF_UNIX** communication channel.

The **sendmsg()** routine lets you send any open file descriptor to a peer application. The file descriptor can refer to a regular file, a pipe, a TLI transport endpoint, or another socket. If the file descriptor refers to a regular file, the receiving application shares the file table entry with the sending application. So, if the receiving application reads or writes to the file, it modifies the file offset of the sending application.

To illustrate, we'll create a routine called **send_fds()** that opens two files and sends the file descriptors to a peer application. In that routine, we do the following:

1. Take the names of two files as arguments.

2. Open each file and store the corresponding file descriptor in an array.

3. Create a socket into the connection-oriented loopback transport provider. We do that by issuing the **socket()** routine specifying the **AF_UNIX** domain, the **SOCK_STREAM** type, and a value of **0** for the protocol.

4. Fill the address of the server into the **sockaddr_un** structure. As mentioned in Section 10.2, the **sockaddr_un** structure contains addresses for the **AF_UNIX** domain. An address in the **AF_UNIX** domain is a UNIX file name. In our application, we simply hard code the address.

5. Connect to the server side of the application by issuing the **connect()** routine. Because we have an unbound socket, the **connect()** routine binds an arbitrary address to our socket.

6. Create the message. We are not sending data, so we set the **iov_base** field and the **iov_len** field of the **iovec** structure to **0**. Also, because our socket is connected, we set the destination address to **0**. Then, we set the **msg_accrights** field to point to the file descriptors to be sent.

7. Issue the **sendmsg()** routine to send the file descriptors to the server side of the application.

The server side of the application reads the file descriptors via the **recvmsg()** routine. We present the code for the server side of the application later in this section.

The code for the client side of the application follows:

```
#include <stdio.h>
#include <fcntl.h>
#include <netdb.h>
#include <signal.h>
#include <sys/types.h>
#include <sys/socket.h>
#include <netinet/in.h>
#include <sys/un.h>
#define SERV_ADDR   "/tmp/example1"

int
send_fds(file1, file2)
char *file1;
char *file2;
```

```
{
    struct msghdr msg;
    struct iovec iov[1];
    struct sockaddr_un servaddr;
    int fd_array[2];
    int sfd;
    int result;

    if ((fd_array[0] = open(file1, O_RDWR)) < 0) {
        return(-1);
    }

    if ((fd_array[1] = open(file2, O_RDWR)) < 0) {
        close(fd_array[0]);
        return(-1);
    }

    /*
     *  Get a socket into the AF_UNIX domain.
     */
    if ((sfd = socket(AF_UNIX, SOCK_STREAM, 0)) < 0) {
        close(fd_array[0]);
        close(fd_array[1]);
        return(-1);
    }

    /*
     *  Fill in the server's address and connect
     *  to the server.
     */

    bzero((char *)&servaddr, sizeof(servaddr));
    servaddr.sun_family = AF_UNIX;
    strcpy(servaddr.sun_path, SERV_ADDR);

    if (connect(sfd, (struct sockaddr *)&servaddr,
            strlen(SERV_ADDR) + sizeof(servaddr.sun_family)) < 0) {
        close(fd_array[0]);
        close(fd_array[1]);
        close(sfd);
        return(-1);
    }
```

```
/*
 *  We are not sending data, so set iov to 0.
 */

iov[0].iov_base   = (char *)0;
iov[0].iov_len    = (char *)0;

msg.msg_iov    = iov;
msg.msg_iovlen = 1;

/*
 *  We are already connected, so we set the address
 *  to 0.  If we were using a connectionless transport
 *  provider, we would specify the address here.
 */

msg.msg_name    = (caddr_t)0;
msg.msg_namelen = 0;

/*
 *  Fill the access rights with the file descriptors.
 */

msg.msg_accrights    = (caddr_t)fd_array;
msg.msg_accrightslen = sizeof(fd_array);

result = sendmsg(sfd, &msg, 0);

close(fd_array[0]);
close(fd_array[1]);
close(sfd);
return(result);
}
```

In this code, we only pass the file descriptors. However, we could have passed data with the file descriptors by filling the **msg_iov** vectors. For example, we could have sent the names of the files, the type of the files, or other information.

As mentioned earlier, the server side of the application reads the information sent via the **sendmsg()** routine by issuing the **recvmsg()** routine. We now present the code that uses that routine.

In the previous code, we created the **send_names()** routine. In that routine, we sent a company name and three employee names in a single message. Now, we can create a routine called **recv_names()** that reads the information.

Our **recv_names()** routine takes the following arguments:

1. A file descriptor corresponding to a socket (the socket must be connected to the client application).

2. A buffer to hold the company name (the caller must allocate these buffers).

3. Three buffers to hold the employee names (the caller must allocate these buffers).

4. An indication of the size of each of the four buffers.

The **recv_names()** routine calls the **recvmsg()** routine to fill the four buffers. It returns **-1** on failure and the number of bytes read on success. The code follows:

```
#include <sys/types.h>
#include <sys/socket.h>

int
recv_names(fd, company, emp1, emp2, emp3, numbytes)
int fd;
char *company;
char *emp1;
char *emp2;
char *emp3;
int numbytes;
{
    struct msghdr msg;
    struct iovec  iov_array[4];

    iov_array[0].iov_base = company;
    iov_array[0].iov_len  = numbytes;

    iov_array[1].iov_base = emp1;
    iov_array[1].iov_len  = numbytes;

    iov_array[2].iov_base = emp2;
    iov_array[2].iov_len  = numbytes;

    iov_array[3].iov_base = emp3;
    iov_array[3].iov_len  = numbytes;
```

```
    /*
     *  Fill in the io vector in the message.
     */

    msg.msg_iov    = iov_array;
    msg.msg_iovlen = 4;

    /*
     *  Set the "name" field to 0 because we don't
     *  want the address of our peer.
     */

    msg.msg_name    = (caddr_t)0;
    msg.msg_namelen = 0;

    /*
     *  We are not reading access rights in this example,
     *  so set them to 0.
     */

    msg.msg_accrights    = (caddr_t)0;
    msg.msg_accrightslen = 0;

    /*
     *  Read the message from the peer application.
     */

    return(recvmsg(fd, &msg, 0));
}
```

In this code, we define an array of four **iovec** structures. We initialize each **iovec**
structure in the array with one of the data buffers passed into the routine. Then, we
assign the array to the **msg_iov** field of the **msghdr** structure. We also set the
msg_iovlen field to **4**, because there are four **iovec** structures in the array. Next,
we call the **recvmsg()** routine to read the data sent by the client side of the application. That routine populates the four buffers in the **iovec** array.

Now let's look at the **msg_accrights** and **msg_accrightslen** fields of the
msghdr structure. These fields let you read specially interpreted data. With sockets in
the **AF_UNIX** domain, these fields let you read file descriptors that another application
sends to you.

To illustrate, we'll create a function named **recv_fds()** that reads two file descriptors from a socket. It implements the server side of the **send_fds()** routine created earlier.

In the **recv_fds()** routine, we do the following:

1. Create a socket into the connection-oriented loopback transport provider. We do that by issuing the **socket()** routine specifying the **AF_UNIX** domain, the **SOCK_STREAM** type, and a value of **0** for the protocol.

2. Fill a **sockaddr_un** structure with our address. As mentioned in Section 10.2, the **sockaddr_un** structure contains addresses for the **AF_UNIX** domain. An address in the **AF_UNIX** domain is a UNIX file name. In our routine, we simply hard code the file name into the application.

3. Bind to our address by calling the **bind()** routine. Because we are using the **AF_UNIX** domain, the **bind()** routine creates the file specified as our address. As long as the file exists, no other application can use that address.

4. Place the socket in the "listen state" by calling the **listen()** routine. We then issue the **accept()** routine to wait for a connection request to arrive. If those routines fail, we unlink the file that the **bind()** routine created. It is the responsibility of the application calling the **bind()** routine to remove the file when it is no longer in use.

5. Allocate a buffer to hold the two file descriptors and assign the buffer to the **msg** structure. And, because the client side of the application does not send any data, we set the **msg_iov** field to **0**. Also, our socket is connected, so we set the source address to **0**.

6. Call the **recvfrom()** routine to read the file descriptors sent by the client side of the application.

7. Return the array of file descriptors.

The code for the **recv_fds()** routine follows:

```
#include <stdio.h>
#include <netdb.h>
#include <signal.h>
#include <sys/types.h>
#include <sys/socket.h>
#include <netinet/in.h>
#include <sys/un.h>

#define SERV_ADDR  "/tmp/example1"
```

```
int *
recv_fds()
{
   struct msghdr msg;
   struct iovec iov[1];
   struct sockaddr_un servaddr;
   struct sockaddr_un client_addr;
   int sfd;
   int recfd;
   int *retval;
   int length;
   static int fd_array[2];

   /*
    *  Get a socket into the AF_UNIX domain.
    */

   if ((sfd = socket(AF_UNIX, SOCK_STREAM, 0)) < 0) {
      return((int *)0);
   }

   /*
    *  Fill in our address and bind to it.
    */

   bzero((char *)&servaddr, sizeof(servaddr));
   servaddr.sun_family = AF_UNIX;
   strcpy(servaddr.sun_path, SERV_ADDR);

   if (bind(sfd, (struct sockaddr *)&servaddr,
          strlen(SERV_ADDR) + sizeof(servaddr.sun_family)) < 0) {
      close(sfd);
      return((int *)0);
   }

   /*
    *  Set the socket up for listening, with a queue
    *  length of 1.
    */

   if (listen(sfd, 1) < 0) {
      close(sfd);
      unlink(SERV_ADDR);
```

```
            return((int *)0);
      }

      length = sizeof(client_addr);
      if ((recfd = accept(sfd,
            (struct sockaddr *)&client_addr, &length)) < 0) {
         close(sfd);
         unlink(SERV_ADDR);
         return((int *)0);
      }

      /*
       *  Now that we have accepted the connection, we
       *  can read the message that contains the file descriptors.
       */

      iov[0].iov_base = (char *)0;
      iov[0].iov_len  = 0;

      msg.msg_iov     = iov;
      msg.msg_iovlen  = 1;

      msg.msg_name    = (caddr_t)0;
      msg.msg_namelen = 0;

      /*
       *  Fill the access rights with the file descriptors.
       */

      msg.msg_accrights    = (caddr_t)fd_array;
      msg.msg_accrightslen = sizeof(fd_array);

      if (recvmsg(recfd, &msg, 0) < 0) {
         retval = (int *)0;
      } else {
         retval = fd_array;
      }

      close(sfd);
      unlink(SERV_ADDR);
      return(retval);
}
```

After we read the file descriptors, they can be used as if we had created them. We can do reads, writes, and all other file operations. We also share the file table entry with the sending process. If we read or write into the file, the file offsets are modified in the client application as well.

Now that we've shown the socket routines, let's create two simple networking applications. The first uses a virtual-circuit communication channel, and the second uses a datagram communication channel.

10.6 A Simple Virtual-Circuit Application

Let's create a simple application that illustrates how to use socket routines over a virtual-circuit communication channel. For our example, we'll write the C code that is specific to the Transmission Control Protocol (TCP).

The application implements the "person query" protocol created in Chapter 8. We implement the same application so you can see the correlation between socket routines and TLI routines.

The following defines what we'll do at each of the upper three layers of the OSI Model:

1. The **application layer** carries out the protocol. The client side of the application sends a user name to the server side of the application. The server side reads the user name and figures out if the user is currently logged onto the system. If the user is logged on, the server returns the "**y**" character. If the user is not logged on, the server returns the "**n**" character. After reading the response, the client side of the application can send another user name to the server. The loop continues until the client side of the application has no more user names to send.

2. The **presentation layer** formats the data. In our application, we only use ASCII characters. However, if we had to send other data types, we could use the methods presented in Section 8.2.

3. The **session layer** synchronizes dialogue. In our application, the client side of the application sends a byte with the **0** value to indicate the end of a user name. Because the response is a single character (a "**y**" or an "**n**"), the client side of the application knows it has the entire response when it reads the single byte.

    As mentioned earlier, the client side of the application can repeat the process as often as it wants. When the client side of the application is finished sending user names, it shuts down the connection (it does this after reading the response from the server, so there is no data in transit). That lets the server side of the application know the client side of the application is finished sending user names.

Therefore, the "over" indication occurs when the client sends a **0** byte, and the "over and out" indication occurs when the client side of the application shuts down the connection.

We begin by presenting the server side of the application.

The Server Code

The following code implements the server side of the application. Because we are using TCP/IP, we define a TCP port number. For this example, we simply hard code the value in the application.

```
#include <stdio.h>
#include <sys/types.h>
#include <sys/socket.h>
#include <netinet/in.h>
#include <sys/errno.h>

#define SERV_PORT   5134

#define MAXNAME     1024

extern int errno;

main()
{
    int socket_fd;          /* file descriptor into transport */
    int recfd;              /* file descriptor to accept      */
    int length;             /* length of address structure    */
    struct sockaddr_in myaddr; /* address of this service     */
    struct sockaddr_in client_addr; /* address of client      */
```

To begin, we call the **socket()** routine to create a socket. We want a communication channel that uses TCP, so we specify the following three parameters:

1. The address family is **AF_INET**. That says we want a socket that uses the TCP/IP protocol suite.

2. The service type is **SOCK_STREAM**. That says we want a communication channel that supplies virtual-circuit service.

3. Because the TCP/IP protocol suite has only one protocol that supplies virtual-circuit service (that is, the TCP protocol), the third argument is **0**.

Next, we have to bind a transport address to the socket. Because we are using the TCP transport provider, we must construct a TCP-specific address.

As mentioned in Section 10.2, SVR4 provides the **sockaddr_in** structure that formats a TCP address. It has the following definition:

```
struct sockaddr_in {
     u_short           sin_family;
     u_short           sin_port;
     struct  in_addr   sin_addr;
     char              sin_zero[8];
};
```

The **sin_addr** field is an **in_addr** structure. The **in_addr** structure is a union that lets you access the 4-byte IP address as four separate bytes, as two short integers, or a a single long integer.

When we create our address, we set the fields of the **sockaddr_in** structure to the following values:

1.   Set the **sin_family** field to the required value of **AF_INET**.

2.   Set the **sin_port** field to the port number defined at the beginning of the application.

3.   Set the **sin_addr** field to **INADDR_ANY**. That value is the special IP address **0.0.0.0**. As explained in Chapter 3, that address binds the transport endpoint to all IP addresses on the machine.

4.   Fill the **sin_zero** array with zeros.

We create our TCP transport address by assigning numeric values to the port number field and IP address field of the **sockaddr_in** structure. As mentioned in Chapter 8, that poses a problem if our machine does not have the data representation assumed by the TCP/IP protocols. The IP protocols assume all addresses are in a predefined ''network representation.'' If we bind to an address that is not in the correct data format, the transport provider functions may fail.

To solve that problem, put the IP address and port number in the network representation. You must use the following TCP/IP specific routines to do the data conversion:

1.   The **htons()** routine converts a short integer (for example, the port number) into the network representation.

2.   The **htonl()** routine converts a long integer (for example, the IP address) into the network representation.

After placing the IP address in the **sockaddr_in** structure, we call the **bind()** routine to bind an address to our socket. The code follows:

```
/*
 *  Get a socket into TCP/IP.
 */

if ((socket_fd = socket(AF_INET, SOCK_STREAM, 0)) < 0) {
   perror("socket failed");
   exit(1);
}

/*
 *  Set up our address.
 */

bzero((char *)&myaddr, sizeof(myaddr));
myaddr.sin_family = AF_INET;
myaddr.sin_addr.s_addr = htonl(INADDR_ANY);
myaddr.sin_port = htons(SERV_PORT);

/*
 *  Bind to the address to which the service
 *  will be offered.
 */

if (bind(socket_fd, (struct sockaddr *)&myaddr,
                        sizeof(myaddr)) < 0) {
   perror("bind failed");
   exit(1);
}
```

Now that our socket is bound to a transport address, we put the socket into the listen state. In our application, we set the **qlen** field to **5**. That lets up to five connection requests arrive on the socket simultaneously.

Then, we loop continuously. Within the loop, we wait for connection requests, accept the connection when one arrives, and create a child process to carry out the protocol. Specifically, we do the following:

1. Issue the **accept()** routine, passing it the socket and a buffer to hold the client address.

2. Check the return value when the **accept()** routine returns. If the routine
    failed, we print the reason for failure and exit the application.

    If the **accept()** routine succeeds, it returns a new socket that has the connec-
    tion to the client side of the application. We can accept the next connection
    request on the original socket.

3. Issue the **fork()** system call to create a child process. The child process
    closes the original socket and calls a subroutine to carry out the protocol. The
    parent process closes the connected socket and continues the loop, waiting for
    the next connection request to arrive.

The code follows:

```
/*
 *   Set up the socket for listening, with a queue
 *   length of 5.
 */

if (listen(socket_fd, 5) < 0) {
   perror("listen failed");
   exit(1);
}

/*
 *   Loop continuously, waiting for connection requests
 *   and performing the service.
 */

length = sizeof(client_addr);
while (1) {
   if ((recfd = accept(socket_fd,
      (struct sockaddr_in *)&client_addr, &length)) < 0) {
      perror("could not accept call");
      exit(1);
   }
   switch (fork()) {

      case -1:
         perror("fork failed!\n");
         exit(1);

      default: /* parent */
```

```
                    close(recfd);
                    /*
                     * Break out of switch and continue loop.
                     */
                    break;

            case 0:  /* child */

                    close(socket_fd);
                    /*
                     *  perform_actions() never returns.
                     */
                    perform_actions(recfd);
            }
        }
}
```

Now, we write the **perform_actions()** routine to implement the protocol. It takes one argument—the socket that has the established connection.

Because the client side of the application can send several user names, we create a loop to read them. Inside the loop, we do the following:

1. Issue the **read()** system call to read the user name from the transport endpoint. However, because TCP does not preserve message boundaries, we continue reading until we see the **0** byte, which indicates the end of the string. We could have used the **recv()** routine instead of the **read()** system call. However, we are not reading expedited data, so it is simpler to use the **read()** system call. Also, note that we place the user name into a buffer containing **BUFSIZ** bytes. Therefore, if we do not see the **0** byte after reading **BUFSIZ** bytes, we exit the child process.

2. If the **read()** system call fails, check the error condition. If the **errno** is set to **ECONNRESET**, then the client closed the connection. That is not an error condition in our example. The client side of the application closes the connection when it has no more data to send. Because that means the client side of the application is finished sending user names, we exit the child process with a success condition. If the **read()** system call fails for any other reason, we exit the child process with an error condition.

3. If the **read()** routine succeeds, keep reading until we get the full user name. Then, figure out if the user is logged onto the system, and send a **y** or an **n** to the client side of the application.

We call the **popen()** routine to figure out if a user is logged onto the system. We could have done that more efficiently by searching the **/etc/utmp** file directly, but the **popen()** routine suffices for our example.

```
int
perform_actions(conn_fd)
int conn_fd;
{
    int done = 0;      /* indicates all data are read        */
    int where = 0;     /* points to where we are in buffer   */
    int nbytes;        /* the number of bytes read           */
    char reply;        /* 'y' or an 'n' to reply to client   */
    char buf[BUFSIZ];  /* buffer to hold the name            */

    char cmd[BUFSIZ];        /* used to figure out if      */
    char junkbuf[BUFSIZ];    /* the user is logged onto    */
    FILE *fp;                /* the system                 */

    for (;;) {
        /*
         *  Read the user name from the client.
         */
        where = 0;
        do {
            if ((BUFSIZ - where) == 0) {
                exit(1);
            }
            if ((nbytes = read(conn_fd, &buf[where],
                                        BUFSIZ-where)) < 0) {
                if (errno != ECONNRESET) {
                    perror("read of data failed!");
                    exit(1);
                } else {
                    exit(0);
                }
            }
            where += nbytes;
            if (buf[where - 1] == '\0') {
                done = 1;
            }
        } while (!done);
```

```
    /*
     *  Determine if the user is logged on...
     */
    sprintf(cmd, "who | grep '^%s '", buf);
    if ((fp = popen(cmd, "r")) == NULL
      || fgets(junkbuf, BUFSIZ, fp) == NULL) {
        reply = 'n';
    } else {
        reply = 'y';
    }

    /*
     *  Send a "y" or an "n" to the client.
     */
    if (write(conn_fd, &reply, 1) < 0) {
        perror("write failed!");
        exit(1);
    }
  }
}
```

Now let's look at the client side of the application. As with the server side, the client side uses the Transmission Control Protocol (TCP).

The client side of the application establishes a connection to the server side. It sends a user name and reads the response, and continues doing so until it has no more names to send. It informs the server that it is finished sending names by shutting down the connection.

The Client Code

The following code implements the client side of the application. The client side takes user names as parameters. For each user name specified on the command line, it sends the name to the server side of the application, reads a response to figure out if that user is logged onto the server machine, and displays the response.

because we are using TCP/IP, we use the TCP port number to which the server side of the application is attached. For this example, we simply hard code the value into the application.

```
#include <stdio.h>
#include <netdb.h>
```

```
#include <signal.h>
#include <sys/types.h>
#include <sys/socket.h>
#include <netinet/in.h>

#define SERV_PORT   5134

#define MAXNAME     1024

main(argc, argv)
int argc;
char **argv;
{
    int fd;                     /* fd into transport provider */
    int i;                      /* loops through user names   */
    int length;                 /* length of message          */
    char buf[BUFSIZ];           /* holds message from server  */
    struct hostent *hp;         /* holds IP address of server */
    struct sockaddr_in myaddr;  /* address that client uses */
    struct sockaddr_in servaddr; /* the server's full addr */
```

To begin, we check that at least one user name is given to the application. Next, we do the following:

1. Create a socket into the TCP transport provider. We do that the in same way as in the server side of the application—by issuing the **socket()** routine, specifying **AF_INET** for the address family, **SOCK_STREAM** as the type of service, and **0** as the protocol.

2. Bind to an arbitrary, unused address. Because we are on the client side of the application, we don't care what address is obtained. No application is going to connect to us, so no application needs to know our address.

   In SVR4, you use the special port of **0** to indicate that you want an unused port number. So, we create our address by specifying **INADDR_ANY** as the IP address and **0** as the port number. Then, we issue the **bind()** routine.

The code follows:

```
/*
 *  Check for proper usage.
 */

if (argc < 3) {
```

```
        fprintf(stderr,
                "Usage: %s host user [user...]\n", argv[0]);
        exit(2);
    }

    /*
     *  Get a socket into TCP/IP.
     */

    if ((fd = socket(AF_INET, SOCK_STREAM, 0)) < 0) {
        perror("socket failed!");
        exit(1);
    }

    /*
     *  Bind to an arbitrary return address.
     */

    bzero((char *)&myaddr, sizeof(myaddr));
    myaddr.sin_family = AF_INET;
    myaddr.sin_addr.s_addr = htonl(INADDR_ANY);
    myaddr.sin_port = htons(0);

    if (bind(fd, (struct sockaddr *)&myaddr,
                                    sizeof(myaddr)) < 0) {
        perror("bind failed!");
        exit(1);
    }
```

We are now ready to make the connection to the server machine. We populate the **sockaddr_in** structure with the transport address to which we want to connect. We fill the fields of the **sockaddr_in** structure as follows:

1. Fill the entire structure with **0** values. That places a **0** in the 8-byte filler area at the end of the structure.

2. Assign the value **AF_INET** to the **sin_family** field. That places the required value of **2** in the first two bytes.

3. Place the predefined port number in the **sin_port** field. As with the server side of the application, we convert that value to network representation by calling the **htons()** routine.

4. Figure out the IP address of the server machine. We do that by calling the
    gethostbyname() routine. That routine is a TCP/IP-specific routine that
    returns a list of IP addresses for a given machine. The addresses are in network
    format, so we don't have to convert them.

    As mentioned in Chapter 8, SVR4 provides no routines to figure out the best
    address to use. So, we use the first address returned by **gethostbyname()**.

After we create the transport address of the server side of the application, we issue the
connect() routine to connect to it. The code follows:

```
/*
 *  Fill in the server's address and the data.
 */

bzero((char *)&servaddr, sizeof(servaddr));
servaddr.sin_family = AF_INET;
servaddr.sin_port = htons(SERV_PORT);

hp = gethostbyname(argv[1]);
if (hp == 0) {
    fprintf(stderr, "could not obtain address of %s\n",
        argv[2]);
    return (-1);
}

bcopy(hp->h_addr_list[0], (caddr_t)&servaddr.sin_addr,
    hp->h_length);

/*
 *  Connect to the server.
 */

if (connect(fd, (struct sockaddr *)&servaddr,
                    sizeof(servaddr)) < 0) {
    perror("connect failed!");
    exit(1);
}
```

Now that we have an established connection, we can carry out the protocol. We loop
through all of the user names given as parameters, and within the loop, we do the following actions:

1. Send the user name to the server machine via the **write()** system call. We make sure to send the **0** byte at the end of the name, because the server uses that to figure out where the name ends.

   We could have used the **send()** routine instead of the **write()** system call. But, because expedited data are not being sent, we use the simpler **write()** system call.

2. Issue the **read()** system call to read the response from the server machine. The response is a single byte (a ''**y**'' or an ''**n**'' character), so we get the entire message with a single **read()** call. The **read()** system call sleeps until the message arrives.

   Here, we could have used the **recv()** routine. But, it is simpler to use the **read()** system call, because the extra features of the **recv()** routine are not needed.

When the loop is completed, we shut down the connection. That lets the server side of the application know we are finished sending user names.

The code follows:

```
for (i = 2; i < argc; i++) {
    /*
     *  Write the user name and read the response.
     */

    length = strlen(argv[i]) + 1;
    if (write(fd, argv[i], length) != length) {
        perror("write failed!\n");
        exit(1);
    }

    if (read(fd, buf, 1) == -1) {
        perror("read failed!\n");
        exit(1);
    }

    if (buf[0] == 'y') {
        printf("%s is logged on server\n", argv[i]);
    } else {
        printf("%s is not logged on server\n", argv[i]);
    }
}
(void) shutdown(fd, 2);
```

```
    exit(0);
}
```

Now that we have seen how to use the socket routines for virtual-circuit transport providers, let's look at an application that uses socket routines over a communication channel that uses a datagram transport provider.

10.7 A Simple Datagram Application

Now let's create a simple application that uses socket routines over a datagram communication channel. For this example, we'll write the C code that uses the User Datagram Protocol (UDP).

The application carries out the same ''person query'' protocol implemented in the connection-oriented application. The following defines what is done at each of the upper three layers of the OSI Model:

1. The **application layer** implements the protocol. The client side of the application sends a datagram containing a user name to the server side of the application. The server side reads the user name and figures out if the user is currently logged onto the system. If the user is logged on, the server returns a datagram containing the ''**y**'' character. If the user is not logged on, the server returns a datagram containing the ''**n**'' character.

2. The **presentation layer** formats the data. In our application, we only use ASCII characters. However, if we had to send other data types, we could use the methods presented in Chapter 8.

3. The **session layer** synchronizes dialogue. Because we are using the User Datagram Protocol, each datagram contains a complete message. So, we coordinate dialogue by incorporating a complete message in a single datagram.

We begin by presenting the server side of the application.

The Server Code

The following code implements the server side of the application. We are using UDP, so we define a UDP port number. For this example, we simply hard code the value in the application.

```
#include <stdio.h>
#include <sys/types.h>
```

```
#include <sys/socket.h>
#include <netinet/in.h>

#define SERV_PORT   5134

#define MAXNAME     1024

main()
{
    int dg_fd;                      /* file descriptor into UDP  */
    struct sockaddr_in myaddr;  /* the addr of this service  */
    int len;                        /* length of address         */
    char buff[MAXNAME];             /* buffer to hold datagram   */
    char reply;                     /* response to the client    */
    struct sockaddr_in client_addr; /* the addr of client        */

    char cmd[BUFSIZ];               /* used to figure out if     */
    char junkbuf[BUFSIZ];           /* the user is logged onto   */
    FILE *fp;                       /* the system                */
```

To begin, we create a socket into the User Datagram Protocol. We call the **socket()** routine, giving it the following arguments:

1. The address family is **AF_INET**. That says we want a socket that uses the TCP/IP protocol suite.

2. The service type is **SOCK_DGRAM**. That says we want a communication channel that supplies datagram service.

3. Because the TCP/IP protocol suite only has one protocol that supplies datagram service (that is, the UDP protocol), the third argument is **0**.

Next, we bind to our transport address. We do that with the following steps:

1. Construct our transport address. As was done in the TCP version of the application, we place that information in the **sockaddr_in** structure. We construct the address as follows:

    a. Fill the structure with **0** values. That places a **0** in the 8-byte filler area at the end of the structure.

    b. Assign the value **AF_INET** to the **sin_family** field. That places the required value of **2** in the first two bytes.

    c. Place the predefined port number in the **sin_port** field. As in the TCP version of the application, we convert that value to network representation by calling the **htons()** routine.

d. Set the **sin_addr** field to **INADDR_ANY**. The **INADDR_ANY** value is
the special IP address **0.0.0.0**. As explained in Chapter 3, that tells IP
to bind to all IP addresses on the machine. We convert the
INADDR_ANY value to network representation by calling the **htonl()**
routine.

2. Call the **bind()** routine to bind the address to the socket.

The code follows:

```
/*
 *  Open a socket into UDP/IP.
 */

if ((dg_fd = socket(AF_INET, SOCK_DGRAM, 0)) < 0) {
   perror("socket failed");
   exit(1);
}

/*
 *  Set up our address.
 */

bzero((char *)&myaddr, sizeof(myaddr));
myaddr.sin_family = AF_INET;
myaddr.sin_addr.s_addr = htonl(INADDR_ANY);
myaddr.sin_port = htons(SERV_PORT);

/*
 *  Bind to the address of this service.
 */

if (bind(dg_fd, (struct sockaddr *)&myaddr,
               sizeof(myaddr)) < 0) {
   perror("bind failed");
   exit(1);
}
```

Now that we've bound to a transport address, we can read datagrams. We loop forever, processing datagrams. Within the loop, we do the following:

1. Issue the **recvfrom()** routine to read a datagram. That routine sleeps until a
datagram arrives and fills the buffer with the data in the datagram. The

    recvfrom() routine also fills the source address of the application that sent
the datagram.

2. Figure out if the user is logged into the machine.

3. Issue the **sendto()** routine to send the results back to the application that sent
the datagram. We give the **sendto()** routine the same address that the
recvfrom() routine returned.

The code follows:

```
/*
 *  Loop continuously, processing datagrams.
 */

len = sizeof(struct sockaddr);
while (1) {
    if (recvfrom(dg_fd, buff, MAXNAME, 0,
            &client_addr, &len) < 0) {
      perror("could not read datagram!");
      continue;
    }

    sprintf(cmd, "who | grep '^%s '", buff);
    if ((fp = popen(cmd, "r")) == NULL
      || fgets(junkbuf, BUFSIZ, fp) == NULL) {
      reply = 'n';
    } else {
      reply = 'y';
    }
    if (sendto(dg_fd, &reply, 1, 0, &client_addr, len) < 0) {
      perror("could not send datagram!");
      continue;
    }
  }
}
```

Now let's look at the client side of the application. As with the server side, the client
side is specific to the User Datagram Protocol.

The client side of the application sends a datagram containing a user name. It then
waits for the response. And, because a datagram transport provider is being used, we
resend the request if a response is not received.

The Client Code

The following code carries out the client side of the application. The client side takes a single user name as a parameter. It constructs a datagram containing the user name, sends the datagram to the server side of the application, and reads a response to see if that user is logged onto the server machine.

The code resends the datagram if it does not get a response. We will not get a response if one of the following happens:

1. The datagram we send to the server side of the application is lost.

2. The datagram containing the response is lost.

To begin, we declare the variables needed. Also, because UDP is being used, we define a UDP port number to which the server is attached. For this example, we hard code that value in the application. We also hard code the number of times we resend the request before giving up. In our example, we resend the request up to **20** times.

The code follows:

```
#include <stdio.h>
#include <netdb.h>
#include <signal.h>
#include <sys/types.h>
#include <sys/socket.h>
#include <netinet/in.h>

#define SERV_PORT   5134
#define MAXNAME     1024

#define NUM_TRIES    20
int timed_out;

main(argc, argv)
int argc;
char **argv;
{
    int fd;                     /* fd into transport provider */
    char buf[MAXNAME];          /* holds message from server  */
    int tries = NUM_TRIES;      /* number of tries to send     */
    int got_it = 0;             /* determines datagram receipt*/
    struct hostent *hp;         /* holds address of server     */
    struct sockaddr_in myaddr;  /* holds the local address     */
    struct sockaddr_in servaddr; /* holds the server addr      */
```

```
int length;              /* length of user name        */
int size;                /* size of sockaddr structure */
void handler();          /* handles time out signals   */
```

The first thing we do is obtain a socket. We do that by calling the **socket()** routine. Because the User Datagram Protocol is being used, we specify the **AF_INET** family, the **SOCK_DGRAM** service type, and the **0** protocol.

Next, we bind an arbitrary transport address to the socket. We don't care what address is obtained, because the system sends our address with the datagram. The server side of the application sends the response to the transport address that originated the request.

As mentioned in the virtual-circuit version of this application, the special port of **0** is used to indicate that we want an unused port number. So, we create our address by specifying **INADDR_ANY** as the IP address and **0** as the port number. Then, we issue the **bind()** routine.

The code follows:

```
/*
 *  Check for proper usage.
 */

if (argc != 3) {
    fprintf(stderr,"Usage: %s user server\n", argv[0]);
    exit(2);
}

/*
 *  Open the socket into UDP/IP.
 */

if ((fd = socket(AF_INET, SOCK_DGRAM, 0)) < 0) {
    perror("socket failed!");
    exit(1);
}

/*
 *  Bind to an arbitrary return address.
 */

bzero((char *)&myaddr, sizeof(myaddr));
```

```
myaddr.sin_family = AF_INET;
myaddr.sin_addr.s_addr = htonl(INADDR_ANY);
myaddr.sin_port = htons(0);

if (bind(fd, (struct sockaddr *)&myaddr,
                          sizeof(myaddr)) < 0) {
   perror("bind failed!");
   exit(1);
}
```

Next, we create the address to which to send the datagram. As was done in the server side of the application, we use the **sockaddr_in** structure to format the UDP transport address. We fill the fields of the **sockaddr_in** structure as follows:

1. Fill the structure with **0** values. This places a **0** in the 8-byte filler area at the end of the structure.

2. Assign the value **AF_INET** to the **sin_family** field.

3. Place the predefined port number in the **sin_port** field. As with the server side of the application, we convert that value to network representation by calling the **htons()** routine.

4. Figure out the IP address of the server machine. We do this by calling the **gethostbyname()** routine. That routine is a TCP/IP-specific routine that returns a list of IP addresses for a given machine. The addresses are in network format, so we don't have to convert them. As mentioned earlier, SVR4 provides no routines to figure out the best address to use. So, we copy the first address into the **sin_addr** field.

The code follows:

```
/*
 *  Fill in the server's UDP/IP address.
 */

bzero((char *)&servaddr, sizeof(servaddr));
servaddr.sin_family = AF_INET;
servaddr.sin_port = htons(SERV_PORT);
hp = gethostbyname(argv[2]);

if (hp == 0) {
   fprintf(stderr,
       "could not obtain address of %s\n", argv[2]);
```

```
        return (-1);
    }

    bcopy(hp->h_addr_list[0], (caddr_t)&servaddr.sin_addr,
        hp->h_length);
    length = strlen(argv[1]) + 1;
    size = sizeof(servaddr);
```

We're now ready to send the datagram. Because our request or the server's reply can be dropped (remember that UDP does not guarantee delivery), we make 20 attempts to get the information needed.

The following code loops 20 times. Within each iteration of the loop, we do the following actions:

1. Send the datagram to the server side of the application.

2. Set the **timed_out** variable to **0**. We then set a signal handler for the **SIGALRM** signal. When we get the **SIGALRM** signal, we call the **handler()** routine. That routine simply sets the **timed_out** variable to **1**. Next, we set an alarm to send ourselves the **SIGALRM** signal in 15 seconds. We then call the **recvfrom()** routine, which sleeps waiting for the reply from the server.

    Here's what we've set up. After 15 seconds, we will get the **SIGALRM** signal. That causes the **handler()** routine to execute (and therefore sets the **timed_out** variable to **1**). It also causes the **recvfrom()** routine to return with an error condition.

    So, if the **recvfrom()** routine succeeds, we have our response. We turn off the alarm, set the **gotit** variable to **1** (that indicates we have a response), and exit the loop.

    If the **recvfrom()** routine fails, we check if the failure was caused by our alarm going off. If it was, then we didn't get a response in 15 seconds. So, we continue the loop, resend the datagram, reset the alarm to send us a signal in 15 seconds, and sleep again waiting for the response. If the **recvfrom()** routine failed for any other reason, we exit the application.

3. Outside the loop, we check the value of the **gotit** variable. If it is **0**, then we know we tried 20 times without getting a response. Otherwise, we display the results to the user.

The code follows:

```
    while (tries --) {
        if (sendto(fd, argv[1], length, 0,
```

```
              (struct sockaddr *)&servaddr, size) != length) {
            perror("sendto failed!\n");
            exit(1);
        }
        /*
         *    Allow 15 seconds for the response to arrive.
         */
        timed_out = 0;
        signal(SIGALRM, handler);
        alarm(15);
        if (recvfrom(fd, buf, MAXNAME, 0,
                    (struct sockaddr *)0, (int *)0) >= 0) {
            alarm(0);
            got_it = 1;
            break;
        }
        if (timed_out) {
            continue;
        }
        fprintf(stderr, "recvfrom failed!\n");
        exit(1);
    }
    if (!got_it) {
        printf("failed %d times, exiting\n", NUM_TRIES);
        exit(1);
    }

    if (buf[0] == 'y') {
        printf("%s is logged on server\n", argv[1]);
    } else {
        printf("%s is not logged on server\n", argv[1]);
    }
    exit(0);
}


void
handler()
{
    timed_out = 1;
}
```

There is one other thing to note about our algorithm. In our example, we only send one user name to the server side of the application and exit the application when we get a result. If we were sending several user names, we would have to modify the algorithm to account for multiple responses to the same query. Section 8.5 discusses the details of the problem and suggests solutions.

Now let's look at some other operations that can be done in socket applications. The following sections explain how to process asynchronous events and how to poll multiple sockets.

10.8 Processing Asynchronous Events

As mentioned in Sections 10.3 and 10.4, your application can run in the synchronous mode or the asynchronous mode. In the synchronous mode, socket routines do not return to your application until the operation is complete. In the asynchronous mode, socket routines return immediately. For example, if your application issues a **read()** routine in the asynchronous mode, that routine returns immediately, even if no data are available.

If your application is running in the asynchronous mode, you may want to know when data arrive so you can read them. You can do that by setting the socket to send you a **SIGIO** signal when normal data arrive and a **SIGURG** signal when expedited data arrive. In that way, your application can do other processing while it waits for data to arrive. And, when it gets the **SIGIO** or the **SIGURG** signal, it can read the data.

There are two things you must do to cause the system to send signals when data arrive:

1.   Associate your process ID with the socket.

2.   Inform the system to send the signal to the process ID associated with the socket.

In BSD systems, you could associate an entire process group with the socket. That caused all processes in the process group to get the signal when data arrived on the socket. That is not true in SVR4. In SVR4, you can only associate your process ID with the socket.

The following code segment shows how to set the socket to deliver the **SIGIO** and **SIGURG** signals to your application when data arrive. In the code segment, we do the following:

1.   Set a signal handler for the **SIGIO** signal. In our example, the application calls the **normal_data()** routine when we get a **SIGIO** signal. The **normal_data()** routine can issue the **read()** system call (or one of the **recv()** routines) to read normal data from the socket.

2. Set a signal handler for the **SIGURG** signal. In our example, the application calls the **expedited_data()** routine when we get a **SIGURG** signal. The **expedited_data()** routine can issue the **recv()** routine to read expedited data from the socket.

3. Associate our process ID with the socket. We do that by calling the **fcntl()** routine, passing it the socket, the **F_SETOWN** value, and the process ID of the application.

4. Set up the socket to send us signals when data arrive. We do that by calling the **fcntl()** routine, passing it the socket, the **F_SETFL** value, and the **FASYNC** value.

The code follows:

```c
#include <fcntl.h>
#include <sys/file.h>

int
setup_signals(socket)
int socket;
{
   int normal_data();
   int expedited_data();

   (void)signal(SIGIO, normal_data);
   (void)signal(SIGURG, expedited_data);

   /*
    *  Associate our process with the socket.
    */

   if (fcntl(socket, F_SETOWN, getpid()) < 0) {
     return(0);
   }

   /*
    *  Tell the system to send us SIGIO or SIGURG when
    *  data arrive.
    */

   if (fcntl(socket, F_SETFL, FASYNC) < 0) {
     return(0);
   }
```

```
    return(1);
}
```

This code segment sits at the beginning of your application. After the code executes, your application will get signals when data arrive on the socket. When normal data arrive, you will get the **SIGIO** signal. When expedited data arrive, you will get the **SIGURG** signal.

Now let's look at how to poll multiple sockets. For compatibility reasons, SVR4 provides the BSD **select()** routine, which does similar actions as the **poll()** system call.

10.9 Selecting Multiple File Descriptors

As mentioned in Chapter 8, SVR4 provides the **poll()** system call to monitor several file descriptors simultaneously. It lets you specify a list of file descriptors to monitor. When you issue the system call, it sleeps waiting for an event to occur on any of the file descriptors. When an event occurs (for example, data have arrived), the **poll()** system call returns. You can use it to monitor any type of file descriptor, including sockets.

For compatibility with BSD systems, SVR4 also provides the **select()** routine, which is the BSD equivalent to the **poll()** system call. If you are creating a socket application that you want to run on BSD systems, use the **select()** routine instead of the **poll()** routine to monitor multiple file descriptors.

As shown in Figure 10.7, you can use the **select()** routine on any file descriptor, not just on file descriptors corresponding to sockets. So, you can create applications that wait for data to arrive on any type of device.

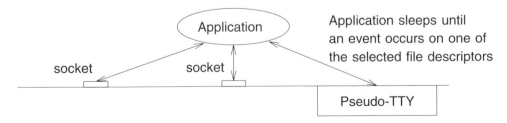

Figure 10.7 Using Select on Multiple File Descriptors

As explained in Chapter 8, the ability to monitor several file descriptors simultaneously simplifies many kinds of applications. For example, consider the TCP/IP **rlogind** process. As explained in Chapter 3, the **rlogind** process is the server side of a remote-login application. That process must monitor two file descriptors. The first file descriptor is a socket connected to the client side of the application, and the second is the master side of a pseudo-terminal device. The **rlogind** process uses the **select()** routine to determine when data arrive on either of the two file descriptors.

Let's take a closer look at the **select()** routine. It has the following syntax:

```
#include<sys/types.h>
#include<sys/time.h>

struct timeval timeout
int            numfds;
fd_set         rfds;
fd_set         wfds;
fd_set         efds;
int            numselected;

numselected = select(numfds, &rfds, &wfds, &efds, &timeout);
```

The **select()** routine monitors several file descriptors, waiting for an event to occur. It returns the number of file descriptors that have events pending. If an error occurs, the **select()** routine returns **-1**.

The arguments to the **select()** routine are as follows:

rfds   Contains a set of file descriptors that you want to monitor for reading (that is, that you want to monitor for incoming data). It is of type **fd_set**. From an application's point of view, **fd_set** is a data type that corresponds to a set of integers, and each integer corresponds to a file descriptor.

For example, suppose you wanted to wait for data to arrive on file descriptors **6**, **7**, and **10**. You could create the set **{6,7,10}** and assign that to the **rfds** argument (we explain how to do that in what follows). The **select()** routine waits for data to arrive on one of the file descriptors. It returns when data arrive or when a specified time passes. If you specify a **NULL** value for this argument, the system interprets it as the empty set.

You specify the amount of time to wait in the **timeout** argument, described in what follows. SVR4 also provides the BSD routines that add file descriptors to a set. We describe those routines shortly.

wfds   Contains a set of file descriptors that you want to select for writing. That
            means you want to wait until you can write data into one of the file
            descriptors. The `select()` routine sleeps until one of the file descrip-
            tors in the set is ready for writing or until a specified time passes.

            For example, flow control restrictions of a transport provider may limit the
            amount of data you can write into the socket. In that case, the file descrip-
            tor is not ready for writing until the transport provider lets you write at
            least one byte of data. If you specify a **NULL** value for this argument, the
            system interprets it as the empty set.

efds   Contains a set of file descriptors that you want to poll for an exceptional
            condition. An exceptional condition occurs when expedited data arrive or
            when a transport-specific exception event occurs.

            The `select()` routine sleeps until one of the file descriptors in the set
            contains an exception condition or until a specified time passes. As with
            the **rfds** and **wfds** parameter, a **NULL** value indicates an empty set.

numfds   Contains the largest file descriptor of all three sets plus one. For example,
            if the **rfds** set contained {**0,1,5**}, the **wfds** set contained {**2,3**},
            and the **efds** set contained {**0,1,2,3**}, then the **numfds** argument
            must contain **6**. The largest value of all three sets is **5**, and the **numfds**
            argument must be one greater than that.

timeout   Specifies how long to wait before the `select()` routine returns to your
            application. It is a **timeval** structure, which has the following
            definition:

```
struct timeval {
        long tv_sec;  /* seconds      */
        long tv_usec; /* microseconds */
};
```

            The **tv_sec** field contains the number of seconds to wait, and the
            tv_usec field contains the additional microseconds to wait. If the
            number of seconds and the number of microseconds pass without a moni-
            tored event occurring, the `select()` routine returns to your application.
            And, because there are no file descriptors that met the conditions you mon-
            itored, the `select()` routine returns a **0** value.

            If the **timeout** argument is NULL, the `select()` routine waits for-
            ever until a file descriptor in one of the sets meets the associated condition.
            However, the `select()` routine will return with an error if your applica-
            tion gets a signal before a specified condition occurs.

Let's look at how to add and remove file descriptors into sets. SVR4 supplies the BSD macros to manipulate sets. The macros follow:

```
#include <sys/types.h>

int fd;
fd_set fdset;

FD_ZERO(&fdset);

FD_SET(fd, &fdset);
FD_CLR(fd, &fdset);

FD_ISSET(fd, &fdset);
```

The SVR4 implementation of sets uses a bit map in an integer, and the macros simply manipulate the bit map. However, from an application's point of view, the macros clear a set, add a file descriptor to a set, remove a file descriptor from a set, and test if a file descriptor is in a set. Specifically, the routines do the following:

FD_ZERO   Initializes a set to the empty set. You should use this macro to initialize the **rfds**, the **wfds**, and the **efds** arguments of the **select()** routine.

FD_SET   Adds the given file descriptor to the specified set.

FD_CLR   Removes the given file descriptor to the specified set.

FD_ISSET   Returns **0** if the given file descriptor is not in the specified set, and nonzero if it is in the set.

Each set is independent of one another. For example, you can create the read set as **{2,5,7}**, the write set as **{0,2,5}**, and the exception set as **{5,8}**. In that case, the **select()** routine sleeps until one of the following conditions is true:

- File descriptor **0** is ready for writing.

- File descriptor **2** is ready for reading or writing.

- File descriptor **5** is ready for reading, ready for writing, or has an exception condition pending.

- File descriptor **7** is ready for reading.

- File descriptor **8** has an exception condition pending.

You can set up the three sets just described with the following code:

```
fd_set rfds;
fd_set wfds;
fd_set efds;

FD_ZERO (&rfds);
FD_ZERO (&wfds);
FD_ZERO (&efds);

FD_SET (2, &rfds);
FD_SET (5, &rfds);
FD_SET (7, &rfds);

FD_SET (0, &wfds);
FD_SET (2, &wfds);
FD_SET (5, &wfds);

FD_SET (5, &efds);
FD_SET (8, &efds);
```

As mentioned earlier, the `select()` routine returns when a monitored event occurs on a file descriptor or when the amount of time specified in `timeout` passes. It returns the number of file descriptors that have an event pending.

The `select()` routine also modifies each set. When it returns, each set only contains the file descriptors that met the criteria. For example, the `rfds` set will only contain the file descriptors that are ready for reading, the `wfds` set the file descriptors that are ready for writing, and the `efds` set the file descriptors that have an exceptional event pending.

To illustrate how to use the `select()` routine, let's create a code segment that selects multiple file descriptors. To begin, let us assume that we have six pieces of information:

1. An array of file descriptors named `read_array`. It contains the file descriptors we want to select for reading.

2. A variable named `num_readarray` that contains the number of elements in the `read_array` array.

3. A second array of file descriptors named `write_array`. It contains the file descriptors we want to select for writing.

4. A variable named **num_writearray** that contains the number of elements in the **write_array** array.

5. A third array of file descriptors named **ex_array**. It contains the file descriptors we want to select for exceptional conditions.

6. A variable named **num_exarray** that contains the number of elements in the **ex_array** array.

Given these three arrays, we can create three sets of file descriptors and use them in the **select()** routine. Specifically, we do the following:

1. Use three sets, named **rfds**, **wfds**, and **efds**.

2. Clear each of the three sets by using the **FD_ZERO()** macro.

3. Place all of the file descriptors in the **read_array** array into the **rfds** set. Also, figure out the largest file descriptor and assign it to the **max_fd** variable.

4. Place all of the file descriptors in the **write_array** array into the **wfds** set. If any of those file descriptors is larger than **max_fd**, we reset **max_fd** to the larger file descriptor.

5. Place all of the file descriptors in the **ex_array** array into the **efds** set. As we did before, if any of those file descriptors is larger than **max_fd**, we reset **max_fd** to the larger file descriptor. At the end of this step, the **max_fd** variable contains the largest file descriptor of all three sets.

6. Increment the **max_fd** variable, because it must be set to the largest file descriptor plus one.

7. Begin a loop that waits for a condition to occur on one of the file descriptors in the sets. Within the loop, we do the following:

   a. Copy each set to a temporary area. We do that because the **select()** routine modifies the sets, and we want to call **select()** with the original set on each iteration.

   b. Call the **select()** routine, specifying an infinite time-out period.

   c. When the **select()** routine returns, check each of the sets. If a file descriptor is in a set, we know the associated condition is true and we act upon the file descriptor.

The code segment follows:

```
fd_set rfds;    /* file descriptors for reading          */
fd_set wfds;    /* file descriptors for writing          */
fd_set efds;    /* file descriptors for exc. conditions */
```

```
fd_set  t_rfds; /* temporary set for reading            */
fd_set  t_wfds; /* temporary set for writing            */
fd_set  t_efds; /* temporary set for exceptions         */
int     max_fd; /* max file descriptor of all sets      */
int     i;      /* loop index counter                   */

if (num_readarray == 0
  && num_writearray == 0
  && num_exarray == 0) {
    /*
     *  No elements in any array...
     */
    return;
}

max_fd = 0;

FD_ZERO(&rfds);
FD_ZERO(&wfds);
FD_ZERO(&efds);

for (i = 0; i < num_readarray; i++) {
   FD_SET(read_array[i], &rfds);
   if (read_array[i] > max_fd)
     max_fd = read_array[i];
}
for (i = 0; i < num_writearray; i++) {
   FD_SET(write_array[i], &wfds);
   if (write_array[i] > max_fd)
     max_fd = write_array[i];
}
for (i = 0; i < num_exarray; i++) {
   FD_SET(ex_array[i], &efds);
   if (ex_array[i] > max_fd)
     max_fd = ex_array[i];
}

max_fd ++;

for (;;) {
   /*
    *  Use a copy so we don't lose the original sets.
    */
```

```
        t_rfds = rfds;
        t_wfds = wfds;
        t_efds = efds;

        if ((n_fds = select(max_fd, &t_rfds, &t_wfds,
                    &t_efds, 0)) < 0) {
            /*  Error condition.  */
            break;
        }
        for (i = 0; i < num_readarray; i++) {
            if (FD_ISSET(read_array[i], &t_rfds)) {
                /*
                 *  Read data from read_array[i].
                 */
            }.
        }
        for (i = 0; i < num_writearray; i++) {
            if (FD_ISSET(write_array[i], &t_wfds)) {
                /*
                 *  Write data to write_array[i].
                 */
            }
        }
        for (i = 0; i < num_exarray; i++) {
            if (FD_ISSET(ex_array[i], &t_efds)) {
                /*
                 *  Process data from ex_array[i].
                 */
            }
        }
    }
```

Now let's look at a way to simplify the server side of your applications. SVR4 provides the BSD **inetd** process that does most of the server work for you.

10.10 Using inetd

SVR4 provides the **inetd** port monitor to help write socket applications. The **inetd** port monitor simplifies the server side of your application by doing most of the socket operations.

The `inetd` process is similar to the SVR4 `listen` port monitor. However, unlike the `listen` port monitor, the `inetd` process only works over the TCP/IP protocols. But, where the `listen` port monitor can only work over virtual-circuit transport providers, the `inetd` process works over both TCP and UDP. It was an integral part of the BSD 4.3 UNIX system, and SVR4 provides it for compatibility with existing socket applications.

For the `inetd` process to work with your application, the administrator of the server machine must create an entry for the server side of your application in the `/etc/inetd.conf` file. The entry contains the following:

1. The name of your service.

2. An indication of whether to use TCP or UDP.

3. An indication of whether to "wait" of not (we'll discuss this in what follows).

4. An indication of the user ID under which to run the service.

5. The path name to your application.

6. The arguments to the application.

The administrator must also put the service name and associated TCP/IP port number in the `/etc/services` file. As mentioned in Chapter 3, the `/etc/services` file contains a mapping of service names to port numbers.

After the administrator enters your application in the `/etc/inetd.conf` file, the `inetd` port monitor manages a socket for you. Figure 10.8 shows the operations of the `inetd` port monitor for services offered over TCP. For each service, the `inetd` port monitor does the following:

1. Issues the `socket()` routine to create a socket into TCP.

2. Opens the `/etc/services` file to find the port number of the specified service. It uses the port number to form the TCP/IP address.

3. Issues the `bind()` routine to bind the address of the service to the socket.

4. Issues the `listen()` routine to put the socket in the listen state.

5. Uses the `select()` routine, waiting for connection requests to arrive on one of the sockets it is monitoring (it puts the sockets in the `rfds` set, because it is waiting for a message to arrive). When a connection request arrives, it issues the `accept()` routine to accept the connection.

6. After it accepts the connection, it issues the `fork()` system call to create a child process. The child process calls the `dup()` system call to duplicate the connected socket onto file descriptors `0`, `1`, and `2`. The child process changes its user ID to that specified in the `/etc/inetd.conf` file and calls `exec()` to start the server side of the application.

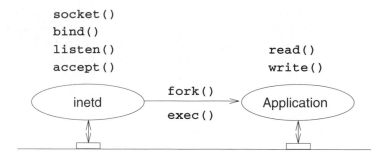

Figure 10.8 Inetd over TCP/IP

If the administrator specified the "wait" option, the **inetd** process waits for the child to complete before it monitors the socket again. If the administrator specified the "nowait" option, the **inetd** process immediately listens for the next connection request.

Most applications use the "nowait" option for TCP services, because it causes the **inetd** process to immediately start monitoring the socket again. However, if your application wants to limit the number of connections or if your application wants to start monitoring the socket itself, it can use the "wait" option.

7. When the application starts, it has a connection to the client side of the application. It does not have to call the socket connection establishment routines and can immediately start issuing the **read()** and **write()** routines. And if needed, you can use the **getpeername()** routine to determine the address of the remote socket. When you complete your application-layer protocol, simply exit the application. When another connection request arrives, the **inetd** process starts your application again.

The **inetd** process can also be used for UDP applications. Figure 10.9 shows the operations of the **inetd** port monitor if your service is offered over UDP. For each service, it does the following:

1. Issues the **socket()** routine to create a socket into UDP.

2. Opens the **/etc/services** file to find the port number of the specified service. It uses the port number to form the UDP address.

3. Issues the **bind()** routine to bind the address of the service to the socket.

4. Uses the **select()** routine, waiting for a datagram to arrive. It puts the sockets in the **rfds** set, because it is waiting for data to arrive.

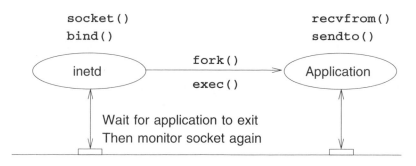

Figure 10.9   Inetd over UDP/IP

5. When a datagram arrives, the **inetd** process does not read the datagram.
    Instead, it issues the **fork()** system call to create a child process. The child
    process calls the **dup()** system call to duplicate the socket onto file descriptors
    0, 1, and 2. The child changes its user ID to that specified in the
    /etc/inetd.conf file and calls **exec()** to start the server side of the
    application. The server side of the application can then read the datagram.

    If the administrator specified the ''wait'' option, the **inetd** process waits for
    the child to complete before it monitors the socket again. If the administrator
    specified the ''nowait'' option, the **inetd** process immediately monitors the
    socket waiting for a datagram.

    Most UDP applications specify the ''wait'' option, because it lets the applica-
    tion have control of the socket when a datagram arrives. Each datagram is a
    complete message, so the application can read the datagram, process it, and wait
    for more datagrams to arrive. If a new datagram does not arrive after a period of
    time, your application can exit, causing the **inetd** process to monitor the
    socket again for you.

Using the **inetd** port monitor has the same advantages as using the **listen** process. The server side of the application:

1. Runs only when a connection request arrives. That reduces the number of
    processes on the server machine.

2. Is much simpler. You don't have to do the connection management routines
    yourself. If you are using TCP, there is an established connection. If you are
    using UDP, there is a socket with a datagram pending.

10.11   Summary

The socket interface contains a set of low-level networking routines that let you create and manage a communication channel. The socket routines are used to establish communication, manage a connection, and transfer data.

The socket routines are simple and easy to use. There is a large base of application written to the socket interface, and SVR4 supplies the socket interface so those applications can port easily.

For Further Reading

1. Leffler, S., McKusick, M., Karels, M., and Quarterman, J., *The Design and Implementation of the 4.3BSD UNIX Operating System*, Addison-Wesley, Reading, MA, 1989.

2. Stevens, R., Chapter 6, Berkeley Sockets, *UNIX Network Programming*, Prentice Hall, Englewood Cliffs, NJ, 1990.

3. Vessey, I., and Skinner, G., "Implementing Berkeley Sockets in System V Release 4," *USENIX Conference Proceedings*, Winter 1990.

Exercises

10.1 Describe the similarities and differences between socket routines and TLI routines. Examine the routines to establish a connection, transfer data, and shut down a connection.

10.2 Describe how to use socket routines over a virtual-circuit transport provider. Detail the steps for connection establishment, data transfer, and connection shutdown.

10.3 Describe how to use socket routines over a datagram transport provider. Detail the steps for sending and receiving datagrams.

10.4 Create a program that passes a file descriptor to an unrelated process using the **sendmsg()** and **recvmsg()** routines. Create the same program using the **ioctl()** system call with the **I_SENDFD** and **I_RECVFD** parameters.

10.5 Write a program that uses sockets to create a ''remote math'' protocol. The client sends two integers and an operation. The operation can be **+** (addition), **–** (subtraction), or ***** (multiplication). The server performs the requested operation on the integers and returns the results.

Index

/dev/ptmx device 46-47
/dev/tty device 49, 84
/etc/hosts file 72, 85-88, 90, 427
/etc/netconfig file 213, 414-416, 418, 420-
  422, 424, 427, 434, 458
/etc/services file 72, 427, 533-534
/etc/uucp/Systems file 111
/var/spool/uucp directory 110, 114, 120-121
/var/spool/uucppublic directory 113, 119

1-to-M multiplexor 32, 34

abrupt shutdown 255-256, 260, 321, 370, 412
accept() routine 454, 459, 461, 463, 475-
  476, 499, 505-506, 533-534
Address Resolution Protocol 54, 60-61
advertise an RFS resource 134-137, 140-141,
  144, 170
AF_INET 325-326, 335-336, 340-341, 347-
  348, 456, 469-471, 473-474, 478,
  503-505, 510-512, 515-516, 519-521
AF_UNIX 457, 469, 471-474, 493-496, 498-
  500
anonymous FTP 83-84
application layer 5-6, 8, 14, 20, 61-62, 64,
  245, 248, 314-315, 320, 322, 338,
  373, 411, 427, 455, 502, 514
ARP (see Address Resolution Protocol)
ARPANET 54, 63, 67, 72
ARPANET Domain Name System 67, 72
asynchronous mode 256-258, 260, 262, 266-
  267, 270, 280, 283-285, 287, 290-
  291, 298, 367, 463-464, 467-468,
  475-476, 481-482, 523
authdes_cred structure 237

authdes_seccreate() routine 236
authsys_create_default() routine
  225
authsys_parms structure 225-226, 229
AUTH_DES authentication flavor 239-240
autopush facility 43-44

Bach 178
Bartoli 20
Berkeley Software Distribution 1, 12, 54, 449
bind() routine 454, 459-461, 465, 473-474,
  499, 505, 510, 516, 519, 533-534
blocking mode 80, 257, 463

cache consistency 134, 138, 160
Cain 107
Cerf 107
Chartok 178
circuit_n flag 213-214
client handle 146-147, 151-158, 198-199,
  214-216, 221-222, 249, 274, 345,
  389-390, 422, 455
client/server model 6-7
clnt_create() routine 212-216, 219,
  221, 225, 235
clnt_destroy() routine 215-216, 222
clnt_freeres() routine 215-216, 222
clnt_pcreateerror() routine 198, 215-
  216, 221
clnt_perror() routine 199, 215-216, 222
clone devices 32, 35-37, 46, 52, 252, 255,
  264, 266, 270, 309, 323, 339, 346,
  353, 361-362, 375, 377
CLONE_OPEN flag 36-37
Comer 107

Common Key in Secure RPC 231-232, 234

communication channel 247, 449-453, 457-459, 465, 467-470, 472-476, 478, 480, 484, 486-491, 493, 502-503, 514-515, 536

connect() routine 454, 459, 461, 465, 467, 474, 477, 494, 512

connection establishment 10, 32, 60, 62, 74, 78, 122, 137, 245, 255, 257, 271-272, 278, 281-284, 291, 313, 315, 330, 333, 336, 368, 379, 385, 388, 397-398, 409, 411, 449, 452, 461, 491, 507, 509, 512, 534-536

connection-oriented service 10-11, 17-18, 213, 245, 370, 375, 377, 417-418, 429, 445-446, 472-473

connectionless loopback transport provider 303, 305-306, 309-310, 312-313, 467, 472

connectionless service 10-11, 18, 213, 245-246, 272, 341, 370, 375, 417, 429, 439-440

connld module 41, 50, 145, 171-172

controlling terminal 18, 49, 99, 105

Conversation Key   188, 232-236

DARPA   (see Defense Advanced Research Projects Agency)

data link layer 60

datagram service 10-11, 20, 59, 62, 70, 296, 346, 413, 417, 441, 448-452, 465, 469-470, 515, 519

datagram_n flag 213-214

Defense Advanced Research Projects Agency 8, 12, 54

device driver 14-16, 21-23, 25, 31-32, 34-35, 37, 43-44, 52, 54, 56, 58-60, 133-134, 145, 160-161, 366, 368

disconnect indication 289, 293-294, 354, 359-360, 388-389, 393, 405

diskless workstation 131, 145, 147

distributed file system 12, 72, 132-133, 160, 162, 166, 178-179

Dougherty 129

downstream 22-23, 25, 38, 51, 367-368

ECONNRESET error 507, 509

endnetconfig() routine 421, 445, 447

equivalent machines 85, 87, 90, 96, 104

ETSDU (see Expedited Transport Service Data Unit)

EWOULDBLOCK error 476, 481-482

expedited data 255, 258, 271-272, 280, 288-290, 331, 336, 452, 461, 463-464, 477-483, 489, 507, 513, 523-525, 527

Expedited Transport Service Data Unit 271

export 149, 159-160, 430

External Data Representation 13, 242

FASYNC flag 524-525

fattach() routine 39, 170

FD_ZERO() macro 530

file and record locking 133, 138, 140, 158

file descriptor passing 34, 39, 46, 52, 144-145, 327, 364, 381, 493, 496, 526-527, 529, 536

file instance number 153

File Transfer, Access, and Management 6

File Transfer Protocol 64, 76, 107

FNDELAY flag 464, 467-468

Forbes 178

freenetconfigent() routine 424

FTAM (see File Transfer, Access, and Management)

ftp 65-66, 68, 76-84, 90-91, 96-100, 104-108, 129

ftpd 76

F_SETOWN flag 524

gethostbyname() routine 333, 335, 345, 347, 512, 520

getmsg() routine 27, 29

getnetconfigent() routine 423-425, 434

getnetpath() routine 421-424

getpeername() routine 454, 485-486, 534

getpmsg() routine 27, 29

getsockname() routine 454, 485

getsockopt() routine 454, 490-491

getty 18, 68-69, 174, 185, 252, 254-255, 265-266, 309, 402, 426, 460-461, 465, 521

Goldberg 178
grade of UUCP jobs 113-114, 119-120
grantpt() routine 46, 49

Hamilton 178
high-priority messages 27, 29, 365, 367, 369
host number 55-59, 65-66, 345, 433
host2netname() routine 236
HOST_ANY flag 430
HOST_BROADCAST flag 430, 440-441
HOST_SELF flag 430-431, 441, 443, 445-
        446, 448
htonl() routine 325, 335, 340, 347, 504,
        516
htons() routine 325, 335, 340, 347, 504,
        511, 515, 520

ICMP (see Internet Control Message
        Protocol)
ID mapping 141-143, 159-161
idempotent operations 11, 20
idload command 141
INADDR_ANY flag 325-326, 340-341, 504-
        505, 510-511, 516, 519-520
inetd 13, 18, 416-418, 532-535
International Organization for Standardization
        4
Internet Assigned Numbers Authority 65, 68
Internet Control Message Protocol 54, 60, 63,
        416, 418, 469
Internet Engineering Task Force 65, 68
Internet Protocol 8, 35, 53-54, 58, 60, 63,
        107, 416, 418, 469
inverse ID mapping 141
iovec structure 480, 484, 493-494, 498
IP (see Internet Protocol)
IP Addresses 55
IPPROTO_IP flag 487
IPPROTO_TCP flag 470, 487
isastream() routine 175
ISO (see International Organization for
        Standardization)
Isreal 52
I_FIND flag 31
I_FLUSH flag 31, 38, 50
I_LINK flag 34-35
I_LIST flag 31

I_LOOK flag 31
I_PLINK flag 35
I_POP flag 23, 25
I_PUNLINK flag 35
I_PUSH flag 23, 25, 41, 48, 172, 409
I_RECVFD flag 39, 41, 172-173, 536
I_SENDFD flag 39, 41, 145, 493, 536
I_SETSIG flag 257, 267, 289, 366-367, 389,
        394, 405
I_SWROPT flag 175

Karels 536
Kerberos 189
keyserv daemon 230
Kleinman 178

layered architecture 3-5
ldterm module 43-44, 47, 49-51
Leffler 536
line discipline 43-44, 47, 49-51
linger structure 489
listen() routine 454, 459-460, 475-476,
        499, 533-534
Luppi 178
Lyon 178

Maximum Transmission Unit 60
McGrath 52
McKusick 536
Melamed 178
memory allocation 211
mergeaddr structure 441
modules 12-16, 18, 21-23, 25-27, 29-32, 34,
        38, 41, 43-44, 47-52, 56, 59-62, 64,
        134, 145, 171-172, 366, 368-370,
        374, 409, 411, 458
mount command 135-137, 148-149, 153, 159,
        162
msghdr structure 479, 483, 491, 493, 498
MSG_DONTROUTE flag 477-479, 488
MSG_OOB flag 477-479, 481-483, 489
MTU (see Maximum Transmission Unit)
multihop 144
multiplexing device driver 31-32, 34-35, 37,
        52
muticast address 58

N-to-1 multiplexor 31, 35
N-to-M multiplexor 34-35
Name-to-Address Mapping 8, 12-13, 16-17,
        19, 71-72, 184, 313, 325, 362-363,
        375-377, 379, 408, 413-417, 424-
        425, 427-428, 432, 443-444, 448,
        453
Named STREAMS 38-39, 41
Narten 107
`nc_perror()` routine 421
nd_hostserv structure 425-426, 430, 433, 445
nd_hostservlist structure 433
ND_MERGEADDR flag 438, 441-443
netbuf structure 249-250, 273, 275, 282-284,
        286, 293-305, 307, 323, 325, 353,
        362, 375, 377, 426, 432, 434-436,
        441
netconfig structure 418, 420-421, 423, 425-
        426, 432, 437, 445
`netdir_free()` routine 437, 445
`netdir_getbyaddr()` routine 432-433,
        437
`netdir_getbyname()` routine 425-427,
        429, 431-432, 437, 441, 443-445,
        448
`netdir_options()` routine 437-438, 440-
        443
`netdir_perror()` routine 426
NETPATH environment variable 213-214,
        422-424
Network File System 12-13, 131, 178
Network Information Center 56
network layer 3-6, 8-9, 58-61, 248, 250, 314-
        315, 320, 411, 455
network name 66-67, 136-137, 159, 181, 188,
        213-214, 229-230, 232, 234, 236-
        237, 240, 362, 375, 413, 416-418,
        427-428, 430, 441
network number 32, 55-59, 237, 250, 252,
        325, 335, 340, 347, 427-429, 504,
        511, 515, 520
Network Selection 12-13, 16-17, 19, 184,
        213, 362, 375-376, 379, 408, 413-
        416, 418, 420-422, 424-425, 427-
        429, 443-445, 448, 453, 458-459,
        470, 473
Network Virtual Terminal 72

newkey command 231
NFS (see Network File System)
NFS recovery 154-155
NIC (see Network Information Center)
nonblocking mode 257, 463
none flavor of authentication 188, 190, 222
normal message 27, 29, 242, 365-367, 369
NVT (see Network Virtual Terminal)

Olander 52
opaque data 209
Open Systems Interconnection Reference
        Model 4, 6, 8-10, 13, 16, 20, 53-54,
        58, 60-62, 64, 109, 245, 248, 282,
        315, 321-322, 338, 373, 411, 413,
        453, 455, 502, 514
open with append mode 133, 140, 157
orderly release 10, 248, 256, 258-260, 278,
        280, 291-293, 321-322, 330-331,
        333, 337-338, 362, 370, 373-374,
        416-417, 419-420, 423, 445, 473
orderly shutdown 256, 260, 272, 291, 412
OSI (see Open Systems Interconnection
        Reference Model)
packet mode 50, 58, 60
Padovano 178
passing file descriptors 34, 39, 46, 52, 144-
        145, 327, 364, 381, 493, 496, 526-
        527, 529, 536
pckt 50
persistent link 35, 52
physical layer 4, 60
ping command 63, 471
`pipe()` routine 37-39, 41
pipemod module 38, 50
pollfd structure 364, 366, 380, 383
`poll()` routine 30, 363-367, 379-380, 444,
        525
`popen()` routine 171, 174, 217, 219, 331,
        371, 388-390, 393, 508
port monitors 13, 17-19, 240, 243, 408-409,
        411, 532-535
port number 65-66, 68-70, 72, 82, 86-87, 108,
        184, 249, 322, 324-325, 333, 335,
        339-340, 344, 346-347, 427, 435-
        436, 441, 456, 490, 503-504, 509-
        511, 514-515, 518-520, 533-534

portmap 183

Postel 107

presentation layer 4-5, 64, 248, 315-316, 320, 322, 338, 373, 411, 455, 502, 514

primary name server 136-137

priority band 29, 365-368

priority messages 27, 29, 365-368

privileged ports 65, 86, 108, 441

protocol family 53, 64, 416-420, 451, 456, 460-461, 469-470, 472, 503, 510, 515, 519

pseudo-device 23

pseudo-terminal 44-46, 49-52, 74, 85, 87, 363-364, 526

ptem module 47-49, 51

`ptsname()` routine 46

`putmsg()` routine 27, 29

`putpmsg()` routine 27, 29

qlen 273-275, 286, 311, 325-326, 341, 351-353, 356-357, 361, 383, 412, 475, 505

Quarterman 536

queued file transfer 109-111, 122, 125-126, 128-129

rcp 13, 64, 90-91, 93, 95-96, 98, 100, 102-104, 162

`recvfrom()` routine 452, 454, 463, 465, 467, 481-482, 489, 499, 516-517, 521, 534

`recv()` routine 452, 454, 461, 463, 465, 467, 480-483, 489, 507, 513, 523-524

`recvmsg()` routine 452, 454, 461, 463, 467, 483-484, 489, 491, 493-494, 496-498, 536

Redman 129

Remote File Sharing 12, 131-147, 149, 161-162, 164, 169-170, 178-179

remote mount model 132-133, 135

Remote Procedure Call 12-13, 159, 181, 183-193, 195-212, 214-217, 221-222, 224-225, 227, 229-232, 235-237, 239-243, 247, 275, 313, 317, 442

resource 1, 5, 14, 134-138, 140-141, 144-145, 240

Reynolds 107

RFS (see Remote File Sharing)

RFS name service 133, 136, 143, 145

Rifkin 178

Ritchie 52

rlogin 13, 64-66, 68, 84-87, 108, 526

rlogind 13, 64-66, 68, 84-87, 108, 526

Rose 20

Routing Protocols 63

RPC (see Remote Procedure Call)

RPC definition language 192-193, 195, 200, 202-204, 206-211, 214, 242

RPC security 187, 224

RPC specification 192-193, 195, 198, 200-201, 204, 206, 210, 242-243, 317

rpcbind 183-185, 190, 199-200, 210, 212, 241-242, 275, 313, 442

rpcgen 192-193, 196-197, 199, 202-203, 205-212, 214-215, 219, 222, 225, 241-243, 316-318

rsh 13, 64-66, 87-90, 95, 108, 162

rshd 87-88, 90

Sabrio 178

SAC (see Service Access Controller)

SAF (see Service Access Facility)

Sandburg 178

secondary name servers 137

secure authentication flavor 159, 188, 229, 235, 237, 243

Secure NFS 159-161

Secure RPC 159, 188, 229-232, 235-237

Secure RPC Domain 230, 236

`select()` routine 525-530, 533-534

`send()` routine 452, 454, 461-462, 465, 467, 476-479, 488, 513

`sendmsg()` routine 452, 454, 461-463, 467, 479-480, 483-484, 488, 491, 493-494, 496, 536

`sendto()` routine 452, 454, 462, 465-466, 478-479, 488, 517, 534

Sequenced Packet Protocol 9, 417, 469, 471, 487

Service Access Controller 13, 19

Service Access Facility 13, 19

service names 8, 65-66, 68, 71-72, 133, 136,
         143, 145, 282, 362, 376-377, 379-
         380, 382-383, 397, 412-413, 417,
         425-427, 430, 432-433, 441, 443-
         446, 448, 533
session layer 4-5, 64, 248, 314-315, 320, 322,
         330, 338, 373, 411, 455, 502, 514
set-user-ID program 142-143
setnetpath() routine 421, 423-424, 445
setsid() routine 49
setsockopt() routine 454, 486, 490-491
Shah 178
share command 135-136, 149, 170
shutdown() routine 454, 463, 484
SIGALRM signal 348, 521-522
SIGCHLD signal 171-172
SIGIO signal 464, 481-482, 523-525
SIGPIPE signal 174-177
SIGPOLL signal 257, 267, 366-368, 389, 393-
         394, 405
SIGURG signal 368, 464, 481-482, 523-525
Skinner 536
SNDZERO flag 175
sockaddr_in structure 325, 335, 340, 346-347,
         455-457, 473-474, 503-505, 511,
         515, 519-520
sockaddr_un structure 457, 473-474, 494, 499
socket() routine 64, 450-451, 454, 458-
         461, 465, 468-472, 491, 494, 499,
         503, 510, 515, 519, 533-534
socketpair() routine 454, 472-473
SOCK_DGRAM flag 469-470, 472, 491, 515-
         516, 519
SOCK_RAW flag 469-471
SOCK_STREAM flag 469-472, 475-476, 491,
         494-495, 499-500, 503, 505, 510-511
sockmod module 51, 458
SO_BROADCAST flag 487
SO_DEBUG flag 488
SO_DONTROUTE flag 488
SO_ERROR flag 491
SO_KEEPALIVE flag 488
SO_LINGER flag 489
SO_OOBINLINE flag 489
SO_RCVBUF flag 489
SO_REUSEADDR flag 489
SO_SNDBUF flag 490

SO_TYPE flag 491
SOL_SOCKET flag 487, 491
SPP (see Sequenced Packet Protocol)
Stallings 20
state information 18, 138, 140, 153-154, 160,
         179, 277
stateless operations 153-154, 161
stat() routine 140-142, 159
Stevens 52, 314, 411, 536
st_dev 140, 159
st_ino 140, 159
stream head 13-16, 22-23, 25-27, 29, 31-32,
         34-35, 38-39, 41, 43-44, 47-48, 170,
         366-369, 409, 458
STREAMS 6, 9, 12-14, 16, 18-19, 21-23, 25,
         27, 29, 31, 34, 37-39, 41, 43-45, 49-
         50, 52, 64, 68-70, 175, 363, 365-366,
         369, 409, 449, 458
STREAMS-based pipes 21, 37, 43
STREAMS-based terminals 21, 37, 44, 47
strrecvfd 172-173
svc_req structure 225-226, 237
synchronous mode 256-258, 260, 262, 266-
         268, 270, 284-285, 289, 291, 298,
         367, 463-464, 467-468, 475-476,
         481-482, 523

taddr2uaddr() routine 433-434
Tanenbaum 20
TCP (see Transmission Control Protocol)
TCP/IP 8-10, 12-13, 16, 18, 34-35, 52-58, 60,
         62-66, 72, 76, 84, 86-87, 90-91, 93,
         100, 107, 109-110, 122, 129, 160,
         184, 249, 322, 324-325, 333, 335,
         340, 346, 378, 413, 427, 430-431,
         434-435, 441-442, 455-457, 469-
         470, 473, 478, 486-487, 489, 503-
         505, 509, 511, 515, 526, 533-534
telnet 64, 66, 72-76, 84, 107-108
telnetd 64, 66, 72-76, 84, 107-108
time skew 139, 157
timeval structure 527
timod module 51
tirdwr module 51, 369-370, 374, 409, 411
TLI (see Transport Level Interface)
TLOOK error 259, 268, 299, 343-344, 350-
         351

`tmpfile()` routine 158

Todino 129

tpi_clts 416, 419

tpi_cots 416, 419

tpi_raw 416, 419, 458

Transmission Control Protocol 8, 34-35, 52-
54, 61, 107, 214, 241, 251-252, 271,
289, 321-322, 333, 351-352, 361,
377, 417, 469, 502, 509

transport address 4, 8, 10-12, 16-17, 27, 65-
66, 68-72, 82, 87, 136-137, 183-185,
190, 200, 210, 215, 241-242, 246-
247, 249-250, 252, 254-255, 259,
262, 264-266, 268, 271-273, 275-
276, 278, 282, 286, 296, 298, 309-
310, 313, 323-325, 327, 333-335,
460-463, 465, 469, 473-474, 477-
478, 481, 496, 503-505, 510-512

transport endpoint 68-70, 246-247, 251-252,
254-255, 257-260, 262, 264-270

transport endpoint states 259-260, 262, 264,
268, 274, 276-280, 284, 287-289,
291-292, 314, 328, 369, 385

transport independence 374

transport layer 4, 6, 8-9, 61-62, 245-246, 248,
250, 314-315, 330, 373, 411, 455,
469-470

Transport Level Interface 9, 12, 16, 27, 29,
51, 64, 137, 245

Transport Protocol Specification 6

Transport Service Data Unit 250, 271, 289-
290, 321

transport user 6, 10-11, 62, 214, 241, 246,
248, 255, 264, 278, 282, 288, 293-
294, 303, 305, 309-310, 312-313,
326, 331, 333, 338-339, 344, 346,
355, 397, 414, 422, 424, 441, 507,
510, 517, 519

transport-level broadcast 313, 363, 438, 487

TSDU (see Transport Service Data Unit)

ttymon 18

`t_accept()` routine 248, 254, 259, 262,
274, 283, 287-288, 301, 327-328,
352, 354-355, 359-360, 380, 385,
409, 444

`t_alloc()` routine 248, 271, 273, 281, 284-
285, 294, 297-302, 304, 307, 309,
323, 327, 334, 339-340, 342, 346,
353-354, 362, 385

t_bind structure 273, 286, 301-302, 309, 323,
325, 340, 351-353, 358, 383, 399,
412

`t_bind()` routine 247, 254-255, 259-260,
262, 265-266, 268, 272-273, 275-
276, 286, 301, 309-310, 323, 326-
327, 334, 340, 353-354, 385, 409,
443-444

t_call structure 281, 283-288, 293-294, 301-
302, 327, 334-335, 353-355, 358,
360, 385, 398-399

`t_close()` routine 247, 255, 259, 262, 268,
276, 407

T_CONNECT event 258

`t_connect()` routine 248, 255, 257-260,
271, 278, 281, 283-285, 301, 334-
335, 397, 444, 474

T_DATA event 258, 267

T_DATAXFER state 260, 262, 264, 278, 288-
289, 291, 369

t_discon structure 294-295, 301-303, 363

T_DISCONNECT event 258-259, 294, 385

t_errno variable 248, 259, 268, 280, 283-284,
287, 291, 294, 298-300, 323, 327-
329, 339, 342-344, 349-351, 354,
356, 359, 382, 387

`t_error()` routine 248, 300

T_EXDATA event 258

`t_free()` routine 248, 302-303, 308

`t_getinfo()` routine 247, 277, 282, 286,
288-289, 291, 294, 296, 301, 362-
363

`t_getstate()` routine 248, 264, 277, 279

T_IDLE state 259-260, 262, 264, 268, 274,
276, 278, 289, 328

T_INCON state 262, 274, 287, 385

t_info structure 270, 272, 277, 282, 288-289,
291, 294, 296, 301, 303, 339, 362

T_INREL state 260, 289, 292

T_LISTEN event 258, 385

`t_listen()` routine 248, 254, 256, 258-
259, 262, 264, 274, 283, 285-288,
294, 301, 327, 352, 354-355, 358,
360, 385, 409, 444, 460, 475

t_look() routine 248, 257-259, 267, 280, 284, 385, 405

T_MORE bit 289-291, 298

t_open() routine 64, 247, 252, 254-256, 259-260, 262, 264, 266-270, 272-273, 276-278, 281-282, 288-289, 291, 294, 296, 301, 309, 323, 327, 334, 339, 346, 353-354, 361-362, 380, 385, 398, 409, 439-441, 443-444, 450

t_optmgmt structure 301-304, 306-309

t_optmgmt() routine 247, 271, 282, 296, 298, 301, 303-308, 312-313, 363

T_ORDREL event 258-259

T_OUTCON state 260, 284

T_OUTREL state 260, 291-292

t_rcvconnect() routine 248, 257-260, 283-285, 301

t_rcvdis() routine 248, 258-260, 262, 272, 294-295, 301, 328, 354, 385

t_rcv() routine 51, 248, 250, 255, 257-260, 262, 290-291, 331, 336-337, 368-370, 388, 390-391, 397, 402-403, 407, 409

t_rcvrel() routine 248, 256, 258-260, 262, 292, 337

t_rcvudata() routine 248, 266-268, 297-299, 301, 310, 342-343, 348-350, 444

t_snddis() routine 248, 255, 259-260, 262, 272, 292-294, 301, 321, 373, 389

t_snd() routine 51, 248, 255, 259-260, 262, 288-290, 336, 368-370, 389, 405, 409, 412

t_sndrel() routine 248, 256, 260, 262, 291-292, 337

t_sndudata() routine 248, 266, 268, 295-297, 301, 343, 444

t_sync() routine 248, 278-280

T_UDERR event 268, 299, 342-343, 349

t_uderr structure 299, 301-303, 363

t_unbind() routine 247, 260, 262, 268, 276

T_UNBND state 259-260, 262, 268

T_UNINIT state 259, 262, 268, 276

t_unitdata structure 296-298, 301-303, 309-310, 342-343, 346-347

uaddr2taddr() routine 436

UDP (see User Datagram Protocol)

universal address 433-436, 442, 448

unix authentication flavor 188, 224-226, 229, 235, 243

UNIX-to-UNIX copy facility 12, 109

unlockpt() routine 46, 49

upstream 22-23, 38, 51

user2netname() routine 236

User Datagram Protocol 35, 54, 62, 65-66, 68, 70, 72, 107-108, 160-161, 245, 338-339, 344, 346-347, 430, 438, 441, 450-451, 469-470, 514-515, 518, 520-521, 533-535

uucico command 110-111, 113-114, 120-122, 130

uucp command 12-13, 109-126, 128-130

uuname command 111-112, 119, 123-124

uupick command 115, 117-118

uuto command 110-111, 115-117

uux command 110-112, 118-121, 130

uuxqt command 111, 120-121, 130

variable-length arrays 206-208

Vessey 536

virtual circuit service 448, 452, 470

void declaration 205, 209

Walsh 178

XDR 13, 186-187, 192, 199, 208, 210-212, 215, 222, 241-242, 316-320, 412

XDR structure 186-187, 199, 208, 211-212, 317-320, 412

XDR_DECODE flag 318-320

XDR_ENCODE flag 318-319

xdr_free() routine 211, 219

xdrmem_create() routine 318-319

XENIX 1

XNS 8-9, 450, 469, 471

Yueh 178